Lecture Notes in Computer Science 13614

More information about this series at https://link.springer.com/bookseries/558

Huayi Wu · Yu Liu · Jianzhong Li ·
Xiaofeng Meng · Qingfeng Guan · Xuan Song ·
Guoqiong Liao · Guoliang Li (Eds.)

Spatial Data and Intelligence

Third International Conference, SpatialDI 2022
Wuhan, China, August 5–7, 2022
Revised Selected Papers

Editors
Huayi Wu
Wuhan University
Wuhan, China

Yu Liu
Peking University
Beijing, China

Jianzhong Li
Harbin Institute of Technology
Harbin, China

Xiaofeng Meng
Renmin University of China
Beijing, China

Qingfeng Guan
China University of Geosciences (Wuhan)
Wuhan, China

Xuan Song
Southern University of Science
and Technology
Shenzhen, China

Guoqiong Liao
Jiangxi University of Finance and Economics
Nanchang, China

Guoliang Li
Tsinghua University
Beijing, China

ISSN 0302-9743 ISSN 1611-3349 (electronic)
Lecture Notes in Computer Science
ISBN 978-3-031-24520-6 ISBN 978-3-031-24521-3 (eBook)
https://doi.org/10.1007/978-3-031-24521-3

This Springer imprint is published by the registered company Springer Nature Switzerland AG
The registered company address is: Gewerbestrasse 11, 6330 Cham, Switzerland

Preface

This volume contains the papers from the 3rd International Conference on Spatial Data and Intelligence (SpatialDI 2022), which was held at the Chaoman Kerry International Hotel, Wuhan, during August 5–7, 2022.

SpatialDI 2022 was sponsored by the ACM SIGSPATIAL China Branch and the ACM SIGMOD China Branch, organized by the China University of Geosciences (Wuhan), and co-sponsored by Wuhan University, Huazhong University of Science and Technology, the China Geographic Information Industry Association Theory and Method Working Committee, and the International Chinese Geographic Information Science Association.

SpatialDI mainly aims to address the opportunities and challenges brought about by the convergence of computer science, geographical information science, AI, and beyond. The main topics of SpatialDI 2022 included Beidou and spatio-temporal big data, spatial intelligence and digital twins, intelligent remote sensing processing and analysis, spatio-temporal data management and information services, spatio-temporal Internet of Things, social perception and urban computing, location services and trajectory big data, new visualization and spatio-temporal cognition, spatial humanities and social geography computing, and other spatial information.

This year, the conference received 77 submissions. Each submission was reviewed by at least three reviewers selected from the Program Committee in a single blind process. Based on the reviewers' reports, 19 papers were finally accepted for presentation at the conference. The acceptance rate was 25%.

In addition to the regular papers, the conference featured a number of invited talks: Deren Li of Wuhan University, China, delivered a talk entitled "On Geospatial Information Science in the Era of IoT", Jianzhong Li of the Harbin Institute of Technology, China, addressed "Computing Methods for Big Data with Limited Computing Resources", Michael Batty of University College London, UK, spoke about "Complexity, Models and Digital Twins in Urban Planning", Xiaofeng Meng of the Renmin University of China addressed "Understanding and Thinking of Data Privacy and Data Governance", Michael Goodchild of the University of California, Santa Barbara, USA, spoke about "Spatial Intelligence: A Geographer's Performance", and Chuang Shi of Beihang University, China, delivered a talk entitled "Beidou Wide Area Real-time Precision Positioning and Time Service System and Application".

The proceedings editors wish to thank our keynote and invited speakers and all the reviewers for their contributions. We also thank Springer for their trust and for publishing the proceedings of SpatialDI 2022.

Huayi Wu
Yu Liu
Jianzhong Li
Xiaofeng Meng
Qingfeng Guan
Xuan Song
Guoqiong Liao
Guoliang Li

The original version of the book was revised: Affiliation of the Editor Huayi Wu has been changed to "Wuhan University". The correction to the book is available at
https://doi.org/10.1007/978-3-031-24521-3_20

Organization

Consultant Committee

Yanxin Wang	China University of Geosciences (Wuhan), China
Deren Li	Wuhan University, China

General Conference Chairs

Huayi Wu	Wuhan University, China
Yu Liu	Peking University, China
Jianzhong Li	Harbin Institute of Technology, China
Xiaofeng Meng	Renmin University of China, China

Program Committee Chairs

Qingfeng Guan	China University of Geosciences (Wuhan), China
Xuan Song	Southern University of Science and Technology, China
Guoqiong Liao	Jiangxi University of Finance and Economics, China
Guoliang Li	Tsinghua University, China

Publication Chairs

Zhiming Ding	Institute of Software, Chinese Academy of Sciences, China
Zhi Cai	Beijing University of Technology, China

Sponsorship Committee Chair

Yong Li	Tsinghua University, China

Publicity Chairs

Kun Qin	Wuhan University, China
Bolong Zheng	Huazhong University of Science and Technology, China

Thematic Forum Chairs

Gang Pan   Zhejiang University, China
Yang Yue   Shenzhen University, China

Finance Chair

Zheng Huo   Hebei University of Economics and Business,
                                  China

Local Arrangements Chairs

Shaoqiang Wang   China University of Geosciences (Wuhan), China
Zhipeng Gui   Wuhan University, China
Xiao Pan   Shijiazhuang Tiedao University, China
Hongzhi Wang   Harbin Institute of Technology, China

Oversea Liaison Chairs

Xinyue Ye   Texas A&M University, USA
Fusheng Wang   The State University of New York at Stony Brook,
                                  USA
Shaowen Wang   University of Illinois at Urbana-Champaign, USA
Song Gao   University of Wisconsin-Madison, USA

Program Committee

Bolong Zheng   Huazhong University of Science and Technology,
                                  China
Zhipeng Gui   Wuhan University, China
Xinghua Li   Wuhan University, China
Binbin Lu   Wuhan University, China
Gang Xu   Wuhan University, China
Qiliang Liu   Central South University, China
Jizhe Xia   Shenzhen University, China
Qingfeng Guan   China University of Geosciences (Wuhan), China
Zeqiang Chen   China University of Geosciences (Wuhan), China
Wenhao Yu   China University of Geosciences (Wuhan), China
Nai Yang   China University of Geosciences (Wuhan), China

Contents

City Analysis

Traffic Management

Coarse-Grained Path Planning Under Dynamic Situational Environment

Mengmeng Chang[1], Zhiming Ding[2(✉)], Lutong Li[1], Nannan Jia[1],
and Jing Tian[1]

[1] Faculty of Information Technology, Beijing University of Technology, Beijing, China
{changmengmeng,lilutong,jianannan,tianj}@emails.bjut.edu.cn
[2] The Institute of Software, Chinese Academy of Sciences, Beijing, China
zhiming@iscas.ac.cn

Abstract. With the enrichment of data acquisition means, large amounts of spatiotemporal data in the traffic network are accumulated in real-time by various sensors and multimedia devices. Through status identification, geographic mapping and statistical calculation, a dynamic situational road network is formed. Existing path planning methods based on the static network are inadequate in coping with the traffic situation, which seriously affects the performance of the path planning in accuracy and ETA. Considering the shortage of above, this paper proposes a coarse-grained path planning method under dynamic situational network. By introducing streaming graph partition and constructing a hierarchical index, the computational cost of path planning is effectively reduced. The pathfinding scope is decreased according to the coarse-grained path by progressively shrinking the minimum containing subarea, converting the pathfinding to a small-scale addressing in the hierarchical index. Meanwhile, the situation update and link reconstruction are performed within each tracking subarea, thus making dynamic perception of the traffic situation during travel. Finally, we conduct simulation experiments on the Beijing traffic dataset to verify the effectiveness of the proposed method.

Keywords: Path plan · Traffic situation · Spatiotemporal environment

1 Introduction

With the continuous urbanization and population growth, the lack of carrying capacity and the rising travel demands of the traffic network have posed a great challenge to the development of cities. Meanwhile, the transport network is not resilient, such as peak traffic, bad weather, and unexpected events can lead to drastic changes in traffic status. Traditional static network-based path planning methods such as Dijkstra [1], A* [2], RRT [3] and their improved algorithms only plan paths based on distance, travel time and even statistics related to vehicle density which cannot respond effectively in a dynamic and changing traffic environment [4]. For example, when vehicles all use the same shortest path planning route, it will cause a sudden increase in traffic flow on the route and induce traffic congestion. Coordinated dynamic urban traffic network can improve the économic and environmental impact of car travel by effectively reducing fuel consumption and pollution [5]. To increase the adaptability of traditional path planning methods for traffic real-time conditions, the study of situational traffic can not only provide reasonable routes, but also contribute to the full utilization of urban traffic at the global level. On the other hand, the method of constructing the path index by precomputation also requires a correction of its structure [6], which is done by deleting the current Shortest Path Tree (SPT) and recomputing it using Dijkstra algorithm. Applying the static network-based path planning method to the situational network will inevitably cause huge network overhead and frequent path oscillations. In addition, the dynamic path planning problem cannot converge to a global optimal solution if the section weights change continuously during the travel. The existing dynamic path planning methods usually receive the status information of the entire network at once, which is extremely inefficient in a continuously changing network.

To address the above problems, this paper proposes a dynamic path planning method based on the traffic situation and subareas partition. Firstly, the network status is integrated into the localized space, by dividing the road network into hierarchical subareas. Node selection and aggregation in subareas according to the graph betweenness reduce the redundant information for pathfinding in the network. The index tree builds a pathfinding profile, allowing the sequence of shortest path between nodes to be quickly adjusted as the subarea situation is updated. Secondly, the path links between hierarchical subareas are modeled using a diffusion approach to analyze the deep connectivity between regions. Finally, we propose a dynamic path planning method for situational network (SA-DPP) based on the subarea status indexed tree (*SA-tree*). The main contributions of this paper are as follows:

(1) To reduce the expensive cost of global computation in dynamic path planning process, a hierarchical partition is used to decompose the road network locally and construct a situational path index. And the hierarchical structure of the subareas is extracted by node betweenness, which effectively reduces the cost of repeated calculations and improves the usability of the path planning model.
(2) A dynamic temporal path projection method is proposed to update the subarea's status changes into the situational indexed tree and search the shortest path according to the hierarchical diffusion direction.
(3) Considering the frequent changes of the situational network, a parallel bidirectional detection is used to enable fast convergence of the pathfinding to a optimal solution, seeking a balance between potential situational changes and travel costs.

The organisation of the rest of the paper is as follows. Section 2 summarises the literature of the path planning based on index and graph partition. Section 3 details our proposed dynamic path planning method based on subareas. Section 4 gives the simulation experiments and result analysis. Finally, Sect. 5 conducts conclusion.

2   Related Work

The research on the situational network focuses on the universality of dynamic network that can adjust quickly when the network status changes. Complex network situation requires path planning methods with the ability to perceive network state changes in real-time. [7] proposed an improved method that incorporates complex road conditions (traffic congestion, the occurrence of accidents, etc.) and Euclidean distance to achieve optimal path planning under their periodic variations. Considering the traffic congestion in urban areas, [8] employed a data dissemination technology to enable the information sharing between roadside units using advanced 5G communication systems. And a real-time path planning method based on the k-shortest paths and fair allocation calculation is proposed. [9] introduced a hierarchical approach to search for sub-environments with maximum expected reward and proposed a dynamic domain reduction method, that enables multi-agent planning for large multi-objective environment. Based on the 2-Hop Cover [10, 11] proposed a pruning algorithm based on the cover labels. The pruned index enables mobile objects to quickly obtain their Top-k shortest paths in a large-scale graph. Furthermore, the index can be dynamically pruned according to the changes of the network status [12].

Recalculating SPT when the status of the network changes is inefficient because it does not take full advantage of the SPT established in the past. [13] proposed the theory of network minimal change, which suggests that after some changes to network topology, the structure of the new SPT does not differ significantly from the original SPT, except for those nodes that are no longer connected to the root via the previous shortest path. The index stability is kept by making the minimal change to the existing SPT according to the network statuses while maintaining the shortest path property. However, the cost of searching and adjusting the SPT is not significantly improved when the network statuses change frequently. To improve the efficiency of SPT construction, [14] combined bidirectional breadth-first search (BFS), with parallel dynamic updates, to handle the SPT update for dynamic network. By avoiding visit the vertices with high degree in the bidirectional BFS process, a partial SPT index is constructed to reduce the search space and maintain stability. In addition, some researchers have tried to improve the speed of SPT construction by replacing the shortest path with distance estimation. [15] proposed a scalable landmark point-based SPT that approximately calculates the path distance between any two nodes via landmark points. This method selects the nodes in the graph that can best cover all shortest paths to construct the index, thus reducing the update cost of SPT. [16] divided the entire graph into smaller subgraphs, reducing the problem of determining k-shortest paths (KSPs) into the computation of partial KSPs in relevant subgraphs. A distributed two-level index is proposed for the efficient identification of related subgraphs. The index is constructed based on virtual paths, so that it is not sensitive to changes in traffic conditions.

To further improve the status update speed and build path query index, some studies in recent years have tried to introduce node importance and graph partitioning methods into dynamic network. Betweenness is used to express the importance of an individual in the overall network, and there is a wide range of applications for path calculation according to the betweenness of different nodes, edges and other structures in the network [17]. [18] proposed a Highway indexed framework based on the betweenness of edges. The module decomposition of the graph is based on Highway, and the shortest path indexes of the nodes in the sub-modules are constructed separately. [19] proposed a dynamic graph update method based on node betweenness, which adds the approximate distance and the weighted edges to the hypergraph and quickly responds to changes in the shortest path between nodes and trigger the betweenness update. Moreover, temporal network betweenness [20,21] provides a new approach to the study of situational road network. Considering that some important nodes act as intermediaries when passing messages in the network, [22] extended the statics network's betweenness to the temporal network and proposed a method for calculating the time-varying betweenness. Similarly, [23] proved that most nodes with high temporal betweenness are located within a specific time window and that most messages sent in this temporal network pass through these small number nodes. On the basis of the large amount of traffic data collected in the past, some researches began to adopt machine learning methods to extract important nodes and edges from the historical data. Based on the traffic congestion probability of the divided grid, [24] proposed a congestion-aware path planning method by identifying network links or paths that affect network traffic congestion. Planning experience gained in the past in the same or similar environments can be used to guide path planning. [25] proposed a neural network-based path planning method that uses a gradient-based self-supervised learning algorithm to predict feasible paths.

The availability of large-scale graph often depends on efficient subgraph partitioning and distributed computation. [26] proposed a dynamic graph extension method that gradually updates the tracked subgraph with the changes in the underlying graph. The sequence of nodes in the subgraph is changed during each update to obtain the best dynamic division. However, these dynamic graph partitioning methods are constantly generating new substructures with the graph status changes, requiring continuous identification and reconstruction of the subgraphs. The partitioning approach for dynamic network prefers a lightweight process, such as streaming graph partitioning [27]. By continuously adjusting the topological relationships and weight changes between nodes in the subgraphs, the properties of the subgraphs can be effectively preserved to improve the performance of the partition.

3   The Coarse-Grained Path Planning Based on Dynamic Situational Subareas

In view of the dynamic changes of the situational network, this paper proposes a pathfinding method based on temporal betweenness, which decomposes the path planning problem in time and space. The planned paths are adjusted along with the network status changes, so as to realize the dynamic path planning under

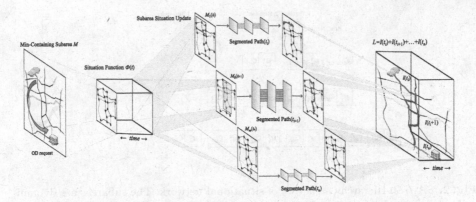

Fig. 1. Partition path planning based on situational traffic.

situational traffic. As shown in Fig. 1, the OD request obtains the minimum containing subarea M by looking up the hierarchy, and the situation function $\Phi(t)$ updates the root of M. The path planning algorithm relies on M. During the path travel, the minimum containing subareas M_1, M_k, M_m are reacquired according to the time period if the situation update occurs. If the change in situation exceeds the threshold, the path is recalculated between the start and end stations in the subarea. Accordingly, $\Phi(t)$ projects the path L as a sequence of segmented paths. Since $\Phi(t)$ is periodically varying, the subsequence of paths L is adjusted separately along with the change of situation. In addition, to improve the efficiency of situation update and path detection, we further reconstruct the areas into subsidiary subareas based on hubs. The $\Phi(t)$ in this subarea can rapidly compute the path sequence $l(t)$.

3.1 Subarea Extraction and Hierarchy Construction

The idea of clustering is to retain relatively cohesive substructures by gradually removing the links between regions. Although the clustering of nodes or edges in the road network improves the addressing efficiency within clusters, the path finding between clusters becomes complicated by the increased division constraints. In this paper, we propose a hierarchical road network partition method based on node betweenness. The higher the betweenness of the nodes, the stronger their transit capacity, indicating that their situation has a greater impact on the network. Thus, the subareas are divided according to the nodes with high degree as hubs with low degree nodes grouped as their subsidiary. The hierarchical partition preserves the complete connectivity between nodes and allows path finding between clusters at different levels.

The mobile object needs to continuously recalculate the optimal path during travel in order to cope with changes in the situation. To improve the efficiency of dynamic path finding, the link situation between nodes are stored in the hierarchy C_M and selectively updated, as shown in Fig. 2. Each branch in the *SA-tree*

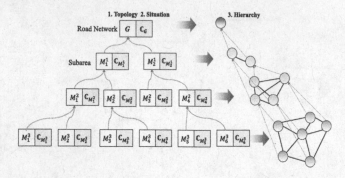

Fig. 2. *SA-tree*: Hierarchy structure of situational network. The subareas are dynamically constructed as a series of spatial status abstractions in the network. Path finding within a subarea is constrained by the sub-environment, and path finding between subareas is dependent on the hierarchy.

represents a subarea and its corresponding situational snapshot in which the path finding is performed. The snapshot of each subarea corresponds to a weighted adjacency matrix, which records the situational distance between neighboring nodes. Assuming that there is no significant change in the situation of the road network, the sub-path sequence can be quickly projected according to the hierarchy combined with $\Phi(t)$. For example, when the OD pair of nodes belongs to the same leaf subarea in the *SA-tree*, the time complexity of computing the shortest path through the situational matrix is O(1). When OD spans multiple areas, the leaf subareas M^o, M^d containing the origin and destination are first identified. The path diffusion is performed starting from the leaf subareas, which meet in the upper level subarea to get the shortest path sequence.

The *SA-tree* divides the road network into a hierarchical subareas of order k. First, the k nodes with the highest rank are calculated and aggregated according to the input G. All the aggregated nodes obtained from the iteration are used as the clustering centers for hierarchical classification. Then the subsidiary nodes at the same level are assigned to subareas according to the Dijkstra distance to the clustering center, and the divided subareas are appended to *SA-tree*.

3.2   Situation Measurement of Subareas

Frequent updates and storage of the entire road network situation are costly. Unlike the raw sampled data, the changes in the regional situation are sparse. Accordingly, for continuous sampling of all changing road statuses in the region, we only store partial information to describe them. Speed is an important indicator to reflect the road load status, here we use the average speed to show the road situation, and map it periodically to the regional situation. In the path planning process, the real-time situation calculation needs to determine the minimum contained subareas of OD and gradually reduce the search scope. In the path sequence, the destination of it in current period is the origin of the next period sequence. We extract the speeds of the dependent regions from the sampled data and update the computed situation into the SA-$tree$. The cost of situation calculation in the subareas on which the path depends decreases with the distance space shrinks. SA-$tree$ organizes subareas as basic units and selects them dynamically with the needs of path planning.

The SA-$tree$ is constructed on the basis of the hierarchical h-$tree$, merging the situational weights in the adjacency matrix of each subarea. The situation update during travel is shown in Algorithm 1, where Q denotes the queue of containing subareas with length l. It corresponds to the Min-containing subarea M_{min}, and its extended field M_l. The situation of the subareas in Q is dynamically tracked and updated. When the path jumps out of this area, it points to the next subarea of Q.

Algorithm 1: Dynamic Local Update of SA-$tree$

Input: SA-$tree$, o, d, situation update period t
Output: Containing subareas M
$subG \leftarrow SA$-$tree.root$;
if $(o, d) \in subG$ **then**
  $\llcorner$ Push $subG$ into Q;

if $subG.left$ is not null **then**
  $leftG \leftarrow subG.left$;
  if $(o, d) \in leftG$ **then**
    $\llcorner$ $MinG(\&leftG, o, d)$;

if $subG.right$ is not null **then**
  $rightG \leftarrow subG.right$;
  if $(o, d) \in rightG$ **then**
    $\llcorner$ $MinG(\&rightG, o, d)$;

return Q;

3.3 Subareas Diffusion Path Planning Based on SA-$tree$

The $\Phi(t)$ projects the OD to the road network as a dynamic path planning process based on the subareas. And the $\Phi(t)$ is updated with the situation period so the projected path sequence also changes with it. For pathfinding within the subarea, the path planning problem is equal to the solution in a static network after reconstructing the links within the subarea according to $\Phi(t)$. We use $l(t)$ to denote the path after the projection of $\Phi(t)$, then the planning process of L is mainly divided into gradient exploration and bidirectional detection, corresponding to the $\Phi^{(1)}(t)$, $\Phi^{(2)}(t)$ defined as follows.

$$\Phi^{(1)}(t) = min \left[SPD(v^{(t)}, u) + \Phi(t-1) \right]. \tag{1}$$

$$\Phi^{(2)}(t) = min \left[SPD(v^o, u^{(t)}) + SPD(u^{(t)}, v^d) \right]. \tag{2}$$

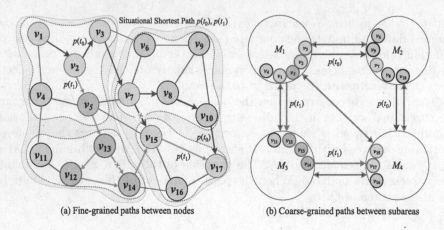

(a) Fine-grained paths between nodes   (b) Coarse-grained paths between subareas

Fig. 3. Diffusion path finding based on subareas. Paths between nodes are converted to coarse-grained paths between subareas, thereby reducing the sensitivity of paths to the changes in situational network.

where $SPD(\cdot)$ is the situational shortest path function between nodes, $v(t)$ denotes the arrival node at t, and u denotes the Hubs with high betweenness in the gradient direction. It gives a heuristic rule for node exploration within the subarea, and performs a bidirectional 2-Hop Cover search based on this rule..

The $\varPhi(t)$ divides the path planning problem in the situational road network into a series of discrete phases. The *SA-tree* is a hierarchical structure with good path finding and status updating performance, which enables fast path finding between nodes in a time-varying road network. The path projection between subareas involves the following definition of the hierarchy subareas.

Definition 3. Subarea *level*. In the hierarchy, the upper *level* subareas serve as the sum of the connection relations and network statuses of the lower *level* subareas.

As shown in Fig. 3, assume that the pathfinding is from v^o in M_1^k to v^d in M_4^k. The subarea diffusion looks along the gradient direction of the coarse-grained path and adds the subarea *hub* to the detection queue Q in turn. The $\bigtriangledown f$ denotes the direction vector from the origin to the destination, and the OD path is gradually spread to the destination node through subareas along $\bigtriangledown f$. If there are no hubs that satisfy the condition, access the upper layer of the *SA-tree* and repeat the above steps. Finally, the situational paths from v^o to *hub* are obtained according to the adjacency matrix with the update period $t \in (t_1, \ldots, t_n)$, and the path with minimum weight is selected as the planning path.

Considering that the shortest path tends to select high-level nodes for transfer, we propose a diffusion path planning method based on *SA-tree* (SA-DPP), which selectively calculates the situation of the containing subarea, thus reducing the search scope for path planning. SA-DPP fuses the situation information of the road network, and the path detection request contains path and cumulative situation weights w^l. The path detection request is sent to the upper subarea from the origin or destination, then advances it subarea by subarea until it reaches the area boundary of the destination or origin. During the travel along the coarse-grained detection path, SA-DPP is able to correct the real shortest path within the subarea accompanied by the road network situation. Algorithm 2 is the coarse-grained multi-path finding process by first obtaining the containing subareas of the origin and destination from M, which are the subareas in the SA-$tree$ as the search scope.

Algorithm 2: Coarse-grained Multi-path Finding

Input: SA-$tree$, o, d, containing subareas M, t
Output: k-$paths$
for M_l in M **do**
    Build Q_f and Q_b based on M_l ;
    push subareas of SA-$tree$ into Q_f and Q_b, along $\bigtriangledown f$;
    while $len(Q_f)$ or $len(Q_b)$ **do**
        if $len(Q_f)$ **then**
            $subG \leftarrow Q_f.pop()$;
            if $subG$ $processed$ **then**
                $midG \leftarrow subG$;
                break;
            for $edge$ $from$ $subG$ **do**
                $\omega \leftarrow subG.\omega + \delta(subG\rightarrow)$;
                if $\omega < D_f[edge]$ **then**
                    $D_f[edge] \leftarrow \omega$;
        if $len(Q_b)$ **then**
            Similar process as Q_f.
    if $t \rightarrow t.next()$ **then**
        break;
    Rebuild fine-grained path p from $\{o\rightarrow midG, midG, midG\rightarrow d\}$;
    k-$paths$.add(p);
return k-$paths$;

---

4   Experimental Verification

The simulation experiments used the Beijing road network provided by Open-StreetMap[1], by further extracting 132,039 road sections and 92,340 nodes. The situation information is based on the average speed of the road section calculated by more than 50,000 taxis with nearly 1.3 billion GPS points in Beijing in December 2012, and the situation update period is 38 s. The experimental

---

[1] www.openstreetmap.org.

environment is Intel(R) Xeon Silver 4210 CPU@2.20 GHz, 64 GB RAM, and Windows 10 64-bit OS.

In the situational road network, the final path can be considered as a prediction of the future path, so the model can be evaluated using the statistical accuracy measure. Prediction error of RMSE and Accuracy are used as evaluation metrics, defined as follows.

$$RMSE = \sqrt{\frac{1}{n} \sum_n (\omega_p - w_{min})^2};$$
$$Accuracy = 1 - \frac{\sum_n (\omega_p - w_{min})}{\sum_n w_{min}}. \tag{3}$$

where w_{min} denotes the situation-based path weight between pairs of ODs, which is calculated by the posterior final path. ω_p denotes the situational weight of the path during actual travel, and n denotes the number of ODs contained in the road network. The smaller the RMSE, the better the flexibility of the model to the situation, and the higher Accuracy means that the result of the situational path is closer to the ideal path.

4.1   Simulation Results and Analysis

We experimentally compare the SA-DPP proposed in this paper with Dijkstra, CH, A* and Dynamic A* path planning methods. To capture the impact of situation on path planning, we conducted experiments on real-time traffic statuses for different time periods. Table 1 shows the RMSE and Accuracy metrics corresponding to path requests for all ODs in the road network at high traffic (8:00 AM), and smooth traffic (14:00 PM).

Table 1. The results on path requests for all ODs

Methods	Travel period	RMSE	Accuracy
Dijkstra	8:00	1640	94.8%
	14:00	492	98.46%
A*	8:00	1640	94.88%
	14:00	492	98.46%
CH	8:00	1640	94.88%
	14:00	492	98.46%
Dynamic A*	8:00	790	97.54%
	14:00	237	99.26%
SA-DPP	8:00	780	97.57%
	14:00	234	99.27%

The static network-based path planning method ignores the change of network status and obtains the final decision path after a successful addressing. Thus, Dijkstra, A* and CH detect the same path and travel according to that path with equal RMSE and Accuracy. Under the change of road network situation, the static method corresponds to the RMSE of 492 in smooth traffic, with an accuracy of 98.46%. The enhancement of the road network situation under high traffic leads to 233% increase in RMSE and 3.77% decrease in Accuracy of the pre-planning method. In contrast, the SA-DPP and Dynamic A* methods combine real-time network status in the process of dynamic path planning to seek the optimal solution under the current situation. The dynamic model significantly reduces the travel cost, with RMSE of 780 and 790, and Accuracy improved by 2.84% and 2.80% compared to the static model at high traffic.

The time-varying nature of the situation causes the estimated time of arrival ETA of the same planned paths to present different, as shown in Fig. 4a. We selected the origin (40.019201, 116.354828) and the destination (39.778991, 116.353455) of the specified OD in Beijing, and executed different path planning methods under high and smooth traffic, respectively. It can be seen that the same method calculates different ETAs under different situations, which is due to the increasing situation leading to a lower capacity of the road network. Under the smooth traffic, there is no significant change in the ETA of different methods, and we can consider that the situation is close to the static road network at this time.

Comparing the ETAs under high traffic shows that as the situation of the road network is enhanced, the static path planning method does not avoid the impacted sections, leading to an increase in travel time. The Dynamic A* and SA-DPP path planning methods can effectively reduce the incremental cost caused by the situation and improve the precision of ETA.

In terms of the performance of path finding, as shown in Fig. 4b and Fig. 4c, the Dijkstra diffusion process uses a greedy algorithm that iteratively computes its shortest path to its nth-order neighbors. The number of detection nodes under high traffic is 51,157, and the average query time for a single detection is 186 ms,

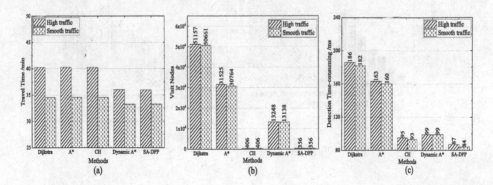

Fig. 4. Comparison of path planning methods under different situational periods.

which has the highest time complexity. The A* and dynamic A* methods use heuristic strategies in the process of path finding to reduce the search space, and the total number of visited nodes is reduced by 38.37% and 74.10% compared to Dijkstra, with a smaller detection time of 99 ms. The CH method improves the path finding performance by reducing the graph dimensions on which the path detection depends through the preprocessing of node contraction. Its total number of corresponding visited nodes is 406, and the detection time is reduced to 93 ms.

The SA-DPP uses hierarchical graph partition, and its detection scope is even smaller than CH's graph snapshot based on global node contraction, so its visited node number and single detection time are better than the above model with 356 nodes and 84 ms. In addition, comparing the two different situational periods, we can see that the detection time and the number of visited nodes do not change significantly, indicating that the impact of the network situation on the performance of the methods is small. The changes in the road network situation also have an impact on the node detection range of the path planning methods. For static path planning methods, path detection is done by a single execution and is only related to the current status snapshot of the road network. Therefore, the path detection of the static methods is less affected by the changes in the situation. As in Fig. 5 and Fig. 6, the performance of Dijkstra, A* and CH is consistent with the number of visited nodes as the detection range increases. For dynamic A* method compared to Dijkstra and A* methods can reach the destination by smaller node visited and detection range. This is due to the fact that the Dynamic A* method can dynamically adjust the direction of path detection in the situational period according to the heuristic function during the travel.

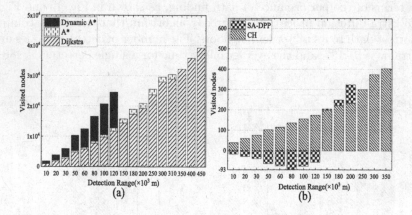

Fig. 5. Comparison of the path detection on low traffic netwrok.

However, the dynamic A* method still needs to visit a large number of nodes for comparison and calculation to make a reasonable decision, so it has a high

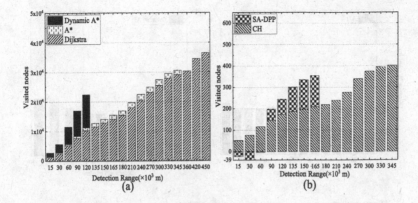

Fig. 6. Comparison of the path detection on high traffic netwrok.

number of node visits. CH contracts the nodes through the preprocessing process, so the total number of visited nodes in shortcuts is lower than that of Dijkstra, A* and Dynamic A*.

In the contraction process of CH, the importance calculation of nodes does not consider the dynamic factors in the situational environment, so its detection range is 345814 higher than that of the Dynamic A*. The SA-DPP combines the advantages of dynamic A* and CH methods to reduce the visited nodes count in the subareas by the hierarchical partition, while effectively reducing the detection range based on the coarse-grained path between subareas. And the detection range can be dynamically adjusted as the situation changes, indicating that the SA-DPP has good robustness to the situational road network.

Figure 7 illustrates the incremental change in the distance weightings of the path planning methods during path detection. With the progression of time, the detection distance is increasing, and finally the distance between ODs is accumulated. The faster the detection distance weights grow, the better the performance of the model. The SA-DPP and CH methods use bidirectional queue detection, when the bidirectional queue meets at a certain moment, that is, the final path between ODs is quickly obtained, which performs best in terms of timeliness. The next is the Dynamic A* method, which arrives at the destination by a smaller time and larger weight increment. This shows that the Dynamic A* method is able to obtain the optimal solution quickly by using a heuristic function with depth transfer between neighboring nodes. The A* also uses the greedy algorithm for path diffusion, however, the distance weights change at a low growth rate over time due to lack of effective decisions for heuristic search.

In addition, it can be seen that the SA-DPP backward lookup reaches a high incremental speed in a short period, while the CH forward lookup reaches within that range subsequently. This is because SA-DPP can quickly locate the spatial relationship between the origin and destination through coarse-grained subarea paths, while CH is still essentially based on fine-grained relationships between nodes for detection. The ability of SA-DPP to reach the destination area faster indicates that the bidirectional subareas detection algorithm of SA-DPP is superior to the node-based detection.

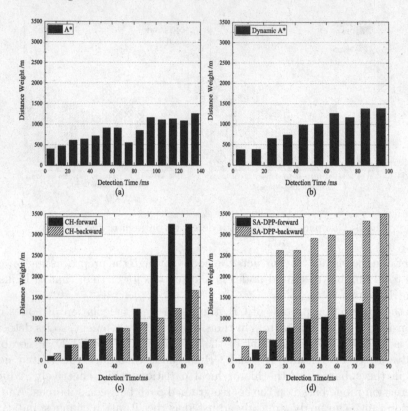

Fig. 7. The cumulative weightings between OD pairs during detection.

5   Conclusion

This paper proposes a diffusion path planning method based on subareas partition applied to solve the vehicle path planning problem in situational network. Through the hierarchical partition of the road network, the indexed tree of the situation updating and path finding is established, and a bidirectional path detection algorithm between subareas is introduced. The simulation experiments on the Beijing road network verified that the spatiotemporal indexed tree helps to model the dynamic network quickly and improve the applicability of the path planning for the situational network.

It is also concluded that path planning methods that do not consider status changes in dynamic network require expensive computational costs, which inevitably lead to optimizing the path planning model from a spatiotemporal perspective to reduce the costs imposed by the situation. The dynamic path planning method proposed in this paper incorporates spatiotemporal status features which is a new extension for the static path planning. The future work is to achieve effective situation avoidance in the dynamic path planning process.

Acknowledgments. This work is supported by the National Key R & D Program of China (No. 2022YFF0503900), the Key R & D Program of Shandong Province (No. 2021CXGC010104), the National Natural Science of Foundation of China (No. 62072016).

References

1. Dijkstra, E.W.: A note on two problems in connexion with graphs. Numer. Math. **1**(1), 269–271 (1959)
2. Hart, E., Nilsson, N., Raphael, B.: A formal basis for the heuristic determination of minimum cost paths. IEEE Trans. Syst. Sci. Cybern. SSC **4**(2), 100–107 (1968)
3. Noreen, I., Khan, A., Habib, Z.: A comparison of RRT, RRT* and RRT*-smart path planning algorithms (2016)
4. Oubbati, O.S., Atiquzzaman, M., Lorenz, P., et al.: SEARCH: an SDN-enabled approach for vehicle path-planning. IEEE Trans. Veh. Technol. **69**, 14523–14536 (2020)
5. Guo, D., Wang, J., Zhao, J.B., et al.: A vehicle path planning method based on a dynamic traffic network that considers fuel consumption and emissions. Sci. Total Environ. **663**(MAY 1), 935–943 (2019)
6. Potamias, M., Bonchi, F., Castillo, C., et al.: Fast shortest path distance estimation in large networks. In: Conference on Information and Knowledge Management, pp. 867–876 (2009)
7. Yan, C.A., Adb, C., Yi, S.B.: Road-condition-aware dynamic path planning for intelligent vehicles. Proc. Comput. Sci. **174**, 419–423 (2020)
8. Ahmad, A., Din, S., Paul, A., et al.: Real-time route planning and data dissemination for urban scenarios using the internet of things. IEEE Wirel. Commun. **26**(6), 50–55 (2019)
9. Ma, A., Ouimet, M., Cortés, J.: Hierarchical reinforcement learning via dynamic subspace search for multi-agent planning. Auton. Robots. **44**(3-4), 485–503 (2020)
10. Cohen, E., Halperin, E., Kaplan, H., et al.: Reachability and distance queries via 2-hop labels. SIAM J. Comput. **32**(5), 542–556 (2002)
11. Akiba, T., Iwata, Y., Yoshida, Y.: Fast exact shortest-path distance queries on large networks by pruned landmark labeling (2013)
12. Akiba, T., Iwata, Y., Yoshida, Y.: Dynamic and historical shortest-path distance queries on large evolving networks by pruned landmark labeling. In: Proceedings of the 23rd International Conference on World Wide Web, pp. 237–248. ACM (2014)
13. Narvaez, P., Siu, K.Y., Tzeng, H.Y.: New dynamic algorithms for shortest path tree computation. IEEE/ACM Trans. Netw. **8**(6), 734–746 (2000)
14. Hayashi, T., Akiba, T., Kawarabayashi, K.I.: Fully dynamic shortest-path distance query acceleration on massive networks (2016)
15. Tretyakov, K., Armas-Cervantes, A., García-Bauelos, L., et al.: Fast fully dynamic landmark-based estimation of shortest path distances in very large graphs. In: ACM International Conference on Information and Knowledge Management. ACM (2011)
16. Yu, Z., Yu, X., Koudas, N., et al.: Distributed processing of k shortest path queries over dynamic road networks (2020)
17. Tsalouchidou, I., Baeza-Yates, R., Bonchi, F., et al.: Temporal betweenness centrality in dynamic graphs. Int. J. Data Sci. Anal. **9**(3), 257–272 (2020)

18. Akiba, T., Iwata, Y., Kawarabayashi, K., et al.: Fast shortest-path distance queries on road networks by pruned highway labeling. In: 2014 Proceedings the Sixteenth Workshop on Algorithm Engineering and Experiments (ALENEX), pp. 147–154. Society for Industrial and Applied Mathematics (2014)

19. Hayashi, T., Akiba, T., Yoshida, Y.: Fully dynamic betweenness centrality maintenance on massive networks. Proc. VLDB Endow. 9(2), 48–59 (2015)

20. Holme, P.: Modern temporal network theory: a colloquium. Eur. Phys. J. B 88(9), 1–30 (2015). https://doi.org/10.1140/epjb/e2015-60657-4

21. Taylor, D., Myers, S.A., Clauset, A., et al.: Eigenvector-based centrality measures for temporal networks. Multisc. Model. Simul. 15(1), 537–574 (2017)

22. Alsayed, A., Higham, D.J.: Betweenness in time dependent networks. Chaos Solitons Fractals 72, 35–48 (2015)

23. Takaguchi, T., Yano, Y., Yoshida, Y.: Coverage centralities for temporal networks. Eur. Phys. J. B 89(2), 1–11 (2016). https://doi.org/10.1140/epjb/e2016-60498-7

24. Lin, C., Han, G., Du, J., et al.: Spatiotemporal congestion-aware path planning toward intelligent transportation systems in software-defined smart city IoT. IEEE Internet Things J. 7(9), 8012–8024 (2020)

25. Kicki, P., Gawron, T., Skrzypczyński, P.: A Self-supervised learning approach to rapid path planning for car-like vehicles maneuvering in urban environment (2020)

26. Zakrzewska, A., Bader, D.A.: A dynamic algorithm for local community detection in graphs. In: Proceedings of the 2015 IEEE/ACM International Conference on Advances in Social Networks Analysis and Mining 2015, pp. 559–564. ACM (2015)

27. Stanton, I., Kliot, G.: Streaming graph partitioning for large distributed graphs. In: Proceedings of the 18th ACM SIGKDD International Conference on Knowledge Discovery and Data Mining, pp. 1222–1230. ACM (2012)

Jointly Modeling Intersections and Road Segments for Travel Time Estimation via Dual Graph Convolutional Networks

Huan Yan[1]([✉]), Guangyin Jin[1], Deng Wang[2], Yue Liu[2], and Yong Li[1]

[1] Department of Electronic Engineering, Tsinghua University, Beijing 100084, China
{yanhuan,liyong07}@tsinghua.edu.cn, jinguangyin96@foxmail.com
[2] AutoNavi, Alibaba Group, Beijing, China
wangdeng.wang@alibaba-inc.com, yue.liu@autonavi.com

Abstract. Estimating the travel time of a given path plays an important role in many urban transportation systems, such as navigation, route planing and ride sharing. However, most existing works focus on modeling either the road segments or intersections, which cannot accurately estimate the travel time. The reason is that, intersections and road segments, as the basic elements of a path, not only include the diverse spatial properties and temporal dynamics, but also have the strong correlations that cannot be captured by modeling one of them. To solve this problem, we propose a novel end-to-end deep learning framework, namely Joint modeling of Intersections and Road segments based on Dual Graph Convolutional Networks (JIR-DGCN), for travel time estimation. Specifically, we design a dual graph convolution approach to capture the complex relations of both intersections and road segments, where the node-wise graph is constructed to explore the inter-section correlations, and edge-wise graph is constructed to characterize the inter-action features between road segments. In order to capture the joint relations of spatial and temporal features, we introduce a spatio-temproal learning approach that incorporates the multi-scale spatial relations integrated from multiple ranges of neighborhoods when capturing the temporal dependencies. We evaluate our JIR-DGCN by extensive experiments on three real-world trajectory datasets, and the results show that our model greatly outperforms several existing methods. Specially, we introduce a new dataset containing the travel time of both road segments and intersections. The experimental results on this dataset show that our model can obtain 8.76%–20.55% improvements of prediction performance.

Keywords: Graph convolutional network · Travel time estimation · Spatio-temporal modeling

1 Introduction

Travel time estimation (TTE), which predicts the travel time for a given path and departure time, is an important problem in many urban transportation system, i.e., routing planing, navigation and ride sharing. Many online map service providers such as

---

H. Yan and G. Jin—Both authors contributed equally to this research.

H. Wu et al. (Eds.): SpatialDI 2022, LNCS 13614, pp. 19–34, 2022.
https://doi.org/10.1007/978-3-031-24521-3_2

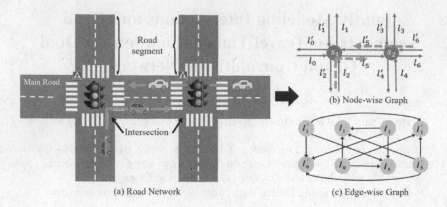

Fig. 1. An example of dual graph construction from the road network.

Google, AutoNavi provide TTE in their applications to help users for intelligent trip planning in advance. How to accurately estimate the travel time is a critical concern for these service providers to improve user experience.

Since a path consists of alternate road segments and intersections (showing in Fig. 1(a)), it is of great importance to characterize the latent features of both the intersections and road segments. To be specific, the intersections, where traffic signals are usually introduced to direct traffic movement to reduce the traffic conflicts, have an impact on the driving speed. According to [21], the delay at the intersections occupies over 10% of the total travel time for buses, which indicates that the influences of intersections cannot be neglected. Meanwhile, the traffic speed of the road segments is closely related to the accuracy of estimation. However, many existing works estimate the travel time of a path by modeling either road segments [6,8,23] or intersections [24]. They do not simultaneously consider the features of the intersections and road segments, which fails to achieve higher accurate estimation.

However, how to jointly model the intersections and road segments is a challenging problem. *First*, there exist the complicated relations of the intersections and road segments. Specifically, two neighboring intersections interact with each other, and their correlations change with the traffic condition. Meanwhile, road segments connected with the same intersection are also correlated, which depends on their upstream or downstream road segments [3]. *Second*, their complex relations contain with the spatial and temporal dependencies. On the one hand, the spatial dependencies are not only related with local traffic properties, but also are influenced by the global traffic patterns in a large scale of regions. For instance, as shown in Fig. 1(b), two different road segments l_2 and l_4 in the network graph do not connect with each other, but they connect with the same main road, i.e., l_5 and l_5'. If traffic congestion occurs on the main road, the spatial dependency tends to be more obvious, e.g., the mean speed on l_2 and l_4 would be similar. On the other hand, the spatial dependencies are not independent with temporal ones, because they are time varying. For example, in the morning rush hours, the mean speed of the road to the downtown is low, but is relatively high in the non-rush hours.

To address the above problems, we propose a novel end-to-end graph convolution network (GCN) based learning framework named JIR-DGCN to estimate the travel time. First, in order to learn the complex relations of the intersections and road segments, we propose a dual graph convolution that not only considers intersection correlations, but also explores the interaction patterns of road segments. We respectively construct the node-wise and edge-wise graph by the adjacency relations of intersections and road segments, e.g., Fig. 1(b–c). Then, we design a multi-range GCN module to integrate the spatial information in different ranges of neighborhoods. Next, a spatio-temporal learning approach is introduced to simultaneously learn the spatial and temporal properties by incorporating the spatial relations when capturing the temporal dependencies. Finally, we adopt a multi-task learning approach to estimate the travel time of the paths, road segments and intersections at the same time.

We summarize our main contributions as follows:

(1) We propose an end-to-end learning framework to estimate the travel time of the paths, road segments and intersections. It is first attempt to jointly model the intersections and road segments based on dual GCNs for travel time estimation.
(2) We propose a dual graph convolution to model the relations of both intersections and road segments. This approach adopts node-wise graph to capture the intersection correlations, and build the edge-wise graph to characterize the interaction features of road segments. Further, we propose to integrate multi-scale spatial information to obtain an aggregated spatial representation, and introduce a spatio-temporal learning approach to fully explore the joint relations of the spatial and temporal features.
(3) We evaluate JIR-DGCN by extensive experiments on three real-world datasets. The experimental results show that our framework is superior to the state-of-art methods under multiple metrics. Particularly, on a new dataset containing the travel time of both road segments and intersections, our model achieves 8.76%–20.55% higher accuracy.

2   Related Works

The existing solutions of travel time estimation are classified into four categories: road segment-based, path-based, learning-based and graph neural network based methods.

Road Segment-Based Travel Time Estimation. There are several works [11, 19, 20, 28] studying on the estimation of the travel time on individual road segments. Since these segment-based methods do not consider the intersections and correlations among road segments, it is difficult to accurately predict the travel time of a whole path.

Path-Based Travel Time Estimation. Path-based methods [17, 18, 23, 26, 29, 31] are introduced to address the above problems. For example, Wang et al. [23] estimate the travel time of a path by finding the nearby historical trajectories based on assumption that paths with similar sources and destinations have similar travel time. Wang et al. [26] adopt a dynamic programming solution to find the optimal concatenation of trajectories so as to estimate a path's travel time. However, these methods cannot effectively capture the complex spatial and temporal patterns of the traffic along the path, which leads to a poor accuracy.

Learning-Based Travel Time Estimation. Recently, deep learning methods become increasingly important in predicting the travel time [9,22,27,32]. For instance, Wang et al. [22] propose an end-to-end deep learning framework to estimate the travel time of a path, which can capture spatial and temporal dependencies along the given path. Zhang et al. [32] use each grid as the feature carrier, and then extract multiple features to predict the travel time by an auxiliary supervision model. DeepIST [9] treats each path as a sequence of images, and uses convolutional neural networks to capture both spatial moving patterns and their temporal patterns for travel time estimation. However, these works do not consider the fine-grained features in road networks.

GCN-Based Travel Time Estimation. Inspired by the advances of GCN, there are several works [3,5,10,13–15,25,30,33] designing spatio-temporal GCN model to encode spatial and temporal information in traffic forecasting. Similarly, GCNs are also adopted in predicting the travel time [6,8]. For example, ConSTGAT [6] employs a graph attention mechanism to capture the joint relations of spatial and temporal information, and applies the convolutions to mine the contextual information of a path. Fu et al. [8] design an online travel time prediction system that uses road network information to learn spatial dependency between road segments by applying a graph attention network. However, these work do not consider the complex relations of intersections and road segments. Different from them, we propose a novel graph neural network that can jointly model the intersections and road segments.

3   Preliminaries

3.1   Definitions

Trajectory: We define a trajectory Y as a sequence of consecutive GPS observations $Y = \{y_1, y_2, ..., y_{|Y|}\}$, each of which includes the location (i.e., latitude ($y_i^{l_1}$) and longitude ($y_i^{l_2}$)) with the timestamp (y_i^t).
Road Network: It can be defined as a directed graph $G = (V, E)$, where V and E denote a node set and an edge set respectively. Node $v \in V$ denotes an intersection in the road network. Edge $e_{i,j} \in E$ represents a road segment connecting intersection v_i and v_j. For convenience, a road segment is also referred to as a link in the following paper.
Path: A path P is a sequence of links and intersections in a road network. We have $P = \{e_{o,1}, v_1, e_{1,2}, v_2, ..., e_{M-1,d}\}$, where $e_{o,1}, e_{M-1,d} \in E$.

3.2   Problem Statement

Given a path P and departure time t_d, we aim to estimate the travel time t_Θ using a historical trajectory dataset D as well as the underlying road network G, which can be expressed as

$$t_\Theta \leftarrow \mathcal{F}(P, t_d, D, G), \tag{1}$$

where $\Theta = \{P, v_P, s_P\}$ represents the set of the entire path and the corresponding links and intersections. $\mathcal{F}(\cdot)$ is the function we need to learn for travel time estimation.

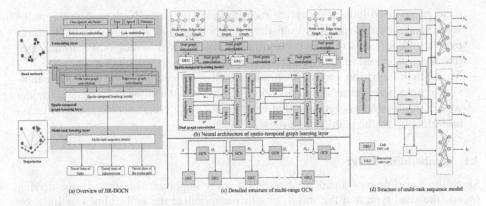

(a) Overview of JIR-DGCN   (b) Neural architecture of spatio-temporal graph learning layer   (c) Detailed structure of multi-range GCN   (d) Structure of multi-task sequence model

Fig. 2. Framework design of JIR-DGCN. (a) is the overview of our proposed model, which includes embedding layer, spatio-temporal graph learning layer and multi-task learning layer. (b) is the architecture of spatio-temporal graph learning layer. The dual graph convolution is adopted to capture the spatial correlation from road networks while the temporal correlation is extracted by GRU. (c) is the detailed structure of a multi-range GCN in spatio-temporal graph learning layer. (d) is the overview of multi-task learning layer. The travel time of links, intersections and the entire path can be estimated simultaneously in this layer.

Note that we cannot directly obtain the paths from the trajectory dataset. Alternatively, we have to convert each trajectory in D into the path based on the road network G, which is expressed as $\{Y, G\} \xrightarrow{\phi} \{P\}$, where ϕ is the map matching function.

4   Proposed Approach

It is challenging to jointly model the intersections and road segments for travel time estimation. First, the intersections and road segments have complex relations. Second, such relations have the complicated spatial and temporal dependencies. Furthermore, these two kinds of features are not independent with each other. To address them, we propose a novel framework JIR-DGCN, which consists of three layers: the embedding layer, spatio-temporal graph learning layer and multi-task learning layer, as shown in Fig. 2(a).

- **Embedding layer.** The quality of initial representations (also referred as the embeddings) of links and intersections are of great importance to effectively learn their complex features in other parts of the framework. One possible way is to use the one-hot representation, but it is too sparse to well distinguish the features of different links and intersections. To deal with it, we initialize their embeddings by integrating external factors (e.g., the types of links and the geo-spatial attributes of intersections). Especially for the intersections, we also incorporate the information of their neighboring links into the intersection embeddings.
- **Spatio-Temporal Graph Learning Layer.** To address the challenge of how the intersections and links are jointly modelled, we first design the node-wise and edge-

wise graph convolutions to capture their complex relations. Next, to capture multi-scale spatial dependencies, a multi-range GCN is proposed to integrate the features from multiple scales of spatial information. Then, a spatio-temporal learning approach is introduced to jointly learn their spatial and temporal features.

– **Multi-task Learning Layer.** To simultaneously estimate the travel time of the individual links, intersections and the entire path, we adopt a multi-task sequence model with a multi-task loss function that can balance local (i.e., intersections and links) and global (i.e., the path) estimations.

4.1 Embedding Layer

Since the travel time of a path is affected by many important factors, e.g., the driving speed, the road type and the travel length, we initialize the embeddings of links by incorporating these factors into our model. To be specific, the embeddings of links at time t can be formulated as follows,

$$h_e(t) = \tanh(W_e \cdot [s_e(t), d_e, p_e]), \tag{2}$$

where $s_e(t)$ is the mean speed estimated at time t, d_e is the length of the link, p_e is the link type, W_e is a learnable parameter matrix, and $[\cdot]$ is a concatenation operator.

Intersections connect with multiple links, thus their embeddings are initialized by aggregating the embeddings of connected links. Meanwhile, they also have their specific geo-spatial attributes (traffic lights on the intersections). Thus, the embeddings of intersections at time t can be expressed as:

$$z_v(t) = \tanh(W_1 \sum_{i \in F(v)} h_i(t) + W_2 \cdot p_v), \tag{3}$$

where $F(v)$ is the set of links connecting with intersection v. p_v denotes whether there exist traffic lights at the intersections. W_1 and W_2 are the learnable parameter matrixes.

4.2 Spatio-Temporal Graph Learning Layer

The core of JIR-DGCN is the spatio-temporal graph learning layer, as shown in Fig. 2(b). Three important components are proposed in this layer, including the dual graph convolution approach, the reinforced GCN and the spatio-temporal learning approach, which together jointly model the intersections and road segments.

Dual Graph Convolution. Existing approaches [6,8] exploit a GCN with a weighted graph to learn the interaction among the road segments, while the intersections connecting the road segments are represented by fixed scalars (e.g., the weighted sum), which neglects the complex interaction between the road segments and their connected intersections. To jointly learn their features, we design a dual graph convolution approach to simultaneously model their complicated relations.

Let $G = (V, E, W)$ denote the node-wise graph, where each node and edge represent an intersection and a road segment respectively. $G' = (V', E', Q)$ is the corresponding line graph (also called edge-wise graph), and the nodes V' of G' are the ordered edges in E, i.e., $V' = (i \rightarrow j), (i, j) \in E$ and $|V'| = |E|$. $\boldsymbol{W}$ and $\boldsymbol{Q}$ are the weighted adjacency matrices that characterize their interactions.

In node-wise graph G, the edge weights between any two neighboring nodes i and j are not the same. Intuitively, if node i and node j have a large number of out-degrees and in-degrees respectively, their edge weight representing the correlation between node i and node j is small. Thus, we compute the edge weights $\boldsymbol{W}$ as follows:

$$w_{i,j} = R_{ij}\exp(-\frac{(d^+(i) + d^-(j) - 2)^2}{\sigma^2}), i \neq j, \tag{4}$$

where $d^+(i)$ and $d^-(j)$ represents the number of out-degree of node i and in-degree of node j, respectively. σ is the standard deviation of node degrees. R_{ij} represents the adjacent relation between node i and node j in the graph. To be specific, for each pair $(i, j) \in V \times V$, R_{ij} is 1 if $(i, j) \in E$ and 0 otherwise.

In edge-wise graph G', the edge weight q_{ij} is defined as the proportion of the traffic from link i to link j. Obviously, if the traffic from link i to link j is larger than that from link i to other neighboring links, the correlation between i to link j is strong. Thus, we compute the edge weights $\boldsymbol{Q}$ as follows:

$$q_{i,j} = R_{ij}\frac{z_{ij}}{\sum_{k \in N(i)} z_{ik}}, i \neq j, \tag{5}$$

where z_{ij} is the number of trajectories traversed from node i to node j. $N(i)$ is the set of the 1-hop neighbors of node i.

Thus, the k-hop dual graph convolution is formulated as:

$$\boldsymbol{Z}^{(l+1)} = \theta^{(l)}_{n*G}[\boldsymbol{Z}^{(l)}, \boldsymbol{MH}^{(l)}], l = 0, 1, ..., k - 1,$$
$$\boldsymbol{H}^{(l+1)} = \theta^{(l)}_{e*G}[\boldsymbol{H}^{(l)}, \boldsymbol{M}^T\boldsymbol{Z}^{(l+1)}], l = 0, 1, ..., k - 1, \tag{6}$$

where θ_{*G} is the graph convolution operation with parameter θ, and $\boldsymbol{M} \in \mathbb{R}^{|V| \times |E|}$ is the incidence matrix that encodes the connections between nodes and edges, defined as: $M_{i,(i \rightarrow j)} = M_{j,(i \rightarrow j)} = 1$ and 0 otherwise. $\boldsymbol{Z}^{(l+1)}$ and $\boldsymbol{H}^{(l+1)}$ denote the output of node-wise graph and edge-wise graph respectively.

Multi-range GCN. One step of graph convolution can aggregate information of 1-hop neighbors [12]. By stacking multiple graph convolution layers, we can expand the receptive neighborhood range. However, as the network goes deep, the nodes tend to have the global traffic patterns, while losing their local patterns. Therefore, we would integrate the multi-scale information to capture both global and local features. To deal with it, we propose a multi-range GCN, which is shown in Fig. 2(c).

To capture the important features from the outputs in previous layers, we use a gated recurrent unit (GRU) [4], which is different from [16] that employs snowball approach to incrementally concatenate multi-scale features. GRU is a simple but effective structure compared with other types of RNN implementation. It can be expressed as:

$$c^{(0)} = \text{GRU}(r^{(0)}, c^{(-1)}), r^{(1)} = \sigma(\boldsymbol{L}r^{(0)}\boldsymbol{W}^{(0)})$$
$$r^{(2)} = \sigma(\boldsymbol{L}[r^{(0)}, r^{(1)}]\boldsymbol{W}^{(1)}),$$
$$r^{(l+1)} = \sigma(\boldsymbol{L}[\text{GRU}(r^{(l-1)}, c^{(l-2)}), r^{(l)}]\boldsymbol{W}^{(l)}),$$
$$l = 2, 3, ..., n - 1, \tag{7}$$

where $L = \widetilde{D}^{-1/2}\widetilde{A}\widetilde{D}^{-1/2}$, $\widetilde{A} = A + I$, $\widetilde{D} = diag(\sum_j \widetilde{A}_{1j}, ..., \sum_j \widetilde{A}_{Nj})$. A is a symmetric adjacency matrix, and I is an identity matrix. σ is a non-linear activation function, and we use function *tanh* in this paper [16]. $r^{(l)}$ is the latent representation of intersection or link at l-th hop. $c^{(l)}$ is the hidden state after we processed the $(l-1)$-hop neighbors, and its initial value $c^{(-1)} = 0$. GRU derives the vector representations of a hidden state, which is expressed as:

$$
\begin{aligned}
u &= \sigma(W_{u_1}r(t) + U_{u_1}c(t-1) + b_{u_1}), \\
x &= \sigma(W_{x_1}r(t) + U_{x_1}c(t-1) + b_{x_1}), \\
c'(t) &= \tanh(W_{h_1}r(t) + U_{h_1}(x \odot c(t-1)) + b_{h_1}), \\
c(t) &= u \odot r(t-1) + (1-u) \odot c'(t),
\end{aligned}
\tag{8}
$$

where $\odot$ is the element-wise multiplication. $W_{u_1}, U_{u_1}, W_{x_1}, U_{x_1}, W_{h_1}, U_{h_1}$ are the parameters to be learned, and $b_{u_1}, b_{x_1}, b_{h_1}$ are biases.

Spatio-Temporal Learning Approach. We use GRU to capture temporal dependency of both intersections and links, as shown in Fig. 2(b). Specifically, we use the historical information of intersections and links to obtain their temporal features, which is formulated as:

$$
\begin{aligned}
s_i(t) &= \text{GRU}(h_i(t), s_i'(t-1)|W_\Omega, U_\Omega, b_\Omega), \\
x_i(t) &= \text{GRU}(z_i(t), x_i'(t-1)|W_\Omega', U_\Omega', b_\Omega'), \\
s_i'(t-1), x_i'(t-1) &= f(G, G', s_i(t-1), x_i(t-1), L),
\end{aligned}
\tag{9}
$$

where $f(\cdot)$ is the function of the dual graph convolution, and L represents the number of layers of the dual graph convolution. $h_i(t)(z_i(t))$ is the representation of i-th intersection (link) at time step t, $s_i(t)(x_i(t))$ is the hidden state after we processed the i-th intersection (link) at time step t. $W_\Omega, W_\Omega', U_\Omega'$ and U_Ω are weight matrices, and b_Ω, b_Ω' are biases, where $\Omega \in \{u, r, h\}$. In particular, inspired by [25], we apply the dual graph convolution operation to both the input and hidden representation of GRU in order to fully exploit the spatial and temporal information.

4.3   Multi-task Learning Layer

As the traffic information is always sequentially dependent, we use the path information that reflects the temporal dependency among links and intersections to further capture it, as seen in Fig. 2(d). For simplicity, we use q to represent both s and x. Thus, the formula can be expressed as:

$$
\begin{aligned}
u &= \sigma(W_{u_2}q_i(t) + U_{u_2}c_{i-1}(t) + b_{u_2}), \\
r &= \sigma(W_{r_2}q_i(t) + U_{r_2}c_{i-1}(t) + b_{r_2}), \\
c_i'(t) &= \tanh(W_{h_2}q_i(t) + U_{h_2}(r \odot c_{i-1}(t)) + b_{h_2}), \\
c_i(t) &= u \odot c_{i-1}(t) + (1-u) \odot c_i'(t),
\end{aligned}
\tag{10}
$$

where $c_i(t)$ is the final representation of i-th road segment or intersection at time step t.

Prediction: To estimate the travel time of each link and intersection, we use a two-layer fully-connected network with the size λ and 1. We define t_{l_i} (t_{v_j}) as the travel time of the i-th link (j-th intersection).

To estimate the travel time of the entire path, we transform the feature sequence $\{c_i\}$ into a fixed length vector.

$$g_P = \sum_{i=1}^{|P|} c_i, \tag{11}$$

where $|P|$ is the total number of links and intersections in Path P.

Finally, we pass g_P to a fully-connect layers with equal size, and obtain the estimation of the entire path.

Loss Function: During the training phase, we use the mean absolute percentage error (MAPE) as our objective functions for travel time estimation of the entire path, which is derived as follows:

$$L_P = \sum_{i=1}^{|D|} \frac{|t_i - \widehat{t_i}|}{\widehat{t_i} + \epsilon}, \tag{12}$$

where t_i denotes the estimated travel time, and $\widehat{t_i}$ is the ground truth for travel time for i-th path. Similar with [22], we add a parameter ϵ to avoid exploded loss value in case that the denominator approaches 0. In this paper, ϵ is set to 5.

For the local path estimation, we define the corresponding loss as the average loss of all local paths,

$$L_l = \sum_{P \in D} \sum_{j=1}^{(|P|+1)/2} \frac{|t_{l_j} - \widehat{t_{l_j}}|}{\widehat{t_{l_j}} + \epsilon}, \tag{13}$$

where $\widehat{t_{l_i}}$ is the ground truth for travel time for i-th link.

For the intersection estimation, we define the corresponding loss as the average loss of all intersections,

$$L_v = \sum_{P \in D} \sum_{j=1}^{(|P|-1)/2} \frac{|t_{v_j} - \widehat{t_{v_j}}|}{\widehat{t_{v_j}} + \epsilon}, \tag{14}$$

where $\widehat{t_{v_i}}$ is the ground truth for travel time for i-th intersection.

Our model is trained to minimize the weighted combination of three loss terms, which is expressed as:

$$L = \alpha L_P + \beta L_l + (1 - \alpha - \beta) L_v, \tag{15}$$

where α and β are used to balance L_P, L_l and L_v.

5 Experiments

We conduct extensive experiments to evaluate our model on two public real-word datasets and a new dataset with more complete information collected by us.

Table 1. The statistics of three datasets.

Dataset	Chengdu	Porto	Beijing
Number of trajectories	15,303	12,683	34,696
Number of links	873	544	714
Number of intersections	807	450	320
Average travel time (s)	246.54	248.49	343.3
Average moving length (m)	1435.34	1394.82	3929.7

Table 2. The statistics of Chengdu datasets in three scenarios, including the suburb, rush and non-rush hours.

Scenario	Suburb	Rush Hrs.	Non-Rush Hrs.
Number of trajectories	8,156	2,867	12,436
Number of links	639	873	873
Number of intersections	291	807	807
Average travel time (s)	242.42	249.81	243.57
Average moving length (m)	1105.42	1435.47	1435.31

5.1 Datasets

We evaluate our proposed model using three real-world datasets: Chengdu dataset [1], Porto dataset [2] and Beijing dataset released by Amap. Chengdu dataset contains taxi trajectories of over 14 thousand taxis in August 2014. Porto dataset contains taxi trajectories of 442 taxis from July 2013 to June 2014. Beijing dataset contains 34,696 anonymous trajectories during 8:00 AM–1:00 PM on December 15, 2020. Different from other two public datasets, the travel time of each intersection is available in this dataset. Table 1 shows the statistics of three datasets used in our experiments.

As the geo-spatial and temporal factors may influence the prediction performance of the travel time, we also choose Chengdu trajectories based on three scenarios to validate the generality of our model, including the suburban areas, rush (7:00–9:00 AM and 5:00–7:00 PM at weekdays) and non-rush hours in the urban areas. At the same time, the scenarios of rush and non-rush hours are defined in the urban areas. Table 2 shows the statistics of Chengdu dataset in three scenarios.

5.2 Experimental Settings

The embedding sizes of intersections and links are set to 20. The number of the multi-range GCN layer is set to 3, and the hop of dual graph convolution is 1 by default. We use the historical information of intersection and link at first 12 time steps with intervals of 5 min to capture their temporal features. The number of fully-connected layers is set to 2, and their hidden sizes are both set to 60. We train the model using Adam optimizer with an initial learning rate of 0.001 on Chengdu dataset and 0.0005 on Porto dataset. We run our model on TITAN Xp GPU with the implementation in Python with Pytorch 1.5, and repeat each experiment for three times.

Table 3. Performance of JIR-DGCN and other methods for estimating the travel time of the paths, links and intersections on three datasets, where the performance improvements of our model are compared with the best of these baseline methods, marked by the asterisk. Especially the predicting results for links and intersections are listed after the symbol '/'.

Method	Chengdu RMSE (sec)	MAE (sec)	MAPE	Porto RMSE (sec)	MAE (sec)	MAPE	Beijing RMSE (sec)	MAE (sec)	MAPE
GBDT	165.03/–	101.68/–	0.5428/–	91.24/–	71.79/–	0.3914/–	372.87/–/–	262.49/–/–	0.6854/–/–
MlpTTE	150.67/–	87.32/–	0.3076/–	59.46/–	44.49/–	0.1783/–	124.92/–/–	79.75/–/–	0.2532/–/–
RnnTTE	155.16/–	89.37/–	0.3011/–	56.45/–	43.32/–	0.1702/–	127.80/–/–	86.59/–/–	0.2924/–/–
DeepTTE	148.30*/–	86.40/–	0.2984/–	57.23/–	43.45/–	0.1686/–	147.60/–/–	92.64/–/–	0.2500/–/–
T-GCN	153.49/ 57.84	87.71/ 24.85	0.2918/ 0.5537	56.35/ 22.48	43.28/ 13.03	0.1678/ 0.5122	129.56/ 47.06/–	85.66/ 23.87/–	0.2758/ 0.5886/–
DCRNN	151.59/ 57.82*	86.14*/ 24.76	0.2884/ 0.5513	54.73*/ 20.59	41.81*/ 11.68	0.1637*/ 0.4605	116.30/ 49.14/–	76.71/ 26.23/–	0.2561/ 0.6366/–
ConSTGAT	152.23/ 58.17	87.10/ 24.55*	0.2845*/ 0.5503*	56.67/ 21.76	43.22/ 12.32	0.1684/ 0.4865	107.58*/ 47.26/–	69.90*/ 21.64/–	0.2288*/ 0.5074/–
GCNAtt	152.95/ 58.26	87.41/ 24.79	0.2898/ 0.5512	55.88/ 19.89*	42.79/ 10.95*	0.1654/ 0.4323*	112.88/ 45.31*/ 22.88*	73.82/ 21.50*/ 10.12*	0.2372/ 0.4884*/ 0.4665*
JIR-DGCN (ours)	140.30/ 55.91	77.60/ 22.88	0.2585/ 0.5122	50.95/ 15.81	40.06/ 8.06	0.1558/ 0.3016	96.27/ 41.34/ 20.60	63.02/ 18.87/ 8.04	0.2145/ 0.4414/ 0.3707
Improvements (%)	+5.39/ +3.30	+9.91/ +6.80	+9.14/ +6.92	+6.90/ +20.51	+4.19/ +26.39	+4.83/ +30.23	+10.51/ +8.76/ +9.96	+9.84/ +12.23/ +20.55	+6.25/ +9.62/ +20.52

5.3 Methods for Comparison

To evaluate the strength of our model, we select 8 state-of-art methods, which are introduced as follows:

- **GBDT** [7]: Gradient Boosting Decision Tree (GBDT) is used for regression.
- **MlpTTE**: A multiple-layer perceptron is adopted to estimate the travel time.
- **RnnTTE**: GRU is utilized as an implementation of the recurrent neural networks for travel time estimation.
- **DeepTTE** [22]: This is an end-to-end deep learning model to capture the spatial and temporal dependencies based on the consecutive sampling GPS points along the query path.
- **T-GCN** [34]: This is a temporal GCN model that combines the GCN and GRU to simultaneously characterize the spatial and temporal dependencies.
- **DCRNN** [14]: It exploits GCN to capture spatial dependency, and then uses the recurrent neural networks to model temporal dependency.
- **ConSTGAT** [6]: This model adopts a graph attention mechanism to explore the joint relations of spatial and temporal information.
- **GCNAtt**: It uses GCN to model the road segments, and adopts an attention mechanism for intersections to address the complex dependencies between road segments.

5.4 Experimental Results

Overall Performance. We compare our model with other baseline methods on three datasets. Table 3 shows the performance of estimating the travel times of the paths. From the results, we find that our model achieves best performance than other methods in terms of all three metrics. This can be explained in two aspects. First, for some graph based methods like T-GCN, DCRNN and ConSTGAT, they only focus on modeling the road segments. However, intersections, as the critical junctions to control the traffic among multiple connected links, also play an important role in travel time estimation. Thus, designing the model without considering the intersections cannot achieve a higher accuracy. Second, for the models like GCNAtt, it has considered the intersections and links, but it does not fully exploit their joint relations that contain much valuable

Table 4. Performance of JIR-DGCN and other methods for estimating the travel times of the paths under three scenarios.

Scenario	Suburb			Rush Hours			Non-Rush Hours		
method	RMSE (sec)	MAE (sec)	MAPE	RMSE (sec)	MAE (sec)	MAPE	RMSE (sec)	MAE (sec)	MAPE
RnnTTE	121.75	76.64	0.2817	126.43	84.87	0.2986	122.50	83.69	0.3020
DeepTTE	114.47	72.55	0.2879	129.45	87.67	0.3121	123.36	83.97	0.2968
T-GCN	121.58	76.38	0.2775	132.05	89.74	0.3039	121.21	83.17	0.2905
DRCNN	120.34	75.40	0.2748	131.22	89.10	0.2976	120.67	82.78	0.2853
ConSTGAT	118.89	72.12	0.2648	128.79	88.06	0.2930	118.64	81.89	0.2821
JIR-DGCN (ours)	**111.87**	**68.63**	**0.2421**	**117.13**	**78.45**	**0.2729**	**105.81**	**71.05**	**0.2579**

contextual information of traffic along the path. Thus, GCNAtt cannot obtain best performance. Unlike them, our JIR-DGCN not only considers both intersections and links, but also captures their complex relations.

Meanwhile, we also conduct experiments to compare our model with other graph learning based methods on predicting the travel times of the links and intersections. Note that only Beijing Dataset has the information of the travel time of intersections, and other models except GCNAtt does not consider the intersections. Thus, we compare our model with GCNAtt for the travel time estimation of the intersections based on Beijing Dataset. As shown in Table 3, we observe that for links, our model obtains better prediction performance on all three datasets. For intersections, there is a significant improvement of 12.23% on RMSE, 20.55% on MAE and 20.53% on MAPE by our model compared with GCNAtt. This is because that our model captures the interaction relations between the links and intersections, which helps to improve the accuracy of estimating the travel time of links as well as intersections.

Performance Improvement Under Different Scenarios. As mentioned above, the geo-spatial and temporal factors have important impacts on the travel time estimation. Specifically, different kinds of regions have different traffic condition. For example, the traffic is usually busy in the downtown, while there are a small number of motor vehicles travelling in the suburb. Meanwhile, traffic condition varies with time. For example, traffic congestion is more likely to occur in the rush hours than in the non-rush hours. Based on the above analysis, we conduct experiments to evaluate our model in estimating the travel time of the paths under three different scenarios, including the suburb, rush hours and non-rush hours. Table 4 shows the obtained results. As we can observe, although traffic congestion may occur during the rush hours, our model can achieve at least 7.36%, 7.56% and 6.86% improvement in RMSE, MAE and MAPE. However, in non-rush hours, our model achieves at least 10.81%, 13.24% and 8.58% improvement in RMSE, MAE and MAPE. Meanwhile, in suburb where there is a small number of trajectories, our model also obtains at least 2.27%, 4.84% and 8.46% improvement of prediction performance in RMSE, MAE and MAPE. Our model has the greatest improvement in the non-rush hours scenario. While, regardless of which scenarios, our model significantly outperforms other methods.

Table 5. Performance of JIR-DGCN and its variants for estimating the travel times of the paths on two datasets.

Method	Chengdu			Porto		
	RMSE (sec)	MAE (sec)	MAPE	RMSE (sec)	MAE (sec)	MAPE
JIR-DGCN_simpleRNN	146.78	82.03	0.2732	51.63	40.82	0.1588
JIR-DGCN w/o RNN	147.48	83.46	0.2764	54.07	41.13	0.1626
JIR-DGCN w/o Intersection	143.82	79.59	0.2642	53.96	41.02	0.1610
JIR-DGCN_simpleGCN	144.56	80.21	0.2709	53.87	40.95	0.1622
JIR-DGCN (ours)	**140.30**	**77.60**	**0.2585**	**50.95**	**40.06**	**0.1558**

Ablation Study. To validate how the spatio-temporal learning approach in JIR-DGCN can effectively capture the joint relations of spatial and temporal properties, we first remove the multi-range GCN from the hidden state of the GRU when processing the sequence. From Table 5, we find that it cannot achieve good performance when compared with JIR-DGCN on two datasets. This is because that the spatial information is incorporated into the temporal dependencies, which demonstrates the effectiveness of our approach. Then, we build JIR-DGCN w/o RNN that removes the temporal part from our model. The results are shown in Table 5, from which we find that there is a obvious decline in prediction performance on two datasets when removing the temporal part. This is because that the temporal part is critical to capture the historical information of traffic along the path, which indicates that purely capturing spatial features cannot obtain better performance. Based on above analysis, it is concluded that our spatio-temporal learning approach can effectively address the spatio-temporal dependencies.

Next, we study how modeling the intersections affects the performance. In JIR-DGCN w/o Intersection, we only model the road segments to estimate the travel time. The results show that regardless of which dataset the performance becomes worse. The reason is that intersections not only contain their own important information, but also have strong correlations with links. Thus, JIR-DGCN w/o Intersection that omits the features of intersections cannot obtain good performance. Further, it demonstrates the importance of modeling both the intersections and links.

Lastly, we show the effectiveness of the multi-range GCN in our model. Specifically, we use a simple GCN [12] instead of the multi-range GCN but with the same number of layers in JIR-DGCN_simpleGCN, and then evaluate its performance. The result shows that using our model with multi-range GCNs can achieve better performance on two datasets. It can be explained that distinct traffic properties exist in different ranges of regions, and capturing them helps to better model the spatial correlations for the travel time estimation. Thus, we conclude that the multi-range GCN is effective in capturing multiple range traffic properties.

Parameter Analysis. To further show the effectiveness of our model, we conduct experiments under different combinations of parameters, including the number of layers of a multi-range GCN (denoted by n) and the number of hops of a dual graph convolution (denoted by k).

Table 6. Performance of JIR-DGCN under different combinations of k and n.

(k, n)	Chengdu			Porto		
	RMSE (sec)	MAE (sec)	MAPE	RMSE (sec)	MAE (sec)	MAPE
(1, 1)	154.11	88.34	0.2975	55.52	42.03	0.1663
(1, 2)	141.60	78.39	0.2653	54.12	41.03	0.1608
(1, 3)	**140.30**	**77.60**	**0.2585**	50.95	40.06	0.1558
(1, 4)	143.78	80.55	0.2689	53.76	40.83	0.1596
(2, 1)	151.67	86.23	0.2865	54.84	41.62	0.1631
(2, 2)	140.52	77.78	0.2596	**51.17**	**38.83**	**0.1544**
(2, 3)	141.22	78.92	0.2612	52.59	40.20	0.1579
(2, 4)	146.75	83.32	0.2756	54.12	41.24	0.1608

Specifically, we evaluate our model under different n for a certain k. As observed in Table 6, we find that in terms of all three metrics, the performance gradually improves when n goes from 1 to 3 under $k = 1$ on the datasets of two cities. However, when $n = 4$, the performance becomes worse. This shows that the higher number of layers of a multi-range GCN does not indicate the better performance. Further, we compare the performance under different combinations of parameters on each dataset. The results show that our model achieves the best performance under $n = 3$ and $k = 1$ on Chengdu dataset, while the optimal performance is obtained under $n = 2$ and $k = 2$ on Porto dataset. This indicates that the number of layers of a multi-range GCN and the number of hops of a dual graph convolution both play a critical role in obtaining a higher accuracy for travel time estimation. To sum up, we conclude that the more layers of a multi-range GCN and the larger hops of a dual graph convolution does not mean better performance, and they should be appropriately chosen according to the corresponding datasets.

6 Conclusion

We proposed an end-to-end framework for travel time estimation, tackling with the problem that road segments and intersections are not considered simultaneously in existing solutions. We adopt a dual graph convolution approach to jointly model road segments and intersections. Moreover, we propose to characterize both the spatial features and temporal dependencies by incorporating the spatial information in modeling temporal sequences. Our model also integrates multi-scale spatial information to capture local and global spatial patterns. Several experiments on three trajectory datasets demonstrated the superiority and generality of our model, as well as the effectiveness of its key designs.

Acknowledgement. This work was supported in part by The National Key Research and Development Program of China under grant 2020YFB2104005.

References

1. Taxi travel time prediction challenge (2016). http://www.dcjingsai.com
2. Kaggle (2020). https://www.kaggle.com/crailtap/taxi-trajectory
3. Chen, W., Chen, L., Xie, Y., Cao, W., Gao, Y., Feng, X.: Multi-range attentive bicomponent graph convolutional network for traffic forecasting. In: Proceedings of AAAI, pp. 3529–3536 (2020)
4. Chung, J., Gulcehre, C., Cho, K., Bengio, Y.: Empirical evaluation of gated recurrent neural networks on sequence modeling. arXiv preprint arXiv:1412.3555 (2014)
5. Derrow-Pinion, A., et al.: ETA prediction with graph neural networks in google maps. In: Proceedings of CIKM, pp. 3767–3776 (2021)
6. Fang, X., Huang, J., Wang, F., Zeng, L., Liang, H., Wang, H.: ConSTGAT: contextual Spatial-Temporal graph attention network for travel time estimation at Baidu maps. In: Proceedings of KDD, pp. 2697–2705 (2020)
7. Hastie, T., Tibshirani, R., Friedman, J.: The Elements of Statistical Learning. SSS, Springer, New York (2009). https://doi.org/10.1007/978-0-387-84858-7
8. Fu, K., Meng, F., Ye, J., Wang, Z.: CompactETA: a fast inference system for travel time prediction. In: Proceedings of KDD, pp. 3337–3345 (2020)
9. Fu, T.Y., Lee, W.C.: DeepIST: deep image-based Spatio-Temporal network for travel time estimation. In: Proceedings of CIKM, pp. 69–78 (2019)
10. Guo, S., Lin, Y., Feng, N., Song, C., Wan, H.: Attention based spatial-temporal graph convolutional networks for traffic flow forecasting. In: Proceedings of AAAI, vol. 33, pp. 922–929 (2019)
11. Jenelius, E., Koutsopoulos, H.N.: Travel time estimation for urban road networks using low frequency probe vehicle data. Transp. Res. B Methodol. **53**, 64–81 (2013)
12. Kipf, T.N., Welling, M.: Semi-supervised classification with graph convolutional networks. arXiv preprint arXiv:1609.02907 (2016)
13. Li, M., Zhu, Z.: Spatial-temporal fusion graph neural networks for traffic flow forecasting. In: Proceedings of the AAAI Conference on Artificial Intelligence, vol. 35, pp. 4189–4196 (2021)
14. Li, Y., Yu, R., Shahabi, C., Liu, Y.: Diffusion convolutional recurrent neural network: data-driven traffic forecasting. arXiv preprint arXiv:1707.01926 (2017)
15. Liang, Y., et al.: Fine-grained urban flow prediction. In: Proceedings of the Web Conference, pp. 1833–1845 (2021)
16. Luan, S., Zhao, M., Chang, X.W., Precup, D.: Break the ceiling: stronger multi-scale deep graph convolutional networks. In: Advances in Neural Information Processing Systems, pp. 10945–10955 (2019)
17. Luo, W., Tan, H., Chen, L., Ni, L.M.: Finding time period-based most frequent path in big trajectory data. In: Proceedings of SIGMOD, pp. 713–724 (2013)
18. Rahmani, M., Jenelius, E., Koutsopoulos, H.N.: Route travel time estimation using low-frequency floating car data. In: Proceedings of IEEE ITSC, pp. 2292–2297 (2013)
19. Rice, J., Van Zwet, E.: A simple and effective method for predicting travel times on freeways. IEEE Trans. Intell. Transp. Syst. **5**(3), 200–207 (2004)
20. Sevlian, R., Rajagopal, R.: Travel time estimation using floating car data. arXiv preprint arXiv:1012.4249 (2010)
21. Tirachini, A.: Estimation of travel time and the benefits of upgrading the fare payment technology in urban bus services. Transp. Res. Part C Emerg. Technol. **30**, 239–256 (2013)
22. Wang, D., Zhang, J., Cao, W., Li, J., Zheng, Y.: When will you arrive? Estimating travel time based on deep neural networks. In: Proceedings of AAAI, pp. 2500–2507 (2018)

23. Wang, H., Tang, X., Kuo, Y.H., Kifer, D., Li, Z.: A simple baseline for travel time estimation using large-scale trip data. ACM Trans. Intell. Syst. Technol. **10**(2), 1–22 (2019)
24. Wang, M.X., Lee, W.C., Fu, T.Y., Yu, G.: Learning embeddings of intersections on road networks. In: Proceedings of SIGSPATIAL, pp. 309–318 (2019)
25. Wang, X., et al.: Traffic flow prediction via spatial temporal graph neural network. In: Proceedings of WWW, pp. 1082–1092 (2020)
26. Wang, Y., Zheng, Y., Xue, Y.: Travel time estimation of a path using sparse trajectories. In: Proceedings of SIGKDD, pp. 25–34 (2014)
27. Wang, Z., Fu, K., Ye, J.: Learning to estimate the travel time. In: Proceedings of SIGKDD, pp. 858–866 (2018)
28. Wu, C.H., Ho, J.M., Lee, D.T.: Travel-time prediction with support vector regression. IEEE Trans. Intell. Transp. Syst. **5**(4), 276–281 (2004)
29. Yang, B., Dai, J., Guo, C., Jensen, C.S., Hu, J.: *PACE*: a *PA*th-*CE*ntric paradigm for stochastic path finding. VLDB J. **27**(2), 153–178 (2017). https://doi.org/10.1007/s00778-017-0491-4
30. Yu, B., Yin, H., Zhu, Z.: Spatio-temporal graph convolutional networks: a deep learning framework for traffic forecasting. arXiv preprint arXiv:1709.04875 (2017)
31. Yuan, J., Zheng, Y., Xie, X., Sun, G.: T-drive: enhancing driving directions with taxi drivers' intelligence. IEEE Trans. Knowl. Data Eng. **25**(1), 220–232 (2011)
32. Zhang, H., Wu, H., Sun, W., Zheng, B.: DeepTravel: a neural network based travel time estimation model with auxiliary supervision. arXiv preprint arXiv:1802.02147 (2018)
33. Zhang, J., Shi, X., Xie, J., Ma, H., King, I., Yeung, D.Y.: GaAN: gated attention networks for learning on large and spatiotemporal graphs. arXiv preprint arXiv:1803.07294 (2018)
34. Zhao, L., et al.: T-GCN: a temporal graph convolutional network for traffic prediction. IEEE Trans. Intell. Transp. Syst. **21**(9), 3848–3858 (2019)

We-Map Orientation Method Suitable for General Public with Weak Sense of Orientation

Xiaolong Wang[1,2,3], Haowen Yan[1,2,3]([✉]), Shan Gao[4], Zhuo Wang[5], and Yang He[1,2,3]

[1] Faculty of Geomatics, Lanzhou Jiaotong University, Lanzhou 730070, China
yanhw@mail.lzjtu.cn
[2] National-Local Joint Engineering Research Center of Technologies and Application for National Geographic State Monitoring, Lanzhou 730070, China
[3] Gansu Provincial Engineering Laboratory for National Geographic State Monitoring, Lanzhou 730070, China
[4] School of Art and Design, Lanzhou Jiaotong University, Lanzhou 730070, China
[5] School of Resource and Environmental Sciences, Wuhan University, Wuhan 430072, China

Abstract. We-Map, a map for the general public, whose core thinking is that cartographers do not need to go through strict professional training to make a map belonged to themselves. The existing maps have strict geographic orientation because their production not only needs cartographers have solid professional knowledge and strict training but also relies on traditional longitude and latitude grid line to determine geographic orientation (i.e. the north, south, east and west) on the map. However, some people in the general public have a weak sense of direction. Although they can understand the geographic orientation on the map, they cannot quickly convert to the geographic orientation in real life. Such kinds of people are obviously impossible to mapping based on geographic directions. Therefore, we-map orientation method suitable for general public with weak sense of direction was proposed to solve the problem. First, general public with weak sense of direction utilize their own position and surrounding spatial objects as a reference to determine map orientation, no longer use a certain direction of the traditional longitude and latitude grid line (i.e. geographic orientation) for orientation; Then, it should be produced from the personal perspective of the map users, not from the perspective of a professional cartographer when a user makes a map; Last, the map will be shared with other users who need it urgently or on one's own social platforms (e.g. WeChat, Facebook, Weibo and Twitter et al.) for the convenience of others after its production is completed.

Keywords: We-map · Map orientation · Weak sense of direction · Cartography

1 Introduction

We-map, a map for the general public, whose core thinking is that cartographers do not need to go through strict professional training to make a map belonged to themselves, i.e. map user can also participate in map production at any time. It can be conveniently used,

© The Author(s), under exclusive license to Springer Nature Switzerland AG 2022
H. Wu et al. (Eds.): SpatialDI 2022, LNCS 13614, pp. 35–41, 2022.
https://doi.org/10.1007/978-3-031-24521-3_3

communicated and fast spread on personal electronic devices (e.g. personal computers, mobile phones, and tablet computers) [1]. The foundations of we-map production are closely related to coordinate system, scale, projection system and orientation system et al. This paper focuses on the research of orientation system because map orientation has a vital to play in recognizing the orientation on the map and understanding the location in real life. Moreover, the existing we-map research rarely involves the orientation of we-map, which mainly concentrate on spread and communication [2, 3], map symbols [4–6] and design [7–11]. Therefore, the issue of we-map orientation demands to be explored urgently.

Some studies have shown that it is not easy for adults to use maps to identify their location and orientation (direction) when they are in a relatively unfamiliar environment [12–14]. In other words, it is difficult for a large number of people to use the map to identify their location and orientation in terms of existing map orientation. This group of people is the general public with a weak sense of orientation (GPWSR). There is a great quantity of GPWSRs among we-map users. Hence, the existing map orientation refers to the geographic orientation of content on the map, which is quite mature but cannot directly be applied to the we-map, i.e. the mature map orientation methods have certain limitations when it be applied to we-map, especially when target group is GPWSRs, the limitations will be magnified.

In a word, this paper proposes a we-map orientation method suitable for GPWSR to provide a novel orientation scheme for GPWSR. They can product maps without professional cartography training, and can use and make maps without being restricted by geographic directions. The issues of we-map orientation are explored to fill gaps in the basic research of we-map mathematics.

2 Method

The reference frame (reference system) is a heuristic used to connect locations, and it is utilized for map orientation [15–17] (Fig. 1). It can help people locate and provide "a sense of direction" [18], which is mainly divided into 3 categories: self-centered reference frame, fixed reference frame and global reference frame. We-map orientation is completely independent of the coordinate system, and uses a self-centered reference frame and a fixed reference frame as the main method of visual expression of spatial objects.

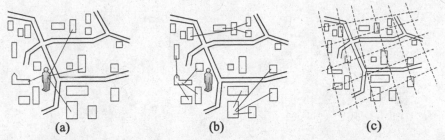

Fig. 1. Reference frame, (a) self-centered reference frame, (b) fixed reference frame, and (c) global reference frame.

The frame of reference, a physical concept related to an observer and the observer's state of motion, is introduced into we-map orientation. A we-map user is viewed as an observer, and the process of the we-map user's wayfinding or orientation is regarded as a motion state, because different users are not in the same location, and the same user is not in the same location in different time periods. Therefore, the we-map users can be considered as an observer, and the process of their wayfinding or orientation is seen as a motion state. When the map is used by its user, in term of the spatial location of the user, the spatial objects within the user's perspective in the space are selected for reference. During this process, the user takes himself as the center to determine the spatial direction (i.e. front, back, left, right, up, down, et al.), which is called self-centered orientation. In this process, if the fixed spatial object is always used as a reference to navigate, find a way or draw a map, it is called a fixed reference orientation.

Existing map orientation is an absolute orientation system, which mainly includes "north orientation" and "oblique north orientation". It needs to be used in combination with the real-life geographical direction (like east, north, west, south, et al.) when a map is used to describe a route. We-map orientation is a relative map orientation. The user only demands to locate the themselves spatial position, and then selects the user itself as a reference, or the space objects around the users as a reference, to perform route description or make a map. Figure 2a is a schematic diagram of an existing map "north orientation", Fig. 2b is a schematic diagram of an existing map "oblique azimuth orientation", Fig. 2c is a schematic diagram of a we-map "self-centered orientation", and Fig. 2d is a we-map "fixed reference orientation" schematic diagram.

(a)

(b)

Fig. 2. Comparison between existing map orientation and we-map orientation, (a) existing map "north orientation", (b) existing map "oblique azimuth orientation", (c) we-map "self-centered orientation", and (d) we-map "fixed reference orientation". **Note:** Figure 2(a) comes from Standard Map Service System, Ministry of Natural Resources of the People's Republic of China (http://bzdt.ch.mnr.gov.cn/), (b) is from Ref. [19], (c) and (d) are derived from improvements in Ref. [1].

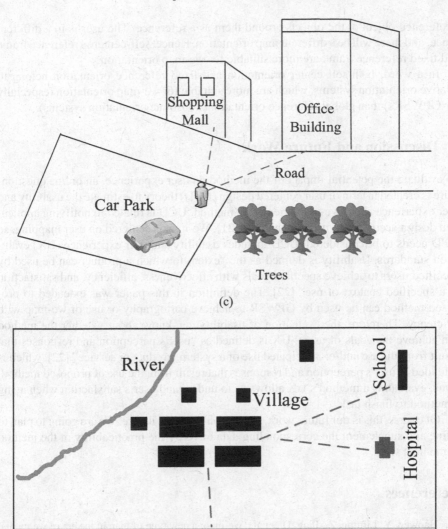

(c)

(d)

Existing maps provide public users with large and comprehensive standardized services. They need to combine the latitude and longitude grid lines for orientation, to aim at the direction on the map is consistent with the geographic direction in the real-life (Fig. 2(a) and (b)). Thus, the global reference frame is more suitable for existing map orientation. We-map neither pursues a large and comprehensive expression, nor does it seek precise geographic orientations like south, east, north, west, and so on. It only demands to allow users to understand how to find or guide the way, to achieve the user's purpose of using a map (either map drawn by others or a map made by himself) to finish his own task in certain space. We-map orientation requires users to view themselves as a reference object or the objects around them as a reference. The user is in a different space, and there will be a different map orientation. Hence, self-centered reference frame and fixed reference frame are more suitable for we-map orientation.

In a word, both self-center orientation and fixed reference orientation belong to relative orientation systems, which are more suitable for we-map orientation (especially for GPWSRs) than global reference orientations (absolute orientation systems).

3   Discussion and Future Work

To evaluate the potential impact of the method on user experience, an online questionnaire is created in term of user centered design (UCD) theory to estimate the usability and user experience about we-map orientation method. UCD is related to notifying application design according to user demand [20, 21]. We-map is centered on user mapping, so UCD needs to be considered. UCD includes usability and user experience (UX) evaluation standards. Usability is defined as the "extent to which a product can be used by specified users to achieve specified goals with effectiveness, efficiency, and satisfaction in a specified context of use" [22]. The definition in this paper was extended to proposed method can be used by GPWSR to achieve cartography or use of we-map with efficiency. Therefore, the evaluation of usability can know about whether the method can achieve the goals of users. UX is defined as "user's perception and responses that result from the use and/or anticipated use of a system, product or service" [22], which is extended to user's perception and responses that result from the use of proposed method. Thus, evaluating a method's UX allows us to understand user's satisfaction when using a method to finish task.

Of course, this is our future work, so we won't discuss it here. We are going to plan to refine and supplement the corresponding data to verify the practicability of the method in the next work.

References

1. Haowen, Y., Liming, Z., Ping, D., et al.: We-map: a new type of map in the era of we media. J. Geomatics Sci. Technol. **33**(5), 520–523 (2016)
2. Jian, Z., Haowen, Y., Haiying, W.: We-map users analysis in multi-dimensional scenario. Sci. Surv. Mapp. **45**(7), 148–153 (2020)
3. Jian, Z.: Users modeling of we-maps in multi-dimensional scenarios. Lanzhou Jiaotong University (2021)
4. Yalan, B., Haowen, Y., Xiaomin, L., et al.: Visual variables of we-maps symbols and their applications. Sci. Surv. Mapp. **46**(7), 182–188 (2021)
5. Daria, B.: Methods of making a symbol library for the we-map. Lanzhou Jiaotong University (2019)
6. Yalan, B.: Visual variables of we-map symbols and their applications, Lanzhou Jiaotong University (2021)
7. Hangyu, W., Haowen, Y., Lei, M., et al.: Generalization method of hand-drawn map line elements in we-map environment. Sci. Surv. Mapp. **44**(10), 117–121 (2019)
8. Huane, D., Zhenghua, Y., Shuwen, Y., et al.: Design of indoor Wifi navigation we-map based on Android system. J. Lanzhou Jiaotong Univ. **38**(4), 109–113 (2019)

9. Hangyu, W., Haowen, Y.: A parallel algorithm for curve segmentation and simplification. Sci. Surv. Mapp. **45**(1), 194–198 (2020)
10. Hangyu, W., Haowen, Y.: Curve generalization method based on area of bends classification using head/tail breaks. Sci. Surv. Mapp. **44**(12), 128–133 (2019)
11. Hangyu, W.: The application of head/tail breaks in the simplification of vector linear feature. Lanzhou Jiaotong University (2020)
12. Qingfen, H., Jing, L.: The combination of self-position and self-orientation in children's map task. Acta Psychol. Sin **48**(9), 1143–1150 (2016)
13. Liben, L.S., Myers, L.J., Kastens, K.A.: Locating oneself on a map in relation to person qualities and map characteristics. In: Freksa, C., Newcombe, N.S., Gärdenfors, P., Wölfl, S. (eds.) Spatial Cognition 2008. LNCS (LNAI), vol. 5248, pp. 171–187. Springer, Heidelberg (2008). https://doi.org/10.1007/978-3-540-87601-4_14
14. Liben, F.S., Myers, R.J., Christensen, R.E.: Identifying locations and directions on field and representational mapping tasks: predictors of success. Spat. Cogn. Comput. **10**(2–3), 105–134 (2010)
15. Tversky, B.: Distortions in memory for maps. Cogn. Psychol. **13**(3), 407–433 (1981)
16. Moar, I., Bower, G.H.: Inconsistency in spatial knowledge. Mem. Cogn. **11**(2), 107–113 (1983)
17. Kitchin, R., Blades, M.: The Cognition of Geographic Space. Ib Tauris, London (2002)
18. Kuipers, B.J.: Modelling spatial knowledge. Cogn. Sci. **2**(2), 129–153 (1978)
19. Jiayao, W.: Principles and Methods of Cartography, 2nd edn. Science Press, Beijing (2014)
20. Robert, R., Kevin, R., Alan, M.E.: User-centered design for interactive maps: a case study in crime analysis. ISPRS Int. J. Geo-Inf. **4**(1), 262–301 (2015)
21. Bartling, M., Robinson, A.C., Resch, B., et al.: The role of user context in the design of mobile map applications. Cartogr. Geogr. Inf. Sci. **48**(5), 432–448 (2021)
22. B.S. Institution: ISO 9241-5 Ergonomic Requirements for Office Work with Visual Display Terminals (VDTS) - Part 5: Workstation Layout and Postural Requirements. https://www.iso.org/standard/16873.html

Feature Extraction and Marking Method of Inertial Navigation Trajectory Based on Permutation Entropy Under Road Constraints

Xiang Li[1]([✉]), Wenbing Liu[2], Xin Liu[3], and Jingyang Li[1]

[1] Information Engineering University, Zhengzhou 450001, Henan, China
ryolx13@126.com
[2] Army Logistics University of PLA, Chongqing 401311, China
[3] Troop 61206, Beijing 100042, China

Abstract. Inertial based intelligent navigation technology is an effective way to solve the problem of "how to realize high-precision intelligent navigation of unmanned vehicles when satellites are unavailable", and it also represents the future development direction. Identifying and understanding a variety of motion behavior modes of inertial navigation is the core problem and key step to complete error matching correction, which has important practical significance. At present, the basic methods of trajectory feature classification and extraction usually rely on a certain mathematical model. The parameter threshold in the extraction process usually adopts estimated or empirical values, which can not truly and accurately identify and extract its features. An inertial navigation trajectory behavior extraction method based on permutation entropy features under road constraints is proposed, starting from the road environment of vehicles, based on the basic inertial navigation trajectory feature elements such as speed and heading angle, the "permutation entropy" is added as a supplementary feature element to describe the trajectory feature classification. At the same time, a one-dimensional convolutional neural network is constructed to train and extract the feature of the original inertial navigation trajectory data, the experimental results show that this method can improve the accuracy of inertial navigation trajectory behavior feature classification and extraction, and can effectively reduce the feature interference caused by random events.

Keywords: Inertial navigation trajectory · Behavioral characteristics · Permutation entropy · Feature classification and extraction · Deep neural network

1 Introduction

In August, 2020, at the closing ceremony of its 22nd Annual Meeting, China Association for Science and Technology released the top ten engineering and technical problems in 2020, including "How to realize high-precision intelligent navigation of unmanned vehicles under the condition of satellites rejection?" [1].

H. Wu et al. (Eds.): SpatialDI 2022, LNCS 13614, pp. 42–57, 2022.
https://doi.org/10.1007/978-3-031-24521-3_4

Inertial-based intelligent navigation technology is an effective way to solve this problem and also represents the future development direction [2] (Shen Chong 2019). However, inertial navigation system ("INS" for short) has obvious shortcomings. Its positioning error will accumulate with time, and the positioning point will deviate from the driving road. Usually, matching correction is required by means of other data sources; (Cisek et al. 2018; Zhao et al. 2019; Chickrin et al. 2020) [3–5]. As a key link in matching and correcting errors, identifying and understanding various motion behavior patterns of inertial navigation has great social and environmental benefits for intelligent transportation applications such as intelligent navigation and positioning, driving safety guarantee, traffic risk assessment, etc. under the condition that satellites are not available.

With more and more consumer-grade vehicle-mounted inertial navigation systems entering the market, a large number of real-time inertial navigation tracks have been accumulated. These trajectory data truly reflect the relationship between vehicles and road environment, and contain rich features of motion behavior (i.e., the motion law of vehicles in different environments and their temporal and spatial features) [6] (Xie Feng et al. 2019). However, the feature expression of trajectory is relatively "implicit". The specific performance is that for any kind of motion state (such as going straight, turning or turning around), it is generally only described as the differentiated value of features such as position, heading, speed and time.

Different from common satellite navigation (Beidou, GPS, etc.) trajectories, inertial navigation trajectories have more dimensions of parameters and feature information. Based on this, this time, on the basis of constructing trajectory behavior feature expression model, the concept of "permutation entropy" feature is further introduced, and deep neural network is used to classify, extract and mark inertial navigation trajectory behavior.

The main contributions of this paper include two aspects:

1 On the basis of the geometric and attribute features of the traditional inertial navigation trajectory, "permutation entropy" is added as a supplementary feature to describe the subtle feature changes of the trajectory due to unexpected accidents;
2 A classification method of inertial navigation trajectory behavior under road constraints is proposed, which does not depend on the traditional mathematical model, and is completely driven by data to identify 11 inertial navigation trajectory behavior features such as turning, turning, lane change, and speed change in real time.

2   Related Work

The existing research methods of trajectory feature recognition and extraction can be divided into manual extraction method and neural network extraction method according to their different operation modes.

(1) Manual extraction method. The method mainly extracts the trajectory features with the most classification function through manual design of relevant rules, including trajectory motion features, shape features, position features and time features [7] (Zhao Zhujun et al. 2017). For example, Douglas-Puke and its derivative algorithm have been widely used as a classical algorithm for vector feature extraction, but they have iterative

calculation, which may lead to low efficiency when facing complex curves [8] (Hu Han et al. 2018). Zheng (2018) summarized the research methods of trajectory and feature recognition, analyzed the basic principles and methods of feature extraction, and classified the technical methods [9]. The author's team put forward the concept of trend features, and extracted features around trend changes to describe the trajectory feature rules more comprehensively and be easier to understand [10] (Li Xiang et al. 2016). Wu et al. (2018) effectively avoided the problem of trajectory aggregation in different driving directions and accurately completed the extraction of geometric features through the trajectory point migration method [11]. Zhu et al. (2014) aiming at the key problem of lack of semantic information in trajectory data, constructed a semantic behavior feature library, analyzed the dependencies between features, and effectively identified the behavior features of trajectories [12]. Thus, manual feature extraction methods have good effects in extraction efficiency and accuracy, but these methods basically rely on certain mathematical models. The parameter thresholds in the extraction process usually adopt estimated values or empirical values, and the models cannot be integrated into new data sources [13] (Angelov et al. 2017), which has certain limitations.

(2) Extraction method based on neural network. In recent years, with the rise of artificial intelligence, many machine learning and depth learning algorithms have been applied to trajectory feature extraction, and a data-driven feature extraction idea came into being [14–16] (Gu et al. 2015; Goodfellow et al. 2016; Zhao et al. 2020). Lu Chuanwei et al. (2020) used generative countermeasure network for deep learning and extracted lane-level features [17]. Yu et al. (2017) and Stavros et al. (2019) used machine learning algorithm to analyze the feature change threshold of instantaneous data [18, 19]. Cui Shumin et al. (2020) used the automatic encoder extracts the depth feature of the trajectory and combines it with the original feature to predict it as the input of Long Short-Term Memory (LSTM for short) [20]. Lv et al. (2018) adopted the idea of convolution neural network and used the trajectory converted into two-dimensional image as input to complete trajectory feature extraction and prediction [21]. In addition, clustering Hidden Markov Model(HMM for short), classical LSTM model, multi-layer perception, bidirectional recurrent neural network and other models have also been used for trajectory feature extraction, and achieved good results [22–24] (Li Mingxiao et al. 2018; Sun Hong et al. 2019; Ji Xuewu et al. 2019). The research object of this article— inertial navigation trajectory, is a kind of time series spatial data, its behavior features have multiple features such as space, time, motion and road environment. However, the above research focuses on the improvement and transformation application of neural network. The learned trajectory features are not comprehensive enough to intuitively express the influence and function of external environment on behavior features and subsequent motion.

3   Acquisition and Preprocessing Method of Inertial Navigation Trajectory Data

3.1   Representation of Inertial Navigation Trajectory Data

Due to temporary parking, measurement errors and other reasons in the process of collecting inertial navigation trajectory data, the obtained data will produce noise data and redundant data, which will have a certain negative impact on the accuracy of subsequent trajectory feature extraction.

The data used in this study are vehicle trajectory data obtained in the Miyun area in Beijing in December 2018. The collection interval is 100 ms, and each record has seven fields, as shown in Eq. (1). p_i represents the position, elevation, heading angle, velocity, acceleration, and time of the inertial navigation output at time i.

$$p_i = (x_i, y_i, z_i, h_i, v_i, a_i, utc_i) \tag{1}$$

3.2 Classification of Inertial Navigation Trajectory Behavior Features

Due to the constraints of roads, vehicles usually travel on roads, and their trajectory features correspond to the changes of road features. With the development of map data, especially the multivariate data represented by high-precision maps entering the field of navigation and positioning, a large number of track features matching with road features are mined and utilized. These features can often change the driving state of the mobile carrier and have a significant impact on the driving behavior of the mobile carrier. It includes not only the shape and topological features (turns, intersections, etc.) based on position coordinates, as shown in Fig. 1; there are also elevation change features (viaducts and underground tunnels) caused by three-dimensional traffic, as shown in Fig. 2; as well as various identification features (speed limit signs, traffic lights, sidewalks) based on traffic rules and driving habits under high-precision map mapping, as shown in Fig. 3.

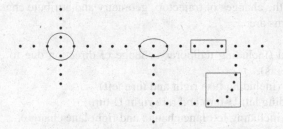

Fig. 1. Geometric features based on shape and topology

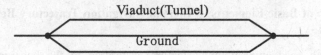

Fig. 2. Elevation features based on stereo traffic

Fig. 3. Identification features based on traffic signs

In this paper, according to the main features in the current road, the following types of features are selected as the focus of extraction. This paper studies 6 kinds of motion behavior patterns and 11 kinds of behavior features that may be generated by inertial navigation mobile carriers, as shown in Fig. 4.

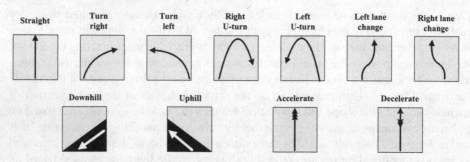

Fig. 4. Inertial navigation trajectory behavior feature classification

According to the changes of trajectory geometry and attribute characteristics, these six types of patterns are:

1. Straight ahead (including temporary change of direction due to driving habits or sudden accidents).
2. Turn a corner (including turn right and turn left).
3. U-turn (including left U-turn and rare right U-turn).
4. Lane change (including left lane change and right lane change).
5. Uphill and downhill.
6. Acceleration and deceleration.

3.3 Selection of Basic Elements of Inertial Navigation Trajectory Behavior Features

Combined with road environmental factors, according to the behavioral features described in Sect. 3.2, it is mainly divided into three categories according to different types:

A Spatial features

Including turning behavior (including left turn and right turn), U-turn behavior (usually left U-turn in China, rarely right U-turn) and lane change behavior (including left lane change and right lane change).

B Elevation features

It mainly includes the large change of elevation in a short period of time, which is caused by vehicles passing through urban interchange traffic (viaduct or underground tunnel, etc.) and undulating terrain areas.

C Motion features

The motion features are mainly speed changes, and there are usually two situations: one is the traffic rule identification features with strong constraints on fixed road sections, such as the fast speed limit sign of expressways; the other is sudden changes according to the actual situation, such as courtesy to pedestrians, traffic congestion or temporary parking on sidewalks.

However, for the classification model, these basic features cannot intuitively express the specific behavior features of the mobile carrier. Only after these basic features are converted into data that can be understood by the classification model through modeling can accurate and effective behavior feature classification be realized. Through the research, analysis and comparison of the existing traditional classification algorithms, it is concluded that the three feature elements of velocity, acceleration and heading angle are effective parameters to distinguish trajectory features, and can be directly obtained from the original data. In addition, the elevation data is collected and described in formula (1), which can also be used as a key element for dividing elevation features.

Of course, the velocity, acceleration, heading angle and elevation information of a single trajectory point cannot effectively reflect the features of this segment or the whole trajectory. Therefore, it is also necessary to calculate the cumulative change of the trend of each element in a certain period of time in combination with the idea of "trend feature" in literature [16].

Let the cumulative trend change of one interval relative to the previous interval be, and the calculation method is:

$$\Delta Tr_i = \begin{bmatrix} \Delta h_i \\ \Delta v_i \\ \Delta a_i \\ \Delta z_i \end{bmatrix} \tag{2}$$

$$\Delta h_i = h_i - h_{i-1} \ (i \geq 1) \tag{3}$$

where h_i, v_i, a_i, and z_i (I = 1, 2, n) represent the heading angle, velocity, acceleration, and elevation, respectively, of the ith track point in the track segment.

3.4 Calculation of Permutation Entropy of Inertial Navigation Trajectory Behavior Features

According to the four types of elements in Sect. 3.3, the inertial navigation trajectory state can be basically described. However, during actual data collection and acquisition, on the one hand, vehicles will inevitably encounter parking conditions such as rush hour traffic jam, comity to zebra crossings and pedestrians, and special conditions such as illegal driving or sudden avoidance. However, it seems that it is impossible to extract and classify trajectory behavior features truly and accurately only by relying on the above feature elements; on the other hand, considering that the inertial navigation trajectory is constantly changing with time, only relying on the above feature elements can only express the general static features of the trajectory, but cannot reflect the time series of the trajectory, and lacks the description of the time series features.

Based on this, referring to the idea of literature [25], this paper introduces the concept of "permutation entropy". Permutation entropy is a feature that represents small changes in time series with entropy. At present, there are some researches on biological signals, mechanical fluctuation prediction, etc. [26].

Permutation entropy is an index used to measure the complexity of time series. Taking the track feature element heading angle as an example, due to the influence of road conditions and drivers' driving habits, the mathematical description of real behavior features is very complicated. The construction of permutation entropy can reflect the hidden features of some trajectories to a certain extent, thus improving the accuracy and robustness of feature classification extraction algorithm.

The calculation method of permutation entropy is as follows:

1. Let the time length of the inertial navigation trajectory segment be N, and its time series can be recorded as u(1), u(2), u(3), ..., u(N), specifying an embedding dimension m and a time delay L;
2. By reconstruct that original time series, each sub-sequence is represent by X(i), where X(i) = u (i), u (i + 1), ..., u (i + (m − 1) L);
3. Then the interior of each X(i) is ordered incrementally, that is, u (i + (j_1 − 1) L) ≤ u (i + (j_2 − 1) L) ≤ ... ≤ u (i + (j_m − 1) L). Where, if the two values are equal, they are sorted according to the subscript i of j. Thus, an X(i) is mapped to (j_1, j_2, j_3, ..., j_m), that is to say, every m-dimensional subsequence X(i) is mapped to one of m! permutations.
4. Through the above steps, the continuous m-dimensional subspace is represented by a symbol sequence, where the number of these symbols is m!. The probability distribution of all symbols is expressed by P_1, P_2, P_3, ..., P_K, where K ≤ m!.
5. Calculate its Shannon entropy, then the permutation entropy of the trajectory time series u(1), u(2), u(3), ..., u(N) is:

$$H(m) = -\sum_{j=1}^{K} P_j \ln P_j \qquad (4)$$

Permutation entropy is an index to measure the complexity of time series. The more regular the time series, the smaller the permutation entropy corresponding to it. The more complex the time series, the greater the entropy of its corresponding permutation. However, this result is based on the appropriate choice of m. If the choice of m is very small, such as 1 or 2, then its arrangement space will be very small. The research shows that the selection of this m should be determined according to the actual situation. Generally speaking, the value suggested by Bandt and Pompe is $m = 3$, ..., 7 [27].

The permutation entropy of velocity, acceleration, heading angle and elevation can be obtained by calculation. These permutation entropies can reflect the order degree of the current inertial navigation trajectory, analyze the hidden features of the trajectory to a certain extent, and can be used as feature elements to enhance the classification of inertial navigation trajectory behavior features.

3.5 Construction of Feature Element Data Sets

In order to ensure the integrity and effectiveness of inertial navigation trajectory behavior features, the dimension of feature elements (including four basic feature elements and four permutation entropy elements) in this paper is 50 dimensions, that is, 50 points are taken as a sub-interval. In order to facilitate expression, it is necessary to normalize the feature vectors. In this paper, the maximum trend change of each attribute vector is taken, and each row of the matrix Tr is divided by this maximum trend change. The feature vector matrix of the four basic elements can be expressed as:

$$Tr' = \begin{bmatrix} \frac{\Delta h_1}{\Delta h_{max}} & \frac{\Delta h_2}{\Delta h_{max}} & \cdots & \frac{\Delta h_{50}}{\Delta h_{max}} \\ \frac{\Delta v_1}{\Delta v_{max}} & \frac{\Delta v_2}{\Delta v_{max}} & \cdots & \frac{\Delta v_{50}}{\Delta v_{max}} \\ \frac{\Delta a_1}{\Delta a_{max}} & \frac{\Delta a_2}{\Delta a_{max}} & \cdots & \frac{\Delta a_{50}}{\Delta a_{max}} \\ \frac{\Delta z_1}{\Delta z_{max}} & \frac{\Delta z_2}{\Delta z_{max}} & \cdots & \frac{\Delta z_{50}}{\Delta z_{max}} \end{bmatrix} \quad (5)$$

Among them, the positive and negative of the cumulative change amount indicates the trend direction relative to the current state of the vehicle, and the same trend is positive, otherwise it is negative.

Since the minimum time interval of inertial navigation trajectory used in this paper is 100 ms, taking the time length of a single trajectory segment as 50, that is, calculating the change of permutation entropy elements within 5 s, the feature vectors of the four permutation entropy elements can be obtained as follows:

$$H' = \begin{bmatrix} H_h(m) \\ H_v(m) \\ H_a(m) \\ H_z(m) \end{bmatrix} \quad (6)$$

By combining formulas (5) and (6) according to time series, the feature element data set can be obtained, which can be used as the input data set of the subsequent depth neural network.

4 Classification and Extraction Method of Trajectory Behavior Features of Feature Inertial Navigation Based on Permutation Entropy

4.1 Construction of Feature Element Data Set

The overall technical flow of the feature inertial navigation trajectory behavior feature classification extraction method fusing permutation entropy is shown in Fig. 5.

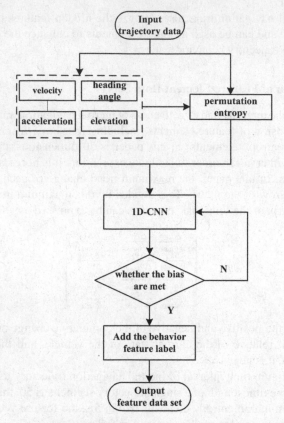

Fig. 5. The general idea of the algorithm

(1) Using the constraints of road environment, four types of feature elements, namely heading angle, velocity, acceleration and elevation, are extracted and calculated from the preprocessed original inertial navigation trajectory data, and combined with the idea of "trend feature", their segmented feature vectors are calculated.

(2) Combining the idea of "permutation entropy", the permutation entropy features of heading angle, velocity, acceleration and elevation are constructed, and the feature vectors are also constructed as corresponding feature elements;

(3) Inputting the combined feature vectors into the one-dimensional convolution neural network as input data, and outputting classification probabilities of different inertial navigation trajectory behavior features through deep learning and training;

(4) Using a data coding method to label the behavior feature labels of each inertial navigation trajectory entering the depth neural network;

(5) Outputting inertial navigation trajectory data set with behavior feature labeling.

4.2 Construction and Training of One-Dimensional Convolution Neural Network

Convolutional Neural Networks (CNN for short) is a kind of feedforward neural networks with convolution calculation and deep structure, and it is one of the representative algorithms of deep learning. Convolution neural network has the ability of representation learning, which can classify input information shift-invariant according to its hierarchical structure, and learn the features of data in the overall structure.

The inertial navigation trajectory data is essentially a set of data sets with time series, which is a simple digital vector of $1 \times N$. However, one-dimensional convolution neural network (1DCNN for short) will not cause a large amount of feature information loss due to dimensional compression of text data, and has achieved excellent results in many data classification fields in recent years. Therefore, this paper chooses 1DCNN as the classification model with feature vectors as input data.

(1) Input layer: input the feature element set into the 1DCNN network and extract features for each T_r.

(2) Convolution layer: Aiming at the geometry, velocity and elevation attributes in the definition of behavior features, the 1DCNN network used in this paper adopts three convolution levels. The output of each convolution layer is activated by the nonlinear function ReLU as the input of the next convolution layer. In order to avoid the loss of key information, pooling layers are not added between convolution layers.

After convolution, bias is usually added, and nonlinear activation function is introduced. Here, bias is defined as b, and activation function is f_a. After the activation function, the result is obtained.

$$Q_i^k = f_a(W_k \times Tr)_i + b \tag{7}$$

(3) Full connection layer: Add a full connection layer at the end for classification, the activation function is softmax, and output the probability that the current trend feature vector is the behavior feature (Fig. 6).

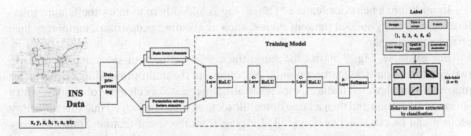

Fig. 6. Basic structure of one-dimensional convolution neural network

4.3 Construction of Behavioral Feature Labels

The behavior feature label of the trajectory data set represents the result of trajectory feature classification and extraction, and can effectively support the subsequent navigation and positioning matching association and error calculation. The specific label construction method is as follows:

The data is divided into 50 trajectory points into a trajectory segment, and each trajectory segment needs to be marked with a behavior feature label.

According to the types of behavior features in Sect. 3.2, tag data is generated by data coding, and the specific corresponding relationship is as follows (Table 1):

Table 1. Comparison table of inertial navigation trajectory behavior feature labels

Behavioral features	Label code	Sub-label code
Go straight	1	1
Turn right	2	0
Turn left	2	1
Right U-turn	3	0
Left U-turn left	3	1
Right lane change	4	0
Left lane change	4	1
Downhill	5	1
Uphill	5	0
Accelerate	6	1
Deceleration	6	0
Other	1	0

The first level label indicates the state of the feature, including 6 states defined in Sect. 3.2; the sub-labels refer to specific feature details, such as left or right, up or down and so on.

In addition, a behavior feature "Other" tag is added here to mark the feature interference caused by sudden random events, such as avoiding pedestrians, temporary lane change and so on.

For example, Fig. 7 shows the same track segment in both sides and faces, with two red track points as starting points. According to the multi-dimensional perspective map, from the elevation features, the elevation of this trajectory changes obviously, with a short uphill section and then a large downhill section. It can be judged that this trajectory section can be classified as downhill. Judging from the speed features, this trajectory segment has dense points and small speed in the uphill segment, and sparse points and large speed in the downhill segment, but the overall change is not very obvious. From the top view, the features of the heading angle can be clearly seen. The trajectory segment is a straight line and the heading angle has hardly changed, so factors such as turning around and turning around need not be considered. Considering comprehensively, the trajectory segment can be classified as downhill, and other features are not obvious enough. To sum up, the label of this track segment is "[5.1]", which corresponds to the behavior features of vehicles going downhill.

In order to solve this problem, we increase the probability weight at the end of the neural network.

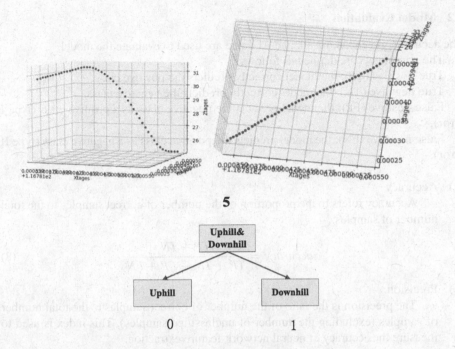

Fig. 7. Example of inertial navigation trajectory segment

The method is described as follows:

$$P = P_{Tr} \cdot W_{Tr} + P_{T_i} \cdot W_{T_i}$$

where P and W represent the weight and probability of classification results respectively, and the behavior feature of the feature with more obvious relative feature is the final behavior feature.

5 Experimental Results and Discussion

5.1 Experimental Environment and Data

The experimental equipment used in the experiment test in this paper is core i7-10510U, 1.80 GHz CPU, 16 GB of memory, the operating system is Windows 10, the neural network is constructed in Python language, the learning framework used is Keras, and the back end is Tensorflow.

The inertial navigation trajectory data set used is the trajectory data of Miyun area in Beijing in 2018, in which each data record contains trajectory data information at the time of acquisition. In the experimental stage, all the data are mixed and disrupted, and 70% of all the data are selected as the training set and 30% of all the data are selected as the test set to train the classification model.

In order to verify the efficiency of the algorithm and the accuracy of feature extraction, experimental analysis is carried out from three parts: evaluation model, accuracy of classification extraction and comparison with other classification extraction methods.

5.2 Model Evaluation

The accuracy, precision, recall, and F1 value are used to evaluate the model.

The parameters are defined as follows:

True positive (TP): the model correctly predicts the positive class.

True negative (TN): the model correctly predicts the negative class.

False positive (FP): the model predicts the negative class as a positive class (type I error).

False negative (FN): the model predicts the positive class as a negative class (type II error).

(1) Accuracy

Accuracy refers to the proportion of the number of correct samples to the total number of samples.

$$accuracy = \frac{TP + TN}{TP + TN + FP + FN} \tag{8}$$

(2) Precision

The precision is the ratio of the number of correct samples to the total number of samples (excluding the number of unclassified samples). This index is used to measure the accuracy of neural network feature extraction.

$$precision = \frac{TP}{TP + FP} \tag{9}$$

(3) Recall

The recall rate is the ratio of the number of samples correctly classified to the total number of samples that should be classified. It is used to measure the integrity of the experimental results.

$$recall = \frac{TP}{TP + FN} \tag{10}$$

(4) F1 value

The F1 value is the harmonic average of the recall rate and accuracy rate. Its value is close to the smallest value of precision and recall.

$$F1 = \frac{2 \times precision \times recall}{precsion + recall} \tag{11}$$

5.3 Experimental Results

(1) The classification extraction effect test of this method

The classification extraction method designed in this paper is used to carry out three rounds of experiments on the preprocessed inertial navigation trajectory data set, and the average value of the two rounds of experimental results is taken as the final effect.

The results of inertial navigation trajectory behavior features are shown in Table 2.

Table 2. Extraction results of several typical trajectory features by this algorithm

Feature class	Sample	Correct	Wrong	Refuse	Accuracy
Left turn	100	92	8	0	92%
Right turn	100	91	9	0	91%
Left U-turn	100	94	6	0	94%
Right U-turn	0	0	0	0	0%
Left lane change	100	89	11	0	89%
Right lane change	100	92	8	0	92%
Uphill	100	90	10	0	90%
Downhill	100	89	11	0	89%
Accelerate	100	92	8	0	92%
Decelerate	100	91	9	0	91%
Others	100	81	19	0	81%
Total	1000	901	99	0	–
Average	100	90.1%	9.9%	0	90.1%

From Table 2, it can be concluded that (1) the classification model proposed in this paper has the best classification and extraction effect for typical behavioral features such as turning and turning, especially the common behavioral feature such as left turning reaches the highest 94%, and its heading angle changes obviously and regularly, which is beneficial for neural networks to learn its features. (2) Because the "permutation entropy" is added to the trajectory feature elements, the feature interference that affects the normal features is divided separately, and the accuracy of extracting other types of behavioral features is increased from the side. However, due to the complexity and particularity of the inertial navigation trajectory, the accuracy of judging feature interference is not very high, only about 80%. (3) Due to the restriction of domestic traffic rules, there are very few samples of right U-turn, which is 0 in this experiment, so it will not be classified separately.

(2) Comparison with other classification extraction methods

Finally, for the same inertial navigation trajectory data experiment, DP, SVM and 1DCNN (no permutation entropy) are used to carry out feature extraction experiments respectively, and the results are shown in Table 3.

As can be seen from Table 3, in the analysis and processing of inertial navigation trajectory, the feature classification extraction algorithm based on neural network has obvious advantages over traditional classification extraction in accuracy, recall rate and F1 value. From. On the other hand, although the effect of adding "permutation entropy" on the accuracy of the results is not obvious enough, it can effectively eliminate some feature interference situations and still has certain research value and significance for classification extraction itself. Therefore, "permutation entropy" is an effective element that can reflect the real trajectory features.

Table 3. Performance comparison of several feature classification extraction models

	Accuracy	Recall	F1
DP	78.70	78.76	78.78
SVM	85.60	85.63	85.66
1DCNN (No permutation entropy)	89.11	89.22	89.24
Our Model	90.90	90.90	90.90

6   Conclusion

In the field of navigation and positioning, classification and extraction of mobile carrier behavior features is a key step to achieve accurate positioning, especially under non-satellite conditions, high-accuracy feature matching can effectively compensate for the location reliability and security under signal missing.

This paper takes inertial navigation trajectory data as the core and drive, based on the basic feature elements such as speed and heading angle, combined with the feature element of "permutation entropy", one-dimensional convolution neural network is used for data training and feature classification extraction, and the accuracy of the result reaches 90%. Compared with other methods, it has a certain degree of improvement, which proves that the method proposed in this paper is feasible and effective.

However, there are still some deficiencies in the labeling of classification results and the cost efficiency of deep learning in the experimental process, such as not considering the combination of multiple behavioral features of the same trajectory, and the coordination among extraction efficiency, accuracy and robustness. Therefore, the next work will focus on the following aspects:

1. Modeling and expression of inertial navigation trajectory combination features;
2. Research on depth learning algorithm model suitable for inertial navigation trajectory classification and extraction;
3. The balance between computational efficiency and accuracy of the algorithm.

References

1. China association of science and technology future oriented science and technology – interpretation of major scientific and engineering technical problems in 2020, pp. 250–261. China Science and Technology Press, Beijing (2020)
2. Shen, C.: Inertial Navigation Intelligent Information Processing Technology, pp. 1–3. Electronic Industry Press, Beijing (2019)
3. Cisek, K., Gryte, K., Bryne, T.H., et al.: Aided inertial navigation of small unmanned aerial vehicles using an ultra-wideband real time localization system. In: 2018 IEEE Aerospace Conference, pp. 1–10. IEEE (2018)
4. Parfiriev, A.V., Dushkin, A.V., Ischuk, I.N.: Model of inertial navigation system for unmanned aerial vehicle based on MEMS. J. Phys. Conf. Ser. **1353**(1), 012019 (2019)

5. Chickrin, D.E., Savinkov, P.A., Kokunin, P.A., et al.: Development of a high-precision satellite local-inertial navigation system for unmanned vehicle control. Izvesti vysih uebnyh zavedenij Priborostroenie 63(12), 1094–1102 (2020)
6. Xie, F., Lou, J.T., Zhao, K., et al.: A research on vehicle trajectory prediction method based on behavior recognition and curvature constraints. Automot. Eng. 41(9), 1036–1042 (2019)
7. Zhao, Z.J., Ji, G.L.: Research progress of spatial-temporal trajectory classification. J. Geo-Inf. Sci. 19(3), 289–297 (2017)
8. Hu, H., Xiang, L.G., Wang, D.H.: Road extraction based on taxi trajectory data. Bull. Surv. Mapp. 496(07), 57–61 (2018)
9. Zheng, Y.: Trajectory data mining: an overview. ACM Trans. Intell. Syst. Technol. 6(3), 29 (2015)
10. Li, X., Zhang, J.S., Ma, J., et al.: Feature extraction algorithm in consideration of the trend changing of track. J. Comput.-Aided Des. Comput. Graph. 28(8), 1341–1349 (2016)
11. Wu, Q.Y., Wu, Z.F., Zhang, L.P.: A road geometric feature extraction method based on taxi trajectory data. CN108776727A
12. Zhu, L., Liu, K.D., Sun, S.Z., et al.: Study on spatial-semantic trajectory based GPS track behavior signature detection. Comput. Appl. Softw. 31(4), 72–74+87 (2014)
13. Angelov, P.P., Gu, X., Principe, J.: Fast feedforward non-parametric deep learning network with automatic feature extraction. In: 2017 International Joint Conference on Neural Networks (IJCNN), pp. 534–541. IEEE (2017)
14. Goodfellow, I., Bengio, Y., Courville, A.: Deep Learning, vol. 1, pp. 326–366. MIT Press, Cambridge (2016)
15. Gu, J., Wang, Z., Kuen, J., et al.: Recent advances in convolutional neural networks. arXiv preprint arXiv:1512.07108 (2015)
16. Zhao, S., Wang, C., Wei, P., et al.: Research on the deep recognition of urban road vehicle flow based on deep learning. Sustainability 12(17), 1–16 (2020)
17. Lu, C.W., Sun, Q., Chen, B., et al.: Road learning extraction method based on vehicle trajectory data. Acta Geodaetica et Cartographic Sinica 49(6), 692–702 (2020)
18. Yu, J., Chen, Z., Zhu, Y., et al.: Fine-grained abnormal driving behaviors detection and identification with smartphones. IEEE Trans. Mob. Comput. 16(8), 2198–2212 (2017)
19. Stavros, G.C., Stratis, K., Alexander, C.: Learning driver braking behavior using smartphones, neural networks and the sliding correlation coefficient: road anomaly case study. IEEE Trans. Intell. Transp. Syst. 20(1), 65–74 (2019)
20. Cui, S.M., Zhang, L., Li, Y., et al.: A deep learning method for taxi destination prediction. Comput. Eng. Sci. 042(001), 185–190 (2020)
21. Lv, J., Li, Q., Sun, Q., et al.: T-CONV: a convolutional neural network for multi-scale taxi trajectory prediction. In: Proceedings of the 2018 IEEE International Conference on Big Data and Smart Computing, pp. 82–89 (2018)
22. Li, M.X., Zhang, H.C., Qiu, P.Y., et al.: Predicting future locations with deep fuzzy LSTM network. Acta Geodaetica et Cartographic Sinica 47(12), 1660–1669 (2018)
23. Sun, H., Chen, S.: Spatio-temporal trajectory prediction algorithm based on clustering based hidden Markov model. J. Chin. Comput. Syst. 40(3), 472–476 (2019)
24. Ji, X.W., Fei, C., He, X.K., et al.: Intention recognition and trajectory prediction for vehicles using LSTM network. China J. Highw. Transp. 32(6), 34–42 (2019)
25. Cao, Y., Tung, W.W., Gao, J.B., et al.: Detecting dynamical changes in time series using the permutation entropy. Phys. Rev. E 70(4), 046217 (2004)
26. Feng, F.Z., Rao, G.Q., Si, A.W., et al.: Application and development of permutation entropy algorithm. J. Acad. Armored Force Eng. 30(02), 34–38 (2012)
27. Liu, G.J., Yang, J.F.: The classification method of traffic trajectory pattern based on deep learning and permutation entropy. J. North China Univ. Technol. 30(02), 76–82 (2018)

Spatio-Temporal Disparity of Traffic Accidents Between the Elderly Involved and Non-elderly Groups in Kumamoto, Japan

Qiaohui Zhou[1]($\boxtimes$) (iD), Riken Homma[2] (iD), and Congying Fang[1] (iD)

[1] Graduate School of Science and Technology, Kumamoto University, Kumamoto, Japan
221d9241@st.kumamoto-u.ac.jp
[2] Faculty of Advanced Science and Technology, Kumamoto University, Kumamoto, Japan

Abstract. Traffic accidents affect people's well-being and it's a complicated issue around the world. This issue becomes even more complicated when the elderly is considered due to their vulnerability to accidents, especially in Japan, where has the most aging population in the world. It is unclear whether spatio-temporal disparity exists between the elderly involved and non-elderly groups, and whether unique characteristic is existed on each group. Therefore, the purpose of this research is to explore the spatio-temporal disparity of traffic accidents between these two groups in a Japanese city. Based on traffic accidents data of the three years that occurred from 2018 to 2020, kernel density estimation, spider plot and comap methods were used to identify spatio-temporal hotspots. Noticeable spatio-temporal disparity of traffic accidents was found between these two groups. It is important for transportation planner to formulate better transportation planning and make targeted transport safety policies to promote traffic safety for the elderly group.

Keywords: Traffic accidents · Spatio-temporal disparity · The elderly · Kernel density estimation

1 Introduction

Traffic accident is a complicated problem and deeply affect people's well-being. Moreover, the problem becomes even more crucial and challenging when the elderly is considered, as they are more vulnerable to traffic accidents and will cause more fatalities and injuries than other groups of people. This is especially critical for Japan which has the most aging population in the world, with an estimated number of people aged 65 and over stood at a record high of 36.4 million, according to the data by the Ministry of Internal Affairs government which released in September 2021. Therefore, it is crucial to identify the characteristic of the elderly involved traffic accidents and distinguish disparity of traffic accidents between the elder involved groups and other groups.

Most studies about traffic accidents analysis just use statistical methods to describe the characteristics of traffic accidents [1, 2, 7–9, 15]. These methods are simple and easy to understand, but they are failed to visualize the spatial pattern and express spatial and temporal connections. Spatial statistics methods can be used to visualize the distribution pattern of traffic accidents and its temporal variation based on GIS spatial analysis and statistic tool [3–6, 11, 12]. However, few studies focus on the spatio-temporal disparity of traffic accidents between different age groups. The first study about spatial and temporal analysis of aging-involved accidents is in Florida [13]. So far, there has been no previous research about spatio-temporal disparity of traffic accidents between the elderly involved and non-elderly groups in Japan, where has the largest aging population among all countries and regions across the world.

With this motivation, the objective of this study is to explore the characteristic of the elderly involved traffic accidents and clarify the spatio-temporal disparity of traffic accidents between the elderly involved and non-elderly groups in Kumamoto, Japan.

2 Method

2.1 Study Area and Data

This paper focused on Kumamoto City, Japan to explore the temporal and spatial pattern of traffic accidents among the elderly involved and non-elderly groups. Kumamoto is the third largest city in Kyushu with an area of 390.32 km^2 and a population of 0.73 million. The population of the elderly is around 0.196 million, which accounts for 26.78% of the total population. Figure 1 shows the population distribution of the elderly and non-elderly people in Kumamoto City in 2020. Both the elderly and the non-elderly were concentrated in Central and East Ward.

This paper was based on data published on the official website of the Kumamoto Prefectural Police Department. Traffic accidents data for the three years that occurred from 2018 to 2020 were included in this study. Figure 2 shows the locations of traffic accidents among the elderly involved and non-elderly people of three years. According to the severity, accidents were divided into three categories: fatality, seriously injury and slightly injury. Figure 3 clearly shows the number of traffic accidents of different severity and the proportion distribution of the elderly involved and non-elderly people. The physical vulnerability of the elderly brought more adverse effects and cause more serious injuries and fatalities. Although the total number of traffic accidents involving the elderly accounted for 15% of all traffic accidents, the elderly involved accounted for more than one-third of serious injuries and nearly half of fatalities.

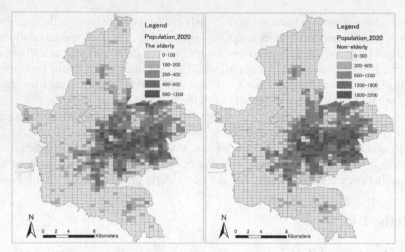

Fig. 1. Population distribution of Kumamoto city for the elderly (left) and non-elderly (right).

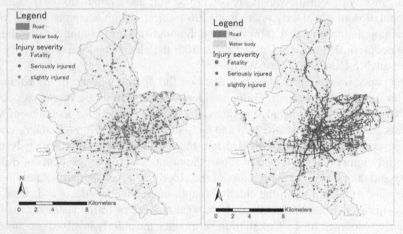

Fig. 2. Spatial distribution of accidents of different severity in Kumamoto city (2018–2020) for the elderly involved group (left) and non-elderly group (right).

2.2 Spatial and Temporal Analysis Method

Kernel Density Estimation (KDE) Method. Kernel density estimation (KDE) is one of the most common and well-established approaches to identify hotspots. Possible uses include analyzing housing density or crime for community planning, exploring intersections and road where traffic accidents occur Frequently. Based on a point dataset, KDE is used to calculate the density of point features around each output raster cell. Each point is covered with a smooth surface. The surface value is the highest at the position of the point, and gradually decreases as the distance from the point increases,

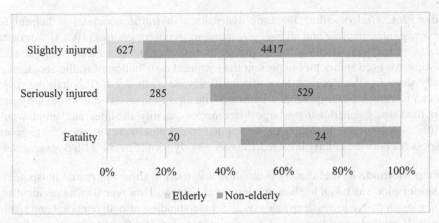

Fig. 3. Frequency and proportion of accidents of different severity among the elderly involved and non-elderly groups.

and the surface value becomes zero at the position where the distance from the point is equal to the search radius. The general equation of kernel density estimation at estimated location was given by the following formula:

$$D = \frac{1}{R^2} \sum_{i=1}^{n} \left\{ \frac{3}{\pi} \left[1 - \left(\frac{d_i^2}{R} \right)^2 \right]^2 \right\} \tag{1}$$

where D is kernel density of the estimated location, $i = 1, \ldots, n$ are the input points which within the search radius distance of the estimated location, d_i is the distance between point i and the estimated location, R is search radius.

Selecting an appropriate search radius is critical to obtain the accurate results. Larger search radius results in smoother and more generalized density grid, whereas narrow search radius yields a detailed density map which displays local effects with all peaks and valleys. This paper used bandwidth estimation formula based on the "Silverman Rule of Thumb," this method of calculating the search radius generally avoids the phenomenon of circular rings around points that often occur in sparse data sets and prevents spatial outliers. The search radius was calculated by the following formula:

$$R = 0.9 \times min\left[SD, \sqrt{\frac{1}{ln(2)}} \times D_m \right] \times n^{-0.2} \tag{2}$$

where R is search radius, SD is standard deviation of the samples, n is the sample size, D_m is the median distance.

In this paper, we plotted the kernel density distribution of all traffic accidents and three different types (vehicle-vehicle collisions, collisions involving pedestrians, single-vehicle collisions) of traffic accidents among the elderly involved and non-elderly groups.

Spider Plot. Understanding the time distribution of traffic accidents is helpful for improving infrastructure and taking corresponding countermeasures [10, 13]. For better visualizing and understanding the frequency of traffic accidents, instead of simple table statistics, we used spider plot to present the temporal distribution of traffic accidents to clearly show in which period the traffic accidents were clustered. Although the spider plot can integrate the temporal distribution of the elderly involved and non-elderly people in the same graph, due to the large difference of quantity, the integrated graph would be difficult to observe. In this paper, we applied spider plot to present accident temporal hotspots for both the elderly involved and non-elderly people over a 24-h day separately.

Comap Method. Kernel density estimation was used to show the spatial hotspot, and the spider plot was taken to show the temporal hotspot. However, Traffic accident is a phenomenon that requires deep analysis and understanding of both temporal and spatial pattern. If multiple accidents occur closely in space but at different time, they may not form significant hotspots. Likewise, multiple accidents occurred at the same time but far apart in space, they also can not represent a significant hotspot. Therefore, it is necessary take a comprehensive consideration to combine temporal and spatial pattern, which can provide a foundation for the better response measures of the traffic improvement. The comap method can well visualize the changes of the spatial hotspots of accidents over time [10, 13]. The time can be selected as needed, including hours, days, months, and seasons, etc. To find out the high accident-incidence moments of the day in our study, we explored the changes in the spatial distribution of traffic accidents between the elderly and non-elderly groups with dividing a day into 8 subsets, which were 0–3, 3–6, 6–9, 9–12, 12–15, 15–18, 18–21, 21–24.

3   Results and Discussion

3.1   Spatial Distribution Difference Between Two Groups (Overall and Type-Based Accidents)

Figure 4 shows kernel density map of all accidents and three different types of collisions for the elderly involved group and non-elderly group. As for all traffic accidents, traffic accidents of non-elderly people were basically distributed near the commercial streets in the downtown area of Central Ward, and the density of other areas were relatively low. Traffic accidents of elderly involved people were more scattered. Except for the most frequent occurrences near the commercial streets in the downtown area, there were certain densities in boundary line areas between East Ward and Central Ward, Kusunoki district and Karikusa district.

For different types of traffic accidents, the differences in spatial distribution were obvious. The traffic accident density value of vehicle-vehicle collisions of non-elderly people was the highest. In addition to the concentration near the commercial street in the downtown area, there was also a large density in adjacent traffic arteries in Central Ward and the side of East Ward which was closer to Central Ward. Comparatively, vehicle-vehicle collisions of the elderly involved people was relatively scattered and two other hotspots were formed in Nagamine district and Kengun district except the largest hotspot near the commercial street in the downtown area. Traffic accidents involving pedestrians of non-elderly people and the elderly involved people were both concentrated near the commercial streets in the downtown area, however, the degree of concentration for non-elderly people was relatively higher. The density value of a single vehicle collision was lowest and the distribution variety of single-vehicle collisions between two groups was the largest. Single-vehicle collisions of non-elderly people were still concentrated near the commercial streets in the downtown area, while the single-vehicle collisions distribution of the elderly was very scatted and forms a wide range, with hotspots concentrated in the left side of the East Ward and the right side of the Central Ward.

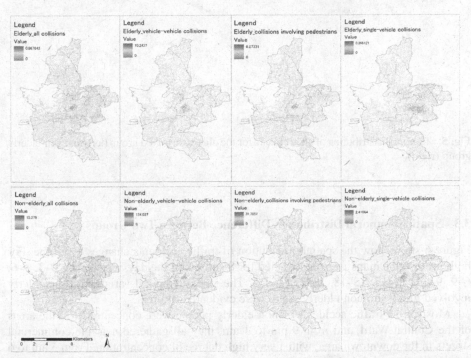

Fig. 4. Kernel density map of all accidents, vehicle-vehicle collisions, collisions involving pedestrians, single-vehicle collisions for the elderly involved group (upper), non-elderly group (lower).

3.2 Temporal Distribution Difference Between Two Groups

Figure 5 shows the temporal distribution of all accidents from 2018 to 2020 for the elderly involved and non-elderly groups. It is evident that the traffic accident peaks of non-elderly people were between 7 am to 9 am and 4 pm to 6 pm (both are commuter peak hours) and the traffic accident peak of the elderly involved was concentrated between 11 am to 4 pm (mid-hours of the day). The traffic accidents frequency of the elderly involved group between 8 pm to 5 am was relatively small and the accident frequency of non-elderly people have a significant decrease from 10 pm and continue to be low till 5 am.

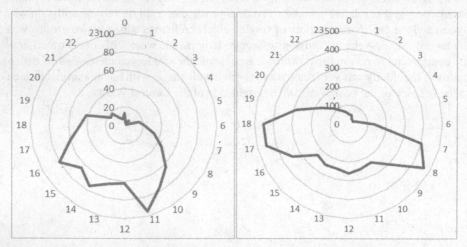

Fig. 5. Temporal distribution of all accidents for the elderly involved group (left) and non-elderly group (right).

3.3 Spatio-Temporal Distribution Difference Between Two Groups

Figure 6 shows how the spatial distribution of traffic accidents changes over time. For both groups, the maps were constructed for 8 subsets of the day, which were 0–3, 3–6, 6–9, 9–12, 12–15, 15–18, 18–21, 21–24. The spatio-temporal variation of the elderly involved group and non-elderly group were evidently different.

Most of the traffic accidents of non-elderly people were concentrated in the areas of the Central Ward, and from 9 pm to 3 am, they all gathered near the commercial streets in the downtown area, with a very high degree of concentration. From 3 am to 6 am, it slowly spread to the surrounding areas and to the East Ward, and the spread was continued to the period of 9 am–12 am. During the period of 12 am–3 pm, it gathered again near the commercial street in the downtown area of Central Ward, and spread to the surrounding area from 3 pm to 6 pm and 6 pm to 9 pm. High density areas were most widely distributed between 6 am to 9 am.

In contrast, the traffic accidents of the elderly involved people was more dispersed. From 9 pm to 6 am, like non-elderly group, traffic accidents were all concentrated near commercial street in the downtown area of the Central Ward. However, the density values of 3 am to 6 am and 9 pm to 12 pm were very low but the density value between 12 pm to 3 am was relatively high. In the daytime, from 6 am to 9 am, although it spread from downtown area to the surrounding areas, the density was not high. The highest density value was formed between 9 am to 12 am, with the hotspots distributed in Central Ward, Nagamine district and Kengun district in the East Ward, meanwhile, the most concentrated areas were not near the commercial streets in the downtown area. From

12 am to 3 pm, the Central Ward and Kengun district still maintained a high density, and from 3 pm to 6 pm, the density increased slightly again, and the area also spread to Shiroyama district, after that the density began to decline again.

3.4 Discussion

This study filled the gap related to the spatio-temporal disparity in the distribution of traffic accidents between the elderly involved and non-elderly people in a Japanese city. Based on the data of all traffic accidents in Kumamoto city from 2018 to 2020, a series of methods including kernel density analysis, spider plot and comap were applied to analyze the spatio-temporal hotspot distribution characteristics of traffic accidents among these two groups. Several important research findings can help urban and transportation planners formulate better policies to support healthier and safer transportation, with a better focus on transportation safety for the elderly group.

The choice of trip time for the elderly is very different from that of the non-elderly. They prefer to concentrate on going out during the day except peak hours. This may be due to the fact that the elderly is more inclined to avoid the peak commuting hours and go out during relatively low traffic flow periods at the middle of the day. This can explain the kernel density estimation value of traffic accidents for the elderly during the period of 12 am to 3 pm remains almost at the same level with the adjacent periods. This is consistent with the results of a previous study which explore the pattern of aging-involved accidents in Florida [13]. Transportation and safety departments, especially in areas with a large proportion of the elderly, should realize that the elderly is an important target of traffic accidents during this period, and pay more attention to the elderly going out and safety during this period.

Compared with non-elderly people, the traffic accidents of the elderly were more dispersed, and the changes of spatio-temporal distribution were more obvious. The traffic accidents of non-elderly people were concentrated in the most dynamic downtown areas, while the traffic accident hotspots of the elderly were also distributed in relatively important areas of each Ward, such as Kengun and Nagamine districts in the East Ward. On one hand, it is related to the fact that the elderly prefers to shop nearby and choose the closest supermarket or commercial street from their residence. On the other hand, the elderly is more likely to have traffic accidents in the case of less traffic, which may be related to the attenuation of their ability to respond to emergencies, including easier collisions at intersections, taking longer time to cross pedestrian crossings, etc. This reminds the traffic department to consider the needs of the elderly when setting policies of traffic lights, minimum speed limit, etc., especially in the areas where the elderly is concentrated.

This paper used Euclidean distance to produce a smooth density surface over the range of land use of road. This may more suitable than producing a smooth density surface over the range of all city. However, a novel network KDE approach may be more suited for characterizing traffic accidents [14]. Therefore, future study is needed to apply network KDE to obtain more accurate density result and help to set for better traffic accident decisions.

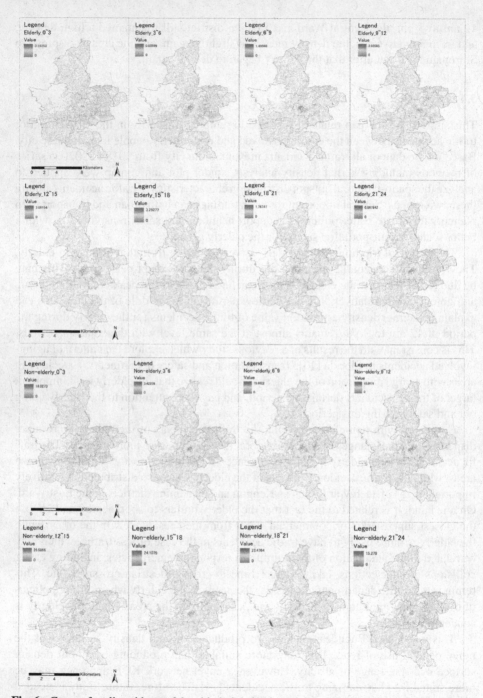

Fig. 6. Comap for all accidents of the elderly involved group (upper), non-elderly group (lower).

4 Conclusions

To clarify the disparity of traffic accidents between the elderly involved and non-elderly groups, and to promote traffic safety by identifying hotspots, we distinguished traffic accident distribution patterns of these two groups. This distinction revealed that there was a noticeable spatio-temporal distribution disparity of traffic accidents between these two groups. Non-elderly traffic accidents were concentrated during the commute peak hours which are 7 am to 9 am and 4 pm to 6 pm, whereas, the elderly involved traffic accidents were concentrated in the mid-hours of the day from 11 am to 4 pm. Besides, these two groups have unique characteristics of traffic spatio-temporal distribution. Accidents of non-elderly people were basically concentrated near commercial street in the downtown area of the Central Ward in all time periods. Traffic accidents of the elderly involved were more dispersed spatially, and the spatio-temporal hotspots changed over time.

These findings have practical implications. They reveal that it is necessary to distinguish disparity of traffic accidents between the elderly involved and non-elderly groups. As this will assist transportation planner to better formulate transportation planning and specify safety policies according to different age groups.

References

1. Ahmed, L.A.: Using logistic regression in determining the effective variables in traffic accidents. Appl. Math. Sci. **11**(42), 2047–2058 (2017)
2. Bargegol, I., Najafi Moghaddam Gilani, V., Abolfazlzadeh, M.: Statistical analysis of the railway accidents causes in Iran. Int. J. Eng. **30**(12), 1822–1830 (2017)
3. Haji Mirza Aghasi, N.: Introducing GIS as legitimate instrument to deal with road accident data: a case study of Iran, Tehran. Spat. Inf. Res. **25**(1), 151–159 (2017)
4. Kingham, S., Sabel, C.E., Bartie, P.: The impact of the 'school run' on road traffic accidents: a spatio-temporal analysis. J. Transp. Geogr. **19**(4), 705–711 (2011)
5. Le, K.G., Liu, P., Lin, L.T.: Determining the road traffic accident hotspots using GIS-based temporal-spatial statistical analytic techniques in Hanoi, Vietnam. Geo-Spat. Inf. Sci. **23**(2), 153–164 (2020)
6. Li, Y., Abdel-Aty, M., Yuan, J., Cheng, Z., Lu, J.: Analyzing traffic violation behavior at urban intersections: a spatio-temporal kernel density estimation approach using automated enforcement system data. Accid. Anal. Prev. **141**, 105509 (2020)
7. Liu, C., Sharma, A.: Exploring spatio-temporal effects in traffic crash trend analysis. Anal. Methods Accid. Res. **16**, 104–116 (2017)
8. Morita, K., Sekine, M.: Analysis of accidents by older drivers in Japan. In: Proceedings of 13th International Pacific Conference on Automotive Engineering, pp. 719–724 (2005)
9. Nishida, Y.: Driving characteristics of the elderly: risk compensation of the elderly driver from the viewpoint of reaction behavior. JSAE Rev. **20**(3), 375–380 (1999)
10. Plug, C., Xia, J.C., Caulfield, C.: Spatial and temporal visualisation techniques for crash analysis. Accid. Anal. Prev. **43**(6), 1937–1946 (2011)
11. Prasannakumar, V., Vijith, H., Charutha, R., et al.: Spatio-temporal clustering of road accidents: GIS based analysis and assessment. Procedia Soc. Behav. Sci. **21**, 317–325 (2011)
12. Romano, B., Jiang, Z.: Visualizing traffic accident hotspots based on spatial-temporal network kernel density estimation. In: Proceedings of the 25th ACM SIGSPATIAL International Conference on Advances in Geographic Information Systems, pp. 1–4 (2017)

13. Vemulapalli, S.S., Ulak, M.B., Ozguven, E.E., et al.: GIS-based spatial and temporal analysis of aging-involved accidents: a case study of three counties in Florida. Appl. Spat. Anal. Policy **10**(4), 537–563 (2017)
14. Xie, Z., Yan, J.: Kernel density estimation of traffic accidents in a network space. Comput. Environ. Urban Syst. **32**(5), 396–406 (2008)
15. Zhang, J., Fraser, S., Lindsay, J., et al.: Age-specific patterns of factors related to fatal motor vehicle traffic crashes: focus on young and elderly drivers. Public Health **112**(5), 289–295 (1998)

Data science

Using DBSCAN-RF Algorithm and Multi-source Features to Model Deep Convection in Hubei, China

Manxing Shi[1](✉) [iD], Xiuguo Liu[1] [iD], Peng Fan[2,3] [iD], Zhipeng Liu[1] [iD], and Qin Li[1] [iD]

[1] School of Geography and Information Engineering, China University of Geosciences, Wuhan, China
shimanxing@cug.edu.cn
[2] NARI Group (State Grid Electric Power Research Institute) Co., Ltd., Nanjing 211106, China
[3] Wuhan NARI Limited Liability Company, State Grid Electric Power Research Institute, Wuhan 430074, China

Abstract. The realistic representation of convection in atmospheric models is paramount for skillful predictions of hazardous weather as well as climate. In order to accurately describe mechanism of deep convection initiation, the forecasting models of thunderstorm occurrence are established from the perspectives of "point to face" and "integration of air and ground", based on Cloud-to-Ground (CG) lightning and convection inducing factors. Firstly, we use the DBSCAN density clustering method to preprocess the discrete CG strokes, eliminating weak convection or noise; then we combine ERA5 with other valuable data sources and use machine learning to predict the probability of thunderstorms. Up to 49 input variables are used, representing, for example, instability, humidity, topography, land-cover. Feature importance derived from random forest (RF) models emphasize the high importance of conditional instability for deep convection. Topographic features accounts for 3%~4% of the total feature contribution, in which geographical position and elevation play a major role. In the comparison experiment of thunderstorm prediction with and without topographic factors, the former can make thunderstorm events and non-events tend to be predicted correctly, reduce false alarm ratio, and improve the overall skill of models. On the 2013–15 independent test, the 2013–15 RF model has a hit rate of 0.79, false alarm ratio is 0.65, and threat score is 0.32. Combining mesoscale reanalysis data with small-scale underlying surface data, the DBSCAN-RF can be used to further study climate trends in convective storms.

Keywords: Deep convection · CG stroke clustering · Multi-source features

1 Introduction

Hazards associated with convective weather (e.g., lightning, large hail, tornadoes, downbursts, and heavy precipitation) cause life threats and huge property damage every year in China (Zheng et al. 2013). Given that these convective systems usually occur and develop on a temporal scale of 1–12 h and a spatial scale of 1–10 kms (Kunz 2007), conventional observation approaches cannot easily capture their meteorological information, resulting in low capabilities of monitoring and forecasting for severe convective weather. Although regional climate models or convection-permitting models can explicitly simulate deep convection, their performance depends largely on the performance of the global model that provides them with initial field and boundary conditions; hence, predictability is limited (Fowle and Roebber 2003; Rajeevan et al. 2010; Weisman et al. 2008).

The current monitoring tools for convective weather mainly include weather radars (Knupp and Cotton 1982; MacGorman et al. 2008; Wilson and Mueller 1993), satellites (Mecikalski and Bedka 2006; Roberts and Rutledge 2003; Vila et al. 2008), ground observation records and lightning location networks (LLNs) (Czernecki et al. 2016; Kaltenböck et al. 2009; Púčik et al. 2015). Although ground observation records are undisturbed by the electromagnetic environment, their observation results are easily affected by various factors, such as weather station environment and background noise (Wapler 2013). The systematic records of convective weather bear the unreliability of observations and the unevenness of spatial and temporal distributions, which limit their accurate estimation of long-term climate trends (Brooks 2013). Compared with Doppler radar and satellite observations, LLNs have the advantages of low maintenance cost, continuous long-term operation, and large spatial coverage (Ukkonen and Mäkelä 2019).

Thermodynamic instability, moisture availability, and the trigger mechanism that lifts the parcel to the condensation height are necessary conditions for thunderstorm occurrence (Doswell III et al. 1996). Statistical techniques based on the potential relationship between thunderstorm ingredients (convective parameters) and storms (Allen and Karoly 2014) have been widely used to develop prediction models for lightning flashes or thunderstorms (Gijben et al. 2017; Rajeevan et al. 2012; Shafer and Fuelberg 2008). However, deep convection forecasting still faces the challenge of high false alarms.

Firstly, the lightning flashes and convective parameters are used to generate class labels according to spatiotemporal criteria. The generation of a thunderstorm event is mainly related to the set time window, space window, and minimum lightning flash threshold. For example, Ukkonen et al. (2017) and Kaltenbock et al. (2009) set the minimum threshold to 1 and 2, respectively. Manzato (2007) and Pucik (2015) adopted the ≥ 3 CG strike threshold, and other studies used the ≥ 10 CG strike criteria (Rasmussen and Blanchard 1998). A large minimum lightning flash threshold reduces the detection errors (Kaltenböck et al. 2009; Manzato 2007; Púčik et al. 2015; Taszarek et al. 2019) produced by the lightning location systems (LLS), but it does not consider the spatiotemporal correlation between adjacent CG strikes. Therefore, grid matching rules considering lightning frequency and topology correlation have stronger statistical significance for deep convection prediction.

Secondly, the above studies only consider the effects of atmospheric environment on the deep convection initiation, but geographic factors also play an important role in triggering convection in the case of weak weather forcing (Shi et al. 2021). Simon et al. (2017) used space, time, and altitude to build a spatiotemporal model of lightning climatology for complex terrain, the altitude effect of the occurrence model suggests higher probabilities of lightning for locations on higher elevations.

In order to accurately predict deep convection in Hubei, we propose a solution based on the DBSCAN-RF algorithm. Reanalysis data, lightning data, and the new generation of GDEM V3 provide rich data for the verification of our method. The DBSCAN algorithm is used to eliminate the discrete noise in CG stroke data, and then the thunderstorm labels with significant or spatial relationship are generated by grid matching. Secondly, the nonlinear relationship between thunderstorms, meteorological factors, and geographical factors is established through RF algorithm. Finally, the primary conditions of deep convection in Hubei are explored and the influence of geographical factors on deep convection is quantitatively evaluated.

2 Study Region and Data

2.1 Study Region

Hubei located in the central part of China and the middle reaches of the Yangtze River. The terrain is an incomplete basin rising on three sides, low in the middle, open to the south, and gapped in the north. There are mountains, hills, and plains accounting for 56%, 24%, and 20% of the total area of Hubei. It has the characteristics of climate in the transition zone between North and South. Due to the complex and diverse landform types, it is easy to form a regional climate with regional differences. Taking 2015 as an example, about 93% of CG lightning occurred in Hubei in the spring and summer seasons, which is significantly related to the climate characteristics of Hubei (Fig. 1).

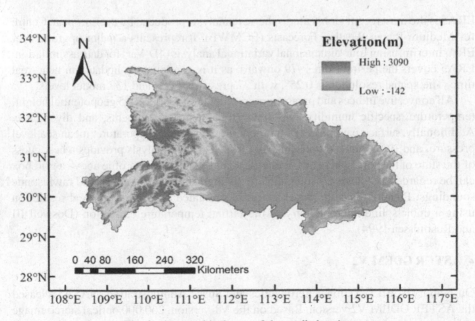

Fig. 1. Geographical map of the studied region.

2.2 Data

• Lightning Data

Lightning is a kind of long-distance electrical discharge and usually occurs during thunderstorms (Srivastava et al. 2017). Lightning can be used to assess the occurrence of deep convection. The advantages of lightning observations are a very high detection efficiency and spatial accuracy. Nearly 20 LLS are distributed in Hubei, and the real-time lightning data are finally stored in the database through the data transmission mode of lightning detection, central, and terminal stations. The LLS built and operated by the State Grid Corporation of China, its dataset contains information on lightning strokes, such as precise time, latitude, longitude, polarity, and peak current. The LLS use both magnetic detection and time-of-arrival location methods to locate the CG strokes (Chen et al. 2002).

Three years (2013–15) of the CG lightning stroke data in Hubei were used in this research. Chen et al. (2012) evaluated LLS in Guangdong with observations of triggered lightning flashes and natural lightning flashes on tall structures. The results showed that the CG flash detection efficiency and CG stroke detection efficiency were about 94% and 60%, respectively. The mean and median for location errors were estimated to be about 710 and 489 m. The absolute percentage errors of peak current estimation were within 0.4%~42%, with arithmetic mean and median values of about 16.3% and 19.1%.

• ERA5 reanalysis

ERA5 is the most recent global atmospheric reanalysis produced by the European Centre for Medium-Range Weather Forecasts (ECMWF). It represents a major upgrade over ERA-Interim, using four-dimensional variational analysis (4D-Var) for data assimilation. ERA5 covers the period from 1979 onward, as it is continuously updated in near–real time. The spatial resolution is 0.25°, with 37 pressure levels and 137 model levels.

All convective indices and parameters are calculated from ERA5 geopotential height, temperature, specific humidity, two-dimensional wind components, and divergence. Additionally, surface parameters of temperature, dewpoint temperature, mean sea level pressure, and 10-m wind components are utilized. The reanalysis provides a best guess of the state of the atmosphere at 1-h intervals, and each vertical profile above a grid box can be regarded as a "pseudo-sounding" to distinguish them from observed rawinsonde soundings. Pseudo-adiabatic parcel ascent is simulated on a 1-hPa vertical resolution using a cubic spline interpolation and the virtual temperature correction (Doswell III and Rasmussen 1994).

• ASTER GDEM V2

On January 6, 2015, National Aeronautics and Space Administration (NASA) released the ASTER GDEM V2 version. Based on the V1 version, 260,000 optical stereo image pairs were added, which are mainly used to improve coverage, improve data resolution, improved water mask processing accuracy. Digital Elevation Model (DEM) is a digital simulation of ground terrain (that is, a digital representation of the shape of the terrain surface) through limited terrain elevation data. It is a solid ground model that uses a set of ordered numerical arrays to represent ground elevation. The spatial resolution of the DEM used in this study is 30 m.

3 Methods

3.1 Preprocess of CG Lightning Using DBSCAN Algorithm

DBSCAN clusters n-dimensional points based on the distance between the points, ϵ, and the minimum number of points necessary to form a cluster (Kriegel et al. 2011). We use the DBSCAN density clustering method to preprocess the discrete CG lightning points, to avoid the grid matching errors, and to improve the accuracy of the prediction and independent variables matching.

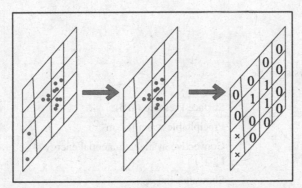

Fig. 2. Combination of DBSCAN and a certain space-time criterion determines the sample category label. The symbol "1" 'indicates a thunderstorm event, the symbol "0" indicates a non-thunderstorm event, and the symbol "x" indicates that it is not a label class.

3.2 Predictand

To develop a classification model for predicting thunderstorm occurrence, class labels first need to be generated by associating lightning with ERA5 by spatiotemporal criteria. In Ukkonen and Mäkelä (2019), ERA5 pseudo-soundings were labeled as "thundery" if at least one lightning flash was observed within the 0.25° × 0.25° grid box during the 1-h period after the analysis time. Compared with the above study, we have used DBSCAN to eliminate discrete strokes. Samples of thunderstorm events (1) and non-thunderstorm events (0) are shown in Fig. 2, where the symbol "×" is excluded from two types of events. The advantage of this is that the response between atmospheric conditions corresponding to thunderstorm events or non-events is higher.

Table 1. Abbreviations, full names, units of measure, data sources and specifications for all input variables.

Abbreviation	Predictor names	Source and specifications
Weather–Reanalysis: pressure level		ERA5 twenty-seven pressure levels (1000, 975, 950, 925, 900, 870, 850, 825, 800, 775, 750, 650, 600, 550, 500, 450, 400, 350, 300, 250, 225, 200, 175, 150, 125, 100 hPa)
Tem	Mean temperature (K)	
RH	Mean humidity (%)	
WS	Mean wind speed (m s^{-1})	
WD	Mean wind direction (decimal degrees)	
Weather–Reanalysis: single level		ERA5 surface or columnar total
SP	Surface Pressure (hPa)	
PW	Precipitable water (kg m^{-2})	
CAPE	Convective available potential energy (J kg^{-1})	
SI	Showalter index	
SWEAT	Strong weather threat index	
VIL	Vertically Integrated Liquid water	
D300	300 hPa Divergence (s^{-1})	
D850	850 hPa Divergence (s^{-1})	
Geographic		DEM and its derivatives, Landcover is derived from MCD12C1 product in MODIS
Ele_mean/Ele_max	Elevation (m) (aggregation type: mean/max)	
Slo_mean/Slo_max	Slope (radian) (aggregation type: mean/max)	
SA_mean/SA_max	Slope aspect (degree) (aggregation type: mean/max)	

(*continued*)

Table 1. (*continued*)

Abbreviation	Predictor names	Source and specifications
TCC_mean/TCC_max	Total cumulative curvature (radian) (aggregation type: mean/max)	
SC_mean/SC_max	Surface curvature (radian) (aggregation type: mean/max)	
PC_mean/PC_max	Profile curvature(radian) (aggregation type: mean/max)	
TR_mean/TR_max	Terrain roughness (aggregation type: mean/max)	
RDLS_mean/RDLS_max	Relief degree of land surface (radian) (aggregation type: mean/max)	
CVE_mean/CVE_max	Coefficient of variation of elevation (aggregation type: mean/max)	
WaterD/WaterA	Water distance/angle	
SuBS/StBS	Sunken/Straight back slope (aggregation type: count)	
CBS	Convex back slope (aggregation type: count)	
FM	Foot of a mountain (aggregation type: count)	
Rep/Che/Dep/Fla/Rid/pea	Ridge/Peak/Replat/Cheuch/Depression/Flat (aggregation type: count)	
LC	Landform characteristics	
Lan	Landcover	
Lat	Latitude (degrees)	
Lon	Longitude (degrees)	
Temporal		
Month	Month of year	
Day	Day of Month	
Time	Time of day	

3.3 Predictors

Although high-resolution atmospheric profiles can be directly used as inputs to the model, doing so would cause dimensional disasters. An alternative approach is to extract feature variables with physical meaning from vertical columns (Ukkonen and Mäkelä 2019). From ERA5 reanalysis, we obtained 12 variables, which characterize the environmental conditions when thunderstorms occur.

DEM is a zero-order digital landform model. Other landform features such as slope, aspect, and slope change rate can be derived the basis of DEM. In order to align all variables with the same spatial resolution, we use thin-plate spline functions to interpolate meteorological data, use aggregation methods to scale up DEM and its derivatives, and finally obtain 49 variables with a spatial resolution of 5 km, as shown in Table 1.

3.4 Classifiers and Metrics

The complexity of the thunderstorm generation mechanism (Manzato 2007), the high imbalance of category samples (Ukkonen and Mäkelä 2019) and the strong correlation between convection parameters (Czernecki et al. 2019) are the main challenges that most statistical methods encounter in severe convection forecasting. The RF can simulate complex interactions, process unbalanced data, and rank variables by importance. Therefore, RF is used in this paper as a classifier to judge whether deep convection occurs.

As described in the contingency Table 2, if a thunderstorm event is forecasted and it is detected in the observation, this is considered as a hit; if a thunderstorm event is detected in the forecast but not observed, this is considered as a false alarm, and if the event is observed but not forecast, this is determined as a miss. Another statistical evaluation is the calculation of proportion correct (PC), the hit rate (H), the false alarm ratio (FAR), false alarm rate (F), the threat score (TS), and the equitable threat score (ETS) (Schaefer 1990). The definition of each index is given in Eqs. (1), (2), (3), (4), (5) and (6) below. Each index can give slightly different information regarding the success of the forecast. The TS is one of indicators for the valuable warning and assumes that an event that is neither predicted nor observed have no consequence.

Table 2. Contingency table.

Event observed	Event forecast	
	Present	Absent
Present	Hit	Miss
Absent	False alarm	Correct negatives

$$PC = \frac{Hit + correct\_negatives}{Hit + Miss + False\_alarm + correct\_negatives} \tag{1}$$

$$H = \frac{Hit}{Hit + Miss} \tag{2}$$

$$FAR = \frac{False\_alarm}{Hit + False\_alarm} \tag{3}$$

$$F = \frac{False\_alarm}{correct\_negatives + False\_alarm} \tag{4}$$

$$TS = \frac{Hit}{Hit + Miss + False\_alarm} \tag{5}$$

$$ETS = \frac{Hit - A}{Hit + Miss + False\_alarm - A}$$
$$A = \frac{(Hit + False\_alarm) \bullet (Hit + Miss)}{Hit + Miss + False\_alarm + correct\_negatives} \tag{6}$$

3.5 Predictor Variable Selection

Disadvantages of RF include possible overfitting of noisy classification and regression tasks, and poor skill when involving a mass of irrelevant variables. In order to accomplish this, optimal predictors are selected based on the backward deletion strategy. The specific steps of this feature selection method are as follows:

Step1: Input all 49 variables into the RF models.

Step2: Sort 49 features according to their importance scores. Remove the 9 features with the lowest scores. For example, in the first cycle, 9 features are deleted and 40 features are retained; in the second cycle, 31 features are retained. By analogy, it should be noted that the number of variables preselected by the tree node m is calculated as $\sqrt{M}$ and M is the total number of features. Because the total number of features input for each iteration is different, m is different.

Step3: For each iteration, evaluate the out-of-bag error score of the training model under this feature combination and the accuracy of thunderstorm prediction based on the independent test set.

Step4: Repeat steps 2~3 until the number of remaining features is equal to or less than 4 and stop the loop. In multiple iteration results, the higher ETS, H, TS, and the lower FAR, F corresponding feature subsets are the optimal predictors for thunderstorm prediction models.

4 Result and Discussion

4.1 Top Predictors

Figure 3 shows the evaluation results of different feature subsets generated during the iterative process based on the RF feature importance ranking method and the "backward deletion" strategy. The three indicators TS, H, and FAR in 2013, 2014 and 2015 are basically the same in terms of change trends. The larger the TS and H, the smaller the FAR, indicating the better the performance of thunderstorm forecasting. The overall change trend of TS and H first increased and then decreased, while FAR showed a change trend of first decrease and then increase. When the predictor number of thunderstorm model in 2013 was 22, TS and H were the largest and FAR was the smallest; TS and H reach a larger value for the 2014 and 2015 thunderstorm models when the number of features was 31, and the FAR was the smallest. In 2015, when the predictor number of thunderstorm model was 4, the hit rate reached the highest, and the false alarm ratio was also the highest. The TS was small, so it could not be used as the optimal feature set for thunderstorm forecasting. The number of features should be chosen for the best prediction performance, not for the least features.

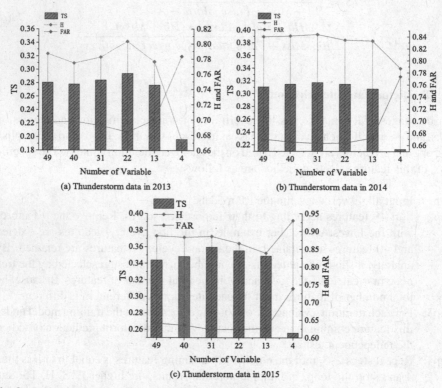

(a) Thunderstorm data in 2013

(b) Thunderstorm data in 2014

(c) Thunderstorm data in 2015

Fig. 3. Evaluation results of feature subsets generated using the "backward deletion" strategy based on 2013, 2014, and 2015 thunderstorm data.

The research results show that with the removal of secondary features, the TS, H, and FAR change more gently. This phenomenon justifies the rationality of the importance ranking of RF feature and the efficiency generated by the combination of "backward deletion" strategy, that is, the removed features are secondary features, which have less impact on the classification results. While retaining features are all high-quality features, which contribute the most important amount of information for classification, so that with the removal of secondary features, the accuracy still maintains a high stability. In addition, it can be found that as the number of features decreases, the accuracy increases first and then decreases. This also indicates that when there are enough features, there will be information redundancy between features and "noise" brought by secondary features. When the redundant information or "noise" is eliminated, the accuracy will increase accordingly. And when excessive features are removed, it will lead to a lack of information, so the accuracy starts to decline.

4.2 Variable Importance

Figure 4 shows the contribution of each factor to the thunderstorm models. The contribution of CAPE in 2013 and 2014 was basically the same, about 18%; in 2015, the contribution of CAPE exceeded one third of the total contribution. Although there are differences, the contribution of CAPE is greater than that of other characteristic factors. CAPE is one of the best characteristics of thunderstorm forecasting, which is consistent with other studies. In the environment where strong convection may occur, CAPE is a thermodynamic variable that is most closely related to the environment, so it is widely used. Previous studies have shown that thunderstorm activity is also strong when CAPE is large (Rutledge et al. 1992; Williams et al. 1992).

It can also be seen from the Fig. 4 that the contribution of meteorological and time factors is much higher than geographic factors in thunderstorm forecasting, but the 300hPa and 850hPa divergence is slightly lower than the latitude and longitude. In the 2013 optimal subset, the geographic feature contribution accounted for 3.56% of the overall contribution; in 2014 and 2015, the geographic factors accounted for 4.18% and

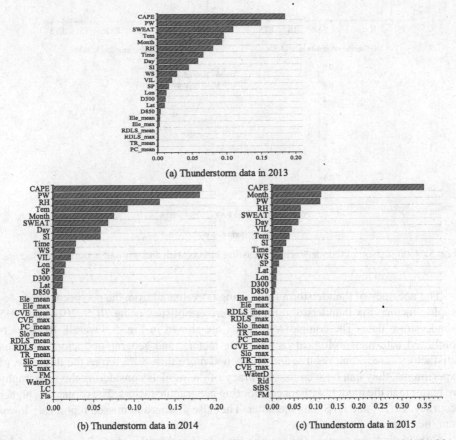

(a) Thunderstorm data in 2013

(b) Thunderstorm data in 2014   (c) Thunderstorm data in 2015

Fig. 4. Contribution of optimal predictors of (a) 2013 thunderstorm forecasting model (b) 2014 thunderstorm forecasting model (c) 2015 thunderstorm forecasting model.

3.15%. Compared with other geographic factors, longitude, latitude, average elevation, and maximum elevation dominate the contribution of thunderstorm forecasting. In 2013, 2014 and 2015, these four features accounted for 78.93%, 76.79%, 78.73% of the total geographic contribution.

4.3 Comparison of Models with and Without Geographic Factors

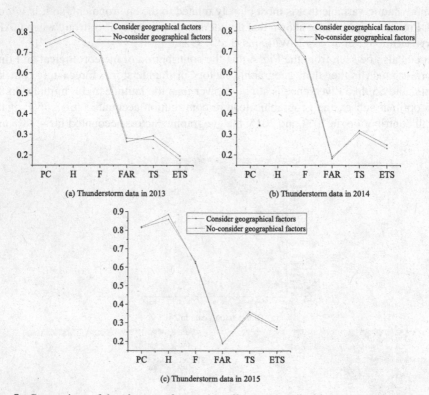

(a) Thunderstorm data in 2013

(b) Thunderstorm data in 2014

(c) Thunderstorm data in 2015

Fig. 5. Comparison of thunderstorm forecasting effects with and without geographical factors.

The accuracy of thunderstorm forecasting is evaluated from the perspectives of geographic factors. Six thunderstorm models were established using 2013, 2014 and 2015 thunderstorm data. The comparison results are shown in Fig. 5. Overall, RF models combined with meteorological factors, time factors, and geographic factors produced satisfactory forecasting results, and H reached more than 80%. From the three sets of experiments, they can be seen that accuracy of the models considering the topography are better than the models without considering geographic factors. The former has higher accuracy, H, TS, and ETS than the latter. The false alarms and missed reports are lower than the latter.

Considering geographic factors, the hit rate increased by about 2%, and the false alarm ratio decreased by about 1%. The overall skill of the thunderstorm forecasting models increased by about 2%, indicating that the increase in geographic features is conducive to the correct discrimination of thunderstorm events and non-events. The hit rate and false alarm ratio are a pair of contradictory indicators. Generally, when the H is increased, the FAR will also increase. Therefore, even though thunderstorm prediction models have a high hit rate, their overall skill score tends to be low. The addition of geographic features can alleviate this contradiction, and make thunderstorm events and non-events lean towards correct forecasting, reduce missed reports and false alarms, and improve the overall skills of models.

4.4 Optimum Model Comparison

It can be seen from Table 3 that the AUC values of thunderstorm models on different independent test sets are all greater than 0.6, indicating that the forecasting capabilities of these models on the corresponding time scales basically meet the requirements. In the 2015 thunderstorm model, the AUC value of the 2013–15 independent test was 0.5709, and the prediction effect was poor. In the 2014 test set, the thunderstorm model obtained the highest hit rate of 0.7923. Accuracy evaluation results of different models on 2013–15 test sets are quite different. For 2013–15 test sets, the 2013–15 model had the highest H, TS, ETS, and AUC value. Comparing the accuracy of thunderstorm models on different time scales, it is found that the accuracy of test sets that the same as the time scale of the model is higher than the cross-time scale.

To sum up, the thunderstorm model established by using annual thunderstorm samples can obtain better forecast results on the same time scale, but the forecast effect will be reduced when forecasting across-time scales. The reason may be that thunderstorms have high time variability, the model in one year may not be suitable for other years. If taking thunderstorm data with a long time to train models, it can avoid the impact of thunderstorm time variability on the model accuracy to a certain extent and improve

Table 3. Results of the accuracy assessment of thunderstorm forecasting models on corresponding independent test sets.

	2013 thunderstorm model		2014 thunderstorm model		2015 thunderstorm model		2013–15 thunderstorm model
	Test in 2013	Test in 2013–15	Test in 2014	Test in 2013–15	Test in 2015	Test in 2013–15	Test in 2013–15
PC	0.8045	0.8329	0.8587	0.8347	0.8831	0.8535	0.8060
H	0.6818	0.5114	0.7923	0.4480	0.7201	0.2047	0.7902
FAR	0.6306	0.6560	0.6063	0.6665	0.5130	0.7045	0.6533
F	0.1769	0.1257	0.1340	0.1154	0.0962	0.0629	0.1919
TS	0.3151	0.2589	0.3568	0.2364	0.4095	0.1376	0.3174
ETS	0.2282	0.1893	0.2935	0.1691	0.3477	0.0892	0.2378
AUC	0.7525	0.6929	0.8292	0.6663	0.8120	0.5709	0.7992

forecasting. Therefore, the 2013–15 thunderstorm model can be applied to thunderstorm forecasting across-time scales. The H and AUC values are 0.7902 and 0.7992.

5 Conclusions

In this paper, we use the DBSCAN-RF algorithm to predict the occurrence of deep convection in Hubei. Firstly, we not only consider the convection parameters that represent environmental conditions, but also input static geographic factors into training models. Secondly, the use of the DBSCAN algorithm can screen out high-density or spatially correlated lightning strokes under the spatiotemporal criterion, and obtain thunderstorm events and non-events through a grid matching strategy. The main findings are summarized as follows:

- Our method can fully mine the correspondence between pseudo-soundings and deep convection, and avoid mismatch between convection parameters and weak convection or noise.
- Geographical factors account for 3% to 5% of the overall contribution of feature factors, with geographic location and elevation playing a major role. Compared with the environmental conditions that are conducive to the development of storms, the uplift of warm and humid air by landform and topography realizes the interaction with the environmental background field. Addition of these factors increases the richness of convective features, thus improving the overall skills of deep convection prediction model.
- Atmospheric environmental factors and time factors play an absolute role in the formation of deep convection. For example, CAPE characterizes the instability of the atmospheric stratification, plays a strong role in regulating the occurrence of thunderstorms.
- The deep convection forecasting models constructed using multi-source features and DBSCAN-RF algorithm have TS between 0.31 and 0.41 and AUC values between 0.75 and 0.85. The overall skills of models constructed in this study are robust, and the recognition of the conditions and development mechanisms of deep convection in Hubei provides a more reliable tool.

In deep convection primary characteristics analysis and prediction technology research has done some work. The occurrence of deep convection is the result of joint action of many different scale factors, its complexity is greatly beyond our imagination. The present research work has obtained certain conclusions, but it is difficult to say we have the universal law of deep convection. In the future, we will study the influence factors of deep convection from the perspective of "sky-space-ground" integration. Incorporating the three aspects of space, air, and ground into one system is bound to be able to better describe and express the conditions under which deep convection occurs.

References

Allen, J.T., Karoly, D.J.: A climatology of Australian severe thunderstorm environments 1979–2011: inter-annual variability and ENSO influence. Int. J. Climatol. **34**(1), 81–97 (2014)

Brooks, H.E.: Severe thunderstorms and climate change. Atmos. Res. **123**, 129–138 (2013)

Chen, L., et al.: Performance evaluation for a lightning location system based on observations of artificially triggered lightning and natural lightning flashes. J. Atmos. Oceanic Tech. **29**(12), 1835–1844 (2012)

Chen, S.M., Du, Y., Fan, L.M., He, H.M., Zhong, D.Z.: Evaluation of the Guang Dong lightning location system with transmission line fault data. IEE Proc.-Sci. Meas. Technol. **149**(1), 9–16 (2002)

Czernecki, B., Taszarek, M., Kolendowicz, L., Konarski, J.: Relationship between human observations of thunderstorms and the PERUN lightning detection network in Poland. Atmos. Res. **167**, 118–128 (2016)

Czernecki, B., et al.: Application of machine learning to large hail prediction-The importance of radar reflectivity, lightning occurrence and convective parameters derived from ERA5. Atmos. Res. **227**, 249–262 (2019)

Doswell, C.A., III., Brooks, H.E., Maddox, R.A.: Flash flood forecasting: an ingredients-based methodology. Weather Forecast. **11**(4), 560–581 (1996)

Doswell, C.A., III., Rasmussen, E.N.: The effect of neglecting the virtual temperature correction on CAPE calculations. Weather Forecast. **9**(4), 625–629 (1994)

Fowle, M.A., Roebber, P.J.: Short-range (0–48 h) numerical prediction of convective occurrence, mode, and location. Weather Forecast. **18**(5), 782–794 (2003)

Gijben, M., Dyson, L.L., Loots, M.T.: A statistical scheme to forecast the daily lightning threat over southern Africa using the Unified Model. Atmos. Res. **194**, 78–88 (2017)

Kaltenböck, R., Diendorfer, G., Dotzek, N.: Evaluation of thunderstorm indices from ECMWF analyses, lightning data and severe storm reports. Atmos. Res. **93**(1–3), 381–396 (2009)

Knupp, K.R., Cotton, W.R.: An intense, quasi-steady thunderstorm over mountainous terrain. Part II: Doppler radar observations of the storm morphological structure. Journal of Atmospheric Sciences **39**(2), 343–358 (1982)

Kriegel, H.P., Kröger, P., Sander, J., Zimek, A.: Density-based clustering. Wiley Interdisc. Rev.: Data Min. Knowl. Discov. **1**(3), 231–240 (2011)

Kunz, M.: The skill of convective parameters and indices to predict isolated and severe thunderstorms. Nat. Hazard. **7**(2), 327–342 (2007)

MacGorman, D.R., et al.: TELEX the thunderstorm electrification and lightning experiment. Bull. Am. Meteor. Soc. **89**(7), 997–1014 (2008)

Manzato, A.: Sounding-derived indices for neural network based short-term thunderstorm and rainfall forecasts. Atmos. Res. **83**(2–4), 349–365 (2007)

Mecikalski, J.R., Bedka, K.M.: Forecasting convective initiation by monitoring the evolution of moving cumulus in daytime GOES imagery. Mon. Weather Rev. **134**(1), 49–78 (2006)

Púčik, T., Groenemeijer, P., Rýva, D., Kolář, M.: Proximity soundings of severe and nonsevere thunderstorms in central Europe. Mon. Weather Rev. **143**(12), 4805–4821 (2015)

Rajeevan, M., Kesarkar, A., Thampi, S. B., Rao, T. N., Radhakrishna, B., and Rajasekhar, M.: Sensitivity of WRF cloud microphysics to simulations of a severe thunderstorm event over Southeast India. In: Annales Geophysicae, pp. 603–619 (2010)

Rajeevan, M., Madhulatha, A., Rajasekhar, M., Bhate, J., Kesarkar, A., Rao, B.A.: Development of a perfect prognosis probabilistic model for prediction of lightning over south-east India. J. Earth Syst. Sci. **121**(2), 355–371 (2012)

Rasmussen, E.N., Blanchard, D.O.: A baseline climatology of sounding-derived supercell andtornado forecast parameters. Weather Forecast. **13**(4), 1148–1164 (1998)

Roberts, R.D., Rutledge, S.: Nowcasting storm initiation and growth using GOES-8 and WSR-88D data. Weather Forecast. **18**(4), 562–584 (2003)

Rutledge, S.A., Williams, E.R., Keenan, T.D.: The down under Doppler and electricity experiment (DUNDEE): Overview and preliminary results. Bull. Am. Meteor. Soc. **73**(1), 3–16 (1992)

Shafer, P.E., Fuelberg, H.E.: A perfect prognosis scheme for forecasting warm-season lightning over Florida. Mon. Weather Rev. **136**(6), 1817–1846 (2008)

Shi, M., et al.: Modelling deep convective activity using lightning clusters and machine learning. Int. J. Climatol. **42**, 952–973 (2021)

Simon, T., Umlauf, N., Zeileis, A., Mayr, G.J., Schulz, W., Diendorfer, G.: Spatio-temporal modelling of lightning climatologies for complex terrain. Nat. Hazard. **17**(3), 305–314 (2017)

Srivastava, A., et al.: Performance assessment of Beijing Lightning Network (BLNET) and comparison with other lightning location networks across Beijing. Atmos. Res. **197**, 76–83 (2017)

Taszarek, M., et al.: A climatology of thunderstorms across Europe from a synthesis of multiple data sources. J. Clim. **32**(6), 1813–1837 (2019)

Ukkonen, P., Manzato, A., Mäkelä, A.: Evaluation of thunderstorm predictors for Finland using reanalyses and neural networks. J. Appl. Meteorol. Climatol. **56**(8), 2335–2352 (2017)

Ukkonen, P., Mäkelä, A.: Evaluation of machine learning classifiers for predicting deep convection. Journal of Advances in Modeling Earth Systems **11**(6), 1784–1802 (2019)

Vila, D.A., Machado, L.A.T., Laurent, H., Velasco, I.: Forecast and tracking the evolution of cloud clusters (ForTraCC) using satellite infrared imagery: methodology and validation. Weather Forecast. **23**(2), 233–245 (2008)

Wapler, K.: High-resolution climatology of lightning characteristics within Central Europe. Meteorol. Atmos. Phys. **122**(3–4), 175–184 (2013). https://doi.org/10.1007/s00703-013-0285-1

Weisman, M.L., Davis, C., Wang, W., Manning, K.W., Klemp, J.B.: Experiences with 0–36-h explicit convective forecasts with the WRF-ARW model. Weather Forecast. **23**(3), 407–437 (2008)

Williams, E.R., Geotis, S.G., Renno, N., Rutledge, S.A., Rasmussen, E., Rickenbach, T.: A radar and electrical study of tropical "hot towers." J. Atmos. Sci. **49**(15), 1386–1395 (1992)

Wilson, J.W., Mueller, C.K.: Nowcasts of thunderstorm initiation and evolution. Weather Forecast. **8**(1), 113–131 (1993)

Zheng, L., Sun, J., Zhang, X., Liu, C.: Organizational modes of mesoscale convective systems over central East China. Weather Forecast. **28**(5), 1081–1098 (2013)

Diversified Top-k Spatial Pattern Matching

Jiahua Xie[1], Hongmei Chen[1,2(✉)], and Lizhen Wang[1,2]

[1] School of Information Science and Engineering, Yunnan University,
Kunming, China
hmchen@ynu.edu.cn
[2] Yunnan Key Laboratory of Intelligent Systems and Computing,
Yunnan University, Kunming, China

Abstract. Spatial Pattern Matching (SPM) is used in various location-based services. SPM usually returns many matches which maybe overlap due to continuous geographic space, while users tend towards diversified top-k matches. Furthermore, existing algorithms to find all matches is low efficient. To solve the above problems, this paper proposes an efficient approximate algorithm DivMatch to attain diversified top-k matches. Firstly, we introduce two metrics $N_{spatial}$ and $D_{spatial}$ to measure the nearness between a match and a query location, and the diversity between two matches. Based on the two metrics, we define an objective function F to select diversified top-k matches. Then, we present an approximate algorithm to efficiently find k matches which maximize the objective function based on level-by-level searching strategy. Experiment results on four real datasets show that DivMatch is more effective and efficient than the algorithm IncMatch.

Keywords: Spatial pattern matching · Diversified top-k matches · Level-by-level searching

1 Introduction

Spatial Pattern Matching (SPM), a kind of spatial keyword query, has attracted researchers and enabled a wide range of location-based services [1–7]. Given a spatial pattern P, SPM returns all matching instances satisfying P in a spatial dataset. SPM is computationally intractable though existing algorithms enhance the performance of SPM by utilizing spatial indexes such as IR-tree, and optimization strategies such as join-order [5,8]. Moreover, SPM usually returns a large number of matches, especially on large scale spatial datasets, while a user only is interested in several matches. So top-k SPM is proposed to find top-k matches closing to a query location [7]. However, it is noted that SPM usually returns many overlapping matches due to continuous geographic space while a user may be interested in diversified matches. This paper presents diversified top-k SPM. Let us see an example shown in Fig. 1.

H. Wu et al. (Eds.): SpatialDI 2022, LNCS 13614, pp. 87–98, 2022.
https://doi.org/10.1007/978-3-031-24521-3_7

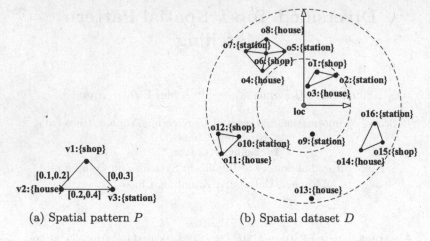

(a) Spatial pattern P (b) Spatial dataset D

Fig. 1. Diversified spatial pattern matching

Example 1. Figure 1 (a) shows a spatial pattern P, in which vertexes describe keyword constraints and edges describes spatial constraints. The spatial pattern P express that a user prefers to a house which has a distance [0.1, 0.2] km with a shop. To avoid noise, the house is at least 0.2 km and at most 0.4 km away from a station. Besides, the distance between the shop and the station is less 0.3 km. In Fig. 1 (b), matching instances satisfying P in the spatial dataset are marked by real lines. We can see that there are 7 matches: $m_1\{o_1, o_2, o_3\}$, $m_2\{o_4, o_5, o_6\}$, $m_3\{o_4, o_6, o_7\}$, $m_4\{o_5, o_6, o_8\}$, $m_5\{o_6, o_7, o_8\}$, $m_6\{o_{10}, o_{11}, o_{12}\}$ and $m_7\{o_{14}, o_{15}, o_{16}\}$. Among these matches, m_2, m_3, m_4 and m_5 are overlapped, for example, m_2 and m_3 share the same house o_4 and the same shop o_6. Given a query location *loc* and a positive integer $k = 4$, top-k SPM will return m_1, m_2, m_3 and m_4 which close to *loc*, while diversified top-k SPM will return m_1, m_2, m_6 and m_7 which not only close to *loc* but also are diversified.

Different from SPM and top-k SPM, diversified top-k SPM has new challenges: How to measure the diversity of the matches? How to balance the diversity of the matches and the nearness between the matches and a query location? How to efficiently find diversified top-k matches? To tackle the above issues, this paper proposes an efficient approximate algorithm DivMatch to attain diversified top-k matches.

In summary, our main contributions are as follows.

- We introduce two metrics $N_{spatial}$ and $D_{spatial}$ to measure the nearness between a match and a query location, and the diversity between two matches. Based on the two metrics, we define an objective function F to select diversified top-k matches by balancing the nearness and the diversity of the matches.
- We present an approximate algorithm DivMatch to efficiently find k matches which maximize the objective function F based on level-by-level searching strategy. We also prove the algorithm has a good approximate bound.

– We experimentally evaluate the performance of DivMatch on four real datasets, and the results show DivMatch outperforms the algorithm IncMatch for top-k SPM on the four datasets.

The rest of the paper is organized as follows. We review the related work in Sect. 2. Section 3 introduces the nearness metric, the diversity metric and the objective function, and formally presents the diversified top-k spatial pattern matching problem. Section 4 details our DivMatch algorithm. We report the experiment results in Sect. 5 and conclude in Sect. 6.

2 Related Work

2.1 Top-k Spatial Pattern Matching

Top-k SPM aims to find k matches of the spatial pattern which are closest to the query location. Existing solutions can be divided into two categories: Ranking After Matching (RAM) and Ranking While Matching (RWM) [17]. RAM first finds all matches of the spatial pattern, then ranks these matches according to the nearness metric and selects top-k matches [14]. [5] proposes a basic method which uses the MSJ algorithm for SPM to find all matches of the spatial pattern, and selects top-k matches based the distance/nearness between the matches and the query location. RWM computes the rank score of the match according to the nearness metric when finding a match, and only retains k matches. Once the rank score of a new match is higher than the smallest score in k matches retained, the match with the smallest score is replaced by the new match. [7] proposes an efficient algorithm IncMatch for top-k SPM based on incremental matching. Different from top-k SPM, we focus on the diversified top-k SPM problem.

2.2 Diversified Graph Pattern Matching

The diversity of the matches is studied in graph pattern matching [9,11]. [9] takes into account the diversity and the relevance of the matches. [11] defines the graph pattern by extending the traditional subgraph isomorphism, and presents the diversity and the relevance metrics. [10] defines the diversity of the matches according to the number of overlapping vertices, addresses the diversified top-k subgraph matching problem in large graphs, and presents the DSQL algorithm to heuristically find the matches based on level-by-level searching. Distinct from the above works, our pattern is the spatial pattern with keyword constraint and spatial constraints such as distance constraint. In the above works, the pattern may be graph simulation [9], subgraph isomorphism [10] and so on.

3 Preliminaries

In this section, we first introduce the nearness metric, the diversity metric and the objective function. Then we formally present the diversified top-k SPM problem.

3.1   Basic Concepts

Definition 1. *(Nearness) Given a set m of spatial objects (e.g. a match of the spatial pattern), and a query location loc, the nearness between m and loc can be defined as follows.*

$$N_{spatial}\left(m, loc\right) = 1 - \frac{\max_{o \in m} |o, loc|}{MaxDist} \qquad (1)$$

where $MaxDist$ is the maximum distance of all spatial objects in a spatial dataset, $|o, loc|$ is the distance between a spatial object o and loc. In this paper, Euclidean distance is used, and it can be replaced by other distance metrics. Obviously, if a spatial object set m is closer to the query location loc, their nearness is larger.

Definition 2. *(Diversity) Given two spatial object sets m_1 and m_2, the diversity between m_1 and m_2 can be defined as follows.*

$$D_{spatial}\left(m_1, m_2\right) = 1 - \frac{|m_1 \cap m_2|}{|m_1 \cup m_2|} \qquad (2)$$

Intuitively, if the spatial objects in m_1 and that in m_2 have higher overlap, the diversity between m_1 and m_2 is smaller.

Based on the above two metrics, we can define an objective function to select k sets of spatial objects by balancing their nearness and diversity.

Given the set of k spatial objects sets $M = \{m_1, m_2, \ldots, m_k\}$, the objective function F can be defined as follows.

$$F(M) = (1 - \lambda) \sum_{m_i \in M} N_{spatial}\left(m_i, loc\right) + \frac{2\lambda}{k-1} \sum_{m_i, m_j \in M, i<j} D_{spatial}\left(m_i, m_j\right)$$

$$(3)$$

where $\lambda \in [0, 1]$ is a parameter set and set as 0.5 in this paper.

3.2   Problem Statement

Let D be a spatial dataset, each spatial object $o \in D$ contains its spatial coordinates and a set of keywords.

Definition 3. *(Spatial Pattern [5]) A spatial pattern is a graph $P = G\left(V, E\right)$, where V is the set of vertices, E is the set of edges, and vertices in V and edges in E have the following constraints.*

- Each vertex $v_i \in V$ has a keyword w_i, if $w_i \in doc\left(o_s\right)$, then the object o_s matches the vertex v_i.
- Each edge $(v_i, v_j) \in E$ has a distance interval $[l_{i,j}, u_{i,j}]$, which specifies the upper and lower bounds of the distance between two objects matching the vertices.

– Each edge $(v_i, v_j) \in E$ is described by one of four signs: $v_i \rightarrow v_j$, $v_i \leftarrow v_j$, $v_i \leftrightarrow v_j$ and $v_i - v_j$. Let o_s and o_t be a pair of objects matching edge (v_i, v_j), i.e., $w_i \in doc(o_s)$, $w_j \in doc(o_t)$, $|o_s - o_t| \in [l_{i,j}, u_{i,j}]$, then the meaning of the four signs is:

  - $v_i \rightarrow v_j$ [v_i excludes v_j]: There is no object in D that has distance less than $l_{i,j}$ from o_s and contains w_j.
  - $v_i \leftarrow v_j$ [v_j excludes v_i]: There is no object in D that has distance less than $l_{i,j}$ from o_t and contains w_i.
  - $v_i \leftrightarrow v_j$ [mutual exclusion]: $v_i \rightarrow v_j$ and $v_i \leftarrow v_j$
  - $v_i - v_j$ [mutual inclusion]: The occurrence of any object pairs (other than o_s and o_t) with keywords w_i and w_j in D with distance shorter than $l_{i,j}$ is allowed.

Definition 4. *(e-match [5]) For an edge (v_i, v_j), a pair of objects o_s and o_t is said to be a e-match of the edge (v_i, v_j) if it matches two vertices v_i and v_j and satisfies the spatial constraints on the edge (v_i, v_j), i.e., the distance interval constraint $[l_{i,j}, u_{i,j}]$ and the sign constraint $(\rightarrow, \leftarrow, \leftrightarrow \text{ or } -)$.*

Definition 5. *(match [5]) Given a spatial pattern $P = G(V, E)$, an object set $S \subseteq D$ is called a match of P, if there exists a surjective $\oslash : V \rightarrow S$, such that for each edge $(v_i, v_j) \in E$, the object pair $(\oslash(v_i), \oslash(v_j))$ is an e-match of e.*

Problem Statement. Given a spatial dataset D, a query location loc, a spatial pattern P and a positive integer k, diversified top-k SPM returns k matches of P which maximize the objective function F.

Obviously, if the number of matches of the spatial pattern P in the spatial dataset D isn't larger than k, all matches will be returned. When the number of matches is larger than k, k matches will be selected by maximizing the objective function F. Since the objective function F balances the nearness and the diversity, maximizing F is computationally intractable [15,16]. So we present an approximate algorithm DivMatch to efficiently to solve the diversified top-k SPM problem.

4   The DivMatch Algorithm

In this section, we first give an overview of the proposed DivMatch algorithm, and then detail the key steps of DivMatch.

In General, the DivMatch algorithm adopts a level-by-level searching strategy because matches of the spatial pattern P far away the query location loc are seldom selected due to the nearness constraint in the objective function F. In each searching level, the DivMatch algorithm selects matches according to the diversity constraint in the objective function F. Specifically, at level $l(l \geq 1)$, DivMatch finds matches in the ring region with the query location loc as center, $(l-1)*r$ as inside radius, and $l*r$ as outside radius respectively. Divmatch selects matches according to the order in which the number $n(0 \leq n < |V|)$ of overlapping vertexes increases. That is to say, DivMatch first selects matches without overlapping vertex, i.e. $n = 0$; then finds matches with one overlapping vertex, i.e. $n = 1$; and so on. If k matches are selected or the whole spatial dataset has been searched, DivMatch exits, otherwise DivMatch searches next level $l + 1$. It is noted that IR-tree on the spatial dataset D is built and the spatial pattern P is refined by using the methods in [5] before calling DivMatch. The inputs and outputs of DivMatch are defined as global variables. The DivMatch algorithm is described in Algorithm 1.

Algorithm 1: DivMatch

Input: D, loc, P, k, the increment of the radius r, the maximum radius mr
Output: the result set M containing k matches of P

1   $inside = 0$; $outside = r$; $flag = true$;
2   **while** $flag$ **do** // at each level l
3   $\quad$ Calculate the ordered list L_1 ;
4   $\quad$ Calculate the ordered list L_2 ;
5   $\quad$ $n = 0$;
6   $\quad$ **while** $n < |V|$ **do** // selecting matches with n overlapping vertexes
7   $\quad\quad$ **for** $i \leftarrow 1$ *to* $|L_1|$ **do**
8   $\quad\quad\quad$ $o = L_1[i]$;
9   $\quad\quad\quad$ $FindMatch(L_2, 1, \{o\}, n)$;
10 $\quad\quad\quad$ **if** $|M| == k$ **then** $flag = false$; *break*; **end**
11 $\quad\quad$ **end**
12 $\quad\quad$ **if** $!flag$ **then** *break*; **end**
13 $\quad\quad$ $n++$;
14 $\quad$ **end**
15 $\quad$ $inside = outside$; $\quad$ $outside = outsice + r$;
16 $\quad$ **if** $inside > mr$ **then** $flag = false$; **end**
17 **end**

In Algorithm 1, Line 1 initializes the *inside* radius and *outside* radius of the ring region, and the searching *flag* at level 1. Based on IR-tree on the spatial dataset D and the refined spatial pattern P, Line 3 calculates the ordered list L_1 in which there are the objects matching a vertex of P and with the least number. Line 4 computes an ordered list L_2 where there are the lists of objects that match the other vertices of P and satisfy the spatial constraints in P with the objects in L_1. Objects in L_1 and L_2 are sorted in ascending order of distances from the query location loc. Line 5 initializes the number n of overlapping vertexes. Line 8 gets the ith object o from L_1 as the start object for searching matches. Line 9 calls the function FindMatch() to find matches of P containing the object o from L_2 and having n overlapping vertexes with matches in M. In Line 10, 12 and 16, DivMatch exits If k matches are selected or the whole spatial dataset has been searched. Otherwise, DivMatch continue to search in Line 13 and 15.

Algorithm 2 describes the function FindMatch(). In Algorithm 2, Line 3 gets the list L_3 of objects which will match the $(i + 1)th$ vertex of P from L_2. Line 6 gets an object o_j from L_3 which matches the $(i + 1)th$ vertex and satisfies the

---

Algorithm 2: FindMatch

Input: L_2, i, m, n, where i is the index of L_2, m is the set of partial matching
objects

Output: Matches containing object o and overlapping n vertices.

1   **if** $|M| == k$ **then** *return*; **end**

2   **if** $|m| < |V|$ **then**

3      $L_3 = L_2[i]$;

4   **for** $j \leftarrow 1$ *to* $|L_3|$ **do**

5   **if** $|M| == k$ **then** *return*; **end**

6         $o_j = L_3[j]$;

7   **if** *the number of overlapping vertexes is not larger than n after joining*
        o_j **then**

8            $m.add(o_j)$;

9            $FindMatch(L_2, i{+}{+}, m, n)$;

10            $m.remove(o_j)$;

11   **end**

12   **end**

13 **else**

14      $M.add(m)$;

15 **end**

---

spatial constraints in P. In Line 9, FindMatch() is recursively called to find an
object matching the next vertex of P. In Line 14, a match is put in the result
set M. In Line 1 and 5, FindMatch() return if k matches are selected.

Theorem 1. *Given a spatial dataset D, a query location loc, a spatial pattern
$P = G(V, E)$ and a positive integer k. If the best solution of the diversified top-k
SPM problem is M_{best}, i.e. M_{best} maximizes the objective function F, the result
set of the DivMatch algorithm is M, then $\frac{F(M)}{F(M_{best})} > \lambda - \frac{2\lambda}{k(k-1)} \sum_{n=0}^{|V|-1} c_n \frac{n}{2|V|-n}$,
where $c_n, 0 \le n \le |V|-1$, is the number of matching pairs overlapping n vertexes
in M.*

Proof. Let UB be the upper bound of F. When $N_{spatial}(m_i, loc) = 1, 1 \le i \le k$
and $D_{spatial}(m_i, m_j) = 1, 1 \le i < j \le k$, then F meets the upper bound
$UB = k$. Then the following formula holds:

$$\frac{F(M)}{F(M_{best})} > \frac{F(M)}{UB} = \frac{F(M)}{k} = \frac{F_N(M) + F_D(M)}{k} > \frac{F_D(M)}{k}$$

where $F_N(M) = (1 - \lambda) \sum_{m_i \in M} N_{spatial}(m_i, loc)$,
$F_D(M) = \frac{2\lambda}{k-1} \sum_{m_i, m_j \in M, i<j} D_{spatial}(m_i, m_j)$

Let $c_n, 0 \le n \le |V| - 1$ be the number of matching pairs overlapping n
vertexes in M, i.e. $c_0 + c_1 + ... + c_{|V|-1} = \frac{k(k-1)}{2}$. Then

$$F_D(M) = \frac{2\lambda}{k-1}[c_0 \times 1 + c_1 \times (1 - \frac{1}{2|V|-1}) + c_2 \times (1 - \frac{2}{2|V|-2}) + ... + c_{|V|-1} \times$$
$$(1 - \frac{|V|-1}{|V|+1})]$$
$$= \frac{2\lambda}{k-1} \left(c_0 + c_1 - c_1 \frac{1}{2|V|-1} + c_2 - c_2 \frac{2}{2|V|-2} + ... + c_{|V|-1} - c_{|V|-1} \frac{|V|-1}{|V|+1} \right)$$

$$= \frac{2\lambda}{k-1}\left(\frac{k(k-1)}{2} - \sum_{n=0}^{|V|-1} c_n \frac{n}{2|V|-n}\right)$$
$$= \lambda k - \frac{2\lambda}{k-1}\sum_{n=0}^{|V|-1} c_n \frac{n}{2|V|-n}$$

Then, the following formula holds:

$$\frac{F(M)}{F(M_{best})} > \frac{F_D(M)}{k} = \frac{1}{k}\left(\lambda k - \frac{2\lambda}{k-1}\sum_{n=0}^{|V|-1} c_n \frac{n}{2|V|-n}\right) = \lambda - \frac{2\lambda}{k(k-1)}\sum_{n=0}^{|V|-1} c_n \frac{n}{2|V|-n}.$$

5   Experimental Evaluation

In this section, we experimentally evaluate the effectiveness and efficiency of the proposed DivMatch algorithm using real spatial datasets and compare with the IncMatch algorithm [7].

5.1   Experimental Setup

Datasets. We use four real spatial datasets and their IR-trees provided by Fang et al [5]. Table 1 shows the statistical information of the datasets.

Table 1. Datasets used in our experiments

Name	Objects	Unique words	Total words
UK	182317	45371	550663
NY	485059	116545	1143013
LA	724952	161489	1833486
TW	2000000	715565	9926629

Spatial Patterns. Following the methods in [5], the 12 pattern structures shown in Fig. 2 are used to generate 240 spatial patterns for each dataset, i.e. 20 spatial patterns for each pattern structure.

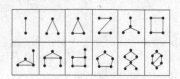

Fig. 2. Structures of spatial patterns

Environment Settings. The algorithms are implemented in Java. The experiments are run on a PC with AMD R5-3600 3.60 GHz CPU and 16 GB Memory.

5.2   Overlap Ratio

We evaluate the effectiveness of the DivMatch algorithm and the IncMatch algorithm by calculating the overlap ratio OR of the objects in k matches of the pattern $P = G(V, E)$, i.e. $OR = 1 - \frac{N_{uo}}{k|V|}$, where N_{uo} is the number of distinct objects in all k matches. Obviously, OR is smaller, the diversity of the result is better. From Fig. 3, we can see that DivMatch always outperforms IncMatch with k changing from 5 to 30 on all datasets. Since IncMatch only considers the distance and does not take into account the diversity, and return the high overlapping matches.

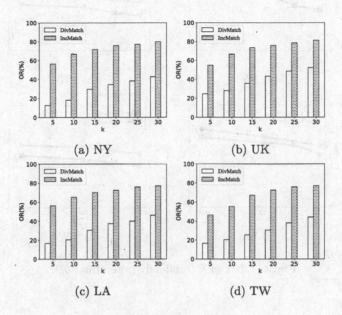

(a) NY

(b) UK

(c) LA

(d) TW

Fig. 3. Overlap ratio

5.3 Effect of k

As shown in Fig. 4, the running time of both DivMatch and IncMatch increases slightly with k changing from 1 to 20. Both DivMatch and IncMatch use the searching strategy based on level-by-level. But, after IncMatch finds an object o, it first finds all matches containing o and then selects top-k matches from these matches. DivMatch finds top-k matches according to the order of the incremental number of overlapping vertexes instead of finding all matches. As a result, DivMatch is slightly more efficient than IncMatch.

5.4 Effect of the Methods for Generating *loc*

DivMatch and IncMatch are all affected by query location *loc* and the distribution of dataset. Two methods are used to generate query locations. The one is randomly generating query locations. Another is generating query locations according to the distribution of the dataset, i.e., locations with more objects have higher probabilities to be selected as query locations. The results are reported in Fig. 4 and Fig. 5 respectively. DivMatch is more efficient than IncMatch whichever method is used. Therefore, DivMatch is efficient and robust.

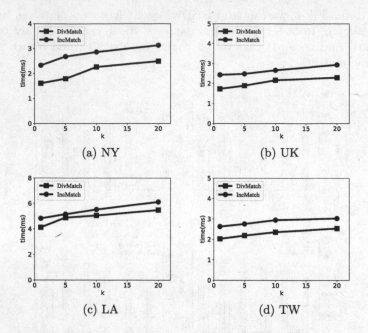

Fig. 4. Effect of k (randomly generating loc)

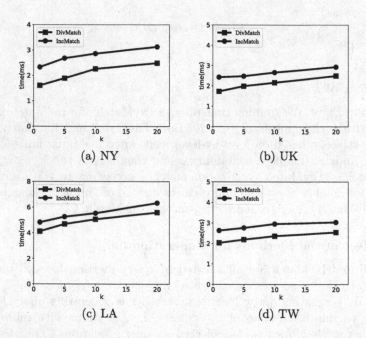

Fig. 5. Effect of k (generating loc according to the distribution)

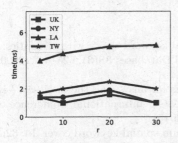

Fig. 6. Effect of r

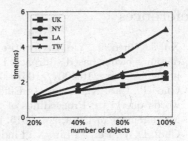

Fig. 7. Scalability

5.5 Effect of r

The DivMatch level-by-level searching strategy uses the increment r of the radius to control the ring region at each level. Figure 6 shows effect of r on the running time of DivMatch. When r changes from 5 km to 30 km, the running time change little. So DivMatch is not sensitive to r.

5.6 Scalability

In order to evaluate the scalability of DivMatch, we randomly selected objects from the original dataset at a ratio of 20%, 40%, 80%, and 100% to generate four subsets. Note that the patterns remain unchanged, which means a pattern may have a keyword which does not appear in a subset, so there is no match for this pattern. The results are depicted in Fig. 7. It can be seen that DivMatch has a good scalability.

6 Conclusion

In order to solve the problem of excessive and overlapping matches in SPM, this paper studies the diversified top-k SPM problem. This paper defines an objective function to effectively select diversified top-k matches by balancing the nearness and diversity of matches, and proposes an approximate algorithm DivMatch to efficiently find diversified top-k matches by a level-by-level searching strategy. Experiment results show that compared with the IncMatch algorithm, the proposed algorithm DivMatch can find more diversified matches in lower time cost.

Acknowledgements. This work is supported by the Open Project Program of Yunnan Key Laboratory of Intelligent Systems and Computing (ISC22Z02), the Program for Young and Middle-aged Academic and Technical Reserve Leaders of Yunnan Province (202205AC160033), the National Natural Science Foundation of China (61966036), Yunnan Provincial Major Science and Technology Special Plan Projects (202202AD080003), and Yunnan Fundamental Research Projects (202201AS070015).

References

1. Xu, J., Chen, J., Yin, L.: Multi-objective spatial keyword query with semantics: a distance-owner based approach. Distrib. Parallel Databases **38**(3), 625–647 (2020). https://doi.org/10.1007/s10619-020-07283-1
2. Guo, T., Cao, X., Cong, G.: Efficient algorithms for answering the m-closest keywords query. In: Proceedings of the ACM SIGMOD International Conference on Management of Data, vol. 2015, pp. 405–418 (2015)
3. Choi, D.W., Pei, J., Lin, X.: Finding the minimum spatial keyword cover. In: 32nd International Conference on Data Engineering (ICDE), pp. 685–696. IEEE (2016)
4. Deng, K., Li, X., Lu, J., et al.: Best keyword cover search. IEEE Trans. Knowl. Data Eng. **27**(1), 61–73 (2014)
5. Fang, Y., Cheng, R., Cong, G., et al.: On spatial pattern matching. In: 34th International Conference on Data Engineering (ICDE), pp. 293–304. IEEE (2018)
6. Chen, H., Fang, Y., Zhang, Y., et al.: ESPM: efficient spatial pattern matching. IEEE Trans. Knowl. Data Eng. **32**(6), 1227–1233 (2020)
7. Fang, Y., Li, Y., Cheng, R., et al.: Evaluating pattern matching queries for spatial databases. VLDB J. **28**(5), 649–673 (2019). https://doi.org/10.1007/s00778-019-00550-3
8. Zou, L., Chen, L., Özsu, M.T.: Distance-join: pattern match query in a large graph database. Proc. VLDB Endow. **2**(1), 886–897 (2009)
9. Fan, W., Wang, X., Wu, Y.: Diversified top-k graph pattern matching. Proc. VLDB Endow. **6**(13), 1510–1521 (2013)
10. Yang, Z., Fu, A.W.C., Liu, R.: Diversified top-k subgraph querying in a large graph. In: Proceedings of the. ACM SIGMOD International Conference on Management of Data, vol. 2016, pp. 1167–1182 (2015)
11. Wang, X., Zhan, H.: Approximating diversified top-k graph pattern matching. In: Hartmann, S., Ma, H., Hameurlain, A., Pernul, G., Wagner, R.R. (eds.) DEXA 2018. LNCS, vol. 11029, pp. 407–423. Springer, Cham (2018). https://doi.org/10.1007/978-3-319-98809-2_25
12. Qin, L., Yu, J.X., Chang, L.: Diversifying top-k results. arXiv preprint arXiv:1208.0076 (2012)
13. Vieira, M.R., Razente, H.L., Barioni, M.C.N., et al.: On query result diversification. In: 27th International Conference on Data Engineering, pp. 1163–1174. IEEE (2011)
14. Zou, L., Chen, L., Lu, Y.: Top-k subgraph matching query in a large graph. In: ACM First Ph. D Workshop in CIKM, p. 139 (2007)
15. Gollapudi, S., Sharma, A.: An axiomatic approach for result diversification. In: WWW (2009)
16. Borodin, A., Lee, H.C., Ye, Y.: Max-sum diversification, monotone submodular functions and dynamic updates. In: Proceedings of the 31st ACM SIGMOD-SIGACT-SIGAI Symposium on Principles of Database Systems, pp. 155–166 (2012)
17. Gupta, M., Gao, J., Yan, X., et al.: Top-k interesting subgraph discovery in information networks. In: 30th International Conference on Data Engineering, pp. 820–831. IEEE (2014)
18. Hassin, R., Rubinstein, S., Tamir, A.: Approximation algorithms for maximum dispersion. Oper. Res. Lett. **21**(3), 133–137 (1997)

Information Diffusion Prediction Based on Deep Attention in Heterogeneous Networks

Xingzhu Zou[1], Lihua Zhou[1]([✉]), Guowang Du[1], Lizhen Wang[1], and Yiting Jiang[2]

[1] School of Information Science and Engineering, Yunnan University, Kunming 650091,
Yunnan, People's Republic of China
lhzhou@ynu.edu.cn

[2] School of Information, Yunnan Normal University, Kunming 650091,
People's Republic of China

Abstract. Understanding how information is spread is critical necessities in many real-world application domains, so the study of information diffusion in social networks has attracted considerable research interest. Compared with the widely studied homogeneous networks, heterogeneous networks can more accurately model the process of information diffusion with multiple channels and more closely match the pattern of information diffusion in the real world. However, the complex structural information and rich semantic information in heterogeneous networks bring challenges to the extraction and utilization of effective information. In addition, the existing heterogeneous diffusion models do not fully consider the different effects of different diffusion channels on information propagation. Therefore, we propose a Heterogeneous Deep Attention Diffusion model (HDAD). HDAD first extracts the information matrix that integrates the network topology and information diffusion state based on the meta-path for simplifying the network and retains the effective information of the network; Secondly we design a deep learning architecture to learn low-dimensional embeddings and capture non-linear relationships; and then attention mechanism is used to learn the importance of different diffusion channels and to combine the low-dimensional embeddings under different semantics in the network rationally. Experiments on the public DBLP and ACM datasets are conducted, and the experimental results show that HDAD can fully exploit the information in the network and the prediction performance is better than the existing models.

Keywords: Heterogeneous networks · Information diffusion · Deep learning

1 Introduction

The rapid growth of online social networks (e.g., Twitter, Weibo) in recent years has dramatically changed the way people obtain and disseminate news, and the ensuing massive amount of network data offers an unprecedented opportunity to explore and exploit the trajectories and direction of the evolution of information diffusion. The study of information diffusion can help people to better understand the law of news dissemination,

H. Wu et al. (Eds.): SpatialDI 2022, LNCS 13614, pp. 99–112, 2022.
https://doi.org/10.1007/978-3-031-24521-3_8

predict the direction of information diffusion, and explore the factors influencing information diffusion. Many application domains have benefited from these studies, such as viral marketing [1], advertising [2], referrals [3], and epidemic prevention and control [4].

Most of the existing information diffusion studies are based on homogeneous networks, but since homogeneous networks contain only one type of node and edge, it can only describe the relationship between homogeneous nodes and represent one kind of diffusion channel directly connected by users. However, users in the real world are connected in a variety of ways, and the diffusion of information in social networks is often dependent on multiple channels. For example, researchers can learn about new research topics from a variety of sources, such as attending academic conferences or reading new papers, and even if two researchers don't know each other, they can influence each other's research topics. Heterogeneous networks contain multiple types of nodes and edges, so they can describe such relationships where two users are not directly connected and represent multiple real diffusion channels. Therefore, the complex structural information and rich semantic information in heterogeneous networks can explore more possibilities of node links in social networks, more accurately simulate the process of information diffusion with multiple channels, and more closely match the law of information diffusion in the real world.

The structure and semantic information of heterogeneous networks can provide a more suitable and effective data foundation for the information diffusion problem. But since most of the heterogeneous network data are large scale high-dimensional sparse data, the work of information diffusion analysis directly based on them faces serious challenges. An effective way to solve the high-dimensional sparse problem is network embedding. Network embedding maps network nodes into a low-dimensional vector space, representing complex network data with denser, low-dimensional vectors for more flexible application to downstream tasks. Some heterogeneous network embedding methods have been proposed, but many of them are shallow models [5–8], which decompose heterogeneous networks into the simpler network for learning embeddings based on meta-paths, neglecting the non-linear relationships in the data. In recent years, deep models based on deep networks [9–11] are widely recognized, due to the ability of mining the rich structural and semantic information in the network as well as learning more accurate and meaningful network embeddings.

However, since the information diffusion problem involves a variety of information such as the news of diffusion, time, channels and the status of nodes, directly applying network structure and node features in a deep embedding model not only is difficult to fuse all information completely, but also generates redundant information that is irrelevant to the specified message. Therefore, the existing deep network embedding model cannot effectively fit the information diffusion problem. In addition, the different channels which the user receives messages have different influences on his/her decision whether to spread the message. The existing models of information diffusion in heterogeneous networks [12–15] either do not explore multiple channels of information diffusion in heterogeneous networks and directly map heterogeneous networks to homogeneous networks for research, or although explore multiple channels of information diffusion but directly mix different channels without distinguishing their influence on the results of information diffusion. These models cannot make good use of the rich semantic information of heterogeneous networks and cannot accurately model the process of message propagation in social networks.

To address the above shortcomings, we propose a Heterogeneous Deep Attention Diffusion model (HDAD) for solving the prediction problem of information diffusion in heterogeneous networks. HDAD first extracts the information matrix to describe the frequency of user interactions in different topics, which integrates the network topology and information diffusion state based on the meta-path; and then we design a deep learning architecture to learn low-dimensional embeddings for mining hidden information between nodes and capturing non-linear relationships; HDAD further utilizes the attention mechanism to automatically learn the weights of different embeddings for extracting the most correlated information. The experimental results show that HDAD can effectively improve the prediction performance of information diffusion, because it learns optimal network embeddings in a hierarchical manner and combines learned embeddings rationally so that the learned network embeddings can better capture the complex structure and rich semantic information in heterogeneous networks.

Our main contributions can be summarized as follows:

(1) We propose a heterogeneous deep attention diffusion model (HDAD). HDAD uses the information matrix to extract and fuse the structural information of the network and the diffusion state of the specific message, as well as learns the optimal network embedding with a deep neural network to achieve the prediction of message diffusion results in a heterogeneous network.

(2) The attention mechanism is utilized to learn the attention values of different diffusion channels for distinguishing the different effects brought by different diffusion channels on information propagation. Based on these learned attention values, HDAD combines reasonably the low-dimensional embeddings under different semantics in the network, and makes full use of the rich semantic information in the heterogeneous network to improve the prediction results.

(3) We conduct extensive experiments on two real datasets to evaluate the performance of the proposed model. The experimental results show the superiority of HDAD by comparing with the state-of-the-art models.

This paper is organized as follows. Section 2 defines and formally describes the concepts involved in the paper and the problem studied. Section 3 elaborates the proposed heterogeneous depth attention diffusion model. Section 4 is devoted to the experimental settings and results on the benchmark real networks. Finally, we conclude the paper in Sect. 5 with some suggestions for further works.

2   Preliminary

In this section, we first list some key definitions for heterogeneous networks and information diffusion, and then provide the statement of the problem.

Definition 1: Heterogeneous networks [7, 16]. A heterogeneous network is defined as $G = \{V, E\}$, where V is the set of vertices and E is the set of edges. A node type mapping function is defined as $\varphi : V \rightarrow A$, an edge type mapping function is defined as $\psi : E \rightarrow R$. A and R denote the sets of predefined vertices types and edges types, where $|A| + |R| > 2$.

Definition 2: Meta-patH [17]. A meta-path Φ is defined as $A_1 \xrightarrow{R_1} A_2 \xrightarrow{R_2} \cdots \xrightarrow{R_1} A_{l+1}$(abbreviated as $A_1 A_2 \cdots A_{l+1}$), where $A_i(i = 1, 2, \cdots l+1)$ is a specific node type and $R_i(i = 1, 2, \cdots l)$ is a specific edge type.

Definition 3: Node activation. An activate action of a node can be represented as a Logical function $f(v, t, \varepsilon)$, where $f(v, t, \varepsilon) = 1$ if node v retweeted the information ε at time t, denoting v is activated by a piece of information ε at time t, v is active node of ε; otherwise $f(v, t, \varepsilon) = 0$, it means that node v did not retweet the information ε at time t, denoting v is not active by ε.

For example, we treat topics of paper as information in the DBLP dataset, if an author v_i wrote a paper related to the topic of "social networks" in 2010, which denotes v_i is activated by "social networks" topic at 2010, and v_i is an active node of "social networks" topic.

Definition 4: Active node set. An active node set is defined as $U_{\varepsilon,t} = \{v \in V | f(v, t, \varepsilon) = 1\}$, it denotes the sets of nodes activated by message ε at time t.

Problem Statement. The information diffusion problem we mainly address is also called the topic diffusion problem. Given a heterogeneous network $G = \{V, E\}$ and its set of meta-paths $\Phi = \{\Phi_1, \Phi_2, \cdots, \Phi_k\}$, for an information ε, we denote the diffusion state of information ε in network G at time t by the active node set $U_{\varepsilon,t}$. The aim of this paper is to predict the diffusion state $U_{\varepsilon,t+1}$ at moment $t + 1$ when $U_{\varepsilon,t}$ is known, i.e., to predict which nodes will be activated at the next moment.

3 The Proposed Model

IN this section, we present our heterogeneous deep attention diffusion model (HDAD). The overall structure of the HDAD is shown in Fig. 1. Given a heterogeneous information network, first, we extract the k information matrices based on k meta-paths to describe the frequency of user interactions based on the meta-path in different topics, which represent the combination of the network structure and the diffusion state of a particular topic under different channels. And then we take k information matrices as input of a deep learning architecture for learning the low-dimensional embedding $\mathbf{Z}_i$, $(i = 1, 2 \cdots, k)$ of each node. Besides, considering that different channels have different impacts on diffusion of different messages, we utilize an attention mechanism to learn weights for fusing the learned embeddings, so as to extract the optimal information $\mathbf{Z}$ for the final prediction task.

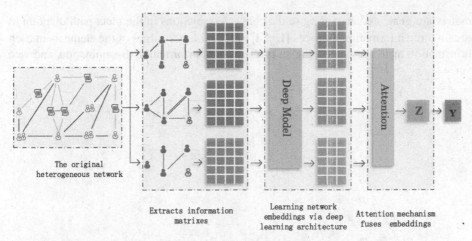

Extracts information
matrixes

Learning network
embeddings via deep
learning architecture

Attention mechanism
fuses embeddings

Fig. 1. The framework of the proposed HDAD.

3.1 Information Matrix

The information diffusion problem involves a variety of information, such as network structure, diffusion messages, time, channel, and node state. HDAD proposes the information matrix to extract and fuse the structural information of the network as well as the diffusion state of the specific message, so as to transform the complex heterogeneous network into multiple low-dimensional homogeneous networks while retain the effective information closely related to the diffusion process of a specific message. Information matrix provides a streamlined and effective data structure basis for subsequent modeling.

Given a heterogeneous network $G = \{V, E\}$ and its set of meta-paths $\Phi = \{\Phi_1, \Phi_2, \cdots, \Phi_k\}$, at each time t, a meta-path graph, representing the connections generated by users under different channels of information diffusion, can be extracted based on the linkage of each meta-path Φ_i. Meanwhile, for the specified information ε, the set of activated nodes $U_{\varepsilon,t}$ can be searched to indicate the diffusion state of information ε in the network G at moment t. We fuse the meta-path graph under each channel with the diffusion states into the information matrix $\mathbf{I}_{\varepsilon,t}^{\Phi_i}$ to describe the frequency of users' contact with information ε in different channels and predict the possibility of information diffusion. We obtain k information matrixes from k meta-paths, denoted as $\{\mathbf{I}_{\varepsilon,t}^{\Phi_1}, \mathbf{I}_{\varepsilon,t}^{\Phi_2}, \cdots \mathbf{I}_{\varepsilon,t}^{\Phi_k}\}$.

Figure 2 is used as an example to explain the specific process. Input an academic heterogeneous network, which contains three types of nodes: authors (A), papers (P), conferences (C), and three types of edges. First, HDAD finds the set of activated nodes $U_{\varepsilon,t} = \{u_1, u_2, u_4\}$ by information from the original heterogeneous network; then according to the three meta-paths of APA, ACA and APPA, three meta-path graphs are extracted, where the edges in the meta-path graph represent the number of times two nodes have generated contact through this channel, e.g., the ACA meta-path graph shows that u_3 and u_4 attended two conferences together; finally, the nodes in $U_{\varepsilon,t}$ are used as the column nodes of the information matrix, and all the nodes in the heterogeneous networks node set V are used as the row nodes, and the values in the corresponding information matrix are generated according to the connected relations in the meta-path diagram to obtain three information matrices $\{\mathbf{I}_{\varepsilon,t}^{\Phi_1}, \mathbf{I}_{\varepsilon,t}^{\Phi_2}, \mathbf{I}_{\varepsilon,t}^{\Phi_3}\}$. Larger values of the elements in each information matrix indicate a higher probability of information dissemination, and vice versa.

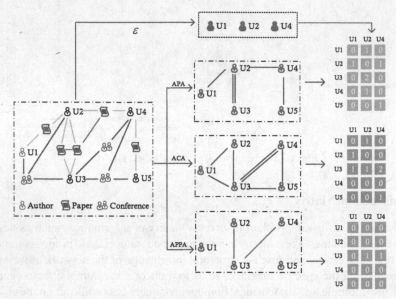

Fig. 2. Example of information matrix extraction process

3.2 Deep Learning Architecture

After obtaining the information matrix, in order to further explore the hidden relationships of the nodes, identify the linear indistinguishable data, and capture the nonlinear data, we use deep neural network to further learn the data embedding. Taking into account the adaptability of the model to the information diffusion task and the dataset, HDAD uses a Multi-layer Perception (MLP) to learn the low-dimensional embedding of the information matrix obtained under each semantics. Some recent studies [18, 19] demonstrated that MPL-based network structures can achieve better results with lower computational costs than today's mainstream neural network models such as CNN, LSTM, and Transformer.

MPL is a fully connected neural network containing at least one hidden layer, and the output of each hidden layer is transformed by an activation function. The number of layers of the multi-layer perceptron and the number of hidden units in each hidden layer are hyperparameters. Using the information matrix under each semantics as input, denotes the number of layers of hidden layers, the output of each hidden layer is $\mathbf{H}_j^{\Phi_i}$, ($j = 1, 2 \cdots l$), is shown as follows:

$$\begin{cases} \mathbf{H}_j^{\Phi_i} = f(\mathbf{I}_{\varepsilon,t}^{\Phi_i} W_h + b_h), j = 1 \\ \mathbf{H}_j^{\Phi_i} = f(\mathbf{H}_{j-1}^{\Phi_i} W_h + b_h), j \neq 1 \end{cases} \tag{1}$$

where h is the number of hidden cells, W_h and b_h are the weight and deviation parameters of the hidden layer, and the function f denotes the activation function.

The output of each output layer is $\mathbf{Z}_{\Phi_i}$, is shown as follows:

$$\mathbf{Z}_{\Phi_i} = \mathbf{H}_l^{\Phi_i} W_o + b_o \tag{2}$$

where W_o and b_o are the weight parameters and deviation parameters of the output layer, W_h, b_h, W_o and b_o are the training parameters in the model. we can optimize the proposed model via back propagation and learn the embeddings of nodes $\mathbf{Z}_{\Phi_1}, \mathbf{Z}_{\Phi_2} \cdots, \mathbf{Z}_{\Phi_k}$.

3.3 Attention Mechanism

Typically, real-world information propagates along multiple diffusion channels, and heterogeneous networks can represent these channels with different semantic information. The node embedding of a particular semantic can only reflect the information contained in the network from one channel. In order to learn the different effects of multiple channels on information diffusion and fuse multiple semantic information together, we apply attention mechanisms to automatically learn the importance of different meta-paths for the prediction task of information diffusion. Taking $\mathbf{Z}_{\Phi_1}, \cdots, \mathbf{Z}_{\Phi_k}$ learned from the deep learning architecture as input, the weights of each meta-path are calculated as shown in Eq. (3):

$$(\beta_{\Phi_1}, \cdots, \beta_{\Phi_k}) = att_{sem}(\mathbf{Z}_{\Phi_1}, \cdots, \mathbf{Z}_{\Phi_k}) \tag{3}$$

Here att denotes the deep neural network which performs the attention. In order to explore the importance of each meta-path the semantic embedding is first transformed nonlinearly using a layer of MLP. The similarity between multiple semantic embeddings is measured by the semantic embedding attention vector q, after which the importance of all specific semantic embeddings is derived as the importance of each meta-path, denoted as w_{Φ_i}, is shown as follows:

$$w_{\Phi_p} = \frac{1}{|V|} \sum_{i \in V} q^T \cdot \tanh(\mathbf{W} \cdot z_i^{\Phi_p} + b) \tag{4}$$

where $\mathbf{W}$ is the weight matrix, b is the bias vector, q is the semantic-level attention vector. After getting the importance of each meta-path, they are normalized by the softmax function. The weight of the meta-path Φ_i is expressed as $\beta_{\Phi i}$, is shown as follows:

$$\beta_{\Phi_p} = \frac{\exp(w_{\Phi_p})}{\sum_{p=1}^{p} \exp(w_{\Phi_p})} \tag{5}$$

Using the weight $\beta_{\Phi p}$ as the coefficient, the node embeddings of each element path are fused to obtain the final embedding $\mathbf{Z}$, is shown as follows:

$$\mathbf{Z} = \sum_{p=1}^{p} \beta_{\Phi_p} \cdot \mathbf{Z}_{\Phi_p} \tag{6}$$

With the final embedding, we can construct the loss function, which is trained in a semi-supervised manner by we can minimize the Cross-Entropy, as follows:

$$L = -\sum_{l \in V} Y^l \ln(C \cdot Z^l) \tag{7}$$

where C is the parameter of the classifier, Y^L and Z^L are the labels and embeddings of labeled nodes. With the guide of labeled data, we can optimize the proposed model via back propagation and learn the embeddings of nodes. Finally, we use linear transformation and SoftMax function to predict the activation of the node.

4   Experiments

4.1   Datasets and Evaluation Measures

To evaluate the effectiveness of the proposed model, we conduct experiments on two real datasets of heterogeneous networks, DBLP and ACM. DBLP is a bibliographic information network on English literature in computing, and ACM is a bibliographic information network of Association for Computing Machinery publications. Since the study requires temporal and topic information of data, we extracted subset networks from the publicly available datasets DBLP citation dataset [20] and ACM citation dataset [20], respectively. The specific description of the data is shown in Table 1.

Table 1. Statistical information about the dataset

Dataset	Paper	Author	Conference	Time	Topic	Meta-path
DBLP	154341	177757	5508	1984~2016	Data mining machine learning social network	APCPA APA
ACM	58985	75468	6950	1951~2010	Data mining machine learning database	ACA APA

For the above two datasets, we can extract a set of data at each time t. In this paper, we use the data from t−4 to t−1 as the training set and the data at t as the test set, and choose the time t = {2001, 2002, 2003, 2004, 2005} for the experiment, and calculate the AUPR (Aurea under Precision-Recall) [21] values for each model on the DBLP and ACM datasets at each time.

AUPR is a widely used evaluation metric because it is applicable to compare the prediction performance between different models in unbalanced data sets. AUPR refers to the area under the PR curve, which means the curve made by recall as the y-axis and precision as the x-axis. The higher the AUPR value is, the better the model is. The specific calculation formulas for recall and precision are as follows:

$$precision = TP/(TP + FP) \tag{8}$$

$$recall = TP/(TP + FN) \tag{9}$$

where TP is true positive, FP is false positive, and FN is false negative. In this paper, TP refers to users who are actually activated and predicted to be activated, FP refers to users who are actually not activated but predicted to be activated, and FN refers to users who are actually activated and predicted to be inactive.

4.2 Baselines

We compare HDAD with some state-of-the-art baselines described as follows.

1. HDD-MLP [13]: HDD is a end to end graph representation learning method in heterogeneous networks, which obtains continuous potential representations of the network by traversing meta-paths and utilizes deep learning architectures to predict the information diffusion. HDD-MLP uses the classical traditional MLP neural network as the deep learning architecture in HDD to realize the prediction of topic diffusion task.
2. HDD-CNNLSTM [13]: HDD-CNNLSTM is a combination of CNN and LSTM as a deep learning architecture in HDD model. The features are aggregated by LSTM based on local features extracted by CNN layer, so that the network can consider local structure as well as global structure to predict the process of information diffusion in the network more effectively.

For our study of topic diffusion in heterogeneous networks, the HDD-MLP and HDD-CNNLSTM models are closely related research works in this field. We choose the above models as comparisons to demonstrate the effectiveness of information matrices for information exploitation and the ability of attention mechanisms to improve prediction performance.

4.3 Implementation Details

For the proposed HDAD, we train a MLP with two hidden layers as the depth architecture module, where the number of hidden units in the first layer is 128, the number of hidden units in the second layer is 32, the output dimension of the last layer is set to 10, and the activation function used is the sigmoid function. We set the optimization model as Adam [22], the learning rate to 0.01, the dropout to 0.5. And we use early stopping with a patience of 20, i.e., we stop training if the validation loss does not decrease for 20 consecutive epochs. For HDD-CNNLSTM and HDD-MLP, we optimize their parameters using the validation set. For HDD-CNNLSTM, the embedding dimension is set to 256, epoch is set to 2, and dropout is set to 0.5. For HDD-MLP, dropout is set to 0.5 and epoch is set to 2. Since the random initialization and early termination of model parameters will have some influence on the results, we use each method to run on each dataset 10 the average of the calculated results is taken.

4.4   Results

Table 2 summarize the experimental results. First, the results in the table show that the proposed HDAD achieves the best performance under all six topics in both datasets. Specifically, compared to HDD-MLP, the AUPR values of HDAD are improved by 0.27 to 0.29 on the DBLP dataset and by 0.20 to 0.29 on the ACM dataset, indicating that the proposed information matrix in the HDAD can better exploit the effective information in the heterogeneous network and thus obtain better performance. Compared with HDD-CNLSTM, the AUPR of HDAD improved by 0.13–0.14 on the DBLP dataset and by 0.12–0.14 on the ACM dataset, indicating that HDAD differentiates the computational weights of embeddings of different paths and can more effectively utilize the rich information in the heterogeneous network to obtain more accurate prediction results.

In addition, analyzing the experimental results also reveals that the performance of HDAD under the machine learning topics in both datasets is lower than the performance under other topics. We calculated the sparseness of data under each topic according to the method proposed by Hoyer in the reference [23] to investigate whether data sparsity has an impact on the prediction results. The method uses the difference between L_1 norm and L_2 norm to measure the sparseness of the data, which is calculated as shown in the following equation:

$$sparseness(X) = \frac{\sqrt{n} - (\sum |x_i| / \sqrt{x_i^2})}{\sqrt{n} - 1} \tag{10}$$

where n is the dimensionality of $\mathbf{X}$. This function evaluates to unity if and only if $\mathbf{X}$ contains only a single non-zero component, and takes a value of zero if and only if all components are equal (up to signs). $sparseness(X)$ is a number between [0,1], and the larger the value, the more sparse it is.

The sparseness of data under each topic is shown in Fig. 3. We can find that the sparsity of data in both DBLP and ACM datasets under the topic of machine learning is higher than other topics, which indicates that the larger data sparsity will lead to more difficulty in HDAD learning and reduce the accuracy of prediction results.

Table 2. AUPR measure of HDAD compared to baselines

Dataset	Topic	Models	Year					AVG
			2001	2002	2003	2004	2005	
DBLP	Data mining	HDD-MLP	0.4421	0.4467	0.4574	0.5011	0.4205	0.4536
		HDD-CNNLSTM	0.5503	0.6081	0.6164	0.6387	0.6223	0.6072
		HDAD	**0.6951**	**0.7648**	**0.7593**	**0.7535**	**0.768**	**0.7481**
	Machine learning	HDD-MLP	0.4345	0.4162	0.4498	0.3756	0.4248	0.4202
		HDD-CNNLSTM	0.5685	0.6232	0.5676	0.4811	0.5692	0.5619
		HDAD	**0.6704**	**0.7311**	**0.6979**	**0.6903**	**0.6808**	**0.6941**
	Social network	HDD-MLP	0.438	0.4688	0.479	0.4431	0.4581	0.4574
		HDD-CNNLSTM	0.5842	0.5787	0.6082	0.6214	0.6215	0.6028
		HDAD	**0.7813**	**0.6339**	**0.721**	**0.7996**	**0.763**	**0.7813**
ACM	Data mining	HDD-MLP	0.4325	0.5636	0.4514	0.467	0.4287	0.4686
		HDD-CNNLSTM	0.5502	0.6209	0.5714	0.5259	0.5118	0.5560
		HDAD	**0.686**	**0.7212**	**0.7449**	**0.6128**	**0.6391**	**0.6808**
	Machine learning	HDD-MLP	0.4508	0.3038	0.5006	0.5012	0.4516	0.4416
		HDD-CNNLSTM	0.5507	0.5604	0.5006	0.5012	0.5016	0.5229
		HDAD	**0.6198**	**0.6154**	**0.6035**	**0.6715**	**0.6924**	**0.6405**
	Database	HDD-MLP	0.4804	0.4915	0.4199	0.5191	0.5067	0.4804
		HDD-CNNLSTM	0.6026	0.6989	0.6013	0.5826	0.6532	0.6277
		HDAD	**0.7877**	**0.7746**	**0.7805**	**0.73**	**0.7798**	**0.7705**

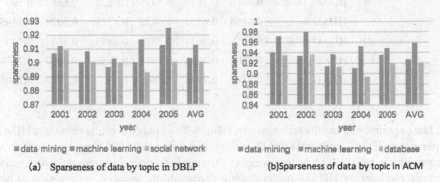

(a) Sparseness of data by topic in DBLP   (b)Sparseness of data by topic in ACM

Fig. 3. Sparseness of data for each topic

4.5 Ablation Studies

We design two variants of HDAD, HDAD_mult and HDAD_weight. HDAD_mult indicates that HDAD is executed using each meta-path parsimony separately, and the single meta-path with the best result is taken as the prediction result, which is used to evaluate the effectiveness of multi-semantics of heterogeneous networks. HDAD _weight denotes the method that does not distinguish between the information matrices under different meta-paths, and the weights are all set to 1, which is used to evaluate the effectiveness of the attention mechanism and to demonstrate the different effects played by different dissemination channels on the diffusion of information in a heterogeneous network.

Table 3. AUPR measure of HDAD compared to ablation experiment

Dataset	Topic	Models	Year					AVG
			2001	2002	2003	2004	2005	
DB LP	Data mining	HDAD_mult	0.6638	0.7391	0.7346	0.7209	0.7586	0.7234
		HDAD_weight	0.6752	0.718	0.7334	0.722	0.7531	0.7203
		HDAD	**0.6951**	**0.7648**	**0.7593**	**0.7535**	**0.768**	**0.7481**
	Machine learning	HDAD_mult	0.6658	0.7064	0.6631	0.6577	0.6568	0.6700
		HDAD_weight	0.6408	0.7103	0.6429	0.5826	0.6159	0.6385
		HDAD	**0.6704**	**0.7311**	**0.6979**	**0.6903**	**0.6808**	**0.6941**
	Social network	HDAD_mult	0.7016	0.6081	0.711	0.7822	0.6845	0.6975
		HDAD_weight	0.6592	0.631	0.6753	0.7528	0.6528	0.6742
		HDAD	**0.7813**	**0.6339**	**0.721**	**0.7996**	**0.763**	**0.7398**
ACM	Data mining	HDAD_mult	0.6796	0.7055	0.7249	0.5951	0.6254	0.6661
		HDAD_weight	0.6827	0.6831	0.7158	0.5625	0.6066	0.6501
		HDAD	**0.686**	**0.7212**	**0.7449**	**0.6128**	**0.6391**	**0.6808**
	Machine learning	HDAD_mult	0.5664	0.5737	0.5034	0.66535	0.6883	0.5994
		HDAD_weight	0.5426	0.5855	0.5035	0.6629	0.6882	0.5965
		HDAD	**0.6198**	**0.6154**	**0.6035**	**0.6715**	**0.6924**	**0.6405**
	Database	HDAD_mult	0.767	0.7631	0.7528	0.6945	0.7251	0.7405
		HDAD_weight	0.7605	0.7656	0.7576	0.7156	0.7197	0.7438
		HDAD	**0.7877**	**0.7746**	**0.7805**	**0.73**	**0.7798**	**0.7705**

The experimental results are shown in Table 3. The analysis results show that HDAD outperforms HDAD_mult and HDAD_weight, indicating that HDAD can get more accurate prediction results by learning weights through heterogeneous semantic fusion and attention mechanism. HDAD_mult cannot utilize multiple semantic information of heterogeneous networks, resulting in a decrease of AUPR values from 2.4% to 4.2% on the DBLP. The AUPR values on the ACM decreased from 1.5% to 4.1%, reflecting the importance of multiple semantic information of heterogeneous networks for information diffusion prediction. HDAD _weight cannot distinguish the weights of different meta-paths, resulting in a decrease of AUPR values from 3% to 4.4% on the DBL, verifying the different effects caused by different diffusion channels on diffusion results.

5   Conclusion

In this paper, we propose a Heterogeneous Deep Attention Diffusion model (HDAD) to predict the problem of information diffusion in heterogeneous networks and. HDAD extracts the information matrix to integrate the network topology and information diffusion state and uses deep learning architectures to capture non-linear relationships, which can better exploit and utilize the effective information in the heterogeneous network. In addition, the HDAD model distinguishes the different influences of different diffusion channels to use attention mechanism, which can improve the prediction performance. Our experimental results on two real datasets verified the effectiveness and efficiency of our methods. As future work, we are interested in reducing the impact of data sparsity on the model to further improve its performance.

Acknowledgments. This work was supported by the National Natural Science Foundation of China (62062066, 61762090, 61966036), Yunnan Fundamental Research Projects (202201AS070015), University Key Laboratory of Internet of Things Technology and Application of Yunnan Province, and the Postgraduate Research and Innovation Foundation of Yunnan University (2021Y024).

References

1. Leskovec, J., Adamic, L.A., Huberman, B.A.: The dynamics of viral marketing. ACM Trans. Web **1**, 5 (2007)
2. Kempe, D., Kleinberg, J., Tardos, É.: Maximizing the spread of influence through a social network. In: Proceedings of the Ninth ACM SIGKDD International Conference on Knowledge Discovery and Data Mining, pp. 137–46. Association for Computing Machinery (2003)
3. Wu, Q., Gao, Y., Gao, X., Weng, P., Chen, G.: Dual sequential prediction models linking sequential recommendation and information dissemination. In: Proceedings of the 25th ACM SIGKDD International Conference on Knowledge Discovery & Data Mining, pp. 447–57. Association for Computing Machinery, Anchorage (2019)
4. Zhao, L., et al.: Online flu epidemiological deep modeling on disease contact network. GeoInformatica **24**(2), 443–475 (2019). https://doi.org/10.1007/s10707-019-00376-9
5. Dong, Y., Chawla, N.V., Swami, A.: metapath2vec: scalable representation learning for heterogeneous networks. In: Proceedings of the 23rd ACM SIGKDD International Conference on Knowledge Discovery and Data Mining, pp. 135–44. Association for Computing Machinery, Halifax (2017)
6. Fu, T.-Y., Lee, W.-C., Lei, Z.: HIN2Vec: explore meta-paths in heterogeneous information networks for representation learning. In: Proceedings of the 2017 ACM on Conference on Information and Knowledge Management, pp. 1797–806. Association for Computing Machinery, Singapore (2017)
7. Shi, C., Hu, B., Zhao, W.X., Yu, P.S.: Heterogeneous information network embedding for recommendation. IEEE Trans. Knowl. Data Eng. **31**, 357–370 (2019)
8. He, Y., Song, Y., Li, J., Ji, C., Peng, J., Peng, H.: HeteSpaceyWalk: a heterogeneous spacey random walk for heterogeneous information network embedding. In: Proceedings of CIKM, pp. 639–48 (2019)
9. Wang, X., Ji, H., Shi, C., Wang, B., Ye, Y., Cui, P., et al.: Heterogeneous graph attention network. In: The World Wide Web Conference, pp. 2022–32. Association for Computing Machinery, San Francisco (2019)

10. Hu, B., Fang, Y., Shi, C.: Adversarial learning on heterogeneous information networks. In: Proceedings of the 25th ACM SIGKDD International Conference on Knowledge Discovery & Data Mining, pp. 120–9. Association for Computing Machinery (2019)

11. Li, Y., Chen, C., Duan, M., Zeng, Z., Li, K.: Attention-aware encoder-decoder neural networks for heterogeneous graphs of things. IEEE Trans. Industr. Inf. **17**, 2890–2898 (2021)

12. Gui, H., Sun, Y., Han, J., Brova, G.: Modeling topic diffusion in multi-relational bibliographic information networks, pp. 649–58 (2014)

13. Molaei, S., Zare, H., Veisi, H.: Deep learning approach on information diffusion in heterogeneous networks. Knowl.-Based Syst. **189**, 105153 (2020)

14. Su, Y., Zhang, X., Wang, S., Fang, B., Zhang, T., Yu, P.S.: Understanding information diffusion via heterogeneous information network embeddings. In: Li, G., Yang, J., Gama, J., Natwichai, J., Tong, Y. (eds.) DASFAA 2019. LNCS, vol. 11446, pp. 501–516. Springer, Cham (2019). https://doi.org/10.1007/978-3-030-18576-3_30

15. Wang, L.-M., Fang, Y., Zhou, L.-H.: Preference-Based Spatial Co-location Pattern Mining, pp. 1–284. Springer, Cham (2022). https://doi.org/10.1007/978-981-16-7566-9. ISBN 978-981-16-7565-2

16. Sun, Y., Han, J.: Mining heterogeneous information networks: a structural analysis approach. SIGKDD Explor. **14**, 20–28 (2012)

17. Sun, Y., Han, J., Yan, X., Yu, P.S., Wu, T.: PathSim: meta path-based top-k similarity search in heterogeneous information networks. Proc. VLDB Endow. **4**, 992–1003 (2011)

18. Guo, M.-H., Liu, Z.-N., Mu, T.-J., Liang, D., Martin, R.R., Hu, S.-M.: Can attention enable MLPs to catch up with CNNs? Comput. Visual Media **7**(3), 283–288 (2021). https://doi.org/10.1007/s41095-021-0240-x

19. Tolstikhin, I.O., Houlsby, N., Kolesnikov, A., Beyer, L., Zhai, X., Unterthiner, T., et al.: MLP-Mixer: An all-MLP Architecture for Vision. CoRR, abs/2105.01601 (2012)

20. Citation Network Dataset. https://aminer.org/billboard/citation

21. Zhu, M.: Recall, precision and average precision, department of statistics and actuarial science, p. 30. University of Waterloo, Waterloo (2004)

22. Diederik, P., Kingma, J.B.: Adam: a method for stochastic optimization. ICLR 2015, pp. 13 (2015)

23. Hoyer, P.O.: Non-negative matrix factorization with sparseness constraints. J. Mach. Learn. Res. **5**, 1457–1469 (2004)

AIS Data Driven CNN-BiGRU Model for Ship Target Classification

Yujun Wang[1], Jian Guo[1], Li Xu[1(✉)], Kexin Li[1], and Zongming Li[2]

[1] Institute of Surveying and Mapping, Information Engineering University, Zhengzhou, China
xuli_1985@yeah.net
[2] 31682 Troops, Lanzhou, China

Abstract. Most traditional methods for classifying marine ship targets using trajectory data rely on manual feature extraction, and it is difficult to consider the influence of spatial and temporal features on the classification results. In this paper, we propose a combination of a convolutional neural network and bidirectional gate recurrent unit (CNN-BiGRU) to classify ship targets using automatic identification system (AIS) data. First, AIS data are pre-processed to obtain valid ship trajectory segments, and basic information of the trajectory points, such as the speed, heading, and time, are used to construct the input feature vectors for the CNN and BiGRU, respectively. Second, the best CNN is trained and combined with BiGRU to obtain the CNN-BiGRU model. The combined model then simultaneously mines the spatio-temporal features contained in the AIS data and fuses the learned deep-level features. Finally, a fully connected layer is used to obtain the classification results of the ship targets. Compared with traditional machine learning algorithms and single deep learning models, the classification method in this study only requires the construction of simple input feature vectors and has different degrees of improvement in the four evaluation indexes of classification accuracy, precision, recall, and f-score, indicating that this method can effectively combine spatio-temporal features to improve the classification effect.

Keywords: Ship target classification · AIS data · Convolutional neural networks · Bidirectional gated recurrent units · Combined classification model

1 Introduction

Trajectory classification has been an important research topic in transportation engineering and traffic geography [1]. The rapid updating of mobile Internet, satellite positioning, and other technologies, as well as the widespread popularity of the 21st Century Maritime Silk Road initiative have accelerated the booming development of the global maritime industry [2]. The rapid development of the global maritime industry has accelerated the growth of ship trajectory data, for which the new open ship data transmission system AIS is an important source. The classification of ship targets based on trajectory data can be used to analyse the movement characteristics and patterns of different ships to help uncover their intrinsic links. This has important application value in identifying abnormal ships [3], providing decision support for shipping analysis and ship scheduling [4], as well as promoting the development of intelligent maritime transportation [5]. Current studies on this problem have mainly extracted multi-dimensional features from ship trajectory segments manually, building a single model based on this to mine the shallow spatial information in the features, and then realise the ship target classification. However, with wide sea waters and the tendency of ship types and structures to diversify, ship classification contains both spatial and temporal dependence of ship target movements and is a relatively complex non-linear mathematical model. Therefore, the simplification of this complex ship target classification task and the construction of an effective classification model are among the main challenges in this field.

Early research focused on the manual extraction of features and the application of traditional machine learning methods for trajectory classification, including a decision tree (DT) [6], support vector machine (SVM) [7] and tree-based ensemble learning models [8, 9]. Some scholars have conducted in-depth studies on the classification of ship targets based on AIS data. Zheng et al. [10] extracted the speed and heading features and applied a BP neural network model to classify and identify the operation mode of fishing vessels. In addition, Sheng et al. [11] extracted 17-dimensional ship motion features and classified cargo ships and fishing vessels using logistic regression models. Kraus et al. [12] extracted multidimensional ship motion features and the addition of geographical features and ship dimensions as auxiliary features to classify ships using a random forest (RF) model. Moreover, Ginolhac et al. [13] extracted 119-dimensional ship motion features and classified multiple types of ships using the XGBoost model. On the one hand, the above methods rely on the manual construction of a tedious feature space, and the classification results are easily affected by a subjective cognition. On the other hand, the use of traditional machine learning methods consider only spatial dependence, ignoring the influence of temporal features on the classification of ship targets, and thus the shallow structure cannot handle the complex non-linear relationships of AIS data, resulting in certain limitations.

Against the background of geospatial artificial intelligence (GeoAI), technological advances in the field of AI have brought about new opportunities for the intelligent development of research in geospatial-related fields [14]. Deep learning methods do not require the extraction of complex features, can better fit nonlinear problems, and have also been gradually used by scholars in recent years to solve trajectory classification problems. Ljunggren et al. [15] used a CNN to mine the spatial dimensional features of AIS data and classify fishing vessels, passenger ships, cargo ships, and oil tankers. Bakkegaard et al. [16] used a recurrent neural network (RNN) to extract the temporal dimensional features of AIS data and classify high-speed ships, tankers, passenger ships, sailing ships, and fishing boats. Although the above methods consider spatial and temporal dependence, respectively, their models are discrete from each other, that is, they do not consider the learning of both spatial and temporal features. Cui et al. [17] constructed distribution and temporal feature vectors for a one-dimensional CNN and a long short-term memory (LSTM) model, respectively, and then fused the ship target classification results of both through weighted voting. Although this method considers the spatio-temporal characteristics of the trajectory data, the process of constructing the input feature vector is more complicated, and the final ship target classification results are not directly obtained by the deep learning model autonomously learning the spatio-temporal features of the trajectory data.

To address the above issues, based on the AIS data, a feature vector consisting of the speed over ground, acceleration, course over ground, and heading is used as the CNN input to extract the spatial features, whereas a feature vector consisting of the time interval, speed over ground, course over ground, and heading is used as the BiGRU input to extract temporal features, followed by a fusion of the deep-level features extracted through both models, and then the direct classification of the ship targets through a fully connected layer. The experiment results demonstrate that the combined model proposed in this study can improve the classification accuracy and effectively achieve the classification of ship targets, providing methodological support for sensing the spatio-temporal movement patterns of ship targets and promoting the development of intelligent maritime transportation.

2   Theory and Methodology

The research basis of this study is presented in Fig. 1. As the data source, the AIS data are first pre-processed, and according to their characteristics and the structure of the deep learning model, the input feature vectors are constructed for the CNN and BiGRU. Then, considering that the learning ability of the two-dimensional CNN for the sequence data is affected by the composition and depth of the model structure, the optimal CNN model is obtained through training, and the combined model is constructed based on the combination of a CNN and BiGRU. Finally, the combined model is used to classify the ship targets, and the classification effects are evaluated in comparison with those of machine learning algorithms and individual deep learning models, based upon which the advantages and applicability of the AIS data-driven CNN-BiGRU model are explored in terms of the ship target classification task.

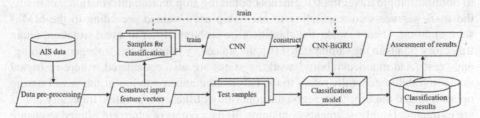

Fig. 1. AIS data driven CNN-BiGRU model for ship target classification research

2.1   AIS Data Pre-processing

AIS data are a sampled sequence with time, position, and other types of information. The 16 fields contained in each row of records of the raw AIS data mainly consist of dynamic and static ship information, as well as ship navigation information [18]. As shown in Table 1, the following information from each row of records was taken to participate in the ship target classification applied in this study.

Table 1. AIS data information

Field name	Descriptions
MMSI	Maritime Mobile Service Identification Number
Time	Timestamp
LAT	Latitude
LON	Longitude
SOG	Speed over ground
COG	Course over ground
Heading	Direction of the bow
Vessel Type	Type of vessel
Status	Status of vessel

The AIS data are noisy owing to an improper operation of the equipment by crew members, equipment failure, and a limited signal transmission distance. Therefore, it is necessary to clean the AIS data, that is, remove missing key segments, time duplications, and out-of-normal range track point records, to provide an accurate and reliable data source for the classification of the ship targets. On this basis, the AIS data are segmented to obtain multiple travel track segments containing ship motion information, i.e. firstly, the track segments corresponding to each ship are obtained according to the MMSI segmentation. Then, to make the classification problem closer to a real situation, retain trajectory points in the sailing state [16], the trajectory points in the 'engaged in fishing' and 'restricted manoeuvrability' working states are also considered, where restricted manoeuvrability generally refers to the restricted manoeuvrability of the vessel during operation, and the trajectory segments consisting of these consecutive trajectory points are extracted. Finally, segments containing 30 data points or more are filtered to ensure that each segment contained sufficient information.

2.2 Input Feature Vector Construction

The pre-processed AIS data contain three types of basic spatio-temporal information, i.e. time, longitude, and latitude, as well as three types of motion information, i.e. SOG, COG, and heading. Basic spatio-temporal information cannot visually express the type of ship targets, and the classification model cannot establish an effective mapping from the spatio-temporal information to such targets. Therefore, before the model can classify the ship targets, the input feature vector needs to be constructed to convert the data into a form that is easily understood by the classification model [19]. The types of features extracted from the trajectory segments can be classified as trajectory point features, trajectory segment features, and self-contained attributes of the applied trajectory data [20]. To avoid extracting too many statistics and an increase the amount of manual computations, as well as relying too much on individual experience cognition, and to give full play to the ability of deep learning models to autonomously learn basic features and deep-level features in ship trajectory segments, the trajectory point features extracted from the basic spatio-temporal information of the AIS data are combined with the three types of motion information of AIS data for constructing the input feature vectors of the CNN and BiGRU models, respectively.

CNN Input Feature Vector Construction. With reference to recent research on trajectory classification [21–23], we selected a total of four effective attributes, namely SOG, COG, heading, and acceleration, to build the input feature vector of a CNN, which is used to learn the local connection and overall features of each trajectory segment. SOG, COG, and heading are the motion information of the AIS data, and thus only the acceleration of the trajectory points needs to be calculated based on the basic spatio-temporal information, the calculation formula of which is as follows:

$$\begin{cases} a_n = \frac{V_n - V_{n-1}}{t_n}; \\ V_n = \frac{d_n}{t_n}; \\ d = 2r \times \sin^{-1} \sqrt{\left(\sin \frac{\Delta \varphi'}{2}\right)^2 + \cos \varphi_1' \times \cos \varphi_2' \left(\sin \frac{\Delta \lambda'}{2}\right)^2}. \end{cases} \quad (1)$$

where a_n denotes the acceleration of the trajectory point (m/s^2); V_n denotes the velocity of the trajectory point (m/s); t_n denotes the time interval between adjacent trajectory points (s); d_n denotes the distance between adjacent trajectory points, which is obtained from the Haversine spherical distance calculation formula d, where r is the radius of the Earth, taken as 6371.393 km; $\Delta \varphi' = |\varphi_1' - \varphi_2'|$; $\Delta \lambda' = |\lambda_1' - \lambda_2'|$; and (λ_1', φ_1') and (λ_2', φ_2') are the positions of the two trajectory points (rad), respectively.

The input vector of the CNN consists of three dimensions: height, width, and depth (channels). The input layer consists of a set of independent samples D with each sample D_i representing a ship trajectory segment containing the SOG, acceleration, COG, and heading. As shown in Fig. 2, each channel has a shape of $(1 \times L)$, and L is the length of each trajectory segment, that is, the number of AIS trajectory points in the trajectory segment, and thus the shape of the input vector is $(1 \times L \times 4)$. To facilitate later CNN model training, the size of the input vector needs to be unified such that the length of all trajectory segments is restricted to a fixed size L, where the longer trajectory segments are segmented, and the shorter segments are filled with values of zero.

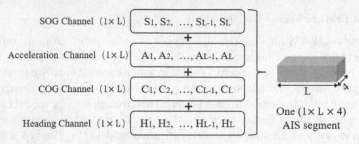

Fig. 2. Input feature vector structure of CNN

BiGRU Input Feature Vector. Construction BiGRU is composed of two gate recurrent units (GRUs) superimposed on the top and bottom to obtain the long-term dependence of the trajectory data on past and future features. Taking into account the characteristics of BiGRU and AIS data, the temporal feature vectors of BiGRU are constructed using four attributes: SOG, COG, heading, and time interval. SOG, COG, and heading all change with time, which helps the model explore the temporal patterns and characteristics of different ship motion information; therefore, the time interval is chosen to enhance the learning of the association between the time and motion information changes of the model.

The input vector of BiGRU consists of two dimensions: feature and the timestep, where the timestep is the input of how many moments of the timestep feature vector generally depend on the length of the trajectory segments of the ship, again limiting all trajectory segment lengths to a fixed size L to simplify the calculation. T For a separate set of samples of the BiGRU input layer, the input feature vector is constituted by a single ship trajectory segment sample T_i, as shown in Eq. (2).

$$T_i = \begin{bmatrix} t_1 & S_1 & C_1 & H_1 \\ t_2 & S_2 & C_2 & H_2 \\ \vdots & \vdots & \vdots & \vdots \\ t_L & S_L & C_L & H_L \end{bmatrix}, \tag{2}$$

where t_i is the time interval, S_i is the speed over ground, C_i is the course over ground, and H_i is the heading.

2.3 Ship Target Classification Model

The main body of the CNN-BiGRU model proposed in this paper consists of two parts: (1) Spatial features in AIS data are extracted using a CNN to portray the spatial dependence of the trajectory segments, and (2) the temporal features in the AIS data are captured using BiGRU to portray the temporal dependence of the trajectory segments. Because the CNN-BiGRU model is a combination of an optimal CNN and a BiGRU, the model structures of the CNN, BiGRU, and CNN-BiGRU are presented separately.

CNN Model Structure. CNNs generally consist of an input layer, an output layer, a pooling layer, a fully connected layer, and an output layer [24]. The parameters of each layer are configured as follows:

(1) Input layer: Sample set D is placed into the input layer, and the CNN network is used to for the spatial feature extraction for each D_i.

(2) Convolutional layer: This study uses a convolutional kernel with a shape of $(1 \times 3 \times C)$, where C is the number of channels in the input vector of each layer. The three-dimensional output shape of each convolutional layer is controlled by three hyperparameters, i.e. the number of convolutional kernels (filters) that determine the depth of the output shape; the length of each step of the convolutional kernel in the input vector, S; and the zero-value padding that controls the size of the output layer. To ensure that the input and output shapes are the same for each layer, $S = 1$ and zero-value padding are used, whereas the number of filters is determined by adjusting them according to the experiments. To achieve a fast convergence and improve the nonlinear feature learning of the network [25], the output of each convolutional layer needs to be activated by the ReLU function and used as input to the next layer.

(3) Pooling layers: To reduce the computational effort and prevent an overfitting, we periodically insert between each convolutional layer a convolutional kernel with a shape of (1×2) and an $S = 1$ Max pooling layer. The output after the max pooling layer is given by Eq. (3).

$$O_{C_l}(l) = \text{pool}\{relu[x_{l,a} \otimes \omega_{C_l}(l) + b_{C_l}(l)]\}; \tag{3}$$

where $O_{C_l}(l)$ is the output after a convolution and pooling by the lth layer using the c_lth filter, l is the depth of the CNN model, $l \in \{1, 2, 3, \cdots\}$, $c_l \in \{1, 2, 3, \cdots, C_l\}$, C_l is the number of filters, pool$(\cdot)$ is the pooling operation, $x_{l,a}$ is the ath feature input vector of the lth layer, $\otimes$ is the convolution operation, $relu$ is the activation function of the filter, and $\omega_{C_l}(l)$ and $b_{C_l}(l)$ are the weight values and bias vectors of the layer l c_lth filter, respectively.

(4) Fully connected layers (FC): Each neuron in the FC is connected to all neurones in the previous layer, and the output data are flattened through element-by-element multiplication. As shown in Eq. (4), all FCs except the last are used to extract the features, and the final extracted high-level features are used in the last FC to conduct the classification task, ensuring that the number of output neurons is the same as the number of classification labels and generating the probability distribution of each type of ship with the help of the softmax activation function.

$$\begin{cases} o_l = \text{flatten}\left[O_1(l), O_2(l), \cdots, O_{C_{l-1}}(l), O_{C_l}(l)\right]; \\ y_{C \cdot NN} = \text{softmax}(\omega_{CNN} O_l + b_{CNN}). \end{cases} \tag{4}$$

Here, 0_l is the high-level feature obtained by flattening the output of the $(l-1)th$ layer, y_{CNN} is the vector of the probability distributions of all ships output by the CNN, *softmax* is the activation function of the filter, and ω_{CNN} and b_{CNN} are the weight values and bias vectors of the layer, respectively.

BiGRU Model Structure. GRU [26] and LSTM [27] are both optimisation models that address the problems of a gradient disappearance and gradient explosion in RNNs [28]. The GRU is a further simplification of the LSTM structure to improve the training efficiency of the model [29]. Because the GRU can only predict the output of the next moment based on the temporal information of the past moment, the output of the current moment is not only related to the past state but also to the future state, and the bidirectional structure can provide the output layer with complete "context" information about each point of the input sequence. BiGRU is used to extract the timing features from the AIS data. The BiGRU structure designed in this study is shown in the Fig. 3. The parameters of each layer are configured as follows:

(1) Input layer: The sample set T is placed into the input layer, and the BiGRU network is used to conduct the temporal feature extraction for each T_i.
(2) BiGRU layer: For each moment t, the input is provided to two GRUs in opposite directions at the same time, and the output is determined jointly by these two unidirectional GRUs. As the right-hand side of Fig. 3 shows, the GRU consists of an input layer, a hidden layer, and an output layer, where the hidden layer consists of an update gate and a reset gate [30, 31]. The memory information H of the hidden layer corresponding to the time-series feature input matrix T_i is as follows:

$$H = (H_1, H_2, \cdots, H_t, \cdots, H_L), \tag{5}$$

where $H_1 - H_L$ are the memory information obtained by the GRU neural network during the 1st to Lth time intervals, respectively. At moment t, the memory information obtained from the current input X_t and $(t - 1)$, the hidden output of the forward state at moment $\vec{H}_{t-1}$, the outputs of the reset and update gates in the GRU neural network can be calculated as R_t and Z_t using the following equations:

$$R_t = \sigma(X_t W_{xr} + H_{t-1} W_{hr} + b_r) \tag{6}$$

$$Z_t = \sigma(X_t W_{xz} + H_{t-1} W_{hz} + b_z), \tag{7}$$

where σ is the activation function, W_{xr} and W_{xz} are the weights selected for the reset and update gates, and b_r and b_z are the bias vectors selected for the reset and update gates, respectively. Based on R_t and Z_t, the candidate hidden state $\tilde{H}_t$ and the current hidden state forward output $\vec{H}_t$ can be calculated using the following equations:

$$\tilde{H}_t = \tanh(X_t W_{xh} + (R_t \odot H_{t-1}) W_{xh} + b_h), \tag{8}$$

$$\vec{H}_t = Z_t \odot \tilde{H}_t + (1 - Z_t) \odot H_{t-1}, \tag{9}$$

where tanh is the activation function; W_{xh} and b_h are the selective memory for the current input X_t of the selected weights and bias vectors, respectively; $\odot$ indicates that the corresponding elements of the operation matrix are multiplied together; $Z_t \odot \tilde{H}_t$ denotes the selective memory of the information that is important at the current node; and $(1 - Z_t) \odot H_{t-1}$ denotes the selective forgetting of information that is not important in the originally hidden state.

Similarly, from the current input X_t and $(t+1)$, the hidden output of the backward state at moment $\overleftarrow{H}_{t+1}$, the backward output of the current hidden state is obtained as $\overleftarrow{H}_t$. Finally, the forward and backward outputs of each time step are stitched together to form the final output of the BiGRU layer.

(3) Dropout layer: To reduce the overfitting problem, a dropout layer is added for regularisation, and the input and output connections are removed from the neural network with probability P = 0.5.

(4) Fully connected layer: The FC is added after the BiGRU layer for feature extraction, and at the end, the FC is added for classification. The probability distribution of the current temporal feature vector corresponding to each type of ship is then output.

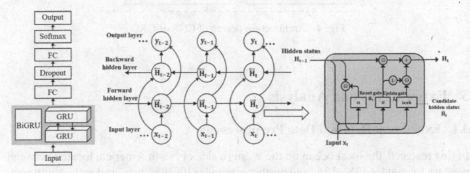

Fig. 3. Diagram of BiGRU structure

CNN-BiGRU Combined Model Structure. To address the problem in which a single model cannot learn both spatial and temporal features of AIS data, as Fig. 4 shows, a combined CNN-BiGRU model was built to classify the ship targets based on the CNN and BiGRU, with the optimal CNN and BiGRU being two branches of the combined model. The specific steps are as follows: First, the feature vectors D_i and T_i are normalised and processed as input data for the CNN and BiGRU, respectively. Second, the spatial and temporal features embedded in the trajectory sequence data are mined using the two models, and the high-level features learned by the two models are fused through the merge layer. Finally, the aggregated features are assigned to the fully connected layer with the softmax activation function to calculate the probability of the distribution of each type of ship target.

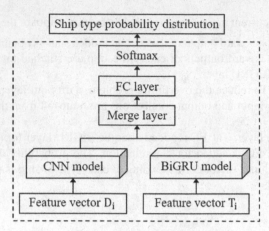

Fig. 4. Architecture design of CNN-BiGRU

3   Experiments and Analysis

3.1   Experiment Data and Data Pre-processing

In this research, the local ocean on the western side of North America, located between western longitudes 126°–138° and northern latitudes 10°–85°, was used as the study area. The experiment data were obtained from the annual yearly AIS data of the National Oceanic and Atmospheric Administration (NOAA) 2015, part of which is shown in Fig. 5. The area consists mainly of cargo ships, fishing vessels, passenger ships, and tugboats, and thus the ships are classified into the above four types.

The raw AIS data contained 31,805,155 track point records, which were pre-processed to obtain 192,226 ship tracks, 33.08% of which are cargo ships, and fishing vessels, passenger ships, and tugboats accounted for 19.80%, 20.15%, and 26.97% of the total, respectively. The trajectories were then constructed with a fixed length of L = 200, a CNN input feature vector consisting of SOG, COG, heading, and acceleration of the four channels with a shape of $(1 \times 200 \times 4)$, and a BiGRU input feature vector consisting of SOG, COG, heading, and time interval the four channels with a shape of (200×4). To speed up the convergence of the deep learning model training, a mean-variance normalisation process was applied to the two-species input feature vectors. Finally, the sample set consisting of two input feature vectors is divided into a training set and a test set at a ratio of 7:3 for classifier construction, training, and validation evaluation.

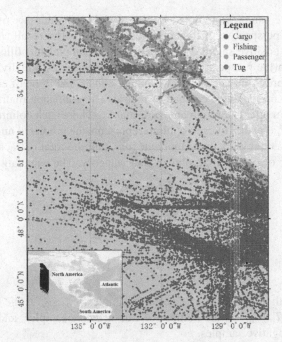

Fig. 5. Visualisation of experiment data

3.2 Experiment Results and Analysis

The running environment of the experiment included an Ubuntu 20.04 Intel i9-10900 k CPU and an RTX3090 GPU and was based on the Keras deep learning library with Tensorflow as the backend. To obtain the optimal CNN and thus build a CNN-BiGRU model, the model needs to be trained to optimise the parameters and minimise the value of the loss function. Adam is a well-suited technique for use in large datasets and parameter optimisation and is widely applied in deep learning methods [32]. Therefore, the Adam optimiser with default settings was used to update the model parameters during backpropagation, that is, i.e., *learning rate* $= 0.001$, $\beta_1 = 0.9$, $\beta_2 = 0.999$, $\varepsilon = 10^{-8}$. The number of data to be batch processed (bath size) was set to 64, and to avoid overfitting problems, early stopping was used to determine the optimal number of iterations (epoch) during the training process.

Evaluation Criteria. In this study, we used the accuracy, precision, recall, f-score, and confusion matrix to comprehensively evaluate the classification effectiveness of deep learning models. The accuracy (A) is the ratio of the number of correctly classified samples in the test set samples to the total number of samples in all test sets, which provides the most intuitive evaluation of the classification performance of the model. In a multiple classification task, the following four types of classification results were obtained by matching the labels of the test set with the predicted results: true positive, true negative, false positive, and false negative. The precision (P) is the ratio of the number of positive samples predicted by the model to the number of actual positive samples from the perspective of the classification result. The recall (R) is the ratio of the number of all positive samples to the number of samples identified by the correct classification from the perspective of the samples themselves. Finally, the f-score (F) is the sum of the precision and recall, which are considered to be of equal importance and are combined into a single evaluation metric. The confusion matrix visualises the above classification effects through an $n \times n$ matrix, where each column represents the predicted category, the total of each column represents the predicted number of positive samples, each row represents the actual category, and the total of each row represents the actual number of positive samples in that category. The calculation formula is as follows:

$$\begin{cases} A = \frac{T_{positive} + T_{negative}}{T_{positive} + T_{negative} + F_{positive} + F_{negative}}; \\ P = \frac{T_{positive}}{T_{positive} + F_{positive}}; \\ R = \frac{T_{positive}}{T_{positive} + F_{negative}}; \\ F = \frac{2PR}{P+R}, \end{cases} \qquad (10)$$

where $T_{positive}$ is the number of true positive samples, $F_{positive}$ is the number of false positive samples, $T_{negative}$ is the number of true negative samples, and $F_{negative}$ is the number of false negative samples.

CNN Training Results. To find the optimal CNN model suitable for ship target classification, it is necessary to avoid the complicated and tedious calculation of the hyperparameters. We refer to the ideas of Dabiri et al. [33] and Simonyan et al. [34] who gradually increased the number of network layers and convolutional kernels according to the classification effect of the model. By contrast, the large amount of weighting and the complex input-output relationship may lead to an overfitting problem of a neural network, and a dropout is the most practical and widely used regularisation method to overcome the overfitting problem in a CNN [35]. Therefore, during the training process, we will try to add more dropout layers to build an optimal CNN model.

The various structural configurations of the CNN and the corresponding training results are listed in Table 2. In Models A–C, the number of convolutional layers is increased from two to six, whereas by increasing the number of filters to capture more deep features, the accuracy of the model is improved by 0.77%. Model D increases the number of fully connected layers to produce an overfitting, and thus the accuracy of the test set decreases rather than increases. To evaluate the effect of the maximum pooling layer, a maximum pooling layer was added after each set of the convolutional layers in model E. The test accuracy improved compared to that of model D; however, the overfitting phenomenon still existed. To alleviate the overfitting problem of the model, Model F added a dropout layer after both the maximum pooling layer and the fully connected layer, but the test accuracy decreased compared to Model E; in addition, an underfitting occurred because the use of too many dropout layers simplified the model and a large number of features were lost, leading to increased classification errors.

Therefore, a proper arrangement of the dropout layers is necessary to strike a balance between the overfitting and underfitting problems. Model G removes the dropout layers from the first and second convolutional layers and achieves a maximum test accuracy of 78.74%. To further validate model G as the optimal CNN model, models H and I add a set of convolutional layers and a fully connected layer to model G. Although a deeper model was created, the test accuracy did not improve, increasing the complexity and computational cost of the model, leading to an increase in training time. Therefore, considering the classification accuracy and efficiency, the optimal CNN structure is found in model G.

Table 2. CNN structure configuration table

Models	A	B	C	D	E	F	G	H	I
Input layer	Feature vector based on AIS data and with shape (1 * 200 * 4)								
Conv layer	32	32	32	32	32	32	32	32	32
Conv layer	32	32	32	32	32	32	32	32	32
Max-Pool layer	–	–	–	–	√	√	√	√	√
Dropout layer	–	–	–	–	–	√	–	–	–
Conv layer	–	**64**	64	64	64	64	64	64	64
Conv layer	–	**64**	64	64	64	64	64	64	64
Max-Pool layer	–	–	–	–	√	√	√	√	√
Dropout layer	–	–	–	–	–	√	–	–	–
Conv layer	–	–	**128**	128	128	128	128	128	128
Conv layer	–	–	**128**	128	128	128	128	128	128
Max-Pool layer	–	–	–	–	√	√	√	√	√
Dropout layer	–	–	–	–	–	√	√	√	√
Conv layer	–	–	–	–	–	–	–	**256**	–
Conv layer	–	–	–	–	–	–	–	**256**	–
Max-Pool layer	–	–	–	–	–	–	–	–	–
Dropout	–	–	–	–	–	–	–	–	–
FC layer	–	–	–	–	–	–	–	–	√
Dropout layer	–	–	–	–	–	–	–	–	–
FC layer	–	–	–	√	√	√	√	√	√
Dropout	–	–	–	–	–	√	√	√	√
FC layer	√	√	√	√	√	√	√	√	√
Accuracy rate A/%	72.44	72.91	73.21	72.32	74.96	74.44	78.74	77.35	78.58
Time t/s	185	277	393	1796	390	419	406	523	416

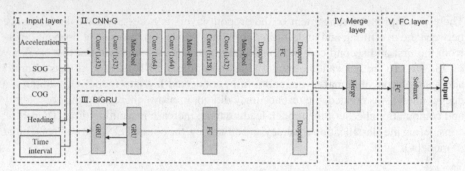

Fig. 6. Overall structure of CNN-BiGRU

CNN-BiGRU Training Results. Combining the optimal CNN model with the BiGRU model yields the CNN-BiGRU model structure shown in Fig. 6. To obtain the optimal number of iterations, the epoch was set to 80, and the model performance was calculated on both the training and test sets for each iteration. When the increase in accuracy of the model reached less than 0.1% after 10 consecutive iterations, training was stopped, and the optimal epoch was obtained. As shown in Fig. 7, the test accuracy stabilised at approximately 79% to 80% after approximately 19 rounds of training, whereas the test loss function remained at approximately 0.51–0.52, reaching a maximum test accuracy of 80.6% and a minimum loss function of 0.507 at the 34th epoch. In the next 10 training rounds after the model reached the maximum accuracy, the test accuracy of the model remained almost constant and did not significantly decrease with an increase in the number of iterations, indicating that the CNN-BiGRU model does not suffer from overfitting problems and can fit the ship target well when mining the spatio-temporal features embedded in the input vector.

To evaluate the performance of the CNN-BiGRU model, Table 3 includes the confusion matrix, classification accuracy, recall, and f-score of the CNN-BiGRU model. In terms of the overall classification, the prediction results for each type of ship are distributed along the diagonal of the confusion matrix, with all classification metrics exceeding 62%, indicating that the combined model can identify the ship targets accurately. In terms of local classification, the classification accuracy and recall of the cargo ships are as high as 94.4% and 94.1% owing to the largest number of sample data, the characteristics of fixed routes, and a constant speed applied at most times. In addition, passenger ships have similar characteristics as cargo ships, and although the classification accuracy of the model can reach 86.6%, the combined model may not be able to learn the movement patterns of passenger ships more fully owing to the smallest number of sample data; thus, the recall is only 73.7%. Tugboats and fishing vessels are more flexible in terms of manoeuvring compared with the two former vessels, and in this study, it is considered that the trajectory points of the vessels during an operational state can cause some difficulties in classification; therefore, the degree of confusion between tugboats and fishing vessels is high, and the lowest classification accuracy and recall of fishing vessels are 66.6% and 62.5%, respectively, whereas the classification accuracy and recall of tugboats with a larger number of samples are 71.1% and 76.3%. The above results show that the classification performance of the combined CNN-BiGRU model is highly correlated with the number of sample instances, and more instances can be considered to be added for identifying passenger vessels as well as distinguishing between tugboats and fishing vessels.

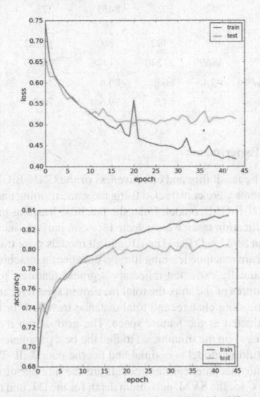

Fig. 7. Training and testing accuracy of models with different epochs

Table 3. Evaluation results of the CNN-BiGRU model

CNN-BiGRU model		Forecast category					
		Cargo ship	Fishing vessel	Passenger ship	Tugboat	Total	Recall /%
Actual category	Cargo ship	**17602**	233	560	243	18638	94.1
	Fishing vessel	352	**7023**	1103	2069	10547	62.5
	Passenger ship	342	592	**8455**	375	9764	73.7
	Tugboat	403	3392	1360	**12652**	17807	76.3
	Total	18699	11240	11478	15339	56756	–
	Accuracy/%	94.4	66.6	86.6	71.1	–	–
	f-score/%	94.3	64.5	79.6	76.3	–	–

3.3 Comparative Experiments

To further evaluate the feasibility and effectiveness of the CNN-BiGRU model, a set of comparison experiments were constructed using the same training and testing trajectory segments as the CNN-BiGRU model. First, the machine learning methods commonly used for multi-classification tasks were selected for comparison, including a K-nearest neighbour (KNN), an SVM, a DT, and an RF, and all models were trained and evaluated based on the scikit-learn machine learning library. Because the machine learning method requires input of manually extracted trajectory segment features, to comprehensively cover the motion features of the ship, the total maximum speed, mean speed, maximum acceleration, mean heading change, and total distance travelled for trajectory segment of each ship are extracted as the feature space. The grid search method and a 5-fold cross validation are used on the training set to find the best parameters for the classifier, ensuring that the resulting model is optimal and fits the data well. The most important parameters of the four machine learning models are the number of neighbours for the KNN, penalty factor C for the SVM, maximum depth for the DT, and number of decision trees for the RF. Finally, the tuned machine-learning models were evaluated on the test set. Second, individual deep learning models were selected for comparison, including a CNN-G, a BiGRU and an LSTM; the combined deep learning model CNN-LSTM was also constructed. The input feature vectors are the same as in the combined model, and the best model was obtained by determining the optimal epochs through the training set and early stopping method, and the best model was evaluated on the test set.

Table 4 lists the optimal parameters for each model within the specified range and the classification performance evaluation results of each model on a total of four metrics: accuracy A, weighted average precision $\overline{P}$, weighted average recall $\overline{R}$, and weighted average f-score $\overline{F}$. Overall, CNN-BiGRU outperforms the other six models under all four evaluation metrics, and its accuracy rate is nearly 15% higher than the average accuracy rate of the other models. From a local perspective, the classification results of the deep learning methods are better than those of the machine learning methods, and the worst-performing LSTM model among the deep learning methods has a 13.3% higher accuracy rate than the best-performing RF model among the machine learning methods. Compared with the CNN, which learns the spatial features of the AIS data, BiGRU and LSTM, which learns the temporal features separately, the combined model can learn both spatial and temporal features to assist in the classification of the ship targets, achieving an accuracy of 1.9% higher than the average of the three deep learning models, effectively improving the classification accuracy. Also, BiGRU can achieve bi-directional mining of AIS trajectory sequences compared to LSTM, so the classification effect of CNN-BiGRU is better than CNN-LSTM.

From the above analysis, it can be concluded that the CNN-BiGRU model can extract advanced features through multi-layer nonlinear processing units better than traditional machine learning algorithms that rely on tedious feature engineering, and by combining the CNN model and BiGRU model, it can effectively mine both spatial and temporal features from the AIS data simultaneously, further improving the classification accuracy of the ship targets.

Table 4. Evaluation of CNN-BiGRU against other algorithms

Models	Parameter name	Parameter range	Parameter values	A/%	$\overline{P}$/%	$\overline{R}$/%	$\overline{F}$/%
KNN	Number of neighbours	[2, 30]	2	56.4	56.4	56.3	56.4
SVM	Penalty factor C	[0.01, 30]	30	59.4	58.2	59.4	56.9
DT	Maximum depth	[1, 40]	19	62.4	69.1	61.8	65.2
RF	Number of decision trees	[2, 200]	100	63.7	75.5	63.6	69.1
LSTM	Epoch	[0, 80]	70	77.0	78.0	76.5	77.0
CNN-G	Epoch	[0, 80]	39	78.7	79.5	78.7	78.8
BiGRU	Epoch	[0, 80]	36	78.3	79.0	78.3	78.3
CNN-LSTM	Epoch	[0, 80]	41	79.1	79.4	79.1	79.0
CNN-BiGRU	Epoch	[0, 80]	34	80.6	81.0	80.6	80.6

4 Conclusions

In this study, we designed a CNN-BiGRU model driven by AIS data for ship target classification. First, the AIS data are cleaned and the ship trajectories are segmented into fixed-length samples. Second, a 4-channel input feature vector is constructed for CNN and BiGRU. Third, the optimal CNN model is trained, and the CNN-BiGRU model is obtained by combining the optimal CNN and BiGRU. Finally, the CNN-BiGRU model is trained based on the two input feature vectors and the ship targets are classified.

The experiment results show that the combined CNN-BiGRU model can effectively achieve an accurate classification and recognition of different ship targets, particularly for cargo ships, with better classification results. Compared with traditional machine learning methods including a KNN, an SVM, a DT, and an RF, this method only requires the construction of simple input feature vectors based on AIS data, which avoids human intervention and complex feature engineering. In addition, the deep learning method has the advantages of autonomously learning and extracting high-level features that represent ship movement patterns contained in AIS data, allowing the CNN-BiGRU model to classify ship targets better than machine learning methods. Finally, compared with deep learning methods including an optimal CNN, a BiGRU, an LSTM and a CNN-LSTM, the CNN-BiGRU model can combine spatio-temporal features to classify the ship targets, effectively improving the accuracy of the ship target classification.

In view of the complexity of the maritime environment and the confusion of the classification owing to similar sailing habits of individual ships, it is necessary to continue to expand the size of the sample database of the ship trajectories and consider adding other details such as static information of the ships or geographical locations of the ports to assist in the classification recognition. Adding AIS data with missing labels and using semi-supervised learning algorithms to further improve the generalisation of the model will be another important direction for future research.

References

1. Chen, J.H., Lu, F., Peng, G.J.: The progress of research in maritime vessel trajectory analysis. China Navig. **35**(3), 53–57 (2012)
2. Deng, Z., Li, Z.F., Duan, W., Li, Z.K.: Spatial-temporal distribution pattern of ship activity in maritime silk road based on AIS data. Econ. Geogr. **41**(4), 15–22 (2021)
3. Liang, Y., Zhang, H.: Ship track prediction based on AIS data and PSO optimized LSTM network. Int. Core J. Eng. **6**(5), 23–33 (2020)
4. Zhou, Y.: Research on collaborative IoT big data processing system in maritime transportation. Naval Sci. Technol. **39**(2), 135–137 (2017)
5. Zhou, L., Zhao, X.S., Wang, J.G., Tang, J.B., Bai, Y.Y.: Research on BDS application in maritime intelligent transport security system. J. Navig. Position. **3**(2), 11–15 (2015)
6. Wang, B., Wang, Y., Qin, K.: Detecting transportation modes based on LightGBM classifier from GPS trajectory data. In: 2018 26th International Conference on Geoinformatics, pp. 32–41. ACM (2018)
7. Li, Z., Sun, J., Ni, X.Y.: Travel mode recognition based on smart phone big data. Appl. Res. Comput. **33**(12), 3527–3529 (2016)
8. Xiao, Z.B., Wang, Y., Fu, K., Wu, F.: Identifying different transportation modes from trajectory data using tree-based ensemble classifiers. ISPRS Int. J. Geo Inf. **6**(2), 57 (2017)
9. Xiong, S.S.: Identifying transportation mode based on improved LightGBM algorithm. Comput. Modernization **126**(10), 68–73 (2018)
10. Zheng, Q.L., Fan, W., Zhang, S.M., Zhang, H., Wang, X.X.: Identification of fishing type from VMS data based on artificial neural network. S. China Fish. Sci. **12**(2), 81–87 (2016)
11. Sheng, K., Liu, Z., Zhou, D.C., He, A.L., Feng, C.X.: Research on ship classification based on trajectory features. J. Navig. **1**, 100–116 (2018)

12. Kraus, P., Mohrdieck, C., Schwenker, F.: Ship classification based on trajectory data with machine-learning methods. In: 2018 19th International Radar Symposium (IRS), pp. 1–10. IEEE (2018)
13. Ginolhac, R., Barbaresco, F., Schneider, J.Y., Pannier, J.M., Savary, S.: Coastal radar target recognition based on kinematic data (AIS) with machine learning. In: 2019 International Radar Conference (RADAR), pp. 1–5. IEEE (2019)
14. Gao, S.: A review of recent researches and reflections on geospatial artificial intelligence. Geomat. Inf. Sci. Wuhan Univ. **45**(12), 1865–1874 (2020)
15. Ljunggren, H.: Using deep learning for classifying ship trajectories. In: 2018 International Conference on Information Fusion, pp. 2158–2164. IEEE (2018)
16. Bakkegaard, S., Blixenkrone, M.J., Larsen, J.J., Jochumsen, L.: Target classification using kinematic data and a recurrent neural network. In: 2018 19th International Radar Symposium (IRS), pp. 1–10. IEEE (2018)
17. Cui, T.T., Wang, G.L., Gao, J.: Ship trajectory classification method based on 1DCNN-LSTM. Comput. Sci. **47**(9), 175–184 (2020)
18. Yuan, J., Zheng, Y., Xie, X., Sun, G.Z.: Driving with knowledge from the physical word. In: Proceeding of the 17th ACM SIGKDD International Conference on Knowledge Discovery and Data Mining, pp. 316–324. ACM (2011)
19. Zheng, Y., Liu, L., Wang, L., Xie, X.: Learning transportation mode from raw GPS data for geographic applications on the web. In: 17th International Conference on World Wide Web, pp. 247–256. ACM (2008)
20. Lu, S.C., Xia, Y.: Dual supervised autoencoder based trajectory classification using enhanced spatio-temporal information. IEEE Access **8**, 173918–173932 (2018)
21. Xiao, G.N., Juan, Z.C., Zhang, C.Q.: Travel mode detection based on GPS track data and Bayesian network. Stat. Decis. **6**, 75–79 (2017)
22. Liu, G.J., Yang, J.F.: The classification method of traffic trajectory pattern based on deep learning and permutation entropy. J. North China Univ. Technol. **30**(2), 67–73 (2018)
23. Broach, J., Dill, J., Mcneil, N.W.: Travel mode imputation using GPS and accelerometer data from a multi-day travel survey. J. Transp. Geogr. **78**, 194–204 (2019)
24. Liu, G.J., Yin, Z.Z., Jia, Y.J., Xie, Y.L.: Passenger flow estimation based on convolutional neural network in public transportation system. Knowl.-Based Syst. **123**, 102–115 (2017)
25. Krizhevsky, A., Sutskever, I., Hinton, G.E.: ImageNet classification with deep convolutional neural networks. In: Advances in Neural Information Processing System, vol. 25, pp. 1097–1105 (2012).
26. Chung, J. Y., Gulcehre, C., Cho, K.H., Bengio, Y.S.: Empirical evaluation of gated recurrent neural networks on sequence modeling. In: 2014 Deep Learning and Representation Learning Workshop, pp. 1–9. Springer (2014)
27. Hochreiter, S., Schmidhuber, J.: Long short-term memory. Neural Comput. **9**(8), 1735–1780 (1997)
28. Schmidhuber, J.: Deep learning in neural networks: an overview. Neural Netw. **61**, 85–117 (2015)
29. Zhang, G.H., Liu, B.: Research on time series classification using CNN and bidirectional GRU. J. Front. Comput. Sci. Technol. **13**(6), 916–927 (2019)
30. Dai, G.W., Ma, C.X., Xu, X.C.: Short-term traffic flow prediction method for urban road sections based on space-time analysis and GRU. IEEE Access **7**, 143025–143035 (2019)
31. Zhao, J.D., Gao, Y., Qu, Y.C., Yin, H.D., Liu, Y.M., Sun, H.J.: Travel time prediction: based on gated recurrent unit method and data fusion. IEEE Access **6**, 70463–70472 (2018)
32. Kingma, D., Ba, J.: Adam: a method for stochastic optimization. In: The 3rd International Conference for Learning Representations, pp. 1–15. Springer (2015)
33. Dabiri, S., Heaslip, K.: Inferring transportation modes from GPS trajectories using a convolutional neural network. Transp. Res. Part C Emerg. Technol. **86**(1), 360–371 (2018)

34. Simonyan, K., Zisserman, A.: Very deep convolutional networks for large-scale image recognition. In: International Conference on Learning Representations, pp. 1–14. Springer (2015)
35. Srivastava, N., Hinton, G., Krizhevsky, A., Sutskever, I.: Dropout: a simple way to prevent neural networks from overfitting. J. Mach. Learn. Res. **15**(1), 1929–1958 (2014)

Heterogeneous Network Representation Learning Based on Adaptive Multi-channel Graph Convolution

Jingwei Du[1], Lihua Zhou[1(✉)], Guowang Du[1], Lizhen Wang[1], and Yiting Jiang[2]

[1] School of Information Science and Engineering, Yunnan University, Kunming 650091,
People's Republic of China
jingweidu@mail.ynu.edu.cn, lhzhou@ynu.edu.cn
[2] School of Information, Yunnan Normal University, Kunming 650091,
People's Republic of China

Abstract. Network representation learning (NRL) is an important technique for network analysis. Heterogeneous information networks (HINs) contain multiple types of nodes and edges, which describe the personalized information of nodes and complex relationships between nodes. In this paper, we propose a Heterogeneous Adaptive Multi-Channel Graph Convolutional Networks (HAM-GCN) for HIN representation learning. In HAM-GCN, we design three channels to extract the specific and common embeddings with respect to each meta-path from node features, topological structures, and their combinations simultaneously. In addition, we design both channel-level attention and semantic-level attention to fuse the low-dimensional representations obtained from different channels and different meta-paths for learning the final representation. A large number of experiments on three benchmark data sets show that HAM-GCN extracts the most relevant information from topological structure and node features, which significantly improves the classification accuracy than other baseline algorithms.

Keywords: Heterogeneous information network · Network representation learning · Attention mechanism · Graph convolutional neural networks

1 Introduction

Network representation learning (NRL) [1, 2] is a generic representation method that maps the nodes in a network to low-dimensional vectors, while retains the inherent features of node attributes and topological structure of the original network. The low-dimensional representations obtained via NRL can be used to serve various downstream tasks, such as node classification [3], node clustering [4] and link prediction [5]. Therefore, NRL has aroused many researchers' interests in recent years.

Graph neural network [6], as a powerful graph representation technique based on deep learning, has been widely used in NRL and obtained superior performance. Especially, graph convolutional network (GCN) [7] has gained great popularity due to its ability of fusing node attributes and structural information through a recursive neighborhood aggregation scheme. For example, to sufficiently embed the graph knowledge, Zhuang & Ma [8] proposed a dual graph convolutional network (DGCN) to embed local consistency-based knowledge (i.e., nearby data points are likely to have the same label) and global-consistency-based knowledge (i.e., data points that occur in similar contexts tend to have the same label) respectively by designing a graph adjacency matrix-based convolution and a positive pointwise mutual information (PPMI) [9] matrix-based convolution. In order to optimally integrate node features and topological structures in a complex graph with rich information, Wang et al. [10] proposed an adaptive multi-channel graph convolutional networks for semi-supervised classification (AM-GCN) to extract the specific and common embeddings from node features, topological structures, and their combinations simultaneously, and used the attention mechanism to learn adaptive importance weights of the embeddings. In this way, AM-GCN adaptively learns some deep correlation information between topological structures and node features. However, DGCN and AM-GCN are designed for dealing with homogeneous information networks (HONs), which consists of only one type of nodes and edges.

In real world, many networks are heterogeneous, i.e. these networks contain multi-types of nodes and edges. In a HIN, different types of nodes have different traits and their features may fall in different feature space. Compared with HONs, HINs contain more detailed information and rich semantics with complex connections among multi-typed nodes. Due to the diversity of node and edge types, the HIN itself becomes more complex, and the diverse connections between nodes also convey more semantic information. Different meaningful and complex semantic information involved in HINs are usually reflected by meta-paths [11], which is a composite relation connecting two objects and has been widely used in NRL for HINs [20, 21, 28]. Depending on different meta-paths, the relation between nodes in a HIN can have different semantics. The heterogeneity and rich semantic information bring great challenges for NRL. How to handle such complex structural and semantic information as well as preserve the diverse feature information simultaneously is an important problem in NRL.

In this paper, we propose a Heterogeneous Adaptive Multi-Channel Graph Convolutional Networks (HAM-GCN) for HIN representation learning. In HAM-GCN, we design three channels to extract the specific and common embeddings with respect to each meta-path from node features, topological structures, and their combinations simultaneously. In addition, we design both channel-level attention and semantic-level attention to fuse the low-dimensional representations obtained from different channels and different meta-paths for learning the final representation. The channel-level attention focus on learning the importance of each channel and assigning different attention values to them, while the semantic-level attention aims to learn the importance of each meta-path and assign proper weights to them. With the learned importance from both channel-level and semantic-level attention, the importance of channel and meta-path can be fully considered. The co-optimization of three channels is beneficial to embed local consistency-based knowledge and global-consistency-based knowledge, as well as to learn some deep correlation information between topological structures and node features. The utilization of two level attention is helpful for selecting the most relevant channels and meta-paths.

In summary, our contributions in this paper can be summarized as follows:

We propose a heterogeneous adaptive multichannel graph convolutional network (HAM-GCN) for NRL in HINs. HAM-GCN consists of three channels to extract the specific and common embeddings with respect to each meta-path from node features, topological structures, and their combinations simultaneously.

A two-level attention mechanism is proposed to distinguish the importance of different channels and meta-paths, such that the most relevant channels and meta-paths can be selected.

We conduct extensive experiments on three real-world benchmark datasets to validate the performance of HAM-GCN. The experimental results show that HAM-GCN outperforms eight baseline methods in classification tasks.

The rest of the paper is organized as follows. Section 2 presents the concepts involved in the paper. Section 3 elaborates the HAM-GCN. Section 4 is devoted to the experimental settings and results. Finally, we conclude the paper in Sect. 5.

2 Related Work

2.1 Graph Convolution Neural Network

Graph neural network (GNN) [6] is a deep learning-based method in the field of graphs. It is widely used in graph analysis tasks because of its excellent performance and better interpretability. Because of the success of CNN in the field of deep learning, more and more people are beginning to define convolution operations on structured graph data. The new research direction of this kind of graph neural network through convolution operation is defined as GCN, which is mainly divided into spectral-decomposition approaches and spatial-structure approaches. On one hand, the method based on spectral decomposition processes the spectral domain correlation representation of the graph. Joan Bruna et al. [12] define the convolution operation in the Fourier domain by calculating the feature factorization of the Laplacian matrix of the graph. Michaël Defferrard et al. [13] proposes the CHEBNET approach, using K-Jump convolution to define graph convolution, and omitting the process of characteristic calculation of Laplace matrix. Kipf et al. [7] proposes the GCN model, by set K = 1 in CHEBNET model, so as to alleviate the problem of local structure overfitting on graphs with large degree distribution range of nodes. On the other hand, the approach of based on spatial-structure can directly defines the convolution operation on the graph, so as to calculate the adjacent fields in space. Federico Monti et al. [14] proposes the spatial domain model Monet, which is applied to the non-Euclidean data domain and can generalize the previous GCN model as the special case of Monet.

2.2 Network Representation Learning

Network Representation learning (NRL) [1, 2] aims to learn to use low-dimensional representations to represent the nodes, edges or subgraphs of the network. In network representation learning, traditional machine learning methods usually rely on manual feature engineering and are limited by high-cost problems. With the success of representation learning, the first representation-based learning method DeepWalk [15] is proposed, which used the SkipGram [16] model in randomly generated paths. For example, methods such as node2vec [17], LINE [18] and TADW [19] have also made follow-up breakthroughs. However, as most of these methods are designed for a single homogeneous network in which nodes and edges are of a single type, the methods for heterogeneous information networks with multiple types of nodes or edges are under development.

2.3 Heterogeneous Information Network Representation Learning

For the problem of node heterogeneity in information networks, an increasing number of approaches on heterogeneous information network representations learning(HINRL) [5] have been proposed in recent years. Fu et al. [20] proposes the HIN2Vec model to learns the representation of different types of nodes and meta-paths simultaneously while performing network tasks. Wang et al. [21] consider the attention mechanism in heterogeneous graph learning, where information from multiple meta-path defined connections can be learned effectively. Ren et al. [22] proposed the unsupervised heterogeneous information network GNN model HDGI inspired by algorithms based on mutual information. The method uses meta-paths to model the semantic information of heterogeneous graph structures and captures the local representation of nodes using a graph convolution module and a semantic-level attention mechanism. Hu et al. [23] propose a novel model, HeGAN, which is the first model to apply adversarial generative networks to the HINRL.

3   Problem Definition

This section mainly introduces the definition of heterogeneous information network.

Definition 1 (Heterogeneous Information Network, HIN) [5]. A heterogeneous information network is defined as an undirected network graph $G = (V, E, Q, U)$, where each node $v \in V$ and link $e \in E$ are respectively associated with their mapping functions $\phi(v) : V \to Q$ and $\varphi(e) : E \to U$, Q and U denote a set of objects and relationship types respectively.

Definition 2 (Meta-path) [11]. In a HIN, two objects can be connected via different semantic paths, which are called meta-paths. A meta-path Φ is defined as a path in the form of $Q_1 \xrightarrow{U_1} Q_2 \xrightarrow{U_2} \cdots \xrightarrow{U_m} Q_{m+1}$ (abbreviated as $Q_1 Q_2 \cdots Q_{l+1}$), which describes relationship types $U = U_1 U_2 \cdots U_l$ and object types $Q_1 Q_2 \cdots Q_{l+1}$ sequence and the length of the meta-path is denoted as m.

Definition 3 (Heterogeneous Information Network Representation Learning, HINRL) [5]. Given a HIN $G = (V, E, Q, U)$, for $\forall v \in V$, HINRL aims to map each node $v \in V$ or edge $e \in E$ to a d-dimensional latent representation vector $r_v \in R^{|V| \times d}$, where $d << |V|$ and $|\cdot|$ is the total number of vertices in the graph G. The low-dimensional representation can retain the essential characteristics of multiple types of nodes or multiple types of link relationships in the original network at the same time.

4 The Proposed Method

Given a HIN $G = (V, E, Q, U)$, a set of meta-paths $\{\Phi_1, \Phi_2, ..., \Phi_m\}$. Let $\mathbf{A} = \{\mathbf{A}^{(1)}, \mathbf{A}^{(2)}, ..., \mathbf{A}^{(m)}\}$ be the set of the adjacency matrices with respect to meta-paths $\{\Phi_1, \Phi_2, ..., \Phi_m\}$, where $\mathbf{A}^{(m)} \in \mathbb{R}^{n \times n}$ describes the connection amongst n nodes via the m - th meta-path. Specifically, the element $\mathbf{A}_{i,j}^m = 1$ indicating that node v_i and v_j are reachable via the m - th meta-path, otherwise not. Let $\mathbf{X} \in \mathbb{R}^{n \times d_\mathbf{x}}$ be the node feature matrix and $\mathbf{P}$ be a positive pointwise mutual information (PPMI) matrix [9], where $d_\mathbf{x}$ denotes the dimension of node features. We assume that nodes are labeled with a total of C categories.

The overall framework of HAM-GCN is shown in Fig. 1. HAM-GCN has three channels with respect to each meta-path, two of them are two independent convolutional modules, designed to learn two specific representations $\mathbf{Z}_\mathbf{A}^{(m)}$ and $\mathbf{Z}_\mathbf{P}^{(m)}$ from adjacency matrix $\mathbf{A}^{(m)}$ and PPMI matrix $\mathbf{P}^{(m)}$ respectively. The third channel is two convolutional modules with share parameters, designed to learn the common representations $\mathbf{Z}_\mathbf{AX}^{(m)}$ and $\mathbf{Z}_\mathbf{PX}^{(m)}$ from $(\mathbf{A}^{(m)}, \mathbf{X})$ and $(\mathbf{P}^{(m)}, \mathbf{X})$ respectively. The discrepancy constraint $\mathcal{L}_\mathbf{A}^{(m)}$ and $\mathcal{L}_\mathbf{P}^{(m)}$ is designed to guarantee the independence between $\mathbf{Z}_\mathbf{A}^{(m)}$ and $\mathbf{Z}_\mathbf{AX}^{(m)}$, $\mathbf{Z}_\mathbf{P}^{(m)}$ and $\mathbf{Z}_\mathbf{PX}^{(m)}$ respectively, while the consistency constraint $\mathcal{L}_{co}^{(m)}$ is designed to enhance the commonality between $\mathbf{Z}_\mathbf{AX}^{(m)}$ and $\mathbf{Z}_\mathbf{PX}^{(m)}$. In addition, we design both channel-level attention and semantic-level attention to fuse the low-dimensional representations obtained from different channels and different meta-paths for learning the final representation $\mathbf{Z}$.

4.1 Independent Convolution Module

GCN Based on Adjacency Matrix $\mathbf{A}^{(k)}$. Given the input adjacency matrix $\mathbf{A}^{(k)}$ and feature matrix $\mathbf{X}$, the output $\mathbf{Z}_\mathbf{A}^{(k,l)}$ of the l - th hidden layer of the network is defined as:

$$\mathbf{Z}_\mathbf{A}^{(k,l)} = \text{GCN}^{(k,l)}(\mathbf{A}^{(k)}, \mathbf{Z}_\mathbf{A}^{(k,l-1)}) = \sigma\left(\left(\tilde{\mathbf{D}}_\mathbf{A}^{(k)}\right)^{-\frac{1}{2}} \tilde{\mathbf{A}}^{(k)} \left(\tilde{\mathbf{D}}_\mathbf{A}^{(k)}\right)^{-\frac{1}{2}} \mathbf{Z}_\mathbf{A}^{(k,l-1)} \mathbf{W}_\mathbf{A}^{(k,l)}\right) \quad (1)$$

where $\tilde{\mathbf{A}}^{(k)} = \mathbf{A}^{(k)} + \mathbf{I}_n$, and $\mathbf{I}_n \in \mathbb{R}^{n \times n}$ is the identity matrix. $\tilde{\mathbf{D}}_\mathbf{A}^{(k)}$ is the diagonal degree matrix of $\tilde{\mathbf{A}}^{(k)}$. $\left(\tilde{\mathbf{D}}_\mathbf{A}^{(k)}\right)^{-\frac{1}{2}} \tilde{\mathbf{A}}^{(m)} \left(\tilde{\mathbf{D}}_\mathbf{A}^{(k)}\right)^{-\frac{1}{2}}$ is the normalized the adjacency matrix to avoid data instability and explosion or disappearance of gradients that may be caused by repeated operations of calculations. $\mathbf{W}_\mathbf{A}^{(k,l)}$ is the weight matrix of the l-th layer in GCN. $\sigma(\cdot)$ denotes an activation function, and $\mathbf{Z}_\mathbf{A}^{(k,0)} = \mathbf{X}$. We denote the last layer output representation as $\mathbf{Z}_\mathbf{A}^{(k)}$.

GCN Based on PPMI Matrix $\mathbf{P}^{(k)}$. A heterogeneous network contains not only first-order topology information defined by the adjacency matrix, but also high-order topology information. Therefore, we will further introduce a convolution method based on PPMI by encoding semantic information. We denote the PPMI matrix as $\mathbf{P}^{(1)}, \mathbf{P}^{(k)}, ..., \mathbf{P}^{(m)} \in \mathbb{R}^{n \times n}$, where $\mathbf{P}^{(k)} \in \mathbb{R}^{n \times n}$ is PPMI matrix of the k - th meta-path. Next, we will introduce how to calculate the PPMI matrix $\mathbf{P}^{(k)}$ in the following two steps.

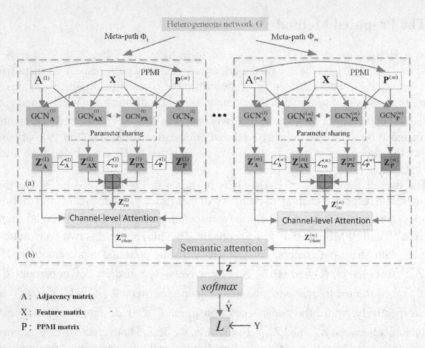

Fig. 1. The framework of HAM-GCN model. Input to different multi-channel GCNs through different meta-paths, and each multi-channel GCN has the same construction (a) $\mathbf{A}^{(1)}$− based and SS-based independent convolution channel. Based on $(\mathbf{A}^{(1)}, \mathbf{X})$ and $(\mathbf{P}^{(1)}, \mathbf{X})$ shared convolution channel. (b) Channel-level attention with fused channel representation, semantic-level attention that fuses meta-paths semantic relations.

Calculating frequency matrix $\mathbf{F}^{(k)}$. In our method, we use a random walk to calculate the semantic similarity between nodes. If the random walker is on the node v_i at time t, we define the state as $s(t) = v_i$. The transition probability of jumping from the current node v_i to one of its neighbors v_j is denoted as $p^{(k)}\big(s(t+1) = v_j | s(t) = v_i\big)$. Thus, given the adjacency matrix $\mathbf{A}^{(k)}$, we define:

$$p^{(k)}\big(s(t+1) = v_j | s(t) = v_i\big) = \frac{A_{i,j}^{(k)}}{\sum\limits_j A_{i,j}^{(k)}} \tag{2}$$

The calculation process of the frequency matrix $\mathbf{F}^{(k)}$ is shown by Algorithm 1, and the time complexity is $O(n\varepsilon L^2)$.

Algorithm 1 Calculating frequency matrix $\mathbf{F}^{(k)}$

---

1.   Input: adjacency matrix $\mathbf{A}^{(k)}$, path length L, window size w, walks of per node ε.

2.   Output: frequency matrix $\mathbf{F}^{(k)} \in \mathbb{R}^{n \times n}$

3.   Initialize matrix $\mathbf{F}^{(k)}$ to zero matrix

4.   for each node $v_i \in V$ do

5.   set v_i as the root node

6.   for $i = 0$ to ε do

7.   S=Random Walk($\mathbf{A}^{(k)}, v_i, L$) $\triangleright$ get a path S using Eq.(2).

8.   Uniformly sample all node pairs $\left(v_i, v_j\right) \in S$ within w

9.   for each pair $\left(v_i, v_j\right)$ do

10. $\mathbf{F}_{i,j}^{(k)} + = 1, \mathbf{F}_{j,i}^{(k)} + = 1$

11.   End for

12.   End for

13. End for

Calculating PPMI. After getting the frequency matrix $\mathbf{F}^{(k)}$, $\mathbf{F}_{i,*}^{(k)}$ is the $\mathbf{F}^{(k)}$ row vector, and $\mathbf{F}_{i,*}^{(k)}$ corresponds to a node v_i. $\mathbf{F}_{*,j}^{(k)}$ is the column vector $\mathbf{F}^{(k)}$, and $\mathbf{F}_{i,*}^{(k)}$ corresponds to a context c_j. $\mathbf{F}_{i,j}^{(k)}$ indicate the number of times that v_i occurs in context c_j.

Then, based on $\mathbf{F}^{(k)}$, we can calculate the PPMI matrix $\mathbf{P}^{(k)}$ as:

$$
p_{i,j}^{(k)} = \frac{\mathbf{F}_{i,j}^{(k)}}{\sum_{i,j} \mathbf{F}_{i,j}^{(k)}}; p_{i,*}^{(k)} = \frac{\sum_{j} \mathbf{F}_{i,j}^{(k)}}{\sum_{i,j} \mathbf{F}_{i,j}^{(k)}}, p_{*,j}^{(k)} = \frac{\sum_{i} \mathbf{F}_{i,j}^{(k)}}{\sum_{i,j} \mathbf{F}_{i,j}^{(k)}}; \mathbf{P}_{i,j}^{(k)} = \max \left\{ pmi_{i,j} = \log \left(\frac{p_{i,j}^{(k)}}{p_{i,*}^{(k)} p_{*,j}^{(k)}} \right), 0 \right\}.
$$

$$(3)$$

According to Eq. (3), we will encode the high-order topology information in $\mathbf{P}^{(k)}$. In other words, $p_{i,j}^{(k)}$ is the probability of node v_i occurs in context c_j. $p_{i,*}^{(k)}$ is the probability of node v_i; and $p_{*,j}^{(k)}$ is the probability of context c_j. According to probability theory and mathematical statistics, if two events are independent of each other, then $p_{i,j}^{(k)} = p_{i,*}^{(k)} p_{*,j}^{(k)}$, and $pmi_{i,j} = 0$. If there is a relationship between v_i and c_j, then $p_{i,j}^{(k)} > p_{i,*}^{(k)} p_{*,j}^{(k)}$, and $pmi_{i,j}$ is positive. If node v_i is unrelated to context c_j, $pmi_{i,j}$ is negative. A common way to improve performance is to assign each negative value to 0, forming a PPMI matrix.

After obtaining $\mathbf{P}^{(k)}$ encoding high-order topology in each meta-path, $\text{GCN}_{\mathbf{P}}^{(k,l)}(\mathbf{X})$ is derived from the similarity defined by $\mathbf{P}^{(k)}$. This convolutional neural network is as follows:

$$
\mathbf{Z}_{\mathbf{P}}^{(k,l)} = \text{GCN}_{\mathbf{P}}^{(k,l)}(\mathbf{P}^{(k)}, \mathbf{Z}_{\mathbf{P}}^{(k,l-1)}) = \sigma \left(\left(\tilde{\mathbf{D}}_{\mathbf{P}}^{(k)} \right)^{-\frac{1}{2}} \mathbf{P}^{(k)} \left(\tilde{\mathbf{D}}_{\mathbf{P}}^{(k)} \right)^{-\frac{1}{2}} \mathbf{Z}_{\mathbf{P}}^{(k,l-1)} \mathbf{W}_{\mathbf{P}}^{(k,l)} \right) \quad (4)
$$

In Eq. (4), $\mathbf{P}^{(k)}$ is the PPMI matrix, and $\left(\tilde{\mathbf{D}}_\mathbf{P}^{(k)}\right)^{-\frac{1}{2}} \mathbf{P}^{(k)} \left(\tilde{\mathbf{D}}_\mathbf{P}^{(k)}\right)^{-\frac{1}{2}}$ is the normalized the PPMI matrix. We denote the last layer output representation as $\mathbf{Z}_\mathbf{P}^{(k)}$.

4.2 Common Convolution Module

The first convolution part consists of the adjacency matrix and the feature matrix for the convolution operation defined as $\mathbf{Z}_{\mathbf{AX}}^{(k)}$, and the second convolution part consists of the PPMI matrix and the feature matrix for the convolution operation defined as $\mathbf{Z}_{\mathbf{PX}}^{(k)}$.

The calculation formula of the first part of the representation $\mathbf{Z}_{\mathbf{AX}}^{(k)}$ is as follows:

$$\mathbf{Z}_{\mathbf{AX}}^{(k,l)} = \text{GCN}_{\mathbf{AX}}^{(k,l)}(\mathbf{A}^{(k)}, \mathbf{X}) = \sigma\left(\left(\tilde{\mathbf{D}}_\mathbf{A}^{(k)}\right)^{-\frac{1}{2}} \tilde{\mathbf{A}}^{(k)} \left(\tilde{\mathbf{D}}_\mathbf{A}^{(k)}\right)^{-\frac{1}{2}} \mathbf{Z}_{\mathbf{AX}}^{(k,l-1)} \mathbf{W}_{\text{co}}^{(k,l)}\right). \quad (5)$$

where, $\mathbf{W}_{\text{co}}^{(k,l)}$ is the shared weight matrix of the l-th layer in $\text{GCN}_{\mathbf{AX}}^{(k,l)}(\mathbf{A}^{(k)}, \mathbf{X})$. $\mathbf{Z}_{\mathbf{AX}}^{(k,l-1)}$ is the node embedding output of the $(l-1)$-th layer, and $\mathbf{Z}_{\mathbf{AX}}^{(k,0)} = \mathbf{X}$. We denote the last layer output embedding as $\mathbf{Z}_{\mathbf{AX}}^{(k)}$.

The calculation formula of the second part of the embedding $\mathbf{Z}_{\mathbf{PX}}^{(k)}$ is as follows:

$$\mathbf{Z}_{\mathbf{PX}}^{(k,l)} = \text{GCN}_{\mathbf{PX}}^{(k,l)}(\mathbf{P}^{(k)}, \mathbf{X}) = \sigma\left(\left(\tilde{\mathbf{D}}_\mathbf{A}^{(k)}\right)^{-\frac{1}{2}} \mathbf{P}^{(k)} \left(\tilde{\mathbf{D}}_\mathbf{A}^{(k)}\right)^{-\frac{1}{2}} \mathbf{Z}_{\mathbf{PX}}^{(k,l-1)} \mathbf{W}_{\text{co}}^{(k,l)}\right). \quad (6)$$

The shared weight matrix $\mathbf{W}_{\text{co}}^{(k,l)}$ can filter out the common features of topological and PPMI. Finally, the representations $\mathbf{Z}_{\mathbf{AX}}^{(k)}$ and $\mathbf{Z}_{\mathbf{PX}}^{(k)}$ obtained by the two parts of the module in the common convolution are fused to obtain the final embedding $\mathbf{Z}_{\text{co}}^{(k)}$ is:

$$\mathbf{Z}_{\text{co}}^{(k)} = \frac{\left(\mathbf{Z}_{\mathbf{AX}}^{(k)} + \mathbf{Z}_{\mathbf{PX}}^{(k)}\right)}{2}. \quad (7)$$

4.3 Attention Mechanism

Channel-Level Attention. We have one common embedding $\mathbf{Z}_{\text{co}}^{(k)}$ and two independent representations $\mathbf{Z}_\mathbf{A}^{(k)}$ and $\mathbf{Z}_\mathbf{P}^{(k)}$. Due to node labels may be associated with a combination of one or more of them, we use the attention mechanism to learn their corresponding importance as follows:

$$\left(\alpha_\mathbf{A}^{(k)}, \alpha_{\text{co}}^{(k)}, \alpha_\mathbf{P}^{(k)}\right) = att_{\text{chan}}\left(\mathbf{Z}_\mathbf{A}^{(k)}, \mathbf{Z}_{\text{co}}^{(k)}, \mathbf{Z}_\mathbf{P}^{(k)}\right), \quad (8)$$

where $\left(\alpha_\mathbf{A}^{(k)}, \alpha_{\text{co}}^{(k)}, \alpha_\mathbf{P}^{(k)}\right)$ are the attention values of n nodes representation $\mathbf{Z}_\mathbf{A}^{(k)}, \mathbf{Z}_{\text{co}}^{(k)}$ and $\mathbf{Z}_\mathbf{P}^{(k)}$, respectively. With respect to node v_i, its representation in $\mathbf{Z}_\mathbf{A}^{(k)}$ is $\mathbf{Z}_{\mathbf{A}_i}^{(k)} \in \mathbb{R}^{1 \times h}$. We will first transform the representation by means of a nonlinear transformation, and then use one shared attention vector $\mathbf{s}_{chan}^{(k)} \in \mathbb{R}^{h' \times 1}$ to get attention value $\omega_{\mathbf{A}_i}^{(k)}$ as follows:

$$\omega_{\mathbf{A}_i}^{(k)} = \left(\mathbf{s}_{chan}^{(k)}\right)^{\mathbf{T}} \cdot \tanh\left(\mathbf{W}_{chan}^{(k)} \cdot \left(\mathbf{Z}_{\mathbf{A}_i}^{(k)}\right)^{\mathbf{T}} + \mathbf{b}_{chan}^{(k)}\right). \tag{9}$$

where $\mathbf{b}_{chan}^{(k)} \in \mathbb{R}^{h \times 1}$ is the bias vector, and $\mathbf{W}_{chan}^{(k)} \in \mathbb{R}^{h' \times h}$ is the weight matrix. According to the above description, we can also get the attention values $\omega_{(co)_i}^{(k)}$ and $\omega_{\mathbf{P}_i}^{(k)}$ for node v_i in the embedding matrices $\mathbf{Z}_{co}^{(k)}$ and $\mathbf{Z}_{\mathbf{P}}^{(k)}$. Next, we normalize the attention values $\omega_{\mathbf{A}_i}^{(k)}$, $\omega_{(co)_i}^{(k)}$ and $\omega_{\mathbf{P}_i}^{(k)}$ with Softmax function to get final weight of Channel-level Attention follow:

$$\alpha_{\mathbf{A}_i}^{(k)} = \mathrm{Softmax}\left(\omega_{\mathbf{A}_i}^{(k)}\right) = \frac{\exp\left(\omega_{\mathbf{A}_i}^{(k)}\right)}{\exp\left(\omega_{\mathbf{A}_i}^{(k)}\right) + \exp\left(\omega_{(co)_i}^{(k)}\right) + \exp\left(\omega_{\mathbf{P}_i}^{(k)}\right)}. \tag{10}$$

Similarly, we can get $\alpha_{(co)_i}^{(k)} = \mathrm{Softmax}\left(\omega_{(co)_i}^{(k)}\right)$ and $\alpha_{\mathbf{P}_i}^{(k)} = \mathrm{Softmax}\left(\omega_{\mathbf{P}_i}^{(k)}\right)$. For the above three weights, $\alpha_{\mathbf{A}}^{(k)} = \mathrm{diag}([\alpha_{\mathbf{A}_i}^{(k)}] \in \mathbb{R}^{n \times 1})$, $\alpha_{(co)}^{(k)} = \mathrm{diag}([\alpha_{(co)_i}^{(k)}] \in \mathbb{R}^{n \times 1})$, and $\alpha_{\mathbf{P}}^{(k)} = \mathrm{diag}([\alpha_{\mathbf{P}_i}^{(k)}] \in \mathbb{R}^{n \times 1})$. Furthermore, the greater $\alpha^{(k)}$ means the more important, on the contrary, the lower the importance. Finally, we fuse the three representations to obtain the channel-level representation $\mathbf{Z}_{chan}^{(k)}$ as follows:

$$\mathbf{Z}_{chan}^{(k)} = \alpha_{\mathbf{A}}^{(k)} \cdot \mathbf{Z}_{\mathbf{A}}^{(k)} + \alpha_{(co)}^{(k)} \cdot \mathbf{Z}_{co}^{(k)} + \alpha_{\mathbf{P}}^{(k)} \cdot \mathbf{Z}_{\mathbf{P}}^{(k)}. \tag{11}$$

Semantic-Level Attention. In order to solve the challenges of meta-paths selection and semantic fusion in HIN, we use semantic-level attention, which automatically learns the importance of different meta-paths and can capture various semantic information behind the HIN.

After obtaining $\mathbf{Z}_{chan}^{(k)}$ of different meta-paths, we use semantic-level attention mechanism to capture the weight of each view:

$$\left(\delta^{\Phi_1}, \delta^{\Phi_2}, \cdots, \delta^{\Phi_k}, \cdots, \delta^{\Phi_m}\right) = att_{sem}\left(\mathbf{Z}_{chan}^{(1)}, \mathbf{Z}_{chan}^{(2)}, \cdots, \mathbf{Z}_{chan}^{(k)}, \cdots, \mathbf{Z}_{chan}^{(m)}\right). \tag{12}$$

In Eq. (12), att_{sem} denotes the semantic-level attention, and $\left(\delta^{\Phi_1}, \delta^{\Phi_2}, \cdots, \delta^{\Phi_m}\right)$ are the attention weights. To learn the importance of each meta-path, we transform semantic-level embedding through a nonlinear transformation, then use one shared attention vector $\mathbf{q}_{sem}^{(k)} \in \mathbb{R}^{h' \times 1}$ to get attention value w^{Φ_k} as follows:

$$w^{\Phi_k} = (\mathbf{q}_{sem}^{(k)})^{\mathbf{T}} \cdot \tanh\left(\mathbf{W}_{sem}^{(k)} \cdot (\mathbf{Z}_{chan}^{(k)})^{\mathbf{T}} + \mathbf{b}_{sem}^{(k)}\right). \tag{13}$$

where $\mathbf{b}_{sem}^{(k)}$ is the bias vector, $\mathbf{W}_{sem}^{(k)} \in \mathbb{R}^{h' \times h}$ is the weight matrix, and the $\mathbf{q}_{sem}^{(k)} \in \mathbb{R}^{h' \times 1}$ is the semantic-level attention vector. After obtaining the importance of each meta-path, it is normalized by the Softmax function to get Semantic-level Attention final weight as follow:

$$\delta^{\Phi_k} = \text{Softmax}(w^{\Phi_k}) = \frac{\exp(w^{\Phi_k})}{\sum_{k=1}^{m} \exp(w^{\Phi_k})}. \tag{14}$$

Equation (14) indicates the contribution of the k - th meta-path Φ_k to the final embedding, and it can be easily seen that if the greater δ^{Φ_k}, the higher the importance of this meta-path. Using the learned weights as coefficients, we can fuse these specific semantic representations to get the final embedding $\mathbf{Z}$ as follows:

$$\mathbf{Z} = \sum_{k=1}^{m} \delta^{\Phi_k} \cdot \mathbf{Z}_{\text{chan}}^{(k)}. \tag{15}$$

4.4 Objective Function

This section still uses the channel where the k - th meta-path is located for the construction of the objective function. For the two independent channel outputs of representations $\mathbf{Z}_{\mathbf{A}}^{(k)}, \mathbf{Z}_{\mathbf{P}}^{(k)}$ and the common convolution modules $\mathbf{Z}_{\mathbf{AX}}^{(k)}, \mathbf{Z}_{\mathbf{PX}}^{(k)}$, this paper is dedicated to designing two constraints that fully capture the consistency and disparity between different representations to further enhance the commonality between representations.

Disparity Constraint. In order to capture the different information between the representations $\mathbf{Z}_{\mathbf{A}}^{(k)}$ and $\mathbf{Z}_{\mathbf{AX}}^{(k)}$, a disparity constraint loss function $\mathcal{L}_{\mathbf{A}}^{(k)}$ is designed. This paper will be use Hilbert-Schmidt Independence Criterion (HSIC) [24], which is an independent measurement method with fast convergence speed. HSIC mainly uses the Hilbert-Schmidt cross-covariance operator, and the empirical estimation of the norm of the operator obtains the independence criterion. The HSIC method used to calculate the disparity constrained loss $\mathcal{L}_{\mathbf{A}}^{(k)}$ is as follows.

$$\mathcal{L}_{\mathbf{A}}^{(k)} = \text{HSIC}\left(\mathbf{Z}_{\mathbf{A}}^{(k)}, \mathbf{Z}_{\mathbf{AX}}^{(k)}\right) = \frac{\text{tr}\left(\mathbf{K}_{\mathbf{A}}^{(k)} \mathbf{H} \mathbf{K}_{\mathbf{AX}}^{(k)} \mathbf{H}\right)}{(n-1)^2}. \tag{16}$$

where $\mathbf{H} = \mathbf{I} - \frac{1}{n}\mathbf{e}\mathbf{e}^{\mathbf{T}}$, $\mathbf{I}$ is an identity matrix, and $\mathbf{e}$ is an all-one column vector. $\mathbf{K}_{\mathbf{A}}^{(k)}$ and $\mathbf{K}_{\mathbf{AX}}^{(k)}$ are the Gram matrix of the observations of $\mathbf{Z}_{\mathbf{A}}^{(k)}$ and $\mathbf{Z}_{\mathbf{AX}}^{(k)}$, they are calculated as follows:

$$\mathbf{K}_{\mathbf{A}_{i,j}}^{(k)} = \text{k}_{\mathbf{A}}^{(k)}\left(\mathbf{Z}_{\mathbf{A}_i}^{(k)}, \mathbf{Z}_{\mathbf{A}_j}^{(k)}\right), \mathbf{K}_{\mathbf{A}_{i,j}\mathbf{X}}^{(k)} = \text{k}_{\mathbf{AX}}^{(k)}\left(\mathbf{z}_{\mathbf{A}_i\mathbf{X}}^{(k)}, \mathbf{z}_{\mathbf{A}_j\mathbf{X}}^{(k)}\right). \tag{17}$$

In the same way, the disparity constraint $\mathcal{L}_{\mathbf{P}}^{(k)}$ calculation method for representations $\mathbf{Z}_{\mathbf{P}}^{(k)}$ and $\mathbf{Z}_{\mathbf{PX}}^{(k)}$ is as follows:

$$\mathcal{L}_{\mathbf{P}}^{(k)} = \text{HSIC}\left(\mathbf{Z}_{\mathbf{P}}^{(k)}, \mathbf{Z}_{\mathbf{PX}}^{(k)}\right) = \frac{\text{tr}\left(\mathbf{K}_{\mathbf{P}}^{(k)} \mathbf{H} \mathbf{K}_{\mathbf{PX}}^{(k)} \mathbf{H}\right)}{(n-1)^2}. \tag{18}$$

Finally, the definition of the disparity constraint loss function $\mathcal{L}_d^{(k)}$ is as follows:

$$\mathcal{L}_d^{(k)} = \mathrm{HSIC}\left(\mathbf{Z}_{\mathbf{P}}^{(k)}, \mathbf{Z}_{\mathbf{PX}}^{(k)}\right) + \mathrm{HSIC}\left(\mathbf{Z}_{\mathbf{A}}^{(k)}, \mathbf{Z}_{\mathbf{AX}}^{(k)}\right). \tag{19}$$

Consistency Constraint. To further enhance the commonality of the common convolution module representation $\mathbf{Z}_{\mathbf{AX}}^{(k)}$ and $\mathbf{Z}_{\mathbf{PX}}^{(k)}$, we design a consistency constraint loss function $\mathcal{L}_C$. We use L_2-normalization to normalize the representation matrix as $\mathbf{Z}_{\mathbf{AX}(norm)}^{(k)}$, $\mathbf{Z}_{\mathbf{PX}(norm)}^{(k)}$. Then, calculate the similarity between the nodes to obtain the similarity matrix $Sim_{\mathbf{AX}}^{(k)}$ and $Sim_{\mathbf{PX}}^{(k)}$. The specific calculation method is as follows:

$$
\begin{aligned}
Sim_{\mathbf{AX}}^{(k)} &= \mathbf{Z}_{\mathbf{AX}(norm)}^{(k)} \cdot (\mathbf{Z}_{\mathbf{AX}(norm)}^{(k)})^{\mathbf{T}} \\
Sim_{\mathbf{PX}}^{(k)} &= \mathbf{Z}_{\mathbf{PX}(norm)}^{(k)} \cdot (\mathbf{Z}_{\mathbf{PX}(norm)}^{(k)})^{\mathbf{T}}
\end{aligned}
\tag{20}
$$

Finally, Constrain the two embedding matrices through the similarity of $Sim_{\mathbf{AX}}^{(k)}$ and $Sim_{\mathbf{PX}}^{(k)}$ to obtain the final consistency loss function $\mathcal{L}_{co}^{(k)}$. The calculation method is as follows:

$$\mathcal{L}_{co}^{(k)} = \left\| Sim_{\mathbf{AX}}^{(k)} - Sim_{\mathbf{PX}}^{(k)} \right\|_F^2. \tag{21}$$

Optimization Objective. In this paper, the final embedding $\mathbf{Z}$ obtained by Eq. (15) is linearly transformed by the Softmax function for multi-label classification tasks, and define the output of predicted labels of n nodes as: $\widehat{\mathbf{Y}} \in \mathbb{R}^{n \times C} = [\hat{y}_{ic}]$, where $\hat{y}_{ic}$ indicates the probability that node v_i is classified into class c. The loss function of the node classification task for the training task is represented by cross entropy [25]:

$$\mathcal{L}_0 = -\frac{1}{|\mathcal{Y}_L|} \sum_{l \in \mathcal{Y}_L} \sum_{i=1}^{C} \mathbf{Y}_{l,i} \ln \widehat{\mathbf{Y}}_{l,i}. \tag{22}$$

where $\mathcal{Y}_L$ is to observe the set of data indices for training, $\mathbf{Y}_{l,i}$ is the real label and $\widehat{\mathbf{Y}}_{l,i}$ is the predicted label. For the cross-entropy loss function, the Adam [26] optimization algorithm is used to minimize the loss, and then the parameters of the model are constantly updated and adjusted, so as to obtain the representation of the low-dimensional node vector. Finally, the node classification loss and constraint conditions are merged to obtain the target loss function as follows:

$$\mathcal{L} = \mathcal{L}_0 + \gamma \sum_{k=1}^{m} \mathcal{L}_{co^{(k)}} + \beta \sum_{k=1}^{m} \mathcal{L}_{d^{(k)}}, \tag{23}$$

where, γ and β are hyper-parameters of consistency constraint and disparity constraint, respectively.

5 Experiments

In this section, we evaluate the proposed HAM-GCN framework in three real-world heterogeneous graphs. We first introduce the datasets and experimental settings, and then we report the model performance as compared to other state-of-the-art competitive methods.

5.1 Datasets

We use the following three real data sets to evaluate our proposed model. The statistics of these data sets are shown in Table 1:

- DBLP [21]: This is a subset of the DBLP-V8 datasets, containing 14,328 papers (P), 4057 authors (A), 20 conferences (C), and 8789 terms (T). Each author submits a conference label for his research field. Node features are terms related to papers, authors, and conferences, and meta-path {APA, APCPA, APTPA} is used to conduct experiments.
- ACM [21]: The datasets contains 3025 papers (P), 5835 authors (A), and 56 conference topics (S). Papers are labeled based on the conference's publication. Paper features correspond to elements of a bag-of-words represented of keywords, and the dimension is 1830. The node characteristics are composed of keywords. We extracted 2 meta-paths {PAP, PSP} from this graph to experiment.
- Yelp [23]: The datasets contains 2614 businesses (B), 1286 users (U), 4 services (S), and 9 rating levels (L). Business nodes are marked according to their category. The node feature is composed of the phrase representation of the keyword. We used meta-path {BUB, BSB, BUBLB, BUBSB} to carry out the experiment.

Table 1. Statistics of the datasets.

Dataset	Node-type	Nodes	Edge-Type	Edges	Feature	Label	Meta-Path
DBLP	Author(A)	4057	A-P	19645	334	4	APA
	Paper(P)	14328	P-C	14325			APCPA
	Conference(C)	20	P-T	88420			APTPA
	Term(T)	8789					
ACM	Paper(P)	3025	P-A	9744	1830	3	PAP
	Author(A)	5835	P-S	3025			PSP
	Subject(S)	56					
Yelp	Business(B)	2614	B-U	12838	82	3	BUB
	User(U)	1286	B-S	4280			BSB
	Service(S)	4	B-L	20529			BUBLB
	Level(L)	2614					BUBSB

5.2 Baseline Methods

We select algorithms for homogeneous and heterogeneous information networks as baseline methods. These methods include unsupervised and supervised ones, and some of them can deal with networks with attributes, while others just can deal with networks without attributes.

Methods for Homogeneous Graphs

Five methods, DeepWalk, ANRL, GCN, DGCN, AM-GCN, are for homogeneous graphs. We run these algorithms on the graph ignoring the heterogeneity of nodes and graphs constructed from every meta-path based adjacency matrix respectively, then report the best result.

- DeepWalk [15]: A random walk-based network embedding method, which is designed for homogeneous graphs without attributes. Here we ignore the heterogeneity and perform DeepWalk on the whole heterogeneous graph.
- ANRL [27]: A single encoder is used to encode node attribute information, and multiple decoders are used to simultaneously construct local structure information and global structure information, so that the final hidden layer can retain certain attribute information through the encoder and obtain some topological structure through the decoder.
- GCN [7]: A semi-supervised graph convolutional network embedding model for homogeneous attribute graphs. GCN integrates node attributes and structural information through a neighborhood aggregation scheme to learn representations of nodes.
- DGCN [8]: A semi-supervised dual GCN for homogeneous attribute graph learning, where two convolutional neural networks are employed to perform graph convolution for embedding the local-consistency-based and global-consistency-based knowledge respectively.
- AM-GCN [10]: A semi-supervised adaptive multi-channel GCN embedding model for homogeneous attribute graphs. AM-GCN extracts the specific and common representation from node features, topological structures, and their combinations simultaneously, and uses the attention mechanism to learn adaptively important weights of the representation.

Methods for Heterogeneous Graphs

- DMGI [28]: A mutual information-based unsupervised network embedding method for attribute multiplex network, which integrates the representation from multiple graphs corresponding to multiple types of relationships between nodes through a consistent regularization framework and a general discriminator.
- HAN [21]: A semi-supervised graph neural network embedding model for HIN. HAN uses the specified meta-path to capture neighbor nodes with different semantic relationships in the network and then employs node-level and semantic-level attentions

to distinguish the importance of different nodes and meta-paths in the process of aggregating neighbor information.

- HeGAN [23]: An adversarial learning-based semi-supervised HIN embedding model, which trains both a relation-aware discriminator and a generalized generator in a minimax game to capture the rich semantics on HINs.

Parameters Setting. In this paper, we use the currently popular deep learning framework PyTorch to implement the coding of the HAM-GCN model and its variants. For these models, we optimize the proposed model using Adam optimizer[26]and the learning rate is set to {0.0005 –0.001}. In the proposed methods, the embedding dimensions of channel-level vector and semantic-level attention vector are both 128, with a dropout rate of 0.5. The coefficient of consistency constraint and disparity constraints are searched in {0.0001,0.001,0.01}and {1e−10, 1e−9,1e−8}. The comparison algorithms in this paper are all initialized with the same parameters suggested in their paper, and the parameters are carefully adjusted to obtain the best performance. All experiments for each algorithm are executed under Ubuntu 18.04 platform with RTX-3090ti GPU and i7-11700K CPU.

5.3   Experimental Results

Node Classification Task. In the node classification task, we conduct the experiments with different training-ratios (10%, 20%, 50%), i.e., 10%, 20%, 50% of the nodes are randomly selected as the training set and the rest of the nodes are used as the test set. As an end-to-end model, the semi-supervised learning methods can directly output the classification result, while for unsupervised methods, we train an SVM [29] classifier to predict labels of nodes. The classifier is trained by using 5-fold cross-validation and the classification process is repeated 10 times. The performance of classification is evaluated by the average Macro-F1 and Micro-F1. The detailed results are shown in Table 2, where bold numbers indicate the best results.

Table 2. Performance evaluation (%) of node classification

Datasets	Type	Methods	10%		20%		50%	
			Mi-F1	Ma-F1	Mi-F1	Ma-F1	Mi-F1	Ma-F1
ACM	A	DeepWalk	80.32	80.65	81.65	81.34	82.77	81.98
	X, A	ANRL	87.23	87.03	87.34	87.28	88.12	88.07
		DMGI	86.45	86.13	87.63	87.49	88.43	88.12
	X, A, Y	HAN	88.72	88.58	88.94	88.82	89.56	89.36
		DGCN	88.34	88.06	88.83	88.54	89.44	88.87
		GCN	86.54	86.18	87.84	87.76	88.54	88.32
		HeGAN	87.94	87.28	88.87	88.54	89.41	89.68

(*continued*)

Table 2. (*continued*)

Datasets	Type	Methods	10%		20%		50%	
			Mi-F1	Ma-F1	Mi-F1	Ma-F1	Mi-F1	Ma-F1
		AM-GCN	87.50	87.18	90.81	90.74	91.10	91.06
		HAM-GCN	**91.54**	**91.37**	**92.44**	**92.03**	**93.29**	**93.18**
DBLP	A	DeepWalk	87.24	86.89	89.13	88.00	90.12	90.56
	X, A	ANRL	86.45	86.13	87.63	87.49	88.43	88.12
		DMGI	89.95	89.18	90.48	90.87	91.50	91.19
	X, A, Y	HAN	91.21	91.21	92.28	91.38	92.47	91.55
		DGCN	89.99	89.32	90.40	90.08	91.71	90.92
		GCN	83.87	82.49	84.44	83.38	86.23	86.01
		HeGAN	89.21	88.88	89.70	89.39	90.33	90.02
		AM-GCN	90.80	89.71	91.10	90.86	91.80	91.85
		HAM-GCN	**91.88**	**91.64**	**92.42**	**92.71**	**93.24**	**93.17**
YELP	A	DeepWalk	73.16	68.68	75.28	70.34	77.12	72.48
	X, A	ANRL	82.45	82.13	82.63	82.49	83.43	83.12
		DMGI	87.71	87.97	87.87	87.81	88.27	88.81
	X, A, Y	HAN	87.81	87.58	88.86	88.49	89.54	89.26
		DGCN	85.51	85.79	85.94	85.89	87.39	88.06
		GCN	85.22	82.52	85.89	83.47	87.78	85.21
		HeGAN	85.44	85.56	86.39	86.44	86.86	86.40
		AM-GCN	85.10	84.37	85.60	85.21	86.90	86.51
		HAM-GCN	**89.96**	**89.57**	**90.11**	**90.34**	**92.67**	**92.63**

From Table 2, we have the following observations and analyses:

- With excellent adaptive learning HIN embeddings capability, HAM-GCN achieves the best classification results on the three datasets, this demonstrates the effectiveness of our proposed model.
- Among single network algorithms, the performance of DeepWalk is relative worst. Because the model only uses topological structure information and does not use feature attributes to learn network representations. This indicates that the feature information of nodes in a HIN helps improve the accuracy of node vectors in classification tasks.
- Compared with single network GNN algorithms, the heterogeneous GNN methods (i.e., HAM-GCN, HAN, DMGI) have better performance, especially by comparing HAM-GCN with AM-GCN, because HAM-GCN can alleviate the problem of heterogeneity and fuse information from every single network. In addition, most of the semi-supervised learning methods in the experiments get higher performance than

the unsupervised learning methods, which indicates that using label information can better improve classification effectiveness.

5.4 Ablation Study

In this section, we will compare HAM-GCN and its six variants on the ACM dataset from different perspectives to verify the effectiveness of the HAM-GCN model. The specific variants are descripted as follows:

- HAM-GCN-CL: HAM-GCN without channel-level attention weights, i.e. each channel is assumed to have the same weight.
- HAM-GCN-SL: HAM-GCN without semantic-level attention weights, that is to say the low-dimensional representation of each meta-path is assumed to be equally important.
- HAM-GCN-W: HAM-GCN whose parameters in the common convolution module are not shared.
- HAM-GCN-C: HAM-GCN only considers the shared consistency constraint $\mathcal{L}_c$, without consideration of the disparity constraint $\mathcal{L}_d$.
- HAM-GCN-D: HAM-GCN only considers the disparity constraint $\mathcal{L}_c$, without consideration of the shared consistency constraint $\mathcal{L}_c$.
- HAM-GCN-C/D: HAM-GCN without disparity constraint $\mathcal{L}_d$ and consistency constraint $\mathcal{L}_c$.

The above variants are divided into three categories. The first category includes HAM-GCN-CL and HAM-GCN-S, which are variants of the attention module, designed to verify the effectiveness of the attention layer. The second category includes HAM-GCN-W, which is a variant of the parameter sharing module. This kind of variant is designed to verify the effectiveness of using the parameter sharing mechanism. The third category includes HAM-GCN-C, HAM-GCN-D and HAM-GCN-C/D, which are designed to verify the effectiveness of difference loss and consistency loss constraints.

The experiment results of HAM-GCN and its six variants in ACM dataset are shown in Table 3, where the boldface indicates the highest performance metrics. The following conclusions can be shown by observing Table 3:

- It can be seen from the comparison of HAM-GCN, HAM-GCN-CL and HAM-GCN-SL, the performance indicators of HAM-GCN are better than those of the two variant models, indicating that assigning weights for different levels of attention mechanisms can fully capture the importance of node embedding from each different channels and meta-paths.
- The comparison results of HAM-GCN and HAM-GCN-W show that designing a common convolution module with shared parameters can fully capture the consistent information of the topological structure and feature structure, and the learned low-dimensional embedding can improve the performance of the node classification task.
- By comparing HAM-GCN and its three variants, i.e. HAM-GCN-C, HAM-GCN-D and HAM-GCN-C/D, we can find that the HAM-GCN-C/D, without disparity constraint $\mathcal{L}_d$ and consistency constraint $\mathcal{L}_c$, has the worst performance. Then, the

performance of HAM-GCN-C and HAM-GCN-D are also lower than that of HAM-GCN, which fully verifies the effectiveness of the co-use of the consistency constraint and the disparity constraint designed in this paper.

Table 3. The experiment results of HAM-GCN and its six variants in ACM dataset.

Datasets	Methods	10%		20%		50%	
		Mi-F1	Ma-F1	Mi-F1	Ma-F1	Mi-F1	Ma-F1
ACM	HAM-GCN-CL	87.53	87.39	89.80	89.59	91.02	90.93
	HAM-GCN-SL	87.54	87.44	90.70	90.62	91.10	91.00
	HAM-GCN-W	87.55	87.35	89.91	89.79	90.84	90.77
	HAM-GCN-C	87.90	87.77	90.89	90.81	91.86	91.82
	HAM-GCN-D	87.61	87.50	90.69	90.60	91.05	90.99
	HAM-GCN-C/D	85.04	84.88	87.95	87.87	89.40	89.33
	HAM-GCN	**91.54**	**91.37**	**92.44**	**92.03**	**93.29**	**93.18**

5.5 Hyper-parameter Study

In the HAM-GCN model, the hyper-parameters γ and β are used for the weights of the consistency constraint loss and the difference loss, respectively. This subsection studies the influence of hyper-parameters on classification performance on ACM data set.

The Hyper-parameter γ of The Consistency Constraint Loss. To explore the influence of hyper-parameter γ (the consistency constraint weight in Eq. (23)) on classification performance, we train HAM-GCN under different γ varying from 0 to 100 and carry out classification task in the ACM data set. The Micro-F1 and Macro-F1 values with respect to different training-ratios (10%, 20%, 50%) are shown in Fig. 2. From which, we can see that both Micro-F1 and Macro-F1 values are basically stable, and curves show similar trends under different training-ratios.

The Hyper-parameter β of The Disparity Constraint Loss. To explore the influence of hyper-parameter β (the different constraint weight β in Eq. (23)) on classification performance, we train HAM-GCN under different β varying from 1e-10 to 0.0001 and carry out classification task in the ACM data set. The Micro-F1 and Macro-F1 values with respect to different training-ratios (10%, 20%, 50%) are shown in Fig. 3. From which, we can see that both Micro-F1 and Macro-F1 values are basically stable when β is less than 1e−6, but the performance drops rapidly when β is greater than 1e−6.

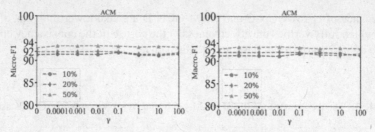

Fig. 2. The Micro-F1 and Macro-F1 values under different γ, where $\beta = 0$

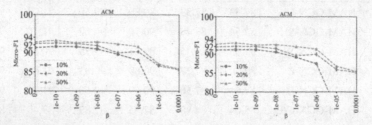

Fig. 3. The Micro-F1 and Macro-F1 values under different β, where $\gamma = 0.001$

5.6 Visualization

For more intuitively demonstrate the effectiveness of the proposed model, we use the t-SNE [30] dimensionality reduction technique on the DBLP dataset to visualize the embeddings learned by HAM-GCN and its five baseline comparison algorithms in a 2D space. The visualization results are shown in Fig. 4. Where the color of a point indicates the class label.

By observing Fig. 4, we can see that HAM-GCN visualization performance is the best, the nodes of the same color in the layout are close to each other, nodes of different colors are far away from each other, and have a clear separation boundary. In the subfigures (a), (b) and (c), corresponding to DeepWalk, ANRL, and GCN, nodes of different colors are clustered together, and the boundary is not clearly separated. Although the separation boundary between DGCN and HAN is clear, some points with the same color are not apart far from, for example, blue points in (d) and yellow points in (e). The visualization results once again prove the effectiveness of the multi-channel adaptive heterogeneous network representation learning model HAM-GCN.

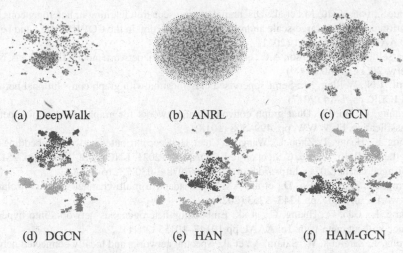

(a) DeepWalk   (b) ANRL   (c) GCN

(d) DGCN   (e) HAN   (f) HAM-GCN

Fig. 4. Visualization of different embeddings on the DBLP dataset

6 Conclusion

In this paper, we propose an adaptive multichannel graph convolution for heterogeneous information network representation learning, called HAM-GCN. It first constructs the adjacency matrices based on different meta-paths and introduces the PPMI matrices to encode the node semantic information, and then uses a multi-channel GCN model to learn the low-dimensional representations of nodes. In addition, it adopts multi-level attention mechanism to self-learn weights with respect to different channels and meta-paths for obtaining the final representations, which can be used in various downstream tasks [31]. Expensive experimental results validate the effectiveness of HAM-GCN on classification task.

Acknowledgments. This work was supported by the National Natural Science Foundation of China (62062066, 61762090, 61966036), Yunnan Fundamental Research Projects (202201AS070015), University Key Laboratory of Internet of Things Technology and Application of Yunnan Province, and the Postgraduate Research and Innovation Foundation of Yunnan University (2021Y024).

References

1. Cui, P., Wang, X., Pei, J., et al.: A survey on network embedding. IEEE Trans. Knowl. Data Eng. **31**(5), 833–852 (2019)
2. Zhang, D., Yin, J., Zhu, X., et al.: Network representation learning: a survey. IEEE Trans. Big Data **6**(1), 3–28 (2020)
3. Wu, J., He, J., Xu, J.: DEMO-Net: degree-specific graph neural networks for node and graph classification. In: KDD, pp 406–415 (2019)
4. Tu, W., Zhou, S., Liu, X., et al.: Deep fusion clustering network. In: AAAI, pp. 9978–9987 (2021)

5. Hou, S., Fan, Y., Ju, M., et al.: Disentangled representation learning in heterogeneous information network for large-scale android malware detection in the COVID-19 era and beyond. In: AAAI, pp 7754–7761 (2021)
6. Scarselli, F., Gori, M., Tsoi, A.C., et al.: The graph neural network model. IEEE Trans. Neural Netw. **20**(1), 61–80 (2009)
7. Kipf, T.N., Welling, M.: Semi-supervised classification with graph convolutional networks. In: ICLR, pp. 1–14 (2017)
8. Zhuang, C, Ma, Q.: Dual graph convolutional networks for graph-based semi-supervised classification. In: WWW, pp. 499–508 (2018)
9. Dong, K., Huang, T., Zhou, L., Wang, L., Chen, H.: Deep attributed network embedding based on the PPMI. In: Jensen, C.S., et al. (eds.) DASFAA 2021. LNCS, vol. 12680, pp. 251–266. Springer, Cham (2021). https://doi.org/10.1007/978-3-030-73216-5_18
10. Wang, X., Zhu, M., Bo, D., et al.: AM-GCN: adaptive multi-channel graph convolutional networks. In: KDD, pp 1243–1253 (2020)
11. Wang, L., Gao, C., Huang, C., et al.: Embedding heterogeneous networks into hyperbolic space without meta-path. In: AAAI, pp 10147–10155 (2021)
12. Bruna, J., Zaremba, W., Szlam, A., et al.: Spectral networks and locally connected networks on graphs. In: ICLR (2014)
13. Defferrard, M., Bresson X, Vandergheynst P.: Convolutional neural networks on graphs with fast localized spectral filtering. In: NIPS, pp 3837–3845 (2016)
14. Monti, F., Boscaini, D., Masci, J., et al.: Geometric deep learning on graphs and manifolds using mixture model CNNs. In: CVPR, pp 5425–5434 (2017)
15. Perozzi, B., Al-Rfou, R., Skiena, S.: DeepWalk: online learning of social representations. In: KDD, pp 701–710 (2014)
16. Onrust, L., Bosch, A.V.D., Hamme, H.V.: Improving cross-domain n-gram language modelling with skipgrams. In: ACL, vol. 2 (2016)
17. Grover, A., Leskovec, J.: node2vec: scalable feature learning for networks. In: KDD, pp 855–864 (2016)
18. Tang, J., Qu, M., Wang, M., et al.: Large-scale information network embedding. In: WWW, pp 1067–1077 (2015)
19. Yang, C., Liu, Z., Zhao, D., et al.: Network representation learning with rich text information. In: IJCAI, pp 2111–2117 (2015)
20. Fu, T.-Y., Lee, W.-C., Lei, Z.: HIN2Vec: explore meta-paths in heterogeneous information networks for representation learning. In: CIKM, pp 1797–1806 (2017)
21. Wang, X., Ji, H., Shi, C., et al.: Heterogeneous graph attention network. In: WWW, pp 2022–2032 (2019)
22. Ren, Y., Liu, B., Huang, C., et al.: Heterogeneous deep graph infomax. CoRR, abs/1911.08538 (2019)
23. Hu, B., Fang, Y., Shi, C.: Adversarial learning on heterogeneous information networks. In: KDD, pp 120–129 (2019)
24. Greenfeld, D., Shalit, U.: Robust learning with the hilbert-schmidt independence criterion. In: ICML, pp 3759–3768 (2020)
25. Du, C., Tu, Z., Jiang. J.: Order-agnostic cross entropy for non-autoregressive machine translation. In: ICML, pp 2849–2859 (2021)
26. Kingma, D.P., Ba, J.: Adam: a method for stochastic optimization. In: ICLR (2015)
27. Zhang, Z., Yang, H., Bu, J., et al.: ANRL: attributed network representation learning via deep neural networks. In: IJCAI, pp. 3155–3161 (2018)
28. Park, C., Han, J., Yu, H.: Deep multiplex graph infomax: attentive multiplex network embedding using global information. Knowl. Based Syst. **197**, 105861 (2020)
29. Cortes, C., Jackel, L.D., Solla, S.A., et al.: Learning curves: asymptotic values and rate of convergence. In: NIPS, pp. 327–334 (1993)

30. Laurens, V.D.M., Hinton, G.: Visualizing data using t-SNE. J. Mach. Learn. Res. **9**(2605), 2579–2605 (2008)
31. Wang, L., Fang, Y., Zhou, L.: Preference-based spatial co-location pattern mining. In: Big Data Management. Springer, Singapore (2022). https://doi.org/10.1007/978-981-16-7566-9(2022)

GWmodelS: A High-Performance Computing Framework for Geographically Weighted Models

Binbin Lu[1,2] and Guanpeng Dong[3,4,5]([✉])

[1] School of Remote Sensing and Information Engineering, Wuhan University, Wuhan, China
[2] Geocomputation Centre for Social Science, Wuhan University, Wuhan, China
[3] Key Research Institute of Yellow River Civilization and Sustainable Development, Henan University, Kaifeng 475001, China
gpdong@vip.henu.edu.cn
[4] Collaborative Innovation Center on Yellow River Civilization Jointly Built by Henan Province and Ministry of Education, Henan University, Kaifeng 475001, China
[5] Key Laboratory of Geospatial Technology for the Middle and Lower Yellow River Regions, Ministry of Education, Kaifeng, China

Abstract. Spatial heterogeneity or non-stationarity is a prominent characteristic of data relationships. In line with Tobler's first law of geography, a number of local statistics or local models have been proposed to explore spatial heterogeneities in spatial patterns or relationships. A particular branch of spatial statistics, termed geographically weighted (GW) models have evolved to encompass local techniques applicable in situations when data are not described well by such global models. Typical GW models and techniques include GW regression, GW descriptive statistics, GW principal components analysis, GW discriminant analysis, GW visualization techniques and GW artificial neural network. These GW models form a generic, open, and continually evolving technical framework to explore spatial heterogeneities from a wide range of disciplines in the natural and social sciences. In this study, we present a high-performance computing framework to incorporate the GW models with parallel computing techniques. We developed a software, namely **GWmodelS** to facilitate a flexible implementation of GW models. This study describes the procedures of geospatial data management, parameter optimization, model calibration and result visualization associated with **GWmodelS**. This software provides free services for scientific research and educational courses in the related domains.

Keywords: Spatial statistics · Spatial heterogeneity · GWR · Exploratory data analysis · CUDA

1 Introduction

Geographical phenomena and processes tend to present complex and diverse patterns in different study area, i.e. spatially heterogeneous or non-stationary characteristics [1]. Thus, local techniques, assuming data relationships to be spatially variant have been

H. Wu et al. (Eds.): SpatialDI 2022, LNCS 13614, pp. 154–161, 2022.
https://doi.org/10.1007/978-3-031-24521-3_11

extensively developed rather than unrealistically regarding them being constant across the study region [2], In line with Tobler's first law of geography [3], Geographically Weighted Regression (GWR) was proposed to investigates spatial non-stationarity in data relationships by incorporating spatial weights into the model calibration process to represent and highlight larger influences of nearby observations in each local regression estimation [4, 5]. It has been become an important local technique and widely applied in studies of regional economics [6], urban planning [7], sociology [8], ecology [9], public health [10] and environmental science [11]. The GWR technique itself has been also largely extended, like generalized GWR [12], multiscale GWR [13–15], robust GWR [16], heteroskedsatic GWR[17], contextualized GWR [18] and geographically and temporally weighted regression [19].

Complying with a hypothetical 'bump of influence' of GWR [17] – for each calibration location, nearer observations were assigned to larger influences in the estimation of local regression coefficients – a particular branch of spatial statistics, termed geographically weighted (GW) models have evolved to encompass a number of local techniques, offering location-wise calculations or estimates for spatially fine-grained descriptions. In addition to GWR and its extensions, GW descriptive statistics [20, 21], GW principal components analysis [17, 22], GW discriminant analysis [23, 24], GW visualization techniques [25] and GW artificial neural network [26, 27] are also developed for covering pluralistic data analysis demands. These GW models form a generic, open, and continually evolving technical framework to explore spatial heterogeneities from a wide range of disciplines and application scenarios.

There are a number of software or packages to provide tools of GW models, mainly focusing on the GWR technique. For instance, GWR3.X [28], GWR4.0 [29] and MGWR [30] provides standalone software for GWR and its extensions. Notably, there are a range of R packages incorporating the GW models listed above, including **spgwr** [31], **mgwrsar** [32], **GWLelast** [33], **spMoran** [34], **gwer** [35], **lctools** [36] and **gwrr** [37]. In particular, an R package namely **GWmodel** [38, 39] incorporated a wide range of GW models or techniques, including GW summary statistics, GW principal components analysis, GW discriminant analysis and various forms of GW regression techniques. As show in Fig. 1, it has been downloaded more than 130,000 times (counted via the R package **cranlogs**) in total, and more than 1500 monthly downloads since 2020.

Despite its popularity, the usage of **GWmodel** is stuck with issues in convenience and computational efficiency. On the one hand, users are required to know the functions well and program with them, which is usually not an easy task for applied researchers. On the other hand, the computational efficiency of **GWmodel** is continually challenged by the greatly increased volume of spatial data sets due to the natural limitation of R, although high-performance solutions have been expediently developed [40]. In this study, we introduce an open, user-friendly and high-performance computational framework to integrate GW models and encapsulate them as a stand-alone software, namely *GWmodelS*.

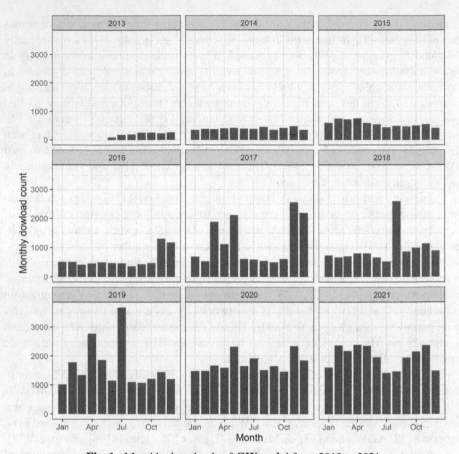

Fig. 1. Monthly downloads of **GWmodel** from 2013 to 2021

2 Development Architecture of GWmodelS

As shown in Fig. 1, we developed **GWmodelS** with C++ programming language, in which four core modules are designed: data/layer management, mapping tools, generic options and GW models. We adopted functions from the geospatial data abstraction library (GDAL) [41] for convenient data operations, QGIS libraries [42] for geovisualization and mapping, and Armadillo C++ library [43] for linear algebra and scientific computing functions. These dependencies largely simplify the subsequent development and integration of new GW modelling tools. In **GWmodelS,** we provide three computational options, i.e. stand-alone, open multi-processing (Open-MP) and the compute unified device architecture (CUDA) solutions, which enables a well fit of application cases with spatial data of various volumes. Note that the former two options have been achieved, while the latter technique with a graphics processing unit (GPU) device is currently under development.

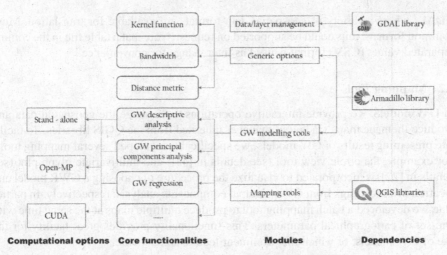

Fig. 2. Development architecture of **GWmodelS**

Fig. 3. The main interface of **GWmodelS**

3   Modules of GWmodelS

As shown in Fig. 2 ang Fig. 3, four main modules are designed in **GWmodelS**, i.e.
data/layer management, mapping tools, generic options and GW models. In this section,
their development will be briefly introduced here.

3.1   Data/layer Management

In **GWmodelS**, the module of data/layer management is developed for handling geospatial data, and currently ESRI shape file, GeoJOSN and GPKG formats could be imported
and exported in a straightforward way. This module is primarily developed from the

GDAL, where a variety of geospatial data formats are available for translation. More common formats, thus could be supported on request. Note that a table file in the comma separated values (CSV) format is used as interchange for convenience.

3.2 Mapping Tools

In **GWmodelS**, we provide interactive operations to visualize the geospatial data and produce thematic maps via layout manager inherited from the QGIS libraries. To facilitate presenting results of GW models, we specifically developed several mapping tools. For example, the circle view tool (see details in [44]) and multivariate glyph plot (see details in [22]) is incorporated to visualize the procedure of choosing a GWR model and location-wise loadings from GW principal components analysis, respectively. In particular, we developed a batch mapping tool to produce multiple maps at the same time with one-set of cartographical parameters. This functionality provides great facility for the use of GW models, of which the prominent feature is mappable.

3.3 Generic Options for GW Models

The essence of a GW model is to conduct location-wise calculations or calibrations by concerning a hypothetical 'bump of influence' via spatial distance-decaying weights. In this sense, distance metric, kernel function and its key parameter (i.e. bandwidth) are three key components for calculating spatial weight, which is fundamental for any GW model. Thus, we developed a substantial collection of options for the three components in **GWmodelS**. In details, flexible choices of distance metrics, including Euclidean distance, great circle distance, Minkowski distance [45], space-time distance [19], network distance [44] and flow distance [46] are available for calibrating GW models. With distances calculated, we provided common choices of kernel functions, including Gaussian, Exponential, Box-car, Bi-square and Tricube, and for each specific kernel function, a fixed or adaptive, optimized or predetermined bandwidth could be defined for various application scenarios.

3.4 GW Models

AS the most important module, **GWmodelS** provide a number of GW models in the current release of **GWmodelS**, including GW descriptive statistics, GW principal components analysis, GW regression and its extensions with applicable to large-scale data set [47], multiscale GW regression [14, 15], geographically and temporally weighted regression [19], robust GW regression [16] and generalized GW regression[12]. The integration of these GW models makes a good start and surely more and more GW models or techniques shall be made available in **GWmodelS**.

4   Concluding Remarks

In this study, we present an open, high-performance and user-friendly computation framework of GW models, namely **GWmodelS**. Four modules are mainly incorporated to cover the entire procedure of conducting a GW model, include geospatial data management, parameter optimization, model calibration and result visualization. The latest release of **GWmodelS** could be downloaded from the URL (http://gwmodel.whu.edu.cn/#/gwmodels/software). Note that there are only a limited number of GW models incorporated, but surely it is not an end but a start open to integrate more and more GW models or techniques in the near future.

Acknowledgements. This study is jointly funded by the National Natural Science Foundation of China (42071368; 42001115) and Hubei Provincial Key Research and Development Program (2021BAA185).

References

1. Goodchild, M.F.: The validity and usefulness of laws in geographic information science and geography. Ann. Assoc. Am. Geogr. **94**(2), 300–303 (2004)
2. Fotheringham, A.S., Brunsdon, C.: Local forms of spatial analysis. Geogr. Anal. **31**(4), 340–358 (1999)
3. Tobler, W.R.: A computer movie simulating urban growth in the detroit region. Econ. Geogr. **46**(2), 234–240 (1970)
4. Brunsdon, C., Fotheringham, A.S., Charlton, M.E.: Geographically weighted regression: a method for exploring spatial nonstationarity. Geogr. Anal. **28**(4), 281–298 (1996)
5. Fotheringham, A.S., Charlton, M.E., Brunsdon, C.: Geographically weighted regression: a natural evolution of the expansion method for spatial data analysis. Environ Plan A **30**(11), 1905–1927 (1998)
6. Cao, K., Diao, M., Wu, B.: A big data-based geographically weighted regression model for public housing prices: a case study in Singapore. Ann. Am. Assoc. Geogr. **109**(1), 173–186 (2019)
7. Cao, X., Liu, Y., Li, T., Liao, W.: Analysis of spatial pattern evolution and influencing factors of regional land use efficiency in China based on ESDA-GWR. Scientific Reports **9**(1), 520 (2019)
8. Yin, C., He, Q., Liu, Y., Chen, W., Gao, Y.: Inequality of public health and its role in spatial accessibility to medical facilities in China. Appl. Geogr. **92**, 50–62 (2018)
9. Liu, S., Dong, Y., Sun, Y., Li, J., An, Y., Shi, F.: Modelling the spatial pattern of biodiversity utilizing the high-resolution tree cover data at large scale: case study in Yunnan province, Southwest China. Ecol. Eng. **134**, 1–8 (2019)
10. Xu, G., Wang, W., Lu, D., Lu, B., Qin, K., Jiao, L.: Geographically varying relationships between population flows from Wuhan and COVID-19 cases in Chinese cities. In: Geo-spatial Information Science, pp. 1–11 (2021)
11. Xiao, R., Cao, W., Liu, Y., Lu, B.: The impacts of landscape patterns spatio-temporal changes on land surface temperature from a multi-scale perspective: a case study of the Yangtze River Delta. Sci. Total Environ. **821**, 153381 (2022)
12. Nakaya, T., Fotheringham, A.S., Brunsdon, C., Charlton, M.: Geographically weighted Poisson regression for disease association mapping. Stat. Med. **24**(17), 2695–2717 (2005)
13. Lu, B., Brunsdon, C., Charlton, M., Harris, P.: A response to 'A comment on geographically weighted regression with parameter-specific distance metrics.' Int. J. Geogr. Inf. Sci. **33**(7), 1300–1312 (2019)
14. Lu, B., Brunsdon, C., Charlton, M., Harris, P.: Geographically weighted regression with parameter-specific distance metrics. Int. J. Geogr. Inf. Sci. **31**(5), 982–998 (2017)

15. Fotheringham, A.S., Yang, W., Kang, W.: Multiscale geographically weighted regression (MGWR). Ann. Am. Assoc. Geogr. **107**(6), 1247–1265 (2017)

16. Harris, P., Fotheringham, A.S., Juggins, S.: Robust geographically weighted regression: a technique for quantifying spatial relationships between freshwater acidification critical loads and catchment attributes. Ann. Assoc. Am. Geogr. **100**(2), 286–306 (2010)

17. Fotheringham, A.S., Brunsdon, C., Charlton, M.: Geographically Weighted Regression: The Analysis of Spatially Varying Relationships. Wiley, Hoboken (2002)

18. Harris, R., Dong, G., Zhang, W.: Using contextualized geographically weighted regression to model the spatial heterogeneity of land prices in Beijing, China. Trans. GIS **17**(6), 901–919 (2013)

19. Huang, B., Wu, B., Barry, M.: Geographically and temporally weighted regression for modeling spatio-temporal variation in house prices. Int. J. Geogr. Inf. Sci. **24**(3), 383–401 (2010)

20. Brunsdon, C., Fotheringham, A.S., Charlton, M.: Geographically weighted summary statistics – a framework for localised exploratory data analysis. Comput. Environ. Urban Syst. **26**(6), 501–524 (2002)

21. Harris, P., Charlton, M., Fotheringham, A.: Moving window kriging with geographically weighted variograms. Stoch. Env. Res. Risk Assess. **24**(8), 1193–1209 (2010)

22. Harris, P., Brunsdon, C., Charlton, M.: Geographically weighted principal components analysis. Int. J. Geogr. Inf. Sci. **25**(10), 1717–1736 (2011)

23. Foley, P., Demšar, U.: Using geovisual analytics to compare the performance of geographically weighted discriminant analysis versus its global counterpart, linear discriminant analysis. Int. J. Geogr. Inf. Sci. **27**(4), 633–661 (2012)

24. Brunsdon, C., Fotheringham, S., Charlton, M.: Geographically weighted discriminant analysis. Geogr. Anal. **39**(4), 376–396 (2007)

25. Dykes, J., Brunsdon, C.: Geographically weighted visualisation: Interactive graphics for scale-varying exploratory analysis. IEEE Trans. Vis. Comput. Graph. **13**, 1161–1168 (2007)

26. Hagenauer, J., Helbich, M.: A geographically weighted artificial neural network. Int. J. Geogr. Inf. Sci. **36**, 1–21 (2021)

27. Du, Z., Wang, Z., Wu, S., Zhang, F., Liu, R.: Geographically neural network weighted regression for the accurate estimation of spatial non-stationarity. Int. J. Geogr. Inf. Sci. **34**(7), 1353–1377 (2020)

28. Charlton, M., Fotheringham, A.S., Brunsdon, C.: Geographically weighted regression: software for GWR. National Centre for Geocomputation (2007)

29. Nakaya, T., Charlton, M., Fotheringham, S., Brunsdon, C.: How to use SGWRWIN (GWR4.0). National Centre for Geocomputation (2009)

30. Li, Z., Oshan, T., Fotheringham, S., Kang, W., Wolf, L., Yu, H., Luo, W.: MGWR 1.0 User Manual. Arizona State University (2019)

31. Bivand, R., Yu, D.: Package 'spgwr' 0.6–34. CRAN (2020)

32. Geniaux, G., Martinetti, D.: A new method for dealing simultaneously with spatial autocorrelation and spatial heterogeneity in regression models. Reg. Sci. Urban Econ. **72**, 74–85 (2018)

33. Yoneoka, D., Saito, E., Nakaoka, S.: New algorithm for constructing area-based index with geographical heterogeneities and variable selection: an application to gastric cancer screening. Sci. Rep. **6**(1), 26582 (2016)

34. Murakami, D.: spmoran: An R package for Moran's eigenvector-based spatial regression analysis. arXiv, 2017, 1703.04467v3

35. Araujo, Y.A., Cysneiros, F.J.A., Cysneiros, A.H.M.A.: gwer: Geographically Weighted Elliptical Regression (2020)

36. Kalogirou, S.: lctools: Local Correlation, Spatial Inequalities, Geographically Weighted Regression and Other Tools. CRAN (2020)

37. Wheeler, D.: gwrr: Fits Geographically Weighted Regression Models with Diagnostic Tools. R package version 0.2–1 (2013)
38. Lu, B., Harris, P., Charlton, M., Brunsdon, C.: The GWmodel R package: further topics for exploring spatial heterogeneity using geographically weighted models. Geo-spatial Inf. Sci. **17**(2), 85–101 (2014)
39. Gollini, I., Lu, B., Charlton, M., Brunsdon, C., Harris, P.: GWmodel: an R package for exploring spatial heterogeneity using geographically weighted models. J. Stat. Softw. **63**(17), 1–50 (2015)
40. Lu, B., Hu, Y., Murakami, D., Brunsdon, C., Comber, A., Charlton, M., Harris, P.: High-performance solutions of geographically weighted regression in R. Geo-spatial Inf. Sci., 1–14 (2022)
41. GDAL/OGR contributors: GDAL/OGR Geospatial Data Abstraction software Library. Open Source Geospatial Foundation (2022)
42. QGIS.org: QGIS 3.22. Geographic Information System Developers Manual. QGIS Association (2022)
43. Sanderson, C., Curtin, R.: Armadillo: a template-based C++ library for linear algebra. J. Open Source Softw. **1**, 1–26 (2016)
44. Lu, B., Charlton, M., Harris, P., Fotheringham, A.S.: Geographically weighted regression with a non-Euclidean distance metric: a case study using hedonic house price data. Int. J. Geogr. Inf. Sci. **28**(4), 660–681 (2014)
45. Lu, B., Charlton, M., Brunsdon, C., Harris, P.: The Minkowski approach for choosing the distance metric in Geographically Weighted Regression. Int. J. Geogr. Inf. Sci. **30**(2), 351–368 (2016)
46. Kordi, M., Fotheringham, A.S.: Spatially Weighted Interaction Models (SWIM). Ann. Am. Assoc. Geogr. **106**(5), 990–1012 (2016)
47. Murakami, D., Tsutsumida, N., Yoshida, T., Nakaya, T., Lu, B.: Scalable GWR: a linear-time algorithm for large-scale geographically weighted regression with polynomial kernels. Ann. Am. Assoc. Geogr. **111**(2), 459–480 (2021)

Spatio-Temporal Variability of Global Aerosol Optical Depth During 2000–2019

Shanshan Lu[1], Fujiang Liu[1(✉)], Fushou Liu[2], Peng Li[1], Jiayu Tang[1], Weihua Lin[1], and Yan Guo[3]

[1] School of Geography and Information Engineering, China University of Geosciences, Wuhan 430074, China
liufujiang@cug.edu.cn
[2] Shanghai Investigation, Design and Research Institute Co., Ltd., Shanghai 200335, China
[3] School of Computer Science, China University of Geosciences, Wuhan 430074, China

Abstract. In the past two decades, the deterioration of air quality around the world has attracted increasing attention. Research of air pollution based on aerosol optical depth (AOD) is particularly significant. In this article, temporal and spatial changes of global aerosol optical depth from 2000 to 2019 are studied based on MODIS AOD product data, in order to reveal the change pattern of global air pollution in the past two decades. As a result of the study, the overall global AOD has been on an upward trend over the period 2000–2019. Changes in AOD during the year have obvious seasonality, in order of which is spring > summer > autumn > winter. Central Africa, South Asia and East Asia have the highest AOD, and therefore the air pollution in these areas is the most serious, however AOD in these areas is generally on the decline.

Keywords: Aerosol optical depth (AOD) · Spatio-temporal variability · Global air pollution

1 Introduction

Over the past two decades, with the rapid development in the world population and the acceleration of global industrialization, global air pollution has spread indiscriminately, seriously affecting human health and social activity. Aerosol is an important indicator reflecting air quality. In general, the aerosol is the liquid or solid suspended particle with a diameter smaller than 10 μm [1, 2]. It plays an essential role in the earth-atmosphere system and has a remarkable influence on global climate change and biogeochemical cycles [3]. Moreover, the underlying surface radiation balance [4], atmosphere, and surface-atmosphere system [5], as well as on all dynamic, physical, and chemical processes in the atmosphere [6] are influenced by the propagation of short-wave and long-wave radiation. Simultaneously, aerosols become one of the principal atmospheric pollutants because it is composed of several chemicals [7, 8] that affect public health [9, 10] and economic activity [11]. Therefore, public health communities and climate researchers realize the importance of understanding the spatio-temporal variations of aerosols. Their

H. Wu et al. (Eds.): SpatialDI 2022, LNCS 13614, pp. 162–174, 2022.
https://doi.org/10.1007/978-3-031-24521-3_12

physical parameters, AOD, and potential causes in the world have attracted increasing attention [12].

Long-term ground measurement of aerosol concentration is feasible for specific locations, but it is challenging on a global scale [13]. The Moderate Resolution Imaging Spectroradiometer (MODIS) products provide a wealth of useful information from global observations, especially the physical properties and radiative forcing which affect climate change, as well as accurate estimates of air pollution [14, 15]. Most of the studies are limited to regions [16–21]. or restrained in the country [22–27]. Some of the studies concentrate on diverse types of surfaces, including plain [7], mountain [28], and desert territories [29–31], as well as urbanized to different degree city [32] and rural areas [33], cities in major rivers basins [34]. The above studies implemented regional analyses to reflect AOD variations based on particular restrict.

Therefore, the purpose of this study is to apply statistical analysis to identify the AOD spatio-temporal variation in the world based on MODIS aerosol products.

2   Materials and Methods

2.1   Study Area

We implemented the spatio-temporal statistical analysis of AOD around the world. The latitude and longitude of the leading research area are $-90°$ S-90° N, $-180°$ W-180° E. The landscape of the world is vast and diverse. The land area is 148,940,000 Km^2, accounting for 29.2% of the global surface area, and the water area is 361,132,000 Km^2, accounting for 70.8% of the global surface area. Meanwhile, the world consists of seven continents, ranked according to size: Asia, Africa, North America, South America, Antarctica, Europe, and Oceania.

2.2   Materials

We obtained Terra MODIS Collection 6.1 Level 3 aerosol products with 1×1 degree cells from March 2000 to February 2020 from NASA Level 1 and the Atmosphere Archive and Distribution System (accessed at https://ladsweb.modaps.eosdis.nasa.gov). MODIS aerosol product has two perfect aerosol retrieval algorithms, including the Dark Target (DT) [35, 36] algorithm over land and ocean, and Deep Blue (DB) [37] algorithm over land. Moreover, a new combined DT and DB (DTB) dataset was introduced over land according to independent MODIS monthly Normalized Difference Vegetation Index (NDVI) products by a simple approach that leverages the strengths of DT and DB algorithms, which can improve the data coverage [36]. According to the research of Wei et al. [38], DTB product performs best in most regions and can obtain the accurate aerosol changes. In this study, we used DTB monthly aerosol datasets at 550 nm from 2000 to 2019 for research.

2.3   Analysis Methods

In this paper, the research objective is to provide quarterly and annual average AOD using all valid values of monthly data for twenty years (2000–2019). We also analyzed year-by-year, and two decades for spatial variation, and month-by-month, quarter-by-quarter, year-by-year for temporal variation of the twenty years. The data averaged from March to December and January to February of the following year was used as annual average data. For the northern hemisphere, spring is considered from March to May, summer from June to August, autumn from September to November, and winter from December to February. In the southern hemisphere, the opposite is true. Autumn is from March to May, winter is from June to August, spring is from September to November, and summer is from December to February. Divide the period from March 2000 to February 2020 into 20 years and process them [26].

3 Results

3.1 Spatial Variation Analysis

Figure 1 shows the 1×1 degree gridded global distribution of the annual average AOD obtained by averaging the AOD values from 2000 to 2019. It shows the ideal annual average hot spots for aerosol, mainly including biomass burning in Africa, dust aerosols in the Saharan desert, and pollution aerosols in India and China also mixed with dust & smoke, which is consistent with Christopher [39]. It also shows that the AOD in many regions is generally low, especially in the southern hemisphere ocean; however, the Atlantic Ocean has a noticeable dust aerosol transport from the Saharan desert from the East to West Atlantic. The high AOD value ($\tau_{MODIS} > 0.8$) mainly occurred over Eastern and Southern Asia and Central Africa. A simple analysis of the annual AOD averages over these 20 years shows that the 20 years can be divided into three stages: low-value zone, mid-value zone, high-value zone, respectively, according to whether there are $\tau_{MODIS} > 1$. Three stages include 2000–2005, 2006–2014, and 2015–2019, respectively.

In the first stage, the low AOD value ($\tau_{MODIS} < 0.2$) mainly occurred over the Pacific Ocean, South America, Atlantic Ocean (not including 30°S-30°N), Indian Ocean (below the equator), Australia, from west to east. The median AOD value ($\tau_{MODIS} > 0.2$ & $\tau_{MODIS} < 0.8$) mainly occurred over southern North America, the center of the Atlantic Ocean, northern and center of Africa, southern and eastern of Asia. The high AOD value ($\tau_{MODIS} > 0.8$) mainly occurred over the Sahara Desert of northern Africa, Delhi of the west-south of Asia, and south of the Hu Line, China.

In the second stage, the AOD values in most of the regions are not much different from the first phase, with the main differences occurring in the Central Sahara Desert in Africa and the Sichuan Basin in China, the Hunan-Hubei border, the eastern coastal cities, the Henan-Hebei-Shandong border. It is clear that after 2006, the air pollution problem in mainland China has become more serious.

In the last stage, the AOD in mainland China was significantly reduced compared to the second phase, i.e., there were almost no cases of AOD values greater than 1 in mainland China. However, very high AOD values still exist in the Sahara Desert in central Africa and southwest Asia.

Next, we observed 10-years AOD spatial variation and the result shown in Fig. 2. From this map, we can see three tangibly increase or decrease from 2000–2009 to 2010–2019. A and B distinct showed a significant decrease; nevertheless, C distinct showed a significant increase. Besides, southern hemisphere ocean parts and central

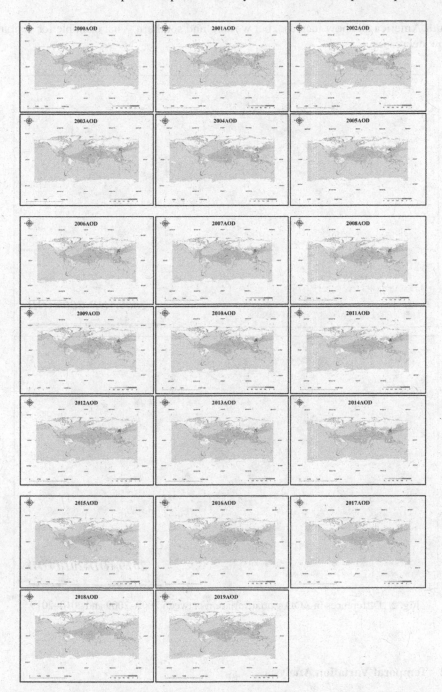

Fig. 1. Spatial distribution of annual AOD (550 nm) overworld during 2000–2019

South America all show increase, but western and southern Asia, example for Tehran, show decrease.

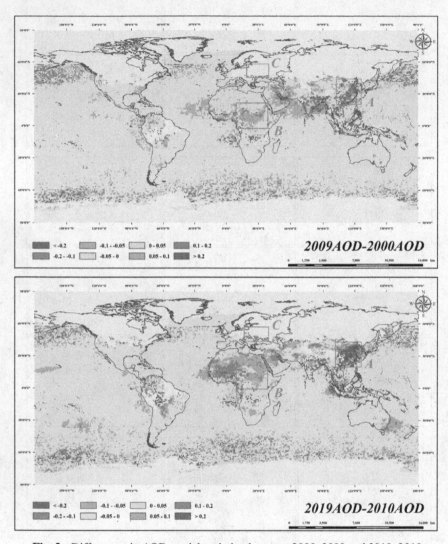

Fig. 2. Differences in AOD spatial variation between 2000–2009 and 2010–2019

3.2   Temporal Variation Analysis

Monthly Variation in AOD. In this paper, we use average monthly AOD values at wavelength 550 nm, obtained with MODIS Terra Spectroradiometer with spatial resolution 1°. In order to investigate the variation of the month, we made a preliminary monthly AOD plot, and the result is shown in Fig. 3. It can be recognized from the graph that the monthly change of AOD has a certain regularity, and the constant conversion between high monthly and low monthly AOD is visible, which is called a sawtooth cycle. AOD on hazy or dust months (peaks in the sawtooth cycle) showed 1–2 times higher than those on clear months (valleys in the sawtooth cycle) [40]. As illustrate in Fig. 3, there has three peak values of AOD. The first data occurred in the May, 2003, the following data presented in the July, 2011, and the last data occurred in August, 2019.

In addition, Fig. 3 shows that the global monthly AOD overall change has shown a slight upward trend during the 20 years. Among them, the fluctuation trend of the peak value is more regular, and it is maintained within a stable fluctuation range. The overall trend of the valley value shows a continuous increase. It can be seen that the rise of the valley value makes the overall trend of global AOD appear to rise.

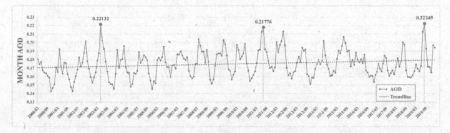

Fig. 3. Monthly AOD variations in the world during 2000–2019

Seasonal Variation in AOD. From Sect. 3.2.1, the result shows a monthly AOD variation cycle like sawtooth, suggesting strong aerosol seasonality. Figure 4 shows the quarterly average AOD of March to May, June to August, September to November and December to February for the northern and southern hemispheres from 2000–2019, as well as a comparison of average AOD of the corresponding spring, summer, autumn and winter for the northern and southern hemispheres.

According to Fig. 4, the seasonal difference in AOD is clearly shown. The northern hemisphere has high AOD in March to May and June to August and low AOD in September to November and December to February, with the highest values generally occurring in March to May and the lowest in December to February. The southern hemisphere shows the exact opposite situation, with high AOD values occurring in September to November and December to February, with the highest values generally occurring in September to November. In addition, the average value of AOD in the northern hemisphere is generally higher than that in the southern hemisphere. The overall trend of the average value of AOD in the northern hemisphere shows a slight decrease, while the average value of AOD in the southern hemisphere shows a clear overall upward trend. It can be seen that the seasonality and development trend of AOD have completely different performances in the northern and southern hemispheres. The reasons are related to the difference in regional temperature at different latitudes, the difference between the north and south seas and land, the difference in topography and climatic conditions, the difference in human activities and the level of economic development, etc.

In order to compare the AOD difference between the northern and southern hemispheres in the same season and the changes in each season in 20 years, the AOD of the corresponding seasons in the southern and northern hemispheres are presented in Fig. 4. The spring AOD is much higher in the northern hemisphere than in the southern hemisphere, but the overall trend of spring AOD in the northern hemisphere has decreased significantly, while the southern hemisphere has increased significantly. Except for spring, AOD of the northern and southern hemispheres in summer, autumn, and winter all showed a similar upward trend, and the overall changes were basically the same. Among them, the AOD in the autumn of the southern hemisphere changes smoothly, and the degree of

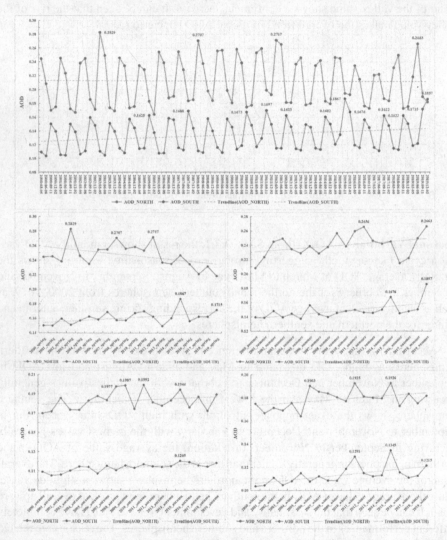

Fig. 4. Seasonal AOD variations in the world during 2000–2019

coincidence with the rising trend line is high, while other seasonal changes are irregular and have multiple maximum values.

In general, in the northern hemisphere, three high values appeared in spring (2003, 2008, 2012) in 20 years, and two high values in summer (2012, 2019). Some high values above 0.17 also appeared in the southern hemisphere. In the past ten years, it has also been concentrated in spring (2015, 2019) and summer (2019).

Annual Variation in AOD. From the previous Sect. 3.2.1 and 3.2.2, we observed monthly variation and quarterly variation of average AOD in the world. Then, we analyze the annual variation of average AOD during 2000–2019, and the result was viewed in Fig. 5. From Fig. 5, the annual average AOD represents an upward trend, and maximum AOD occurred in 2015. This point is a very motivating mutation point, 2014–2015, a sudden massive increase, and 2015–2016, a significant decrease.

In addition, air pollution was at a low level from 2000 to 2005, and it was basically flat from 2006 to 2010 and air pollution was at a medium level. After 2010, the annual average AOD showed irregular rise and fall.

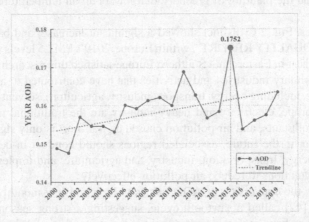

Fig. 5. Annual AOD variations in the world during 2000–2019

4 Discussion

In this article, we explored the spatial variation of the AOD by the MODSI AOD product on a global scale. We also conducted a statistical analysis on the global scale to explore the decades, annual, quarterly, and monthly variations over the world.

Spatially, high aerosol concentration is detected in the Saharan desert of Africa, South Asia, and East Asia. According to Christopher [39], high AOD value in Africa is strongly impacted by biomass burning and dust. In South Asia, high aerosol concentration mainly impacted by biomass burning emissions [41] and pollution aerosol [39]. In East Asia, high AOD value mainly below in the Hu Line of China, where experience the fastest social-economic development, anthropogenic activities, and rapid industrialization conduct gas emission. However, low aerosol concentration, mainly in the southern hemisphere ocean where keep away from the urban center, which indicates ocean winds and direction, and less human activities can reduce aerosol concentration, but, the Atlantic Ocean has a noticeable dust aerosol transport from Saharan desert from the East to West Atlantic. In Australia, low AOD may be due to its proximity to the sea and its tiny population, which is less affected by human activities. As a result of the 2019 forest fires, forests burned and produced large amounts of smoke and dust resulting in higher AOD values on the eastern side of Australia. The decade's difference, Fig. 2 A and B distinct, showed a significant decrease, which indicates that leaders of those regions have already taken steps to implement effective prevention and air quality optimization. Figure 2 A district represented east of Asia, according to "State of the Global Air 2019", China had introduced and implied Air Pollution Prevention and Control Action Plan, which has achieved air quality significant improvement in the past five years, and is consistent with the experiment results. Figure 2 B district represented the center of Africa, mainly in DR Congo, where has a humid tropical climate. The FAO "Greener Cities" project in Kinshasa, launched in 2000, to beautify the environment through waste management and the planting of greenery that lowers urban temperatures and purifies the air.

Nevertheless, Fig. 2 C distinct showed a significant increase, and based on "2019 WORLD AIR QUALITY REPORT", within Europe, 2019's PM2.5 levels were generally found to be highest in Eastern and Southern Europe satisfied this research. Over the past 20 years, the primary industries and activities that have contributed to air pollution in western Europe, including energy, transport, industry, agriculture, solvent use. In central and Eastern Europe, electricity and heavy industry are the traditional major emitting sectors of air pollutants, and air pollution caused by transport is only significant in the major cities. So, in the future, associated regions should conduct in-depth studies in the fields of energy, transportation, industry, and agriculture, and implement effective policies and regulations to reduce air pollution effectively.

Temporally, the conversion of AOD values of high and low monthly is evident in what Jia et al. [42] called a sawtooth cycle, suggesting a strong seasonality of AOD variation. AOD on hazy or dust months (peaks in the sawtooth cycle) showed 1 - 2 times higher than those on clear months (valleys in the sawtooth cycle), suggesting the presence of inter-monthly AOD variation as well, this consistent with Guo [40]. Quarterly, the AOD value was higher in spring and summer. High AOD in spring is primarily due to frequent breakouts of spring sand-dust storms [41]. During summer, photochemical interactions resulted in higher air temperatures, which could increase aerosol values [43]. Although air pollution triggered by aerosols is not that obvious in summer because of sharp solar radiation, and frequent precipitation facilitate the periodical removal and dispersal of aerosols in the atmosphere [44]. In winter, the global AOD is mostly at a quarterly minimum due to the slowing down of market economic activities, lower air temperatures, less diffusion of exhaust gases from industrial production at low temperatures, and relatively low human activities. The above seasonality is partly a result of the slow meteorological circumstances [40] and the sandstorm phenomenon. Annually, the average AOD represents an upward trend, and maximum AOD occurred in 2015.

This point is a very motivating mutation point, 2014–2015, a sudden massive increase, and 2015–2016, a significant decrease. According to WMO's 2015 State of the Global Climate Statement, 2015 experienced the warmest year on record, rising nearly half of the 2 degree Celsius limit from pre-industrial times, and produced one of the most robust levels of El Niño on record, causing global AOD values to reach their highest in 2015 since 2000 [44].

This article obtains the result of spatio-temporal variability of global AOD during 2000–2019, and discusses its potential causes, which makes an essential contribution to our long-term goals. Meanwhile, this application research may be useful for another researcher and government meteorological and environment departments.

5 Conclusion

In this paper, MODIS AOD data used to study the spatio-temporal variability of average AOD across global during 2000–2019. Significant temporal and spatial variations have been detected in the variability of high, medium, and low AOD values using monthly satellite-retrieved AOD. Some valuable findings were found as follows:

The overall global AOD has been on an upward trend over the period 2000–2019. Among them, air pollution was at a relatively low level from 2000 to 2005, and was basically the same at a medium level from 2006 to 2010. After 2010, the annual average AOD increased irregularly, especially the sharp increase in 2014–2015 and the sharp decline in 2015–2016. The extreme variation of AOD and the abrupt change of global climate show a similar pattern, and it also reveals that global air pollution is becoming more and more serious.

Changes in AOD during the year have obvious seasonality. Regardless of the northern and southern hemispheres, in order of AOD is spring > summer > autumn > winter. In spring, there are frequent dust storms and serious air pollution; in summer, there are frequent human activities, the temperature rises and the air pollution is more serious; in winter, there are fewer human activities, the temperature decreases and the air pollution level is relatively low.

The overall upward trend of monthly AOD is mainly due to the continuous increase in the low value of AOD. The high value of global AOD in a year mainly occurs between March and August, most of which are concentrated in July.

Central Africa, South Asia and East Asia have the highest AOD, and therefore the air pollution in these areas is the most serious. Among them, Central Africa, represented by the Sahara Desert, is mainly affected by dust aerosols. South Asia, where productivity is relatively lagging, is mainly due to biomass combustion emissions leading to severe air pollution. East Asia, with China as the main representative, is mainly due to the rapid development of social economy and industrialization, as well as the huge population, which has brought violent human activities and caused serious air pollution. However, judging from the overall trend of the time series, AOD in these areas has shown a downward trend and air quality has improved.

References

1. Carmichael, G.R., Adhikary, B., Kulkarni, S., D'Allura, A., Tang, Y.H., Streets, D., et al.: Asian aerosols: current and year 2030 distributions and implications to human health and regional climate change. Environ. Sci. Technol. **43**(15), 5811–5817 (2009)
2. Deng, X.L., He, D.Y., Pan, D.L., Sun, Z.B.: Analysis of aerosol characteristics over the China Sea by remote sensing. J. Remote. Sens. **14**(2), 294–312 (2010)
3. Satheesh, S., Krishnamoorthy, K.: Radiative effects of natural aerosols: a review. Atmos. Environ. **39**(11), 2089–2110 (2005)
4. Bian, H., Chin, M., Rodriguez, J.M., Yu, H., Penner, J.E., Strahan, S.: Sensitivity of aerosol optical thickness and aerosol direct radiative effect to relative humidity. Atmos. Chem. Phys. **9**(7), 2375–2386 (2009)
5. Sellers, W.D.: A global climatic model based on the energy balance of the Earth-Atmosphere system. J. Appl. Meteorol. Clim. **8**(3), 392–400 (1969)
6. Seinfeld, J.H., Pandis, S.N., Noone, K.: Atmospheric chemistry and physics: from air pollution to climate change. Phys. Today **51**(10), 88–90 (1998)
7. Xia, X.A., Chen, H.B., Goloub, P., Zong, X.M., Zhang, W.X., Wang, P.C.: Climatological aspects of aerosol optical properties in North China Plain based on ground and satellite remote-sensing data. J. Quant. Spectrosc. Ra. **127**, 12–23 (2013)
8. Hu, J.L., Wang, Y.G., Ying, Q., Zhang, H.L.: Spatial and temporal variability of PM2.5 and PM10 over the North China Plain and the Yangtze River Delta. China. Atmos. Environ. **95**, 598–609 (2014)
9. Watts, N., Adger, W.N., Agnolucci, P., Blackstock, J., Byass, P., Cai, W.J., et al.: Health and climate change: Policy responses to protect public health. Lancet **386**(10006), 1861–1914 (2015)
10. Thurston, G.D., Ahn, J., Cromar, K.R., Shao, Y., Reynolds, H.R., Jerrett, M., et al.: Ambient particulate matter air pollution exposure and mortality in the NIH-AARP diet and health cohort. Environ. Health Persp. **124**(4), 484–490 (2016)
11. Huang, J.P., Ji, M.X., Xie, Y.K., Wang, S.S., He, Y.L., Ran, J.J.: Global semi-arid climate change over last 60 years. Clim. Dynam. **46**(3–4), 1131–1150 (2016)
12. He, Q.Q., Zhang, M., Huang, B.: Spatio-temporal variation and impact factors analysis of satellite-based aerosol optical depth over China from 2002 to 2015. Atmos. Environ. **129**, 79–90 (2016)
13. Luo, Y.X., Zheng, X.B., Zhao, T.L., Chen, J.: A climatology of aerosol optical depth over China from recent 10 years of MODIS remote sensing data. Int. J. Climatol. **34**(3), 863–870 (2014)
14. van Donkelaar, A., Martin, R.V., Brauer, M., Kahn, R., Levy, R., Verduzco, C., et al.: Global estimates of ambient fine particulate matter concentrations from satellite-based aerosol optical depth: development and application. Environ. Health Persp. **118**(6), 847–855 (2010)
15. Cao, C.X., Zheng, S., Singh, R.P.: Characteristics of aerosol optical properties and meteorological parameters during three major dust events (2005–2010) over Beijing. China. Atmos. Res. **150**, 129–142 (2014)
16. Cheng, L., Li, L., Chen, L., Hu, S., Yuan, L., Liu, Y., et al.: Spatiotemporal variability and influencing factors of aerosol optical depth over the Pan Yangtze River Delta during the 2014–2017 period. Int. J. Env. Res. Pub. He. **16**(19), 3522 (2019)
17. Chi, Y.F., Zuo, S.D., Ren, Y., Chen, K.C.: The spatiotemporal pattern of the aerosol optical depth (AOD) on the canopies of various forest types in the exurban national park: a case in Ningbo city, eastern China. Adv. Meteorol. **2019**, 1–12 (2019)
18. Kuang, Q., Wang, Y.: Spatial-temporal characteristics of the aerosol optical depth (AOD) derived from longterm (1980–2018) MERRA-2 over Guangdong. ISPRS Archives **XLII-3/W9**, 103–108 (2019)

19. Shen, X., Bilal, M., Qiu, Z., Sun, D., Wang, S., Zhu, W.: Long-term spatiotemporal variations of aerosol optical depth over Yellow and Bohai Sea. Environ. Sci. Pollut. Res. **26**(8), 7969–7979 (2019). https://doi.org/10.1007/s11356-019-04203-4

20. Xue, R., Ai, B., Lin, Y.Y., Pang, B.B., Shang, H.S.: Spatial and temporal distribution of aerosol optical depth and its relationship with urbanization in Shandong Province. Atmosphere-Basel **10**(3), 110 (2019)

21. Yang, Q.Q., Yuan, Q.Q., Yue, L.W., Li, T.W., Shen, H.F., Zhang, L.P.: The relationships between PM2.5 and aerosol optical depth (AOD) in mainland China: about and behind the spatio-temporal variations. Environ. Pollut. **248**, 526–535 (2019)

22. Feng, Y., Chen, D.M., Zhang, X.H.: Atmospheric aerosol pollution across China: a spatiotemporal analysis of satellite-based aerosol optical depth during 2000–2016. Int. J. Digit. Earth **12**(7), 843–857 (2018)

23. Filonchyk, M., Yan, H., Zhang, Z.: Analysis of spatial and temporal variability of aerosol optical depth over China using MODIS combined Dark Target and Deep Blue product. Theoret. Appl. Climatol. **137**(3–4), 2271–2288 (2018). https://doi.org/10.1007/s00704-018-2737-5

24. He, Q.Q., Gu, Y.F., Zhang, M.: Spatiotemporal patterns of aerosol optical depth throughout China from 2003 to 2016. Sci. Total Environ. **653**, 23–35 (2019)

25. Islam, M.N., Ali, M.A., Islam, M.M.: Spatiotemporal investigations of aerosol optical properties over Bangladesh for the period 2002–2016. Earth Syst. Environ. **3**(3), 563–573 (2019)

26. Xie, G.Q., Wang, M., Pan, J., Zhu, Y.: Spatio-temporal variations and trends of MODIS C6.1 dark target and deep blue merged aerosol optical depth over China during 2000–2017. Atmos. Environ. **214**, 116846 (2019)

27. Kumar, A.: Spatio-temporal variations in satellite based aerosol optical depths & aerosol index over Indian subcontinent: Impact of urbanization and climate change. Urban Clim. **32**, 100598 (2020)

28. Li, Z.Q., Zhao, S.H., Edwards, R., Wang, W.B., Zhou, P.: Characteristics of individual aerosol particles over Ürümqi Glacier No. 1 in eastern Tianshan, central Asia, China. Atmos. Res. **99**(1), 57–66 (2011)

29. Che, H.Z., Wang, Y.Q., Sun, J.Y., Zhang, X.C., Zhang, X.Y., Guo, J.P.: Variation of aerosol optical properties over the Taklimakan Desert in China. Aerosol. Air Qual. Res. **13**(2), 777–785 (2013)

30. Ge, J.M., Huang, J.P., Xu, C.P., Qi, Y.L., Liu, H.Y.: Characteristics of Taklimakan dust emission and distribution: a satellite and reanalysis field perspective. J. Geophys. Res. Atmos. **119**(20), 11772–11783 (2014)

31. Zong, X.M., Xia, X.A., Che, H.Z.: Validation of aerosol optical depth and climatology of aerosol vertical distribution in the Taklimakan Desert. Atmos. Pollut. Res. **6**(2), 239–244 (2015)

32. Che, H.Z., Xia, X.A., Zhu, J., Wang, H., Wang, Y.Q., Sun, J.Y., et al.: Aerosol optical properties under the condition of heavy haze over an urban site of Beijing, China. Environ. Sci. Pollut. R. **22**(2), 1043–1053 (2015)

33. Wang, Y.F., Zhang, W.Y., Kong, L.B., Wang, J.J.: Analysis of applicability and characteristics of MODIS aerosol products in agricultural regions (in Chinese). Remote Sens. Technol. Appl. **28**(03), 505–510 (2013)

34. Song, W.Z., Jia, H.F., Huang, J.F., Zhang, Y.Y.: A satellite-based geographically weighted regression model for regional PM2.5 estimation over the Pearl River Delta region in China. Remote Sens. Environ. **154**, 1–7 (2014)

35. Levy, R.C., Remer, L.A., Mattoo, S., Vermote, E.F., Kaufman, Y.J.: Second-generation operational algorithm: retrieval of aerosol properties over land from inversion of Moderate Resolution Imaging Spectroradiometer spectral reflectance. J. Geophys. Res. Atmos. **112**(D13), D13211 (2007)

36. Levy, R.C., Mattoo, S., Munchak, L.A., Remer, L.A., Sayer, A.M., Patadia, F., et al.: The collection 6 MODIS aerosol products over land and ocean. Atmos. Meas. Tech. **6**(11), 2989–3034 (2013)

37. Hsu, N.C., Jeong, M.J., Bettenhausen, C., Sayer, A.M., Hansell, R., Seftor, C.S., et al.: enhanced deep blue aerosol retrieval algorithm: the second generation. J. Geophys. Res. Atmos. **118**(16), 9296–9315 (2013)

38. Wei, J., Peng, Y.R., Guo, J.P., Sun, L.: Performance of MODIS Collection 6.1 Level 3 aerosol products in spatial-temporal variations over land. Atmos. Environ. **206**, 30–44 (2019)

39. Christopher, S., Gupta, P.: Global distribution of column satellite aerosol optical depth to surface PM2.5 relationships. Remote Sens.-Basel **12**(12), 1985 (2020)

40. Guo, J.P., Zhang, X.Y., Wu, Y.R., Zhaxi, Y.Z., Che, H.Z., La, B., et al.: Spatio-temporal variation trends of satellite-based aerosol optical depth in China during 1980–2008. Atmos. Environ. **45**(37), 6802–6811 (2011)

41. Srivastava, R.: Trends in aerosol optical properties over South Asia. Int. J. Climatol. **37**(1), 371–380 (2017)

42. Jia, Y.T., Rahn, K.A., He, K.B., Wen, T.X., Wang, Y.S.: A novel technique for quantifying the regional component of urban aerosol solely from its sawtooth cycles. J. Geophys. Res. **113**(D21), D21309 (2008)

43. Dickerson, R.R., Kondragunta, S., Stenchikov, G., Civerolo, K.L., Doddridge, B.G., Holben, B.N.: The impact of aerosols on solar ultraviolet radiation and photochemical smog. Science **278**(5339), 827–830 (1997)

44. WMO: Provisional WMO statement on the status of the global climate in 2016. World Meteorological Organization (2016)

City Analysis

Research on the Prediction Model of Sites in Kashgar Based on Logistic Regression Analysis

Wan Jiang(✉) and Huaguang Gao

National Museum of China, Beijing, China
wande412@whu.edu.cn

Abstract. By applying the GIS spatial analysis function, 547 sites in Kashgar of Xinjiang before the Ming and Qing dynasties were selected as research objects, 540 non-site points were generated using GIS spatial analysis method. Geographical environment variables such as the elevation, slope, orientation, land-cover types, degree of relief, distance to the ridge line, distance to the valley line and the distance to the river of the site and non-site points were obtained respectively. 274 site points and 270 non-site points were randomly selected as training set, the logistic binary regression analysis was used to establish a site prediction model. Cross-validation and Kvamme's gain statistics method were adopted to verify the model accuracy. The result showed that: the overall prediction accuracy of the model is 70.29%, the prediction ability of the non-site points in the low probability area is strong, and the prediction ability of the site points in the high probability area is strong too. It can provide reference for field archaeological investigation, archaeological research and cultural heritage protection.

Keywords: GIS · Spatial analysis · Historical and cultural sites · Logistic regression analysis · Kashgar area

1 Introduction

The predictive model of site points is to build a mathematical model in the study area by analyzing the geographical environment factors of the identified sites, to find out the statistical laws and characteristics of their distribution, and then predict the probability value of the possible existence of sites in the unknown area. The earliest establishment of site prediction model can be traced back to the 1950s and 1960s, when American archaeologist Willey conducted research on prehistoric settlements in the Virú Valley of Peru [1]. After the 1960s, quantitative analysis methods gradually emerged. In 1973, Green used the multiple linear regression method to establish a prediction model for the prehistoric Maya sites in northern Honduras [2]. Later, with the development of computer technology, statistics and spatial analysis began to be applied to the construction of site prediction models. Scholar such as Kvamme [3, 4], Kohler and parker [5], Judge and Sebastian [6] have published many related monographs and books. After the 1990s, with the popularization of spatial analysis software applicaions such as ArcGIS, Grass,

H. Wu et al. (Eds.): SpatialDI 2022, LNCS 13614, pp. 177–188, 2022.
https://doi.org/10.1007/978-3-031-24521-3_13

Moss, the research on site prediction model has been carried out in an all-round way. The application of logistic regression analysis to the study of site prediction models in China mainly includes Ni, J.S. [7], Peng, S.Z. [8], Qiao, W.W. [9], Dong, Z. [10] and Cao, Y.W. [11], research areas were concentrated in Shandong Shuhe River Basin, Wensi River Basin, Zhengluo Area, Yanbian Area and Conghua Liuxi River Basin. This paper took the Kashgar region of XinJiang as the research area, took the site points before the Ming and Qing dynasties as the research object, used the logistic binary regression analysis method to establish the site prediction model, generated the probability distribution map of the site, verified the accuracy of the model and analyzed the relationship between the site distribution and the environment.

2   Overview of Research Area and Data Processing

2.1   Study Area

Kashgar was called Shule, Renru, and Shufu in ancient times. It is located in southwestern Xinjiang. It is an ancient town on the westernmost frontier of China. It is an important part of the Silk Road and the largest oasis in the Tarim Basin. Its jurisdiction includes 1 county-level city, 10 counties and 1 autonomous county, with a width of about 750 km from east to west, and a length of about 535 km from north to south, with a total area of 162,000 square kilometers, accounting for 9.75% of the total area of the Xinjiang Uygur Autonomous Region. Geographically spans $74°27'49''$–$79°51'47''$ east longitude and $35°26'54''$—$40°15'27''$ north latitude. It is bordered by the Pamirs on the west, the Taklimakan Desert on the east, the Tianshan Mountains on the north, and Tibet on the south by the Kunlun Mountains. The altitude is 750 m—8374 m, with an average of 2494 m. In terms of climatic conditions, this area belongs to the warm temperate continental arid climate zone, with dry climate and little precipitation. It mainly relies on the melting of glaciers and snow in the mountainous areas to create oasis suitable for human life. The landforms are alternately distributed with mountain grasslands, deserts and oases. Kashgar can be divided into 3 geographical units, namely: Pamir Plateau (southwest), Yarkand River Oasis (central) and Kashgar Oasis (northwest).

2.2   Source and Processing of Site Data

The site data used in this article was from the "Chinese Cultural Relics Atlas"(Xinjiang Uyghur Autonomous District Book) [12] and the third national cultural relics census. We calculated the temporal and spatial distribution information of the sites, and selected the sits before the Ming and Qing dynasties as the basic data, including 365 sites from the third national cultural relics census and 182 sites from the atlas. Sites from the third national cultural relics census carries GPS latitude and longitude coordinates, which were converted into point coordinates in ArcGIS software after being entered into excel. The sites in maps were vectorized after the georeferncing of maps in the cultural relics atlas. A total of 547 sites were finally sorted out.

2.3 Source and Processing of Map Data

The digital elevation model (DEM) (Fig. 1a) used in this paper was from ASTER GDEM (advanced spaceborne thermal emission and reflection radiometer global digital elevation model) with a spatial resolution of 30 m. The land cover data was from the National Science and Technology Infrastructure Platform-National Earth System Science Data Sharing Service Platform (http://www.geodata.cn) [13–15]. The slope surface analysis(slope) and orientation surface analysis (aspect) function of the ArcGIS spatial analysis were adopted to process the DEM data to get the slope map (Fig. 1b) and orientation map (Fig. 1c) respectively. The hydrology word module was used to extract the river network based on the undulations of the surface morphology [16]. In the calculation process, the threshold was set to 30000, and the raster river network needs to be vectorized (Fig. 1d). The land-cover data combined with the national land-cover classification system and the landform characteristics of Kashgar area, we divided land cover types into 12 categories (Fig. 1e). What needs to be mentioned is that Tumshuk city, which is not administratively part of Kashgar area, is geographically included within the Kashgar area. Considering the continuity of changes in topographical factors, this article took Tumshuk into consideration when conducting spatial analysis. Topographic factors within the geographic area of the city were also counted.

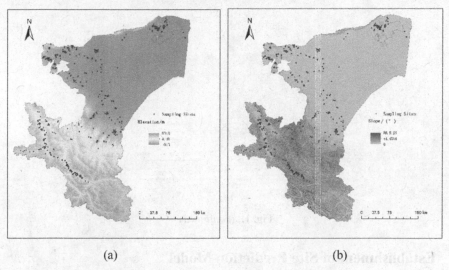

(a)   (b)

Fig. 1. The superimposed relationship between sites and geographical environment elements before the Ming and Qing dynasties in Kashgar area. (a) shows elevation; (b) shows slope; (c) shows orientation; (d) shows water system; (e) shows land-cover types

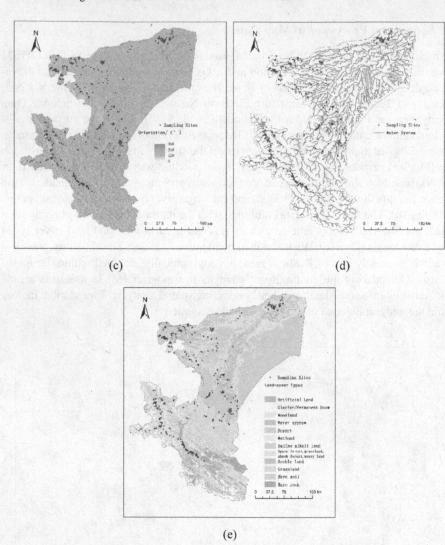

(c)   (d)

(e)

Fig. 1. (*continued*)

3   Establishment of Site Prediction Model

3.1   Logistic Regression Method

Logistic regression method is a popular multivariate quantitative statistical analysis method in machine learning, which belongs to probabilistic nonlinear regression. A binary variable logistic regression model refers to a logistic regression model in which the dependent variable is a binary classification. The logistic regression model has no assumptions about the distribution of the independent variables, thus avoiding the various difficult assumptions faced in the analysis. Kvamme's research showed that the binary variable logistic regression model is more robust than many other statistical methods in construction of site prediction models [17]. Therefore, this paper adopted the logistic binary regression model to model the sites in Kashgar area.

Let P be the probability that the site exists, its value range is [0, 1], and the probability of non-site is $1 - P$. Perform logit transformation on P, that is, take the natural logarithm of the contrast number $1/(1 - P)$, the record it as logit P. Set up a linear regression equation with logit P as the dependent variable:

$$\text{logit } P = \theta_0 + \theta_1 x_1 + \theta_2 x_2 + \cdots + \theta_n x_n \tag{1}$$

In the formula, θ_0 is the offset eigenvalue, which is a constant. $[x_1, x_2, \cdots, x_n]$ are the environment variables that affect the distribution of sites in this study. $[\theta_1, \theta_2, \cdots, \theta_n]$ are the regression coefficients of geographic factors. The regression model of the existence probability of the sites can be obtained by transforming the formula (1):

$$P = \frac{1}{1 + e^{-(\theta_0 + \theta_1 x_1 + \theta_2 x_2 + \cdots + \theta_n x_n)}} \tag{2}$$

Taking each environmental factor variable and the corresponding P value (1 for site sites and 0 for non-site sites) as input, the offset eigenvalues and regression coefficients can be calculated to build a logistic regression model. This model is a binary variable logistic regression model, which is a generalization of the ordinary multiple linear regression model, but its error term obeys a binomial distribution rather than a normal distribution.

3.2   Selection of Model Samples

This paper randomly selected 274 sites from the total 547 sites as the training set, and the remaining 273 sites as the testing set (Fig. 2a). The non-site point data were generated by the random point generation tool in ArcGIS software, with a total of 540 points, of which 270 points were randomly selected as the training set, and the other 270 points were used as the testing set (Fig. 2b). The logistic binary regression analysis used the training set of site points and non-site points as a sample set to construct the site prediction model.

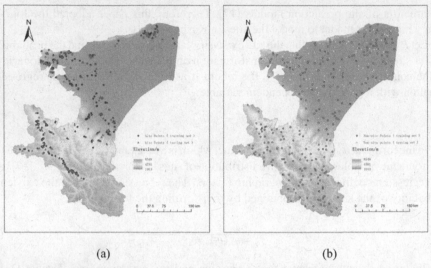

(a)   (b)

Fig. 2. Distribution map of sample set in Kashgar. (a) shows training set and testing set of site points; (b) shows training set and testing set of non-site points

3.3 Selection of Model Variables

The dependent variable of the logistic regression model is a binarized value, that is, the P value of the site point is 1, and the P value of the non-site point is 0.

Based on the analysis and researches on the spatial distribution of sites, 8 geographical environment factors including elevation, slope, orientation, land-cover types, degree of relief, distance to the ridge line, distance to the valley line and the distance to the river were adopted as candidate factors. The sample set and various candidate factor layers were superimposed and extracted in ArcGIS respectively. In order to facilitate the regression convergence, the natural breaks method(Jenks) was used to divide the values of different factors, and then reassigned them as 1–12. The classification of the training set and the testing set of site points was shown in Fig. 3.

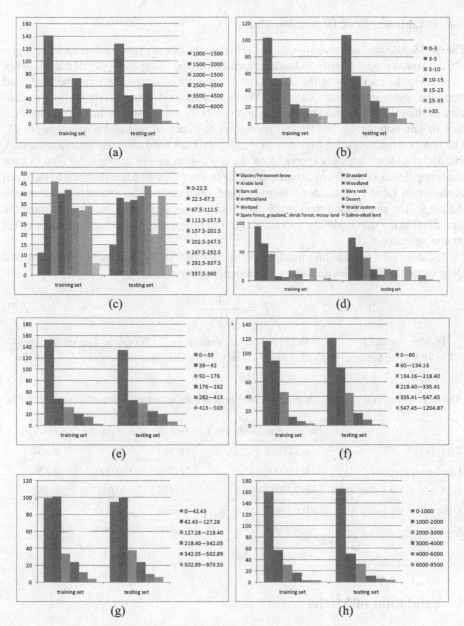

Fig. 3. Statistical analysis diagram of training set and testing set of site points. (a) shows the statistical result of elevation. (b) shows the statistical result of slope. (c) shows the statistical result of orientation. (d) shows the statistical result of land-cover types. (e) shows the statistical result of degree of relief. (f) distance to the ridge line. (g) shows the statistical result of distance to the valley line. (h) shows the statistical result of distance to the river.

3.4 Establishment of Regression Model

The SPSS software was used to realize the establishment of dichotomous variable logistic regression model of sites in Kashgar area before the Ming and Qing dynasties. After comparing the accuracy of the models established by different methods, the backward stepwise selection method (Backward Wald) was adopted. The overall prediction accuracy of the selected method for sample points was 72.8%, of which the prediction accuracy of site points was 79.2%, and prediction accuracy of non-site points was 66.3%. The independent variables were screened using the backward stepwise selection method. The independent variables entered into the regression model through the significance test were elevation, land-cover types, distance to the valley line and distance to the river, as shown in Table 1. The other 4 factors: slope, orientation, degree of relief, distance to the ridge line were failed the significance test, which was determined to optimize the equation during the modeling process and did not mean that these factors had no effect on site selection.

Established a regression model for predicting sites in Kashgar before the Ming and Qing dynasties based on the selected independent variables.

$$P = \frac{1}{1 + e^{-z}} \tag{3}$$

In the formula, $z = -0.217948 \times$ elevation $- 0.156608 \times$ landcovertypes $- 0.238983 \times$ distance to the valley line $- 0.679696 \times$ distance to the river $+ 3.254784$.

Table 1. Prediction model parameters of sites in Kashgar before the Ming and Qing dynasties

	Regression coefficients	Test factor	Salience	Odds ratio
Elevation	−0.217948	10.360	0.001	0.804
Land-cover types	−0.156608	26.736	0.000	0.855
Distance to the valley line	−0.238983	6.425	0.011	0.787
Distance to the river	−0.679696	63.663	0.000	0.507
Constant	3.254784	93.310	0.000	25.914

4   Validation of Model

4.1   Cross-Validation Method

In this paper, the semi-cross-validation method in the cross-validation method was used to verify the site model. The testing set of site points and non-site points were substituted into the regression model for probability calculation. The judgment threshold was 0.5. When the probability value of point was greater than 0.5, it was judged as a site point, otherwise it was a non-site point. After calculation, 221 points in the testing set of site points (273) were correctly classified, the classification accuracy was 80.95%. 161

points in the testing set of non-site points (270) were correctly classified, the classification accuracy was 59.63%. The overall prediction accuracy of the model was 70.29%. This showed that the overall accuracy of the site prediction model is good, and it was feasible to use the logistic binary regression model to establish a site prediction model in Kashgar before the Ming and Qing dynasties.

4.2 Kvamme's Gain Statistics Method

Kvamme's gain statistics method was adopted to verify the accuracy of the site prediction model too. The calculation formula is:

$$Gain = 1 - \frac{E_a}{E_s} \tag{4}$$

In the formula, $Gain$ is the gain value, E_a is the ratio of the probability area to the area of the study area, E_s is the ratio of the number of sites in the probability area to the total number of sites in the study area. If the probability area is small and there are many site points, the gain value will be large and the model accuracy will be high. When the gain value is close to 1, it indicates that the model has strong positive predictive ability; when it is close to 0, it indicates the model has weak predictive ability; when the gain value is negative, the reverse predictive ability is strong, that is, the probability of predicting non-site points is strong [18].

The raster calculator was used in ArcGIS software to calculate the probability of site existence in the entire Kashgar area according to the established logistic regression model. The natural breaks method (Jenks) was adopted to classify the probability values into three levels: low, medium and high. The higher the level, the higher the probability of the sites exists, as shown in Fig. 4. The Kvamme gain value of each probability area was counted and shown in Table 2.

Table 2. Kvamme's gain statistics of site prediction model

The level	Probability distributions	Area(grid number of 30 m × 30 m)	Percentage of total area	Number of sites	Percentage of total sites	Gain
Low-level	0.35%–28.43%	45,228,371	36.38%	41	7.50%	−3.85
Middle-level	28.43%–57.88%	38,349,835	30.84%	144	26.33%	−0.17
High-level	57.88%–87.67%	40,753,420	32.78%	362	66.18%	0.50

As shown in the Table 2, in the area of high-level area which accounts for 32.78% of the study area, 66.18% of the site points were distributed. The Kvamme gain value is 0.50, indicated that the site prediction model has a strong forward prediction ability in the high-level area. In contrast, the Kvamme of the low-level is −3.85, which indicated the model has a strong reverse prediction ability in the low-lever area.

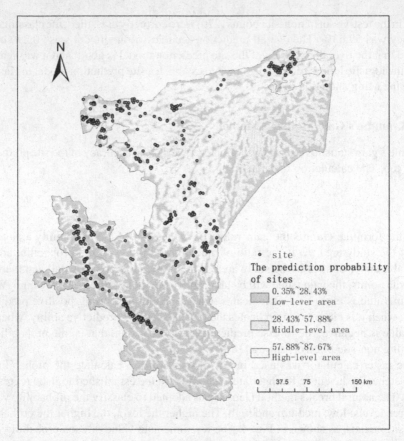

Fig. 4. Probability map of site distribution in Kashgar before the Ming and Qing dynasites

5   Conclusion

Kashgar has a long history and diverse cultures. It is the intersection of the four civilizations of ancient India, Greece-Roman, Persia, and Han and Tang Dynasties. It has formed a complex and creative regional culture and is an important part of Chinese culture. Investigating the spatial distribution of sites in this area can further reveal the ancient people's choice and dependence on the environment in Kashgar, and provide an important reference for further research and protection of ancient sites.

The spatial analysis method of ArcGIS software and the logistic regression method of SPSS data software were adopted to establish the site prediction model in Kashgar before the Ming and Qing dynasities. The geographical elements: the distance to the river, the distance to the valley line, elevation, land-cover types have a significant impact on the distribution of sites, and their influences are ranked from high to low.

The cross-validation method and the Kvamme gain statistics method were adopted to verify the site prediction model and the results showed the accuracy was high. The site prediction model gives the probability distribution of sites in Kashgar area before the Ming and Qing dynasties, further reveal the spatial distribution of the site. It can be shown in the site distribution probability map, the higher probability distribution area is concentrated in the basins of four major rivers, including the Kashgar River, the Yarkand River, the Tiznafu River and the Tashkurgan River, especially the oasis area of the Yarkand River and the Kashgar River. The lower probability area is concentrated in the non-river distribution area on the Pamir Plateau.

The application of GIS and statistical testing methods has transformed archaeological research from qualitative to quantitative research and provided new methods and perspectives for settlement archaeology. However, due to the limitations of source data, the elements included in the analysis in this study are limited to geographical environment elements. The next step will consider the influence of social, cultural and other factors on the distribution of site points, so that the prediction model can provide reference for further investigation work and assist field archaeology more effectively.

References

1. Willey, G.R: Prehistoric settlement in the Virú Valley, Peru. Bureau of American Ethnology Bulletin 155, Washington (1953)
2. Green, E.L.: Location analysis of prehistoric Maya sites in Northern British Honduras. Am. Antiquity **38**, 279–293 (1973)
3. Kvamme, K.L.: Computer processing techniques for regional modeling of archaeological site locations. Adv. Comput. Archaeol. **1**, 26–52 (1983)
4. Kvamme, K.L.: Development and testing of quantitative models.Judge J W, Lynne Sebastian. Quantifying the Present and Predicting the Past: Theory, Method and Application of Archaeological Predictive Modelling. U. S. Department of Interior, Bureau of Land Management. Denver, pp. 325–428(1988)
5. Kohler, T.A., Parker, S.C.: Predictive models for archaeological resource location. Adv. Archaeol. Method Theory. **9**, 397–452 (1986)
6. Judge, J.W., Sebastian, L.: Quantifying the present and predicting the past: theory, method and application of archaeological predictive modelling. U. S. Department of the Interior, Bureau of Land Management, Denver (1988)
7. Ni, J.S.: Prediction model of archaeological sites in the upper reaches of the Shuhe River in Shandong. Progr. Geogr. **28**(04), 489–493 (2009). 倪金生.山东沭河上游流域考古遗址预测模型. 地理科学进展 **28**(04), 489–493 (2009)
8. Peng, S.Z., Zhang, W., Chen, D.D.: Model prediction of dawenkou culture archaeological site in wensi valley. J. Taishan Univ. **32**(06), 34–39 (2010). 彭淑贞,张伟,陈栋栋.汶泗流域大汶口文化考古遗址模型预测. 泰山学院学报 **32**(06), 34–39 (2010)
9. Qiao, W.W., Bi, S.B., Wang, Q.F., Guo,Y.: Prediction model of Longshan cultural site in Zhengluo area. Sci. Surv. Mapp. **38**(06), 172–174+181 (2013). 乔文文,毕硕本,王启富,郭忆.郑洛地区龙山文化遗址预测模型. 测绘科学 **38**(06), 172–174+181 (2013). https://doi.org/10.16251/j.cnki.1009-2307.2013.06.023
10. Dong, Z., Jin, S.Z.: Prediction research on Bohai Kingdom ruins in Yanbian area based on the logic regression model. J. Yanbian Univ. (Nat. Sci.) **41**(02), 179–184 (2015). 董振,金石柱.基于Logistic回归模型的延边地区渤海国遗址预测研究. 延边大学学报(自然科学版) **41**(02), 179–184 (2015). https://doi.org/10.16379/j.cnki.issn.1004-4353.2015.02.018
11. Cao, Y.W.: Prediction model of ante-qin dynasty sites in conghua liuxi river basin based on logistic regression analysis. Geomat. Spat. Inf. Technol. **44**(05), 124–127+131 (2021). 曹耀文.基于Logistic回归分析的从化流溪河流域先秦时期遗址预测模型. 测绘与空间地理信息 **44**(05), 124–127+131 (2021)

12. National cultural heritage administration.: Atlas of Chinese Cultural Relics, Xinjiang Uyghur Autonomous District Book. Cutural Relics Press, Beijing (2012). 国家文物局. 中国文物地图集,新疆维吾尔自治区分册. 文物出版社 (2012)

13. Wu, B.F., Yuan, Q.Z., Yan, C.Z., et al.: The land-cover changes in the first ten years of the 21st century in China. Quat. Res. **34**(4), 723–731 (2014). 吴炳方, 苑全治, 颜长珍, 王宗明, 于信芳, 李爱农, 马荣华, 黄进良, 陈劲松, 常存, 刘成林, 张磊, 李晓松, 曾源, 包安明. 21世纪前十年的中国土地覆盖变化. 第四纪研究 **34**(4), 723–731 (2014)

14. Zhang, L., Jia, K., Li, X., Yuan, Q., Zhao, X.: Multiscale segmentation approach for object-based land-cover classification using high-resolution imagery. Remote Sensing Letters **5**(1), 73–82 (2014)

15. Zhang, L., Wu, B.F., Li, X.S., et al.: China land-cover classification system based on carbon budget. Acta Ecologica Sinica **34**(24), 7158–7166 (2014). 张磊, 吴炳方, 李晓松, 邢强. 基于碳收支的中国土地覆被分类系统.生态学报 **34**(24), 7158–7166 (2014)

16. Tang, G.A., Yang, X.: ArcGIS Geographic Information System Spatial Analysis Experiment Tutorial. China Science Press, Beijing (2012). 汤国安, 杨昕. ArcGIS 地理信息系统空间分析实验教程. 科学出版社 (2012)

17. Kvamme, K.L.: The fundamental principles and practice of predictive archaeological modeling. In: Mathematics and Information Science in Archaeology: A Flexible Framework, Bonn, pp. 257–295 (1990)

18. Vaughn, S., Crawford, T.: A predictive model of archaeological potential: an example from northwestern Belize. Appl. Geogr. **29**(4), 542–555 (2009)

Research on the Spatial Characteristics of High-Density Urban Road Network and Functional Agglomeration Taking the Northern Part of Macau as an Example

Liang Zheng and Yile Chen(✉)

Faculty of Humanities and Arts, Macau University of Science and Technology, Avenida Wai Long, Taipa 999078, Macau, China
2009853GAT30001@student.must.edu.mo

Abstract. Multi-source data analysis and calculation is an important part of urban planning and urban governance. Taking the Northern District of Macau as an example, this study combines spatial syntax with POI data based on multiple indicators such as the integration, selectivity, and depth of the urban road network, and aggregates the spatial characteristics and functions of urban roads on the basis of multi-source data. The spatial coupling relationship is evaluated, and suggestions for optimizing the urban road network and functional layout are proposed, aiming to provide methodological reference and guidance for the urban planning, functional layout, and development and construction of high-density urban areas.

Keyword: High-density city · Road network · City function layout · Multi-source data

1 Introduction

The road network is one of the basic elements of the structure of a city, and to a certain extent reflects the city's spatial characteristics, economic conditions, human settlements, social structure, and cultural heritage. With the development of urban modernization, the urban road network and spatial structure continue to grow and change with the needs of modernization. The vigorous development of emerging economies and the increasing population expansion have made high-density urban agglomeration an inevitable trend [1]. On the one hand, high-density cities enrich the diversity of residents' lives, improve the efficiency of work and life, and reduce the per capita cost of urban supporting construction. On the other hand, high-density cities have problems such as uneven business distribution, inefficient use of buildings, and traffic congestion due to their high capacity and complex functional layout.

H. Wu et al. (Eds.): SpatialDI 2022, LNCS 13614, pp. 189–206, 2022.
https://doi.org/10.1007/978-3-031-24521-3_14

This article takes the Northern District of Macau as an example (Fig. 1). It is located to the north of the Macau Peninsula and includes the Ilha Verde District (Zone A), Fai Chi Kei District (Zone B), Toi San District (Zone C), Povoação de Mong-Há and Reservatório de Água Area (Zone D), Iao Hon and Areia Preta Area (Zone E), and Novos Aterros da Areia Preta Area (Zone F).

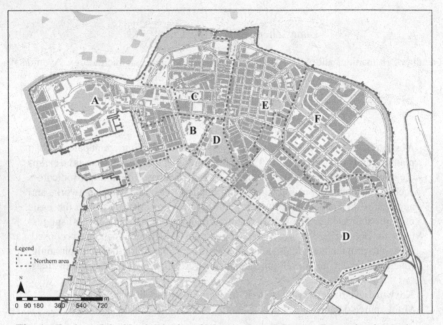

Fig. 1. Zoning of the North District of Macau. (Image Source: Drawn by the Author)

Since the beginning of the 20th century, the Macau government has started a series of land reclamation projects in the North District to meet the needs of economic development. Reclamation project. Due to economic setbacks, the reclamation plan was once stagnated. However, small-scale reclamation was carried out in Zone D in 1966. Until the 1980s, due to the economic recovery and booming development, the demand for land increased greatly. The large-scale land expansion project started again. In 1985, the previously reclaimed land in Zone B, Zone C and Area E was expanded. In 1990, the land reclamation project in Zone F was completed, which has now formed the geographic area of the Northern District of Macau [2]. The Northern District of Macau covers an area of 3.2 square kilometres, accounting for 34.4% of the area of the Macau Peninsula. It has a population of 246,600 and a population density of 77,000 per square kilometre. The per capita green area and recreation area is only 1.47 square meters, making it the most populous area in Macau. [3]. In response to the needs of social development and the positioning of the future city, with the opening of the Guangdong-Macau New Corridor (Edifício Posto Fronteiriço de Macau do Posto Fronteiriço QingMao) in September 2021, the North District has three cross-border ports: Qingmao, Gongbei, and Ilha Verde. The North District's land use, block integration and urban image renewal are highly concerned. Recently, the Macau Special Administrative Region Government's Urban Administration has launched a plan for the North District to develop a master plan and design guidelines [4] to create an internationally featured venue for the North District and realize the regional economy, The sustainable development of ecology and society has brought new opportunities.

In recent years, the research on road network structure and spatial format is gradually showing the trend of quantification and scientificization along with the development of analysis technology. At present, many scholars use Bill Hillier's spatial syntax theory to conduct research on urban road networks: ① From the perspective of research, they mainly use multi-source data as the background, combined with quantitative statistical analysis tools to analyze the laws and rules of road networks. Features [5–7]. ② In terms of research content, the built-up areas of cities or villages are the main ones, mainly involving road optimization [8], behavioral activity analysis [9], comparative city research [10], road plan evaluation [11], site selection research [12] Wait. ③ In terms of research methods, use spatial syntax theory and technology to construct models of urban road network axes, line segments and convex spaces, use integration, selectivity, and depth algorithms to study the characteristics of urban road networks, and combine points of interest (POI) [13], geographic location data (LBS) [14], geographic information system (GIS) [15], statistical product and service solution (SPSS) [16], etc. to conduct data coupling comparison and comprehensive evaluation.

The research needs to deepen the direction: First, from the research perspective, most of the multi-source data comes from open platforms, such as OpenStreetMap, etc., which lack official and authoritative data support, which affects the accuracy of the analysis results. Second, the research objects are mostly low-, medium-, and high-density cities. The research on ultra-high-density cities (population density exceeding 25,000 people per square kilometer) [17] pays little attention to the impact of urban population density on roads and business types. The impact is greater, so the ultra-high-density city as the research object has more prominent main characteristics. Third, in terms of research methods, some scholars ignore the influence of search radius in the technical application of space syntax, and only analyze and study the research area, lacking attention to the peripheral road network, and cannot accurately summarize the parameters of the space syntax in the area. Therefore, this study takes representative ultra-high-density cities as the research object, and uses multi-source data based on geographic information data of the Macau Cadastral Bureau to set micro (500 m), meso (1500 m), and macro (5000 m)) And many other search radii, combined with spatial syntax, GIS, POI and other research methods to conduct quantitative research on it, respond to the government's development plan for the area and provide theoretical basis and technical indicators for urban design and urban planning.

2   Research Scope and Data

2.1   Area of Research

The scope of this article is the northern part of the Macau peninsula, from left to right along with Rua da Doca Seca, Rua da Bacia Sul, and Rua do General Ivens Ferraz from left to right, Avenida do General Castelo Branco, Avenida do Coronel Mesquita, Estrada do Reservatório, Avenida da Amizade, and Zhuhai City to the north Connected to the east and west of the Marina (Fig. 2), it is one of the most densely populated areas in Macau. Among them, the Iao Hon and Areia Preta Area (Zone E) have a median population of 170,953 per square kilometre at the Macau Statistics Bureau. The density of people is representative of ultra-high-density cities. Identifying and analyzing the characteristics of the road network structure and business layout of the Northern District of Macau has important reference value for optimizing the spatial structure of the Northern District of Macau and even the Macau Peninsula. It can provide a reference for the study of the spatial structure of ultra-high-density cities.

Fig. 2. Satellite Map of Northern District of Macau. (Image Source: The author is intercepted from Macau GIS)

2.2   Data Sources

This article is mainly based on GIS data and POI data. The GIS data comes from the 2019 digital map of the Macao Special Administrative Region provided by the Cartography and Cadastre Bureau of the Macao Special Administrative Region. The data is rich in types, highly targeted, fair and scientific, and can ensure the accuracy and representativeness of this research. The map POI data is taken from the AutoNavi Maps Open Map API in September 2021. AutoNavi Map is the mainstream electronic map platform with fast data acquisition, short update cycle, timeliness and comprehensiveness. According to the road network data in the GIS, all the POI points in the northern area of Macau are selected, a total of 8,939, and a total of 20 categories. This research divides it into 8 categories after screening by POI data: commercial (58.74%), corporate (12.76%), transportation (10.81%), residential area (10.20%), education (2.95%), government Institutions (2.73%), scenic spots (1.29%), public facilities (0.51%). On the basis of the mainstream POI classification, the diversity of POI data is retained, and the POI data of the map in the study area is finally obtained (Table 1).

Table 1. Map POI data classification.

POI category	Number of points	Category
Catering Service	1621	Commercial
Sightseeing	115	Attractions
Public facilities	46	Public facilities
Corporate Enterprise	1141	Corporate Enterprise
Leisure Services	129	Commercial
Traffic facilities	36	Transportation
Residential complex	912	Residential complex
Living Services	838	Commercial
Accommodation Service	13	Commercial
Shopping Service	1494	Commercial
Transportation facility service	930	Transportation
Financial Insurance Services	152	Commercial
Science, Education and Cultural Services	264	Education
Motorcycle Service	44	Commercial
Healthcare Services	652	Commercial
Government agencies and social organizations	244	Government agencies
Car Service	163	Commercial
Car repair	107	Commercial
Car sales	38	Commercial

3   Research Methods

3.1   Space Syntax

Space syntax is one of the quantitative analysis methods of spatial form. Through the quantitative description of spatial structure, it studies the relationship and laws between people and spatial organization, and is widely used in the fields of urban form and urban spatial structure. There are four types of spatial syntax component models, namely, horizon model, convex space model, axis model, line segment model, etc. The line segment model is based on the real distance of the road and the road turning angle as the main calculation factors, which is considered to have higher The credibility of, has a significant advantage in calculating the different distance radii of the road. In addition, related studies have proved that the line segment model is closer to the actual situation in road analysis [7], so this study chooses the axis model as the analysis model.

In terms of analysis parameters, this article uses variables commonly used in space syntax: integration, selectivity, and depth. The specific meaning of each variable is: ① Integration is also called integration degree, which describes the degree of agglomeration or dispersion between spaces in the system. The closer the space units in the system are, the less the barriers between spaces are., The higher the concentration of the space, the higher the publicity and convenience in the road system. ② Choice is a description of the traversability of a road, which means the number of times that can be crossed between roads, that is, the degree to which one can be selected in an ideal state. The higher the degree of choice, the greater the traffic potential. ③ Total depth is the depth of the description of the location. The global depth represents the sum of the minimum distance between nodes and other nodes in the system. The smaller the depth value, the higher the road convenience. The local depth indicates the relative closeness of the local radius to the central area. The value of local integration is positively related to the convenience of the road, and the value of global integration is negatively related to the convenience of the road [18].

3.2   Nuclear Density Analysis

Nuclear density is to describe the density of the elements in the system. The POI density is calculated by the kernel density analysis method, the distribution law of the analysis elements in the space is studied according to the standard difference level method, and the attenuation function is used to study the specific analysis of the elements. The distribution and agglomeration conditions are combined with GIS to visually express the analysis results in the form of heat maps to study the vitality of the space. The higher the nuclear density of each element in the system, the higher the vitality.

4   Results and Analysis

4.1   Structural Characteristics of Urban Road Network

Based on the analysis method of space syntax, extract the central axis of the Macau Peninsula in the GIS, construct the line segment model, set the search radius to N meters (global scope), 500 m, 1500 m, 5000 m and other analysis parameters of different distances, among which A 500-m radius represents a walking distance of 5 to 10 min, a 1500-m radius represents a walking distance of 15 to 20 min, and a 5000-m radius represents the maximum diameter of the Macau Peninsula, which is in line with the need for the analysis of the radius division in the space syntax boundary effect. Under different search radii, the integration, selectivity, and depth are analyzed, and the analysis results of 4 search radii are obtained respectively (Table 2).

Table 2. Spatial syntax parameter analysis results

Spatial syntax variables (line segment model)		Average index					
		Zone A	Zone B	Zone C	Zone D	Zone E	Zone F
Integration	Overall situation	635	718	743	636	738	706
	R = 500	29	38	49	42	63	56
	R = 1500	97	196	194	134	236	166
	R = 5000	612	710	737	614	724	687
Selectivity	Overall situation	142514	171031	543389	311226	322135	506633
	R = 500	418	741	382	1031	995	1030
	R = 1500	5237	12604	13326	21119	13666	12441
	R = 5000	98632	208918	242221	255208	173263	267003
Depth	Overall situation	94682	77914	79873	92617	78452	82408
	R = 500	179	253	156	259	356	177
	R = 1500	3060	7760	4768	4888	4784	2021
	R = 5000	65033	61996	60785	76647	65606	63107

The results of the integration analysis of the northern area of Macau are shown in Fig. 3. The central area is southerly.

Specific analysis of the degree of integration:

① In the overall degree of integration, the core integration is zone C, followed by zone B and zone E, and the remaining zones are gradually attenuating. Therefore, for the large-scale and global structure of motor vehicle travel, the highly integrated areas are generally the arterial roads in the central part of the North District, reflecting the characteristics of the North District's motor-driven city.

② In the local integration within a radius of 500 m, as a walking destination, the overall integration is weak, and the areas with the highest accessibility are concentrated in Zone E. Secondly, the Avenida da Amizade along the coast of Zone F connects many roads, and the degree of integration is the second highest. Zone E and Zone F are ideal areas within a 5 to 10-min walking distance.

global integration   integration(R=500)

integration(R=1500)   integration(R=5000)

Fig. 3. Analysis of the Integration Degree of the Northern District of Macau. (Image Source: Drawn by the Author)

③ In the local integration within a radius of 1500 m, the overall integration has been improved, and the integration of the Zone E has been significantly improved, indicating that whether it is a short walk of 5 to 10 min or a long distance of 15 to 20 min During walking, E area has good spatial penetration.

④ In the local integration degree with a radius of 5000 m, the integration degree is similar to the global integration degree. All in all, the core integration of the North District is concentrated in Zone C and Zone E, among which Zone C is better for motor vehicle access, and Zone E is better for long and short walks.

The results of the analysis of the selectivity of the Northern District of Macau are shown in Fig. 4. Both the global and local selectivity are relatively weak.

Specifically: ① In the global selection degree, the areas with higher selection degree are Zone C and F. Among them, the Avenida De Artur Tamagnini Barbosa in the Zone C and the Avenida da Amizade in the Zone F show higher values, making the area The average value has been improved, indicating that in terms of vehicle-based travel, Avenida De Artur Tamagnini Barbosa and Avenida da Amizade have the highest degree of passability and are the main traffic arteries.

② In the local selectivity with a radius of 500 m, the areas with the highest selectivity are Zone D, Zone E, and Zone F. The road network in Zone E is denser and therefore has a high degree of travel, while the roads around the ponds in Zone D The distance between the nets is relatively close, which increases the degree of passability. Zone F is because the

global choice   choice(R=500)

choice(R=1500)   choice(R=5000)

Fig. 4. Analysis of the degree of selection in the Northern District of Macau. (Image Source: Drawn by the Author)

Avenida Doutor Ma Man Kei on the right is the only road connecting Reclamation Zone A and the Hong Kong-Zhuhai-Macao Port, which significantly improves the degree of passability. Excluding the interference factors of zone D and F, in short-distance walking, zone E has good conditions for passing through.

③ In the local selectivity with a radius of 1500 m, the area with the highest selectivity is Zone D. The Rua de Francisco Xavier Pereira on the west side has a higher value, which makes the overall selectivity significantly improved, indicating that in long-distance walking, Rua de Francisco Xavier Pereira has a high potential for passing traffic.

④ In the local selectivity with a radius of 5000 m, each area has a higher selectivity except for Zone A. Since Zone A is in a relatively isolated position, it contributes less to the travel of each area, which reduces the overall travelability. So the potential for passable traffic in Zone A is low. All in all, Zone C and Zone F have better passability for motor vehicle-based trips, while Zone E has better passability for pedestrian-based trips.

The in-depth analysis of the northern area of Macau is shown in Fig. 5. The central area is southerly.

Specifically: ① In the global depth, the areas with the highest depth are Zone A, Zone D and Zone F. These three zones are located at the edge of the North Zone, relatively far away from the central area of the Macau Peninsula, with longer distances and greater convenience.

② In the local depth with a radius of 500 m, because the local integration degree is positively correlated with the road convenience, the area with the highest local depth is the Zone E, which is similar to the analysis result of the local integration degree under the same radius. The Zone E is more effective for short-distance walking. The high degree of convenience.

③ In the local depth with a radius of 1500 m, the deepest area is concentrated at the junction of Zone B, Zone C, Zone D and Zone E. This area is closer to the central area of the Macau Peninsula and is within a long walking distance shorter and more convenient.

④ In the local depth with a radius of 5000 m, the area with the highest depth in Zone D. Because the centre of the depth is shifted to the area of Colina da Guia Mountain, which is closer to Zone D, the depth of Zone D presents a higher value, but The central area is contrary to the actual situation, and the local depth of this radius is not highly referenced. All in all, for pedestrian-based travel, the coastal areas of Zone A, Zone F and Zone D have low access to the central area, while the junction of Zone B, Zone C, Zone D and Zone E leads to the central area convenience is high.

Fig. 5. In-depth analysis of the Northern District of Macau. (Image Source: Drawn by the Author)

4.2   The Spatial Distribution of Functional Business Clusters

The distribution of POI data in the Northern District of Macau is shown in Fig. 6. Different types of POI have different spatial layouts:

① From the data point of view, commercial POI accounts for 58.74% of the total data, and is the main type of POI.

② From the perspective of layout, it is mainly distributed in Zone E, forming an obvious high-density POI zone, followed by Zone F, Zone C and Zone B forming a POI medium-density zone. Among them, the POI in Zone F is unevenly distributed, with more POI in the southwest and the northeast. Less. The distribution of POI in Zone A and Zone D is less, which is a low density zone of POI.

③ From the point of view of site selection, it is mainly distributed along the street, with more residential areas and less coastal areas.

④ In general, the distribution of POI in the North District has a significant dual-center structure, with the Zone E as the main center and the Zone B as the secondary center, and the surrounding POI density gradually decreases.

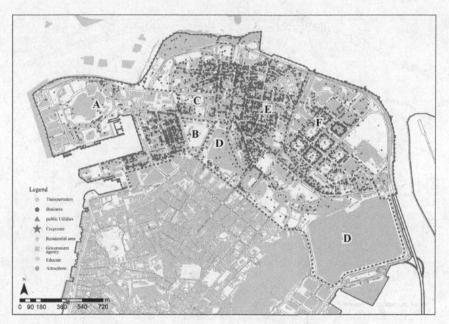

Fig. 6. Distribution of POI Data in Northern District of Macau. (Image Source: Drawn by the Author)

Perform nuclear density analysis on the above-mentioned POI data, and obtain the analysis results in Fig. 7, 8, 9, 10, 11, 12, 13 and 14. The characteristics of each category of POI in the Northern District of Macau:

① The commercial POI core density presents a dual-center structure with spatial imbalance. Zone E is the main commercial center and Zone B is the secondary commercial center.

② The company's corporate POIs are mainly distributed in the north of Zone D, which is mainly the industrial building clustering area along the Avenida de Venceslau de Morais.

③ The distribution of POIs in transportation, residential quarters, government agencies, scenic spots and public facilities is similar to commercial POIs, which are mainly distributed in Zone B and E, indicating that transportation, housing, and public facilities are related to commerce.

④ Education POIs are distributed in a multi-point manner. Each district has a gathering point for education distribution, mainly concentrated in Rua de Lei Pou Chôn in Zone C and Avenida da Longevidade in Zone E.

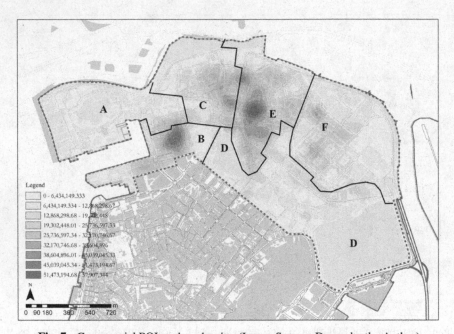

Fig. 7. Commercial POI nuclear density. (Image Source: Drawn by the Author)

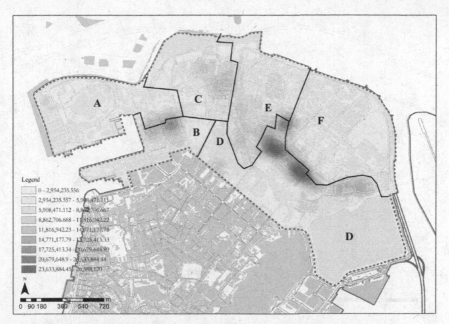

Fig. 8. Corporate POI nuclear density. (Image Source: Drawn by the Author)

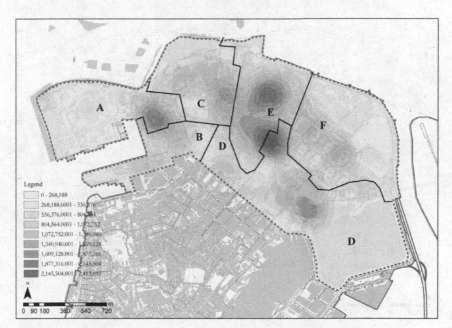

Fig. 9. Transportation POI nuclear density. (Image Source: Drawn by the Author)

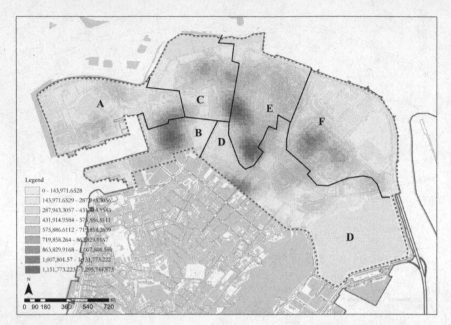

Fig. 10. Residential district POI nuclear density. (Image Source: Drawn by the Author)

Fig. 11. Education POI nuclear density. (Image Source: Drawn by the Author)

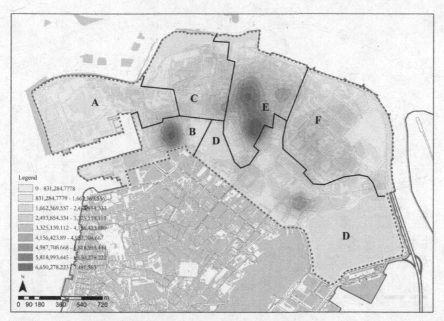

Fig. 12. Government agencies POI nuclear density. (Image Source: Drawn by the Author)

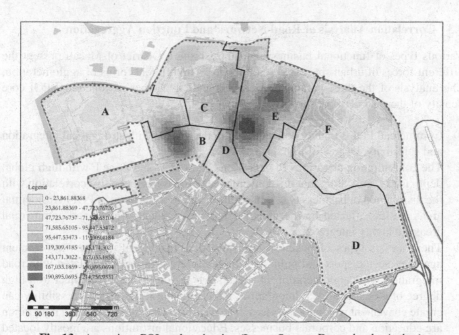

Fig. 13. Attractions POI nuclear density. (Image Source: Drawn by the Author)

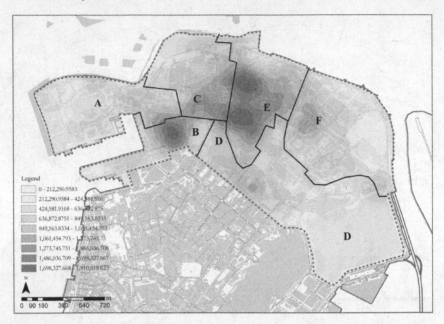

Fig. 14. Public facilities POI nuclear density. (Image Source: Drawn by the Author)

4.3 Correlation Analysis of Road Network and Function Aggregation

Various types of functional businesses in the Northern District of Macau present the different forces of urban space and road networks in different forms of agglomeration. The analysis of the three-parameter variables and eight types of functional POI core density of the road network shows:

① Commercial POI is mainly concentrated in the Zone E with strong local integration and selectivity. Degree of influence.

② The concentration of various POIs in Zone A, Zone D and Zone F with high global depth is low, indicating that the convenience of roads has a positive correlation with the distribution of business types. In addition, the concentration of POI in residential areas are less affected by the global depth, and residential areas and commercial areas are highly integrated.

③ There are six types of business, transportation, residential quarters, government agencies, scenic spots and public facilities that are positively correlated with road integration. The agglomeration of these six types of business is subject to a high degree of global and local integration, indicating that it has good accessibility can create convenient residents' services. The weaker correlations with road integration are education and corporate businesses. Educational institutions are mostly located in living quarters, while corporate businesses have a clear location division and are less affected by traffic arterial hubs.

④ Zone A and Zone F have a high degree of integration and selectivity. For example, the Ilha Verde in Zone A and Avenida Doutor MA Man Kei in Zone F have high development potential, but the concentration of commercial POI in this area is relatively low. The commercial vitality is insufficient and needs to be continuously developed.

⑤ In general, the degree of integration, choice, and depth of roads in the North District, that is, the accessibility, passability, and convenience of the roads will affect commerce, transportation, residential communities, government agencies, scenic spots, and public The agglomeration of 6 types of functional business formats such as facilities, among which the degree of local integration and choice has an obvious effect on commercial agglomeration, while the distribution of education and companies is less affected by roads. The agglomeration of residential quarters and commerce is highly integrated. The permeability of the district is high, and the residential district has no clear directionality.

5 Conclusion

The distribution characteristics of urban POI data reflect the level of vitality of different regions. Scientific analysis tools can be used to objectively and quantitatively analyze the characteristics of urban spatial structure and function distribution. Taking the northern area of Macau as an example, combining the research methods of space syntax and POI nuclear density, it is found that: ① The northern area of Macau has a significant double-centre structure, namely the Iao Hon and Areia Preta Area (Zone E) and Fai Chi Kei District (Zone B), and is positively correlated with road integration and selectivity, and global depth is negatively correlated with commercial distribution. ② Ilha Verde District (Zone A) on the west side of the North District and the new reclamation area of Novos Aterros da Areia Preta Area (Zone F) on the east side are unevenly distributed, but the local roads have certain traffic advantages in terms of integration and choice. Targeted development will activate the commercial vitality of the area. ③ In the road structure indicators, it is shown that the degree of local integration and the degree of local selection has a great impact on commercial agglomeration, reflecting the close relationship between the accessibility and passability of pedestrian traffic and the commercial distribution of the North District, and sustainable optimization of the pedestrian traffic network The structure and road environment promotes a more balanced type and distribution of block functions.

This study shows that different types of data and their analysis results have certain differences. The comparative study of multi-source data can be used to make the analysis results more accurate. Combining space syntax and POI data to study urban spatial structure is feasible, providing a theoretical and technical basis in functional layout, shop location, urban design, etc., and improving the scientificity and objectivity of research in related fields.

Acknowledgement. This paper is supported by Macao Special Administrative Region Government Higher Education Fund Special Funding Program for Research on Humanities and Social Fields in Macao Higher Education Institutions (No. HSS-MUST-2020–9).

References

1. Dong, C.: High-density architecture. Beijing: China Building Industry Press (2012)
2. Huang, J., Rong, X.: Macau takes land from the sea.Macau: Overseas Chinese News (1998) (013)
3. Statistics and Survey Bureau of the Macau Special Administrative Region Government. Demographic Information Database Homepage. https://www.dsec.gov.mo/Censos WebDB/#!/main?lang=moAccessed 21 Sept 2021
4. Municipal Administration of the Government of Macao Special Administrative Region. Project Information Homepage. https://www.iam.gov.mo/project/c/info/Projectquote.aspx? quotetype=1. Accessed 21 Sep 2021
5. Yanqun, Y., Kun, C., Yingzi, W.: Research on the vitality of historical districts based on the comprehensive measurement of space syntax and Baidu heat map. Chin. Foreign Arch. **08**, 101–106 (2021)
6. Yao, S., Zhuo Jian, W., Zhiqiang,: Precise urban design: a city morphology oriented to the precise promotion of social effects. Times Arch. **01**, 26–33 (2021)
7. Hengyu, G., Duo, H., Tiyan, S., Xiaoling, Q.: Research on spatial syntax model verification and application in urban design driven by multi-source urban data. Planner **35**(05), 67–73 (2019)
8. Chang, L.: Optimization strategy for walkability of public service facilities under the background of aging. Shanxi Arch. **44**(21), 10–12 (2018)
9. Luo, Q., Wen, Z., Yu, L.: Research on the strategy of improving the street space vitality of small towns under the guidance of environmental behavior: taking zihu town as an example. Urban Dev. Res. **26**(02), 20–24 (2019)
10. Qiang, S., Haishan, X., Xing, L.: An empirical study on the cross-section passenger flow between subway stations by space syntax——taking Beijing, Tianjin and Chongqing as examples. Urban Plan. **42**(06), 57–67 (2018)
11. Sheng, Q., Zhou, C., Kaiwan, K., Lu, A., Shao, M.: Data-based urban design based on spatial syntax model: taking the design of Chaoyang plaza in Jilin City as an example. Landscape Arch. **6**(02), 103–113 (2018)
12. Qiang, S., Yang Zhensheng, L., Le Anhua, C.: Application of network open data in syntactic analysis of urban commercial vitality space. New Arch. **03**, 9–14 (2018)
13. Zhou, Y., Zhang, C., Cui, M., Li, N., Chen, P.: Research on the layout of urban commercial outlets based on spatial syntax and POI information: taking longquanyi district of Chengdu as an example. Sichuan Arch. **34**(06), 15–18 (2014)
14. Xinhua, H., Ying, L., Miao, S., Peng, W.: Beijing street vitality: measurement, influencing factors and planning and design enlightenment. Shanghai Urban Plan. **03**, 37–45 (2016)
15. Huang Mengzhen, G., Hengyu, C.Z.: The influence of road network shape on the spatial distribution of urban internal park system: taking Nansha district of Guangzhou as an example. J. South Chin. Normal Univ. (Nat. Sci. Ed.) **50**(03), 78–84 (2018)
16. Qian, L., Xingzhao, L., Xinxin, L., Sainan, L., Jiaxin, L.: Research on the accessibility of park green space in Nantai Island, Fuzhou based on space syntax. J. Guangxi Normal Univ. (Nat. Sci. Ed.) **39**(04), 181–195 (2021)
17. Heping, L., Zhi, L.: Analysis of the temporal and spatial evolution of urban density and high-density development in China-from 1981 to 2014. Urban Dev. Res. **26**(04), 46–54 (2019)
18. Asami, Y., Kubat, A., Kitagawa, K.: Introducing Third Dimension On Space Syntax: Application On The Historical Istanbul1 (2003)

Hot Public Appeal Extraction and Visual Analysis Combined BERT and Spatio-Temporal Location

Wei Fan[✉] and Ruhong Yang

Wuhan Natural Resources and Planning Information Center, Wuhan 430014, China
124542264@qq.com

Abstract. Analyzing the temporal and spatial distributions of public appeal can contribute to understanding issues of public concern. However, how to find hidden and valuable for early warning information and intelligence clues in large-scale text data remains a challenging task, especially with the explosion of public appeals. This paper proposes an intelligent extraction model of hot public appeal based on BERT and Spatio-Temporal location. For the unstructured appeals and its address, the fusion model is trained after extracting the keywords by word segmentation. Taking Baibuting Community as an example, experimental results show that the text representation model and text clustering method proposed in this paper have better topic detection effect than traditional methods. Combining spatial and temporal information with the classification results, We analyze the spatial and temporal distribution characteristics of hot topics in different regions. It will assist the grass-roots level in the rapid discovery, rapid response and coordinated disposal of the main problems of public appeal, and improve the refinement and intelligence level of grass-roots social governance.

Keywords: BERT · Time series · Public appeal · Intelligence extraction · Visual analysis

1 Introduction

In recent years, with the continuous development of the Internet and the increasing enthusiasm of the public to participate in social governance, the number of public appeals has increased sharply. At present, Wuhan has basically built a series of information service projects that benefit people's livelihood, including people's special line, micro-neighborhood, urban message board, smart urban management, etc. These can receive public appeals by telephone, Wechat and Website. At the same time, according to the requirements of government information disclosure, the whole process of the disposal of such public appeals can be read, queried and commented on websites and Wechat. These public appeals come from the grass-roots level, including all aspects of social development and people's livelihood services. The appeal theme is broad, which generally includes location, events and other information. It has the characteristics of interactivity, real-time and sociality, and the public appeal themes in different regions are different.

H. Wu et al. (Eds.): SpatialDI 2022, LNCS 13614, pp. 207–217, 2022.
https://doi.org/10.1007/978-3-031-24521-3_15

How to focus on the specific content of social demands from the public perspective and accurately obtain and perceive the distribution of demands has become the difficulty of current research.

At the same time, the conductivity and liquidity of the new social contradiction risk are continuously enhanced, and the cycle from brewing and fermentation to centralized outbreak is continuously shortened. So it puts forward new requirements for the scientificity of social governance decision-making and the accuracy of risk prevention and control. How to accurately and timely perceive the demands of the public and respond in a timely and effective manner has become an important measure to promote the fine governance of grass-roots society. At present, there is a lack of effective hot topic mining methods based on location dimension. This paper proposes a hot public appeal extraction method integrating geographical location and incremental clustering, mining hot appeal in different regions, helping grass-roots staff identify common and hot issues of public concern in their jurisdiction, and improving the refinement of grass-roots social governance.

2 Related Works

2.1 BERT Model

In recent years, natural language processing model has achieved bettle results in text semantic analysis. The Bidirectional Encoder Representations from Transformers (BERT) training model was proposed by Google in 2018. It is a large-scale multi task language model with deep two-way and unsupervised language representation. It is a model that only uses plain text corpus for pre training. The goal of BERT model is to use large-scale unlabeled corpus to train and obtain the representation of text containing rich semantic information. It is a self-coding language model (Auto-encoder LM), that designs two tasks Masked Language Model (MLM) and Next Sense Prediction (NSP) to pre-train the model. MLM is to randomly select some words to be predicted when entering a sentence, and then replace them with a special symbol mask [1], and then let the model learn the words to be filled in these places according to the given label. NSP adds a sentence level continuity prediction task on the basis of the two-way language model, that is, to predict whether the two text segments input into BERT are continuous text. The introduction of this task can better enable the model to learn the relationship between continuous text segments.

Compared with the traditional model, BERT can execute concurrently, extract the relational features of words in sentences, and extract the relational features at multiple different levels, so as to reflect the sentence semantics more comprehensively. It can also obtain the word meaning according to the sentence context, so as to avoid ambiguity. At the same time, the disadvantages are obvious. There are too many model parameters, and the model is too large. It is easy to over fit when training with a small amount of data.

2.2   Incremental Clustering

With the rapid development of information processing technology, text clustering is increasingly attracting our attention. Feature extraction is a key element of text clustering. Good text features can reflect the nature of text better and improve the clustering result. Proposed term frequency based feature word selection method (TF) [2], that is, select according to the order of the total word frequency of feature words in the corpus. The higher the word frequency, the more important the feature words are. The feature word selection method based on document frequency (DF) [3] proposed by Azam n et al. Selects according to the order of document frequency of feature words in the corpus. The higher the document frequency, the more important it is. Some researches are based on the combination of the above two methods for feature selection, such as the two-stage feature selection method proposed by Wang y et al. [4], term frequency inverted document frequency (TF-IDF) [5] and its improved method proposed by Zheng y et al. TF-IDF method is an idea based on text classification, that is, the higher the word frequency and the lower the document frequency, the better the distinction of words in the text database and the higher its importance.

Although clustering algorithm has some challenges in processing high-dimensional data in processing static data, it can get ideal results by using different preprocessing [6–8]. However, in the current era of rich web applications, when new data appears, non-incremental clustering will have to re cluster all data, which is bound to reduce efficiency and waste computing resources. As an algorithm to remove the redundant noise features of high-dimensional data, feature extraction algorithm, combined with clustering algorithm, can reduce the clustering calculation load and improve the clustering speed while maintaining the accuracy of clustering results. Therefore, applying feature extraction algorithm to the preprocessing of incremental clustering will play a positive role in clustering.

Yiming Yang proposed a solution algorithm [9] using the combination of average clustering algorithm and agglomerative clustering algorithm, which can trace the precursor events. Trieschnigg D et al. Proposed an improved text aggregation hierarchical clustering algorithm based on text incremental hierarchical clustering algorithm [7] in terms of hierarchical clustering algorithm for hot spot discovery, which integrates the remaining text into the acyclic directed graph system according to the value range of similarity, and the remaining text into the acyclic directed graph system according to the value range of similarity. The text whose similarity is greater than the set threshold will be embedded into the acyclic directed graph as its own class cluster, and the text whose correlation is less than the set threshold will be determined as a new class cluster. As a classical incremental text clustering algorithm [10], single pass algorithm has been widely used in text clustering and topic discovery.

3   BERT Model Based on Spatio-Temporal

Analyzing the specific information of each appeal, we can know the appeal information, including appeal content, appeal location, appeal time, etc. From the perspective of text, this information belongs to short text. If we deal with short text based on the concept of words, we can only stay at the level of the text itself, and there will be a large deviation in the mining of hot event topics. It ignores the topic relevance between sentences. That is, when extracting topics, many topics may be the same one which describing one appeal, while similar topics occurring in different places should be two topics. Therefore, this paper proposes a BERT model combining time information and geographical location to mine urban regional hot events, so as to make the distribution of hot events more real-time.

3.1   Construction of Model

The BERT semantic vector model based on Spatio-Temporal information describes the appeal event information as a spatio-temporal change vector, which is described by four elements: space, time, attribute and topict. Its data model is expressed as

$$PA = f (S, T, A, HT) \qquad (1)$$

PA represents the public appeals, S represents the spatial location, T represents the time, A represents the event attribute, and HT represents the hot topic (see Fig. 1).

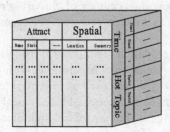

Fig. 1. BERT semantic vector model based on spatio-temporal

The general idea of the model construction is to extract the address of the public appeals. Through the standard address matching in the geographic information database, it give each appeal the spatial location such as longitude and latitude, which can divide it into different community management units. So the spatial location vector of BERT Semantic Vector Model is obtained. We can obtain the time vector of occurrence of this appeal. The Spatio-Temporal vector of model is constructed.

According to the Time Interval, different appeal events are divided into several equal interval time slices. The keywords and weights of the extracted text in each time slice are extracted, and the BERT model of the text is constructed. Set ω, σ and ρ as the word vector, text vector and position vector of BERT model. When the BERT semantic feature vector is trained, the N-dimensional vector representation of any word is output. The BERT semantic feature vector D_m is defined as:

$$D_m = W_{ij}(\omega + \sigma + \rho) \qquad (2)$$

Finally, the first two vector models are spliced to obtain BERT semantic vector model based on Spatio-Temporal of each appeal.

3.2 Cluster Analysis and Heat Calculation

Unlike online public opinion, similar appeals occur in different places should be two things. Therefore, grid partition and text clustering are used together to determine different events. According to the place where the appeal occurs, all appeals are divided into different grids. And then text clustering is used. In order to improve the calculation speed, the time period is equally divided into multiple time slices. We get a list appeal according to time vector of model in such time period.

The incremental clustering method is adopted to judge whether it is the same topic through cosine similarity, and each topic with its vector model is obtained in different time slices of each region.

Cosine similarity is calculated as:

$$\cos(u, v) = \frac{u \cdot v}{|u| \cdot |v|} = \frac{x_1 \cdot y_1 + x_2 \cdot y_2 + \ldots x_n \cdot y_n}{|u| \cdot |v|} \qquad (3)$$

where u and v are two vectors and x_i y_i are the weights of the corresponding words.

Then, the topics of all time slices are aggregated and classified to get different events. At the same time, spatial location vector of each appeal are used to distinguish event with similar topics.

Next the event heat is calculated. Count the hottest time of each topic in the current topic set. If an event is composed of one or more topics, then counting the hottest time of a topic can better express the development process of an event. The topic heat is calculated according to the complaint heat in a time slice and the public opinion heat of Internet users. The final topic set is the spatial vector model of the topic and the set of the hottest time and heat. The heat is calculated as:

$$
\begin{aligned}
hot_n &= hot_d * w_1 + hot_w * w_2 \\
&= \sum_{c=1}^{K} \left(\frac{d_{nc}}{\sqrt{\sum_{i=1}^{T} D_{ic}^2}} * e^{\frac{d_{nc}}{d_c}} \right) * w_1 + e^{\frac{0.5*\sum_{i=1}^{N} m_i + \sum_{i=1}^{N} cn_i}{\sum_{i=1}^{N} m_i + \sum_{i=1}^{N} cn_i}} * w_2
\end{aligned}
\qquad (4)
$$

where hot_d and hot are the heat of complaints and the heat of netizens' public opinion;

K: The total amount of all complaint channel corresponding to appeal in the time slice;

d_c: The number of appeal texts in the c complaint channel;

d_{nc}: The number of appeal texts related to topic n in complaint channel c;

$d_c d_c$: The number of appeal texts of the topic i in complaint channel c;

rn: The total number of times topic n was read in time slice T;

cn: The total number of times topic n was queried in time slice T;

N: The number of appeal texts contained in topic N;

rn_i :The number of times to read the text of each appeal;

cn_i: The number of queried progress times of each appeal.

According to the heat of appeals, it arranged in reverse order of popularity of hot appeals. It is the whole workflow (see Fig. 2).

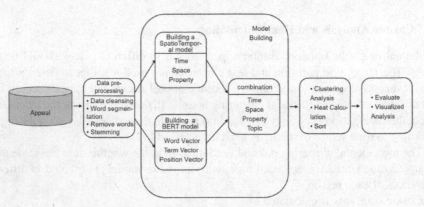

Fig. 2. The workflow of experimental implementation

4   Experiment and Results

4.1   Data Preprocessing

The platform of "Wuhan MinHuWoYing" is aggregated from all channels, including by telephone, Wechat and Website.That's where the data comes from. Meanwhile, Wuhan has divided the urban space into grid units of a certain size according to population density, forming a multi-level grid of city, district, street, community and grid [11]. In this experiment, Abort 6.19 million appeals from all channels in the city in 2020 gathered by this platform were used. People name, contact information, appeal content, appeal address, grid of occurrence and other information arc obtained.The appeals were divided into management units of different communities according to grid. More than 150000 appeals were extracted from Baibuting community.

The specific process is as follows: First, get the text of appeal content. Then carry out word segmentation, filter punctuation and numbers, and text denoise at the same time including synonym merging, full names and abbreviations consolidation, Stop words (such as for, etc.) removing and eliminating proprietary descriptions words (such as compare, involve, etc.).

4.2   Calculation of Model

Using the Bert model to embed words in the preprocessed data, the Bert semantic feature vector is constructed. In the transformer encoder unit, multi head self-attention is used to obtain vector. After the residual connection and normalization, the semantic feature vector of Bert is extracted. Input the segmented document into the model, and each word is mapped into three vectors, which are word vector, text vector and position vector of text. The transformer encoder learns and stores the semantic relationship and grammatical structure information of the document. By means of vector splicing, the Bert semantic feature vector and spatio-temporal location vector are superimposed to form a new input vector, which contains both word meaning features and space-time features. The appeals in different places belong to different events. Different events are obtained through spatial clustering and text incremental clustering.

After the cosine similarity calculation is completed, the calculation threshold of document similarity is set to 0.8. If the similarity is greater than 0.8, it seems that the two documents are the same appeal.

The heat of appeal is reflected in the heat of appeal and the heat of netizens' public opinion. In general, repeated complaints are events of public concern, and netizens often have some invalid comments. When calculating the sum of hot spots, the weight of appeal heat and netizen public opinion heat shall be distributed in the proportion of 4:1.

We can see the top three topics in different communities from January to December 2020 (see Fig. 3).

4.3   Evaluation of Model

The coherence of topic modeling and the contour coefficient of clustering are used to test the effect of this model. This paper uses a method to measure topic coherence whether the meaning of characteristic words in the same topic arc coherent. This method is proposed by Newman David from University of California Irvine(UCI) in 2010 [12]. The basic principle of this method is to calculate the Pointwise Mutual Information (PMI) of all word pairs (one set segmentation) in a given subject word based on the sliding window, and indirectly obtain the coherence by using the normalized point wise mutual information and cosine similarity, which is used for, and its value range is [0,1].

$$C_{UCI} = \frac{2}{N * (N - 1)} \sum_{i=1}^{N-1} \sum_{j=i+1}^{N} PMI(\omega_i, \omega_j) \qquad (5)$$

The contour score is used to evaluate the clustering effect of the model, and its value range is [−1, 1]. The higher the values of coherence and contour coefficient, the better the effect of the model.

community		January	Februar	March	April	May	June	July	August	September	October	November	December
1	Xingfashidai Neighborhood Committee	prevention and control	epidemic situation	enterprise	epidemic situation	blood glucose	Jingdong	wink	WeChat	report	sort out	activity	fitness
		epidemic situation	enterprise	WeChat	enterprise	diabetes	Driver training schools	mortgage	work	WeChat	age	lovely	Mirinda
		work	supermarket	work resumption	WeChat	consult	Safe	victory	service	Fill in the wrong	WeChat	xujing	work
2	First Neighborhood Committee	Neighborhood Committee	epidemic situation	epidemic situation	epidemic situation	WeChat	WeChat	work	advantage	sink	red packet	past due	work
		Neighborhood	buy vegetables	WeChat	contact	work	work	salary	salary	check in	sink	leadership	fitness
		lily	anju	recover	WeChat	consult	red packet	subsidy	WeChat	party member	work	clean out	Mirinda
3	modern city	beike	epidemic situation	Neighborhood	epidemic situation	consult	consult	square	WeChat	flow	sort out	clean out	fitness
		go out	district owner	modern city	diabetes	WeChat	Driver training schools	voice	work	scan QR codes	Happy	business	Mirinda
		hospital	enterprise	work	WeChat	diabetes	safe	business street	service	yuanbao	work	Each household	work
4	Daishan	epidemic situation	epidemic situation	epidemic situation	enterprise	market	Driver training schools	parental instructions	loans	work	extract	take up an occupation	supply heating
		prevention and control	Neighborhood	enterprise	epidemic situation	scene	Sign up	family tradition	enterprise	reportreport	watch	activityi	register
		pneumonia	mask	product	mask	detection	technology	accumulation fund	hot weather	activity	extract	recruit	cost
5	Jiangbei	fever	neighbourhood	epidemic situation	diabetes	QR code	policy	funeral	loans	report	Sign up	jiangbei	rush to repair
		neighbourhood	hujin	WeChat	work resumption	diabetes	start school	happy	enterprise	inoculate	distribute	recruit	coordinate
		Hujin	real estate	product	epidemic situation	blood glucose	work	service center	hot weather	family	hujin	outstanding	panic
6	Dandong	secretary	neighbourhood	epidemic situation	enterprise	epidemic situation	driving school	accumulation fund	friend	rubbish	Qingdao	homework	activity
		country	epidemic situation	WeChat	epidemic situation	maintain	Sign up	social security	loans	environment-al sanitation	Return to wuhan	Welding and cutting	party member
		development	buy vegetables	enterprise	mask	activity	distribution	friend	hot weather	party member	extract	activity	video

Fig. 3. Top three topics in different communities from January to December 2020

Table 1. Comparison of model evaluation.

Evaluation of model	TF-IDF	LDA	BERT	BERT model based on Spatio-Temporal
Coherence	0.514	0.471	0.468	0.532
Silhouette Score	0.008	/	0.073	0.136

From the model evaluation results in Table 1, the three methods have little difference in subject coherence, and the BERT model based on Spatio-Temporal information is slightly better. However, the contour coefficient of the other two methods is low, and there are many overlaps among the subject categories, so it is difficult to distinguish the edges between the subject categories. The comparison results show that the clustering effect of BERT model based on Spatio-Temporal information is significantly improved.

4.4 Visual Analysis

Time-Series Analysis. From the perspective of time, the hot words from January to May in each region were related to the epidemic, while those from June to August were related to the resumption of work and school, reflecting that the hot issues that residents were concerned about during the epidemic period had shifted from fighting the epidemic and living during the epidemic to the resumption of work and production after the epidemic, and gradually returned to the normal order of life. The hot cases identified from September to December 2020 involve people's livelihood services and the environment, enabling the government to grasp the main contradictions, focus on the main problems, and mobilize the main forces to realize the focus on solving the demands of the people.

We also find four top topics in Baibuting Community. According to the document–topic probability distribution matrix, the topic category of each appeals was obtained, and the spatial and temporal statistical analysis (See Fig. 4 and Fig. 5) under different topics was conducted.

The heat of WeChat peaked in April, May and August respectively. The heat of Work peaked in June and August respectively. The heat of Epidemic situation peaked in April and decreased month by month. The heat of Mask peaked in January and decreased month by month (See Fig. 4). It reflects the livelihood needs of community residents.

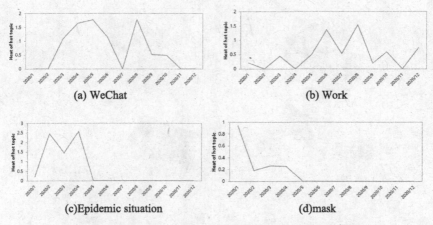

(a) WeChat   (b) Work

(c)Epidemic situation   (d)mask

Fig. 4. Time-series of the monthy under different of hot topic

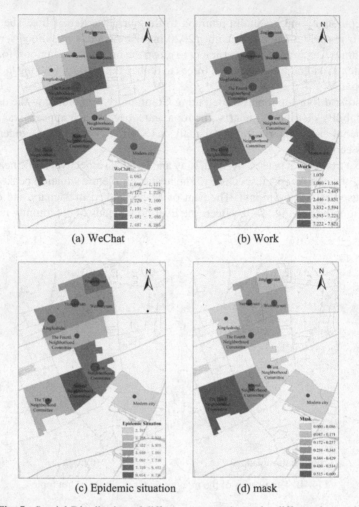

Fig. 5. Spatial Distribution of different community under different hot topic

Spatial Distribution of the Hot Topics. The spatial patterns of public opinion topics 1–4 were aggregated and distributed, most of which were clustered.

The First, Second, Third and Forth Baibuting Comminity are old communities for more than ten years. A lot of low-income people who need help are living in communities of Jinglanyuan, Yujingyuan, Wenhuiyuan. Xinfushidai and the modern city have some commercial block, where a little self-employed households live. We can see people living in old communities are more concerned about the demand for masks and work.

5   Conclusions

Through the spatial information extraction of public appeal hot event data and the quantitative analysis of public appeal pieces in various regions and industries, valuable early warning information and intelligence clues can be generated to study and judge the change trend and development law of public appeal. This paper makes a qualitative analysis on the temporal and spatial characteristics of hot topics. In the next step, we can further analyze the correlation between hot topics, living environment and population density.

References

1. Devlin, J., Chang, M.W., Lee, K., et al.: BERT: pre-training of deep bidirectional transformers for language understanding. In: Proceedings of the 2019 Conference of the North American Chapter of the Association for Computational Linguistics: Human Language Technologies. Stroudsburg, PA: Association for Computational Linguistics, pp. 4171–4186 (2019)
2. Yan, Y.: Text representation and classification with deep learning. University of Science and Technology Beijing, Beijing (2016). (in Chinese)
3. Tongrui, Y., Ran, J., Xiaozhen, H., et al.: Review of pre-training models for natural language processing. Comput. Eng. Appl. **56**(23), 12–22 (2020). (in Chinese)
4. Ibrahim, O., Landa-Silva, D.: Term frequency with average term occurrences for textual information retrieval. Soft. Comput. **20**(8), 3045–3061 (2016)
5. Azam, N., Yao, J.T.: Comparison of term frequency and document frequency based feature selection metrics in text categorization. Expert Syst. Appl. **39**(5), 4760–4768 (2012)
6. Yang, Y., Picrce, T., Carboncll, J.: A study on retrospective and on-line event detection. In: Proceedings of the 21st Annual International ACM SIGIR Conference on Research And Development in Information Retrieval, CMU, USA:ACM, pp. 28–36 (1998)
7. Tricschnigg, D., Kraaij, W.: TNO Hierarchical topic detection report at TDT 2004. In: Topic Detection and Tracking Workshop Rcport (2004)
8. Papka R., Allan, J.: On-line new event detection using single pass clustering. University of Massachusetts, Amherst, pp. 37–45 (1998). LNCS Homepage. http://www.springer.com/lncs. Accessed 21 Nov 2016
9. Dang, Y., Xu, Z., Liu, L., et al.: Research on incremental clustering algorithm of online public opinion text based on single-pass algorithm. J. Inner Mongolia Univ. Technol. **36**(5), 364–372 (2017)
10. Wu, G.S., Zhang, Y.: An improved density peak algorithm for micro-learning unit text clustering based on LSA model. Comput. Eng. Sci. **42**(04), 722–732 (2020). (In Chinese)
11. Li, Z., Peng, M., Pan, C.: Construction of social management innovation platform based on temporal spatial big data. Geospatial Inf. **14**(9), 1–5 (2016). (in Chinese)
12. Newman, D., Lau, J.H., Grieser, K., et al.: Automatic evaluation of topic coherence. In: Human Language Technologies: Conference of the North American Chapter of the Association of Computational Linguistics. DBLP (2010)

Study on the Differences of Urban Thermal Environment Under the Framework of Local Climate Zones

Shuyue Wang[1], Ziyue Fan[1,2], and Wenyou Fan[1,3(✉)]

[1] China University of Geosciences, Wuhan 430074, Hubei, China
mapsuv@126.com
[2] Sun Yat-sen University, Zhuhai 519000, Guangdong, China
[3] The Greatmap Company Limited, Beijing 100085, China

Abstract. The urbanization process causes the urban heat island effect and affects the urban climate change. The urban heat island intensity is often used to describe the urban thermal environment, but how to objectively and scientifically obtain the urban heat island intensity is a research difficulty. This paper uses remote sensing data, OpenStreetMap data, climate data and other data, based on the local climate zones framework, combined with surface temperature retrieval, GIS spatial analysis and other methods, to study the urban thermal environment differences in Wuhan. The research shows that the rapid acquisition method of the area of interest based on OpenStreetMap data can better realize the local climate classification. The overall accuracy is 77.1% and Kappa coefficient is 0.75, which meets the accuracy requirements. On this basis, by superimposing the results of surface temperature retrieval from remote sensing images, the thermal characteristics of ground objects of different local climate types in the city can be obtained, thereby comprehensively reflecting the differences in the thermal environment in the city.

Keywords: Local climate · Heat island intensity · Temperature retrieval

1 Introduction

Since the Industrial Revolution, urbanization is proceeding at an unprecedented speed all over the world. According to the prediction of the United Nations, 68% of the world's population will live in cities by 2050 [1]. The stable and rapid urbanization process leads to population aggregation, and the underlying surface of the city changes to varying degrees, which has an impact on the local thermal environment and microclimate. The interaction of various conditions leads to the Urban Heat Island (UHI). It refers to the phenomenon that the urban temperature is higher than that in the suburbs [2], while the temperature difference between cities and suburbs is called Urban Heat Island Intensity (UHII). Under the background of global warming, the combined effect will occur due to the combination of UHI and a variety of weather events, affecting the urban ecology and living environment, which go against the sustainable development [3–6]. With the aggravation of UHI, it has become a primary problem in urban environmental research.

© The Author(s), under exclusive license to Springer Nature Switzerland AG 2022
H. Wu et al. (Eds.): SpatialDI 2022, LNCS 13614, pp. 218–230, 2022.
https://doi.org/10.1007/978-3-031-24521-3_16

However, in the previous researches, there is often a lack of scientific description and quantitative analysis for UHII. At present, the most commonly UHII calculation method is using the temperature difference between cities and rural areas directly to describe the UHII [7–10], whereas the problem is that it is unable to scientifically define cities and suburbs, as well as objectively obtain the temperatures of them. Furthermore, UHI is closely related to the urban form. Compared with sparsely populated cities, the underlying surface and land use mode of densely populated cities are more complex and changeable. Therefore, the traditional urban heat island research cannot well reflect the actual urban thermal environment [11]. Therefore, how to scientifically characterize UHII is a difficulty in the study of urban heat island. Compared with areas of sparse population, the underlying surface and land use mode of dense population areas are more complex and changeable. Hence, the traditional researches cannot reflect the actual urban thermal environment well [11]. From this point of view, how to scientifically characterize UHII is a difficult point in the investigation of urban heat island.

In view of the above background, Stewart and Oke [12] divided the urban land use into 17 categories (as shown in Table 1), which is called Local Climate (LCZ), according to the building types and surface cover types in the city. The classification system comprehensively considers the impact of urban form on the thermal environment, which aims to provide a scientific UHII calculation method for UHII research on a global scale, and to achieve a standardized comparison of global UHII. At present, the research on urban thermal environment based on LCZ has been carried out in many cities at home and abroad [13–17]. For example, Geleti et al. [18] mapped Prague in the Czech Republic by the LCZ framework and found that the local surface temperature of LCZ 10 type is about 15.0 K higher than that of LCZ A. Yuan et al. [19] monitored LCZ building types and indicated that the temperature of high-rise buildings is lower than that of medium and low-rise buildings. Moreover, the temperature difference can be more than 1.5k. Benjamin et al. [20] established LCZ classification database in many cities around the world by using remote sensing technology.

Table 1. LCZ types.

LCZ building types		LCZ land cover types	
LCZ 1	Compact high-rise	LCZ A	Dense trees
LCZ 2	Compact midrise	LCZ B	Scattered trees
LCZ 3	Compact low-rise	LCZ C	Bush, scrub
LCZ 4	Open high-rise	LCZ D	Low plants
LCZ 5	Open midrise	LCZ E	Bare rock or paved
LCZ 6	Open low-rise	LCZ F	Bare soil or sand
LCZ 7	Lightweight low-rise	LCZ G	Water
LCZ 8	Large low-rise		
LCZ 9	Sparsely built		
LCZ 10	Heavy industry		

To sum up, LCZ is a new quantitative calculation method of UHII, which is more reasonable than the traditional UHII calculated by using the data from urban and suburban weather stations. Under the framework of LCZs, considering the low acquisition efficiency of the Region of Interests (ROI) in the traditional LCZ classification workflow, we propose a method which can quick obtain the urban LCZ type ROI based on OpenStreetMap data. Furthermore, by using surface temperature retrieval, spatial analysis and other methods, combined with remote sensing images and meteorological data, it is applied to the study of thermal environment in Wuhan, the capital city of Hubei Province, and provides a reference for land and space planning as well as building a livable city.

2   Survey of Study Area

Wuhan is located in the center of China, the east of Hubei Province, and the intersection of the Yangtze River and the Han River. The geographical location is $113° 41'–115° 05'$ E and $29° 58'–31° 22'$ N [21]. The climate is a north subtropical monsoon humid climate with abundant rainfall and sufficient sunshine. Due to lots of lakes, the weather is hot in summer and cold in winter. Up to 2020, Wuhan has a built-up area of 885.11 km^2 with 10.3927 million urban population.

In this study, the central urban area of Wuhan is selected as the study area, which includes not only the urban built-up area, but also the connecting zone outside. The differentiation law of urban thermal environment is discussed under the framework of local climate zones.

3   Data and Method

3.1   Data Sources and Preprocessing

This study is based on OpenStreetMap data (OSM data), remote sensing data and meteorological data (as shown in Table 2). The OSM data is used to classify the study area by LCZ, the remote sensing images are used to invert the urban surface temperature, and the meteorological data are used to test the reliability of the retrieval results of the surface temperature. Based on the climate characteristics of Wuhan, Landsat-8 OLI data of the central urban area in summer (April to August) and winter (November to December) from 2015 to 2020 with great imaging quality (cloud cover <5%) are selected. The image data information is shown in Table 3.

Before using the OSM data, firstly, the vector data of Wuhan administrative region are used to cut the OSM data, and the cut data is reprojected to the WGS_1984_UTM_Zone_Under 50N coordinate system; Before using the remote sensing image, ENVI FLASSH atmospheric correction module is used to eliminate the influence of water vapor. Then, through geometric correction, image mosaic, and using the reprojected OSM data as a mask, the study area data can be obtained.

Table 2. Data sources and descriptions.

Data type	Source	Description
OSM data	http://download.geofabrik.de/asia/china.html	Up to November 2021
Remote sensing data	https://earthexplorer.usgs.gov/	Operational Land Imager (OLI) and Thermal Infrared Sensor (TIRS), with resolutions of 30 m and 100 m respectively
Meteorological data	https://rp5.ru/	Temperature, air pressure, humidity, etc.

Table 3. Imaging information.

Data identification	Imaging time	Transit time	Cloud cover (%)
LC81230392015330LGN02	2015-11-26	10:56:27 AM	4.55
LC81230392016205LGN00	2016-07-23	10:56:17 AM	0.41
LC81230392017207LGN00	2017-07-26	10:56:13 AM	1.66
LC81230392017351LGN00	2017-12-17	10:56:36 AM	0.5
LC81230392020120LGN00	2020-04-29	10:55:47 AM	2.63
LC81230392020360LGN00	2020-12-25	10:56:37 AM	0.8

3.2 Remote Sensing Image Classification Based on LCZ Framework

World Urban Database and Access Portal Tools (WUDAPT) is a new method to realize urban LCZ classification. WUDAPT aims to acquire and disseminate climate-related data of urban physical geography for modeling analysis and classification of cities, and establish a high-resolution database of world urban forms and urban functions on a global scale [15]. Since its establishment in 2015, urban climate researchers around the world have applied WUDAPT to LCZ studies [22–26]. Consider that the traditional WUDAPT workflow needs visual interpretation for images to obtain the ROI, resulting in low efficiency. Therefore, this study attempts to use a new method to replace the traditional visual interpretation to quick obtain the ROI of study area, so as to efficiently obtain the LCZ classification results.

Association Between LCZ Type and OSM Type. In this study, we intend to obtain the urban LCZ classification by OSM data. Since OSM data contains detailed surface attributes, first consider associating LCZ type with OSM attribute value. It is worth mentioning that owing to OSM data is updated daily, data obtained at different times will also be different. Hence, this step must be repeated over time. Table 4 shows the association between LCZ types and OSM types considered in the study area.

Table 4. Association of LCZ and OSM.

LCZ type	OSM attribute key	OSM attribute value
LCZ A or B	Landuse (polygon)	Forest
LCZ C	Landuse (polygon)	Scrub
LCZ D	Landuse (polygon)	Grass, farmland
LCZ G	Waterway (line)	Canal, drain, river, stream
LCZ 1to10	Roads (line)	Cycleway, living_street, motorway, motorway_link, path, pedestrian, primary, primary_link, residential, service, secondary_link, tertiary_link, tertiary, trunk, trunk_link, unclassified
	Building (polygon)	All
	Pois (polygon)	Pitch, school, track, public_building, restaurant, hospital, college, mall, hotel, supermarket, stadium, kindergarten, library, playground, museum

Extraction of LCZ Building Types. Some attributes in OSM data are represented by line elements, such as roads, railways and rivers. To map these attributes to LCZ categories, we need to convert them to face features. The conversion process is as follows: ① The line feature representing the road is divided into segment L_i along the break point to calculate the nearest distance; ② For the line segment L_i, given the search radius R and calculate the nearest distance D_i from the line segment to the surrounding buildings; ③ Consider that some roads in the suburbs are far away from buildings, the nearest distance is set as d for buildings outside the search radius; ④ Take the nearest distance of each road as the radius, generate the buffer area, and merge the buffers of each road; ⑤ Merge the road buffers and building layers, then the impervious surface features obtained.

After that, intersect the impervious surface features with a 200 m × 200 m grid of the study area, then calculate the ratio of the impervious surface area in each grid unit to the whole unit area, which is the Impervious Surface Fraction (ISF). Similarly, intersect the building surface features with a 200 m × 200 m grid, and calculate the proportion of the building area in each grid unit to the whole unit area, which is the Building Surface Fraction (BSF).

By the above steps, for LCZ building type (LCZ 1–10), information about buildings and impervious surface can be obtained from OSM data. According to the research of Stewart et al. [12], the value ranges of ISF and BSF of different LCZ types are not the same. Therefore, the impervious surface features are classified according to the values of ISF and BSF of each surface element. The value range of ISF and BSF for each LCZ building type is shown in Table 5.

Table 5. Value ranges of ISF and BSF.

LCZ type	BSF (%)	ISF (%)
LCZ 1	40–60	40–60
LCZ 2	40–70	30–50
LCZ 3	40–70	20–50
LCZ 4	20–40	30–40
LCZ 5	20–40	30–50
LCZ 6	20–40	20–50
LCZ 7	60–90	<20
LCZ 8	30–50	40–50
LCZ 9	10–20	>20
LCZ 10	20–30	20–40

Note that the membership degree of BSF and ISF to LCZ category is interval type, so the quadratic parabolic function is selected as the membership function by formula (1).

$$A(x) = \begin{cases} \left(\frac{x-a}{b-a}\right)^k, & a \leq x < b \\ 1, & b \leq x < c \\ \left(\frac{d-x}{d-c}\right)^k, & c \leq x \leq d \\ 0, & x < a \ or \ d < x \end{cases} \tag{1}$$

Consider the logical relationship of indicators, BSF and ISF belong to the same category only when the relationship of them is intersection, that is, they meet the value range of BSF and ISF at the same time. For example, when $BSF_i \in [0.4, 0.6]$ and $ISF_i \in [0.4, 0.6]$, the feature belongs to LCZ 1. Therefore, we select the Fuzzy Set Standard Intersection Operation (FSSIO) for calculation. The expression is shown in formula (2).

$$\mu_{A \cap B}(u) = \min\{\mu_A(u), \mu_B(u)\} \tag{2}$$

By FSSIO, the membership degree of each impervious surface element to LCZ1–10 is calculated, and the fuzzy matrix $F = \{a_{1i}, a_{2i}, a_{3i} \ldots a_{ni}\}$ is obtained, where a_{ni} represents he membership of the n th impervious surface element to LCZ_i. For each element, the category corresponding to its maximum membership is the LCZ category.

Extraction of LCZ Land Cover Types. Since the attribute values of OSM data are related to LCZ land cover types directly, specific OSM attribute values can be considered to represent LCZ land cover types. The conversion process for LCZ a (dense trees) and LCZ B (sparse trees) is as follows: ① From the landuse attribute of OSM, filter out the polygon features whose value is forest; ② Intersect the polygon features element with a

200m × 200m grid, and calculate the ratio of the intersecting area in each grid unit to the entire unit area, that is, the tree density; ③ Given a threshold t, the polygon features area features with tree density greater than t belong to LCZ A (dense trees), and the polygon features area elements smaller than t belong to LCZ B (scattered trees).

For LCZ C (shrubs bush and dwarf trees scrub) and LCZ D (dwarf vegetation low plants), select the corresponding attribute values (see Table 3 for details). While for LCZ G (water body), the data are usually line elements (the attribute name is waterway), so that it is necessary to generate buffers for line elements according to the actual situation of the study area, and the area elements obtained finally belong to LCZ G.

3.3   Land Surface Temperature Retrieval

Compared with the Thematic Mapper (TM) and Enhanced Thematic Mapper (ETM +) of Landsat 7 satellite, the TIRS of Landsat 8 satellite has two thermal infrared bands (Band10 and Band11), and the spectral filter of TIRS has narrower bandwidth than the thermal wave band on onboard TM and ETM +, which can capture more fine surface information [27–29]. Therefore, in this paper, an improved Split-Window Algorithm called Dual Channel Nonlinear Split Window, which proposed by Chen et al. in 2015 [30], is used for Land Surface Temperature Retrieval with Landsat-8 data. This algorithm has been widely used in surface temperature retrieval inversion from multiple sensors due to it does not need accurate information about the atmospheric profile during satellite acquisition. The calculation method is shown in formula (3).

$$T_s = b_0 + \left(b_1 + b_2 \frac{1-\varepsilon}{\varepsilon} + b_3 \frac{\Delta\varepsilon}{\varepsilon^2}\right)\frac{T_i + T_j}{2} + \left(b_4 + b_5 \frac{1-\varepsilon}{\varepsilon} + b_6 \frac{\Delta\varepsilon}{\varepsilon^2}\right)\frac{T_i - T_j}{2} + b_7(T_i - T_j)^2 \qquad (3)$$

where T_i and T_j are observed brightness temperature of two channels, b_i $(i = 0, 1...7)$ are coefficients determined by the moisture content of atmosphere air column.

3.4   Calculation of Urban Heat Island Intensity Between LCZ Classes

Stewart and Oke [12] proposed to use the temperature difference between LCZ categories to characterize the urban heat island intensity, and the commonly selected reference area is LCZ D (low vegetation category). The calculation formula of Urban Heat Island Intensity $UHII_{LCZX}$ between LCZ classes is shown in formula (4).

$$UHII_{LCZX} = LST_{LCZX} - LST_{LCZD} \qquad (4)$$

where LST_{LCZX} represents the average temperature of LCZ building type, LST_{LCZD} represents the average temperature of LCZ D type.

4   Results and Discussion

4.1   Spatial Distribution Characteristics of Local Climate

According to the method of quick extracting ROI proposed in this paper, the LCZ classification diagram of the study area is obtained by using LCZ generator [22] (Fig. 1). By sampling the results of LCZ classification, 3476 sampling points are randomly selected on Google Earth image, moreover the confusion matrix and accuracy of classification results are calculated for accuracy evaluation. The overall accuracy is 77.1% and Kappa coefficient is 0.75, which meets the accuracy requirements.

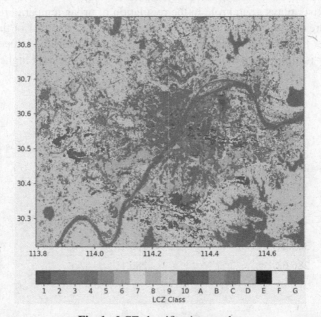

Fig. 1. LCZ classification results.

From the results, the urban area is dominated by LCZ building type, while the suburbs are dominated by LCZ land cover type. In terms of building density, most of the buildings in the urban area are open (LCZ 4–LCZ 6), and there are few dense buildings. In dense buildings, LCZ 1 type is mostly distributed in Jiang An District and Jiang Han District, and LCZ 2 and LCZ 3 expand outward from the central urban area. Most buildings in the suburbs are dense low-rise buildings, and the large low-rise buildings (LCZ 8) and scattered buildings (LCZ 9) are mainly distributed in the suburbs. From the perspective of natural landscape, low vegetation (LCZ D) accounts for a large proportion, whereas dense trees (LCZ A) are less in the central urban area, and most of them are distributed in the transition areas between central and suburban areas. In addition, due to the large number of lakes in Wuhan and the Yangtze River, the water body also accounts for a large proportion in the LCZ classification results.

4.2 Spatial Characteristics of Urban Heat Island Intensity

The Retrieval results of land surface temperature are shown in Fig. 2. The results are compared with the data of Wuhan Tianhe meteorological station (114.21E, 30.79N, station Id: 57494099999), which are shown in Table 6. It shows that the maximum error of surface temperature Retrieval results is 2.1k, the minimum is 0.09k, and the average error is 0.43k. The accuracy is high, indicating that the result is relatively reliable. As a whole, whether in summer or winter, the urban surface temperature in the center of the study area is significantly higher than that in the suburbs. The temperature in the area covered by buildings is higher, and the urban heat island is significant. Vegetation coverage area and water are the main low-temperature areas. It is worth mentioning that the Yangtze River plays a vital role in the regulation of urban temperature. In summer, the temperature of the Yangtze River is significantly lower than that of the city center, and also lower than the temperature of urban lakes. In winter, the temperature of the Yangtze River is higher than that of the city center and significantly higher than that of urban lakes.

Table 6. Evaluation of temperature retrieval accuracy.

Time	Retrieval of temperature (K)	Measured temperature (K)	Error (K)
2015/11/26	283.93	282.37	1.56
2016/07/23	307.05	309.15	−2.10
2017/07/26	313.36	312.15	1.21
2017/12/17	282.30	280.93	1.37
2020/04/29	305.24	305.15	0.09
2020/12/25	286.62	286.15	0.47

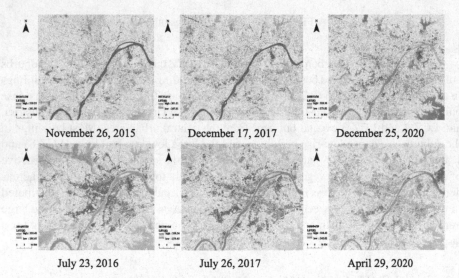

November 26, 2015   December 17, 2017   December 25, 2020

July 23, 2016   July 26, 2017   April 29, 2020

Fig. 2. Retrieval results of LST in Wuhan.

4.3 UHII Between Urban LCZ Classes

The average temperature of LCZ D (Low plants) at different times is shown in Table 7. Due to few samples, The UHII of LCZ 7 was not calculated. Finally, the results of the UHII between urban LCZ classes (UHII-LCZ) in the study area in summer and winter are shown in Table 8 and Table 9.

Table 7. Average temperature of LCZ D (low vegetation) at each time (unit: K).

Time	The average temperature of LCZ D (Low plants)
November 26, 2015 (Winter)	285.27
July 23, 2016 (Summer)	306.39
July 26, 2017 (Summer)	313.59
December 17, 2017 (Winter)	282.87
April 29, 2020 (Summer)	304.49

Table 8. UHII-LCZ in winter (unit: K).

LCZ built type	July 23, 2016	July 26, 2017	April 29, 2020	Average
1	0.14	−0.08	0.70	0.26
2	0.33	0.32	1.29	0.65
3	−0.21	0.02	0.97	0.26
4	0.24	0.21	0.88	0.44
5	0.00	−0.09	0.82	0.24
6	0.15	0.18	0.70	0.34
8	0.97	1.23	1.79	1.33
9	−0.30	−0.37	0.43	−0.08
10	2.10	2.07	2.56	2.24

From the overall results, the UHII-LCZ in summer is significantly higher than that in winter. The average UHII-LCZ in summer is 4.87k and that in winter is 0.63k. Both in summer and winter, heavy industry (LCZ 10) contribute UHII-LCZ, which is 6.58k and 2.24k respectively. Due to the different heights of buildings in the vertical direction and different densities in the horizontal direction, the contributions of buildings with different forms to UHII-LCZ are different. From the horizontal direction, the UHII-LCZ of compact buildings is higher than that of open buildings. In winter, the UHII-LCZ of compact buildings is 0.39k and that of open buildings is 0.34k. In summer, the UHII-LCZ of compact buildings is 6.17k and that of open buildings is 4.13k; From the vertical direction, the results show that in both winter and summer, owing to the heat of high-rise buildings is dispersed everywhere by airflow while absorbing solar radiation, the heat

Table 9. UHII-LCZ in summer (unit: K).

LCZ built type	November 26, 2015	December 17, 2017	December 25, 2020	Average
1	8.05	4.71	5.90	6.22
2	8.80	5.01	7.30	7.04
3	6.76	3.98	5.06	5.27
4	5.99	2.34	5.14	4.49
5	6.16	3.05	5.42	4.88
6	4.15	1.62	3.28	3.02
8	6.10	4.76	5.80	5.56
9	1.11	−0.69	1.89	0.77
10	8.98	4.16	6.59	6.58

island intensity is lower than that of middle-rise buildings and higher than that of low-rise buildings, which are 0.35k and 5.36k respectively. For low-rise buildings (LCZ 8) without shielding solar radiation, the heat island intensity is higher than other low-rise buildings (LCZ 2, LCZ 6).

5   Conclusions

At present, the extreme climate is sweeping the world and has a great impact on human survival. The urban heat island intensity is becoming more and more intense with the continuous process of urbanization. China is committed to exploring a sustainable economic growth mode to make great contributions to carbon neutralization and carbon peak. Local climate provide a new idea for the study of the urban thermal environment. According to the framework of local climate , this paper studies the thermal environment of the central urban area of Wuhan and quantitatively analyzes the UHII-LCZ of different types in local climate areas. The results show that:

(1)   The central urban area of Wuhan is dominated by LCZ built types, while the suburbs are dominated by LCZ land cover types.
(2)   Whether in summer or winter, the temperature in the center of the study area is significantly higher than that in the suburbs, and the temperature in the area covered by buildings is high as well as the heat island intensity is significant.
(3)   The Yangtze River plays an important role in the regulation of urban temperature. In summer, the temperature of the Yangtze River is significantly lower than that of the city center and lower than the urban lakes. In winter, the temperature of the Yangtze River is higher than that of the city center and significantly higher than that of urban lakes.
(4)   The UHII-LCZ in summer is significantly higher than that in winter, and the contribution of different forms of buildings to the UHII-LCZ is different. From the horizontal direction, the UHII-LCZ of compact buildings is higher than that of

open buildings. From the vertical direction, the UHII-LCZ of middle-rise buildings is the highest, while that of low-rise buildings is the lowest.

To sum up, from 2015 to 2020, whether in winter or summer, there is an obvious urban heat island in Wuhan, and there are obvious differences in the UHII-LCZ with different forms of urban buildings. For urban planning in the future, vegetation and water should be used reasonably to cool the city. In addition, good urban architectural form and layout can help to alleviate the urban heat island intensity. Therefore, it is necessary to reasonably design the architectural form and layout new buildings, strictly limit the height, so as to ensure the sustainable development of the urbanization process.

References

1. World Urbanization Prospects: The 2018 Revision (2018)
2. Manley, G.: On the frequency of snowfall in metropolitan England. Q. J. Roy. Meteorol. Soc. **84**, 70–72 (1958)
3. X, A., J, T., X, Z.: The synergistic effect of urban heat and heatwave in Shanghai and its influencing island factor. J. Geogr. Sci. **14** (2019)
4. Ward, K., Lauf, S., Kleinschmit, B., Endlicher, W.: Heat waves and urban heat islands in Europe: a review of relevant drivers. Sci. Total Environ. **569–570**, 527–539 (2016)
5. Yang, X., et al.: Contribution of urbanization to the increase of extreme heat events in an urban agglomeration in east China. Geophys. Res. Lett. **44**, 6940–6950 (2017)
6. Georgescu, M., Moustaoui, M., Mahalov, A., Dudhia, J.: Summer-time climate impacts of projected megapolitan expansion in Arizona. Nat. Clim. Change **3**, 37–41 (2012)
7. Zhou, D.C., Zhao, S.Q., Liu, S.G., Zhang, L.X.: Zhu: Surface urban heat island in China's 32 major cities: spatial patterns and drivers. Remote Sens. Environ. **2014**(152), 51–61 (2014)
8. Zhao, L., Smith, R.B., Oleson, K.: Strong contributions of local background climate to urban heat islands. Nature **511**, 216–219 (2014)
9. Kolokotroni, M., Ren, X., Davies, M., Mavrogianni, A.: London's urban heat island: Impact on current and future energy consumption in office buildings. Energy Build. **47**, 302–311 (2012)
10. Tomlinson, C.J., Chapman, L., Thornes, J.E., Ba Ker, C.J.: Including the urban heat island in spatial heat health risk assessment strategies: a case study for Birmingham, UK. Int. J. Health Geogr. **10**, 1–14 (2011)
11. Yan, Z., Shepherd, J.M.: Atlanta's urban heat island under extreme heat conditions and potential mitigation strategies. Nat. Hazards **52**, 639–668 (2010)
12. Stewart, I.D., Oke, T.R.: Local climate for urban temperature studies. Bull. Am. Meteorol. Soc. **93**, 1879–1900 (2012)
13. Chung, S.C., Chao, R.: Outdoor thermal comfort in different urban settings of sub-tropical high-density cities: an approach of adopting local climate zone (LCZ) classification. Build. Environ. **154**, 227–238 (2019)
14. Kotharkar, R., Bagade, A., Ramesh, A.: Assessing urban drivers of canopy layer urban heat island: a numerical modeling approach. Landsc. Urban Plann. **190**, 103586 (2019)
15. Ran, W.A., Meng, C.A., Chao, R., Bb, D., Yong, X.E., Ena, B.: Detecting multi-temporal land cover change and land surface temperature in Pearl River Delta by adopting local climate zone. Urban Clim. **28**, 100455 (2019)
16. Wang, C., Middel, A., Myint, S.W., Kaplan, S., Brazel, A.J., Lukasczyk, J.: Assessing local climate in arid cities: the case of Phoenix, Arizona and Las Vegas, Nevada. ISPRS J. Photogram. Remote Sens. **141**, 59–71 (2018)

17. Mushore, T.D., et al.: Remotely sensed retrieval of local climate and their linkages to land surface temperature in Harare metropolitan city, Zimbabwe. Urban Clim. **27**, 259–271 (2018)
18. Geleti, J., Lehnert, M., Dobrovoln, P.: Land Surface temperature differences within local climate, based on two central European cities. Remote Sens. **8**, 788 (2016)
19. Yuan, S., Ka-Lun, L.K., Chao, R., Edward, N.: Evaluating the local climate zone classification in high-density heterogeneous urban environment using mobile measurement. Urban Clim. **25**, 167–186 (2018)
20. Benjamin, B., et al.: Mapping local climate for a worldwide database of the form and function of cities. Int. J. Geo-Inf. **4**, 199–219 (2015)
21. Wuhan Municipal Bureau of Statistics: Wuhan Statistical Yearbook 2021. China Statistics Press, Beijing (2021)
22. Demuzere, M., Kittner, J., Bechtel, B.: LCZ generator: a web application to create local climate zone maps. Front. Environ. Sci. **9**, 637455 (2021)
23. Danylo, O., See, L., Bechtel, B., Schepaschenko, D., Fritz, S.: Contributing to WUDAPT: a local climate zone classification of two cities in Ukraine. IEEE J. Sel. Top. Appl. Earth Observ. Remote Sens. **9**, 1841–1853 (2017)
24. Hidalgo, J., Schoetter, R., Petit, G., Bocher, E., Dumas, G.: Comparing WUDAPT level 0 cartography with a more detailed urban database. Some examples for French cities using the MAPUCE database (2017)
25. See, L., et al.: Generating WUDAPT's specific scale-dependent urban modeling and activity parameters: collection of level 1 and level 2 data (2015)
26. Yong, X., Chao, R., Meng, C., Edward, N., Wu, T.: Classification of local climate using ASTER and landsat data for high-density cities. IEEE J. Sel. Top. Appl. Earth Observ. Remote Sens. **10**, 1–9 (2017)
27. Rozenstein, O., Qin, Z., Derimian, Y., Karnieli, A.: Derivation of land surface temperature for landsat-8 TIRS using a split window algorithm. Sensors **14**, 5768–5780 (2014)
28. Jimenez-Munoz, J.C., Sobrino, J.A., Skokovic, D., Mattar, C., Cristobal, J.: Land surface temperature retrieval methods from landsat-8 thermal infrared sensor data. IEEE Geosci. Remote Sens. Lett. **11**, 1840–1843 (2014)
29. Wang, S., He, L., Hu, W.: A temperature and emissivity separation algorithm for landsat-8 thermal infrared sensor data. Remote Sens. **12**, 9904–9927 (2015)
30. Chen, D., Ren, H., Qin, Q., Meng, J., Zhao, S.: A practical split-window algorithm for estimating land surface temperature from landsat 8 data. Remote Sens. **7**, 647–665 (2015)

Response of Urban Park Visitor Behavior to Water Quality in Beijing

Wen Jiang[1,2], Yaobin Meng[2(✉)], Yuan Zhang[1], Jiaxin Wu[1], and Xiang Li[1]

[1] Faculty of Geographic Science, Beijing Normal University, Beijing 100875, China
[2] School of National Safety and Emergency Management, Beijing Normal University, Beijing 100875, China
yaobin-meng@bnu.edu.cn

Abstract. Based on the big data of remote sensing observation and mobile phone signaling, we put forward two quantitative indices that objectively characterize visitor visiting behavior—Park Visiting Hours (PVH) and the probability of visitor attendance (PVA). We hope to answer whether the water quality of urban landscape water will affect PVH and how different it will be for various groups. The findings are as follows: (1) Sensory Pollution Index (SPI) has a very significant negative correlation with HPV. The conclusion that the deterioration of water quality will shorten PVH is statistically significant. However, water quality is not the main factor affecting that. (2) Visitor visits decrease with the deterioration of water quality, and this trend is more evident with the extension of PVH. (3) There are significant differences in PVH between various groups when the water quality is excellent or poor. Generally speaking, when the water quality is good, the younger visitors will have a higher PVH, while when the water quality is poor, the more youthful visitors will have a lower PVH.

Keywords: Urban water landscape · Water quality · Visitor behavior · Various groups

1 Introduction

As one of the most fundamental elements required for human survival and economic development, water resources are limited and irreplaceable primary natural resources [1, 2]. However, there is an urgent freshwater shortage problem in China [3], and the water resources per capita are only 2,100 m^3, which is one-quarter of the world average [4, 5]. Simultaneously, water resources are much scarcer than before [6, 7] and the urban water environment has been deteriorated sharply given the rapid urbanization, industrialization, and the growth of the urban population [8, 9]. As a result, environmental problems, especially those relating to water, have become the most significant challenge restricting the sustainable development of society today [10–12]. Therefore, the Chinese government has made great efforts to control water pollution and improve surface water quality [13], including implementing a series of policies, laws, and regulations [13]. For instance, the *Action Plan for Water Pollution Prevention and Control* was issued

H. Wu et al. (Eds.): SpatialDI 2022, LNCS 13614, pp. 231–249, 2022.
https://doi.org/10.1007/978-3-031-24521-3_17

in April 2015 to implement a comprehensive strategic deployment of China's water pollution prevention and control actions [14].

Although the academic circles have made rich explorations on the effectiveness of water pollution control [15–17]. While they mainly focus on achieving Engineering "performance" with environmental pollution load as the primary quantitative index [18, 19]. To what extent can the urban surface water ecosystem improve urban residents' happiness and sense of acquisition? The existing research is less involved and is still in the stage of scale questionnaire or small sample exploration [20, 21]. Therefore, exploring simple and effective indicators can quantitatively measure this sense of acquisition, which is also essential content for evaluating the effectiveness of water pollution control.

The research attempts to refine the following self-evident hypothesis (H0) into two verifiable technical hypotheses (H1 and H2):

H0: The water quality of urban landscape water will affect visitor sightseeing behavior.
H1: The apparent water quality of urban landscape water bodies will affect the length of visitor visits.
H2: The apparent water quality of the water landscape will affect the state of visitors in the park.

H0 has high reliability. H1 and H2, as the derivative technical expressions of H0, express the conceptualized water quality as apparent water quality and concretize the visitor tour behavior into "tour duration" and "in park state" in the water landscape parks, so that the utility evaluation of urban water quality improvement is advanced from subjective feeling analysis to objective index analysis. The goal of this paper is to determine whether and to what extent the tour time of water landscape changes with the change of apparent water quality index and the difference of its influence on various groups.

Therefore, we used the following data to participate in the analysis: (1) we obtained the vector data of 592 parks in Beijing from the Baidu map platform, screened them according to their general area, water surface area, overall reputation, and visitor visits, and analyzed four typical water feature parks in the central urban area, such as Beihai Park, Shichahai Park, Longtan Lake Park, and Taoranting park. (2) The length of stay of visitors and the probability of staying in the park are calculated by using the time of entering the park, the time of leaving the park, and the number of visitor records of mobile signaling data. (3) The remote sensing index of the sentry-2 satellite is used as the substitute index of apparent water quality. We hope that around the comprehensive goal of urban environmental governance and improvement, it can provide technical support for evaluating the water environment service quality improvement effect brought by water quality improvement. Moreover, at the same time, it can partially provide an indirect basis for reducing the benefits of health and ecological risks brought by water quality improvement.

2 Data and Methodology

2.1 Study Area

Water landscape parks are large-scale urban wetland parks whose water surface area exceeds 30% of the park's total area, and the water landscape provides the core leisure service function. According to this standard, we selected four water landscape parks located in the downtown area of Beijing as sample parks for analyzing the PVH: Shichahai Park, Beihai Park, Longtanhu Park, and Taoranting Park (Fig. 1).

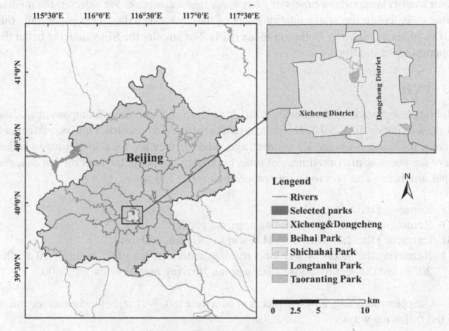

Fig. 1. Local of the study area.

The parks we selected have four advantages:

(1) Water landscape is the key feature of these parks, which can better evaluate the influence of water quality on visitor behavior.
(2) These parks provide open water surfaces, ensuring the accuracy of calculating apparent water quality data based on Sentinel-2.
(3) Mobile phone data shows that more than 80% of visitors are local, which reduces the interference of sightseeing behavior to enjoy the scenery.
(4) These parks are free of charge or deficient charge, which is beneficial to exclude the influence of economic factors.

2.2 SPI

Since lack of monitoring water quality data, we decided to replace it with reliable remote sensing data. Sentinel-2 of the European Air Force can provide global remote sensing products since August 2015. The so-called 2BDA value is calculated by the ratio of the fifth and fourth bands of the satellite band (B5/B4), which is widely considered to be significantly related to the chlorophyll-a concentration [22, 23] and can be used as an apparent water quality index related to eutrophic water pollution [24, 25].

Based on the Google earth engine platform, we obtained the data of Sentinel-2(2A) in July 2019. To ensure the reliability of the value of 2BDA, we extracted the center water quality comparison pixels of each water landscape park. We selected the median value to calculate the water quality index of the park every day. This paper calls this 2BDA index the Sensory Pollution Index (SPI). The smaller the SPI value, the better the apparent water quality.

2.3 PVH

Mobile phone signaling data comes from China Unicom Smart Steps Company, including 31 days of data in July 2019. The data has a total of 469,151 records. One record for each visitor, including a unique ID number, age, whether they are local to Beijing, whether there are peers, admission time, exit time, number of people in the park on that day, and other attributes. The preprocessing procedures are as follows:

(1) Removing duplicate values.
(2) Removing the record without an apparent gender.
(3) Extracting the data whose PVH is within [30 min, 360 min].
(4) Removing the record whose label naming "entering park time" before 8:00 or after 20:30 and the record whose label naming "leaving park time" after 21:00.

After preprocessing, 254,440 pieces of data were left. We divide the dataset according to the following ways:

(1) Dividing dates into weekdays (WD) and weekends (WE).
(2) Classifying visitors according to their age: i) Under 23 years old, young students (YSS). ii) Aged between 23 and 45: young professionals (YPS). iii) Aged between 23 and 45: middle-aged professionals (MPS). iv) Over 60 years old, the retired groups (RG).

Because the research aims to propose a simple and easy quantitative indicator to characterize the visitor behavior influenced by water quality, it is not necessary to divide the dataset too complicated to ensure the universality of the needle.

2.4 The Probability of Visitors Attendance (PVA)

PVA multiplies the total number of people visiting an urban water landscape park on a particular day to get the number of people in the park at every specific time. This practical value can estimate the number of visitors to a park at different times (Fig. 2).

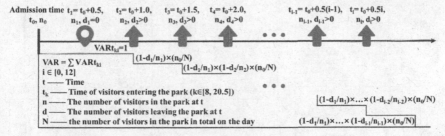

Fig. 2. The illustration of PVA

2.5 Meteorological and Air Quality Data

Considering that climate suitability and air quality are also factors that may affect the presence of visitors in the park, we acquired the surface meteorological parameters and air quality index (AQI) in July 2019 from China meteorological data sharing service system (http://data.cma.cn) and Beijing air quality release platform (https://aqicn.org/data-platform/register/) respectively. The climate comfort index (CCI) is calculated as follows:

$$CCI = (T - 21.5) + 0.04(RH - 55) + 0.5(WSP - 2.0) \tag{1}$$

where, T is the air temperature (°C), RH is the relative humidity (%), and WSP is the wind speed (m/s).

3 Results

3.1 Description of Visitor Stay Status

Overall, The average PVH is about 120–150 min, and the standard deviation is 55–75 min. The average PVH on working days is about 13 min shorter than on weekends. The female's PVH is 6.62 min longer than the male's. According to various groups, the average PVH decreased gradually with age.

Moreover, the probability of women in the park is higher than that of men. The probability of staying in the park on weekends is generally higher than that on weekdays, and its peak value is half an hour later than that on weekdays (Fig. 3).

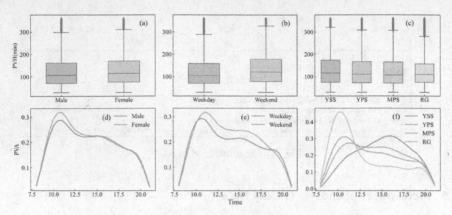

Fig. 3. The description of PVH and PVA for various groups

There are significant differences in the park probability curves of different age groups. The probability of retirees in the park in the morning is higher, and the peak appears at about 10:00. Teenagers are more likely to be in the park in the afternoon, and the peak occurs at about 16:00. The curves of young professionals and middle-aged professionals are relatively similar, and the peak appears from 10:30 to 11:00. YPS has a lower probability of being in the park in the morning and a higher probability of being in the park in the afternoon than MPS (Table 1).

Table 1. Probability of visitors in the parks to the time[1]

Groups	Models	R^2	Adjust_R^2	Sig
Entirety	$p = -0.004t^2 + 0.1093t - 0.4892$	0.698	0.673	<0.001
YSS	$p = -0.0064t^2 + 0.1924t - 1.1444$	0.965	0.962	<0.001
YPS	$p = -0.005t^2 + 0.1402t - 0.7218$	0.866	0.855	<0.001
MPS	$p = -0.0035t^2 + 0.0944t - 0.3799$	0.614	0.581	<0.001
RG	$p = -0.0007t^2 - 0.0001t + 0.3536$	0.449	0.404	0.001

3.2 The Relationship Between Water Quality and Visitor Presence Status

We do a Pearson correlation analysis between daily SPI and PVH mean value. It can be seen that there is a significant negative correlation between them, and the correlation coefficient is about 0.3. The worse the water quality, the shorter the length of stay of

---

[1] "t" means the time within the range of [8:00, 21:00].

"p" means the probability of tourists in the parks.

visitors in the park. Women's PVH is more vulnerable to SPI than men from different groups. The correlation between PVH and SPI on weekdays was stronger, about −0.473, and was statistically significant at 0.01. The correlation between them is weak at the weekends and fails to pass the statistical test. There are some differences in the correlation between PVH and SPI in different age groups. The correlation between PVH and water quality in the middle-aged occupational population is the strongest, and that in the retired population is the weakest (Table 2).

Table 2. The correlation analysis between SPI and PVH for various groups[2].

Groups	r	Groups	r	Groups	r
Entirety	−0.319***	Male	−0.322***	Female	−0.339***
WD	−0.473***	WE	−0.147	YSS	−0.238***
YPS	−0.309***	MPS	−0.351***	RG	−0.164**

We use the natural breakpoint method to divide the data set into three parts according to the value of SPI. When $0.893 < SPI \leq 0.961$, it is good water quality, when $0.961 < SPI \leq 1.014$, it is medium water quality, and when $1.014 < SPI \leq 1.12$, it is poor water quality. PVH was divided into 11 intervals at an interval of 30 min. We count the number of visitors visiting events in different PVH periods under various water quality conditions and calculate the proportion. It is not difficult to find that the number of sightseeing events decreases with the deterioration of water quality, and this trend is more evident with the extension of PVH.

What's more, the Mann-Kendall trend analysis is carried out for the proportion sequences of different groups of tourism events under three water quality conditions. When the water quality is good, the proportion of tour events with large PVH generally shows a significant increasing trend, with an average increase of 1.29% for every 30 min. The upward movement of the YPS group was faster, with an average rise of 1.38% for every 30 min. The rising trend of the YSS group is the slowest, and the proportion increases by 0.69% every 30 min. The upward trend began to slow down when PVH reached 150–180 min. Teenagers were earlier, and the change occurred in 120–150 min. The retired groups are later, and the change happens at 180–210 min. When the water quality is moderate, the proportion of tour events with large PVH generally shows a significant downward trend, and the ratio decreased by 0.53% every 30 min. The downward trend becomes slower when PVH reaches 90–120 min. For every 30 min increase in average PVH, the proportion reduces by 0.22%. When the water quality is poor, the proportion of tour events with large PVH generally shows a significant downward trend. The decline is faster than that when the water quality is moderate. The ratio of PVH decreases by 0.78% every 30 min. The downward trend becomes slower when PVH is

---

[2] *** Significant at 1% level.
    ** Significant at 5% level.
    * Significant at 10% level.

210–240 min, and the proportion reduces by 0.45% for every 30 min increase of PVH (Fig. 4).

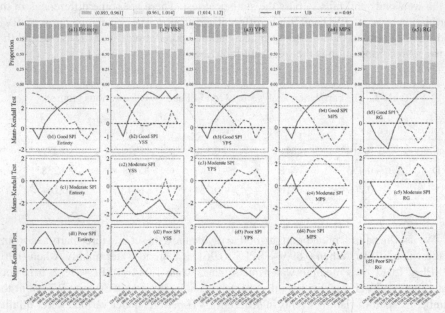

Fig. 4. Changes in the proportion of tour events under different water quality and PVH conditions

Due to the data set does not meet the conditions of variance analysis, we employed the Kruskal-Wallis Test to compare the PVH of four groups under different water quality conditions.

In the same age group, there are significant differences in PVH under different water quality conditions. PVH gradually decreases with the deterioration of water quality. The PVH differences between the two under the three water quality conditions have passed the statistical test. Under the same water quality condition, the difference in the PVH among the four groups is statistically significant. When the water quality is good or moderate, the younger visitors tend to have more length of stay. When the water quality is poor, the retired groups have the longest PVH, and the PVH of YPS is close to that of MPS (Table 3).

Table 3. Comparison of PVH under different water quality and population conditions

Test variable	Control variable	N	Statistic	Sig.
SPI	YSS	23796	84.131	<0.001
	YPS	121555	552.570	<0.001
	MPS	65526	255.240	<0.001
	RG	43563	41.143	<0.001
Age	Good SPI	103797	89.232	<0.001
	Moderate SPI	92943	61.830	<0.001
	Poor SPI	57700	24.062	<0.001

From the perspective of PVA, when the water quality is poor, higher PVA will appear in the early morning than in other water quality conditions. When the water quality is good, higher PVA will appear in the afternoon (Fig. 5).

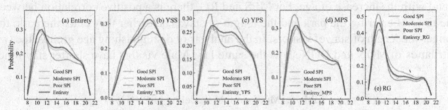

Fig. 5. Comparison of PVA in various groups under three water quality conditions

In the related samples, Friedman's two-way analysis of PVA for different age groups under three kinds of water quality shows that the difference among each group is not statistically significant (Table 4).

Table 4. Comparison of PVA in different groups

Groups	N	Statistic	Sig.
Entirety	27	2.741	0.254
YSS	27	0.889	0.641
YPS	27	2.741	0.254
MPS	27	2.889	0.236
RG	27	3.852	0.146

3.3 Modeling

From the Pearson correlation results in Sect. 2.1, it can be seen that there is a significant negative correlation between PVH and SPI. With the deterioration of apparent water quality, visitors tend to reduce the length of time they visit the park in a sense of expectation. However, this relationship cannot rule out the illusion that it is under the mixed influence of climate comfort and air quality factors. Therefore, it is necessary to identify the factors that affect residence time through multivariable regression.

This paper divides the factors affecting the PVH into two categories: visitor attributes and the surrounding environment. Through variable screening, we include the three variables of admission time (EPK), visitor gender (MON), and whether it is a working day (DON) as visitor attributes in the model. SPI, CCI, AQI, and the average population in the park on that day as environmental factors in the model.

From other explanatory variables, the CCI of YPS and MPS show a significant negative relationship with PVH. In contrast, except for adolescents, the AQI of different age groups shows a meaningful positive relationship with PVH. The younger groups such as YSS and YPS have a significant negative correlation with PVH. The earlier they enter the park, the shorter the stay time of visitors, but this correlation shows a downward trend with the increase of age. For MPS and RG, there is a positive correlation between the time of entering the park and the length of stay. The earlier they enter the park, the longer the length of stay of visitors. In the analysis of distinguishing age groups, the two attributes of MON and DON show the same law. Male visitors have shorter stay times

Table 5. Multivariable modeling of PVH[3]

	Entirety	YSS	YPS	MPS	RG
SPI	−92.393***	−123.442***	−112.887***	−97.370***	−30.955**
CCI	−0.149	−1.244***	−0.546**	−0.125	0.230
AQI	0.039*	−0.035	0.042*	0.036*	0.063***
POP	0.005***	0.004***	0.003***	0.004***	0.005***
EPT	1.895**	−7.164***	−2.770**	0.976	3.949***
MON	−6.033***	−9.749***	−6.800***	−4.300***	−4.390***
DON	−8.118***	−4.983**	−11.172***	−7.599***	−4.216***
Constant	185.402***	358.267***	277.696***	203.795***	91.532***
R^2	0.628	0.458	0.597	0.534	0.457
Adj_R^2	0.617	0.442	0.585	0.520	0.440
Sig.	<0.001	<0.001	<0.001	<0.001	<0.001

---

[3] POP, the number of people in the park.

  EPT, time to enter the park.

  MON, male or not.

  DON, workdays or not.

than female visitors, with an average reduction of 6.033 min. Working days have more temporary stays than weekends, with an average decrease of 8.118 min (Table 5).

3.4 Robustness

We test the robustness of the above model by numerical transformation, replacing the actual value with the approximate weight and taking a small proportion of samples. The results show that the negative relationship between PVH and SPI is robust to a wide range of alternate specifications, shown in Tables 6, 7, 8, 9, 10 and 11.

Log-Log Specification. Table 6 presents results from a log-log specification, regressing the value in the log of PVH on the log of SPI and the log of the other continuous variables. The results again reveal the law between PVH and SPI.

Table 6. Robustness of results to a log-log specification

	Entirety	YSS	YPS	MPS	RG
SPI	−0.740***	−0.981***	−0.889***	−0.774***	−0.275**
CCI	−0.011	−0.051***	−0.026**	−0.008	0.002
AQI	0.021**	−0.012	0.021*	0.018*	0.035***
POP	0.082***	0.071***	0.042***	0.058***	0.086***
EPT	0.221**	−0.714***	−0.335**	0.094	0.411***
MON	−0.048***	−0.072***	−0.053***	−0.034***	−0.036***
DON	−0.069***	−0.038**	−0.089***	−0.066***	−0.042***
Constant	3.617***	6.368***	5.403***	4.120***	3.009***
R^2	0.592	0.439	0.573	0.483	0.406
Adj_R^2	0.580	0.422	0.560	0.468	0.388
Sig	<0.001	<0.001	<0.001	<0.001	<0.001

Reduce the Time Accuracy of PVH to 30 min. The PVH of each record is divided at an interval of 30 min and replaced by the median value of each interval (11 values of 45, 75, 105,..., 315, 345). It can be seen that the five regression models have passed the significant test. There is a significant negative correlation between SPI and PVH, but this negative relationship decreases gradually with age.

Table 7. Robustness of results to the 30 min precision alternative PVH

	Entirety	YSS	YPS	MPS	RG
SPI	−89.566***	−114.127***	−109.071***	−98.130***	−29.684**
CCI	−0.118	−1.072***	−0.474*	−0.100	0.148
AQI	0.035*	−0.040	0.043*	0.034	0.042*
POP	0.005***	0.004***	0.003***	0.004***	0.005***
EPT	1.894**	−6.976***	−2.605**	0.926	3.774***
MON	−6.063***	−9.905***	−6.560***	−4.478***	−5.028***
DON	−7.775***	−4.235**	−10.812***	−7.238***	−4.224***
Constant	184.820***	347.302***	272.793***	207.428***	97.518***
R^2	0.626	0.459	0.591	0.527	0.423
Adj_R^2	0.614	0.442	0.579	0.513	0.406
Sig.	<0.001	<0.001	<0.001	<0.001	<0.001

Transform the Threshold of PVH. To eliminate the interference of the selection of the upper and lower limits of PVH on the regression results, we selected 120 min, 180 min, 240 min, and 300 min as the upper limit of PVH to form four data sets. We established regression models to test the relationship between PVH and SPI. The results prove that the PVH tends to shorten with the deterioration of water quality.

Only Non-local Visitor Records are Extracted for Analysis. Only the data of non-local visitors are taken out for analysis, which accounts for only 4.87% of the total data. Although the overall variance interpretation of the model is only 0.302, the five models have passed the significance test. According to the regression results, it can be found that there is a negative correlation between PVH and SPI in different groups. The SPI coefficient of the retired population is not significant, and the adjusted R^2 of the model is only 0.039, which may be due to the insufficient amount of data because the data records of the retired population account for only 8.3% of the data set.

Only Non-single Visitor Records are Extracted for Analysis. Only samples of visitors with peers are taken for re-inspection. The data set accounts for 3.08% of the original data. It can be seen from Table 10 that the five regression models have passed the significance test, and SPI still shows a negative correlation with PVH. This correlation is statistically significant in the data of the other four groups except for the retired population.

5% of the Samples were Randomly Selected for Analysis. Finally, 5% samples are randomly selected from the original data to form a new data set, namely 12722 data. After regression analysis, it can be seen that the five regression models have passed the significance test, and except for the retired population, the SPI of other models has a significant negative correlation with PVH.

Table 8. Robustness of results to the PVH thresholds

	Entirety	YSS	YPS	MPS	RG
30 min ≤ PVH ≤ 120 min					
SPI	−5.585**	−12.880*	−5.279	−7.186**	3.912
CCI	0.075*	0.215	0.002	0.039	0.108
AQI	0.000	−0.032**	0.002	0.000	−0.008
POP	0.001***	0.001***	0.001***	0.001***	0.002***
EPT	−0.851***	−2.243***	−1.877***	−0.212	−0.879***
MON	−1.898***	−3.062***	−1.756***	−2.056***	−1.626***
DON	−1.165***	−1.126	−2.217***	−0.293	0.259
Constant	92.790***	124.2***69	109.023***	84.387***	81.092***
R^2	0.728	0.326	0.587	0.434	0.444
Adj_R^2	0.719	0.305	0.574	0.417	0.428
Sig.	<0.001	<0.001	<0.001	<0.001	<0.001
30 min ≤ PVH ≤ 180 min					
SPI	−25.870***	−65.566***	−32.750***	−25.012***	5.174
CCI	−0.047	−0.334	−0.260**	−0.078	0.303**
AQI	0.011	−0.042**	0.015	0.003	0.019
POP	0.002***	0.002***	0.001***	0.002***	0.003***
EPT	−0.892***	−4.334***	−2.560***	−0.759*	−0.703*
MON	−3.401***	−5.247***	−4.054***	−2.874***	−1.682***
DON	−3.999***	−3.789***	−6.084***	−2.560***	−0.599
Constant	133.765***	230.641***	168.923***	129.439***	92.070***
R^2	0.728	0.462	0.676	0.522	0.515
Adj_R^2	0.720	0.445	0.666	0.507	0.501
Sig.	<0.001	<0.001	<0.001	<0.001	<0.001
30 min ≤ PVH ≤ 240 min					
SPI	−52.129***	−89.402***	−64.455***	−56.473***	−12.146
CCI	−0.061	−0.546*	−0.301*	−0.186	0.260
AQI	0.020	−0.034	0.025	0.012	0.026*
POP	0.004***	0.003***	0.002***	0.003***	0.004***
EPT	0.599	−5.799***	−2.173***	−0.211	1.259**
MON	−4.359***	−5.841***	−5.089***	−3.247***	−3.294***
DON	−5.950***	−3.344**	−8.530***	−4.649***	−3.171***

(*continued*)

Table 8. (*continued*)

	Entirety	YSS	YPS	MPS	RG
Constant	150.409***	285.263***	207.082***	165.318***	97.594***
R^2	0.686	0.497	0.642	0.541	0.492
Adj_R^2	0.676	0.481	0.631	0.527	0.477
Sig.	<0.001	<0.001	<0.001	<0.001	<0.001
	30 min ≤ PVH ≤ 300 min				
SPI	−77.203***	−119.699***	−92.252***	−84.186***	−22.875**
CCI	−0.186	−0.699**	−0.523**	−0.274	0.279
AQI	0.030*	−0.038	0.037*	0.023	0.040**
POP	0.004***	0.004***	0.003***	0.003***	0.005***
EPT	1.392*	−4.875***	−2.403**	0.242	3.403***
MON	−5.471***	−7.754***	10.457***	−3.441***	−4.842***
DON	−7.592***	−3.851**	6.338***	−6.852***	−4.182***
Constant	173.229***	310.354***	230.827***	196.103***	88.165***
R^2	0.642	0.452	0.605	0.537	0.485
Adj_R^2	0.631	0.436	0.593	0.523	0.469
Sig.	<0.001	<0.001	<0.001	<0.001	<0.001

Table 9. Robustness of results to the dataset containing only non-local visitors

	Entirety	YSS	YPS	MPS	RG
SPI	−138.330***	−183.993***	−156.781***	−172.947***	−82.849
CCI	0.439	−0.672	0.397	0.761	2.188
AQI	0.070	−0.166	0.039	0.142*	0.134
POP	0.004***	0.008***	0.002*	0.004**	0.008***
EPT	−3.131**	−1.768	−5.526***	−2.388*	−1.222
MON	−5.569***	1.150	−4.592*	−8.645**	−9.142
DON	−8.220***	1.246	−11.073***	−10.219**	3.302
Constant	301.155***	326.999***	359.082***	321.501***	197.358**
R^2	0.323	0.117	0.265	0.180	0.071
Adj_R^2	0.302	0.088	0.243	0.155	0.039
Sig.	< 0.001	< 0.001	< 0.001	< 0.001	< 0.001

Table 10. Robustness of results to the dataset containing only visitors with peers

	Entirety	YSS	YPS	MPS	RG
SPI	−137.967***	−180.576*	−147.013***	−225.253***	−92.841
CCI	−1.178**	−6.635***	−0.862	−1.098	−0.708
AQI	0.044	−0.187	0.176**	−0.065	0.081
POP	0.003**	−0.007*	0.003	0.003*	0.002
EPT	−1.291	−6.805***	−3.427***	−4.821***	−4.461***
MON	−7.074***	−10.532	−3.991	−8.897*	−9.961*
DON	−13.359***	−9.439	−17.538***	−7.565	−7.040
Constant	286.458***	495.105***	317.767***	418.844***	264.899***
R^2	0.248	0.215	0.221	0.190	0.101
Adj_R^2	0.225	0.179	0.198	0.165	0.071
Sig.	<0.001	<0.001	<0.001	<0.001	<0.001

Table 11. Robustness of results to the samples randomly selected 5% from the original dataset

	Entirety	YSS	YPS	MPS	RG
SPI	−119.577***	−131.107**	−123.782***	−174.922***	−37.031
CCI	−0.481	−1.710	−0.440	−0.702	0.300
AQI	0.014	−0.123	0.017	0.032	0.077
POP	0.004***	0.003	0.003***	0.003**	0.004**
EPT	−1.848	−3.619**	−4.571***	−2.349*	−1.236
MON	−4.707***	−20.762***	−5.320**	−3.013	−1.896
DON	−7.579***	−5.213	−11.191***	−4.673	−6.669
Constant	266.540***	334.615***	313.446***	326.108***	161.766***
R^2	0.353	0.137	0.298	0.143	0.068
Adj_R^2	0.334	0.108	0.277	0.117	0.040
Sig.	< 0.001	< 0.001	< 0.001	< 0.001	< 0.001

4 Discussions

4.1 A Discussion on SPI

Our sensory pollution index SPI of a water body is the band reflectivity B5/B4 of the Sentinel-2 satellite. According to literature research [23, 26, 27], there is a simple linear relationship between SPI and chlorophyll-a concentration in water ($R^2 = 0.90$):

$$[Chl - a\,(\mu g/L)] \approx 71 \times SPI - 58 \quad (Chl - a \in (5, 65)) \tag{2}$$

According to the rule that PVH changes with the sensitivity of SPI of −92.393 found in this study, and the ratio between Chl-a and SPI is calculated as 71, it can be inferred that when Chl-a is in the appropriate range, PVH will change with the sensitivity of Chl-a of about 0.768, that is, every increase of Chl-a in the water body of the park µg/L, visitors will tend to shorten the tour duration of about 1.302 min. When the chlorophyll surge such as water bloom occurs, the Chl-a increases by 100 µg/L, visitors will generally shorten the tour duration to approximately 130 min, which is the loss of the recreational service capacity provided by the water body.

The concentration of Chl-a is an important symbol of phytoplankton biomass in the water body, which can be used as one of the indexes to judge the eutrophication degree of a water body. The input of nitrogen and phosphorus nutrient load and the rapid convergence of endogenous load caused by it are the key factors of water body eutrophication. Although the relationship between TP and Chl-a may be different with different regions, climatic conditions, and seasons, it is still relatively consistent from the review or seasonal comparison worldwide [28, 29]. We take the linear model structure commonly used in literature and substitute it with the coefficient of four seasons average in literature (formula (2)), which is not much different from the formula obtained by summarizing the research in various countries, and should have certain reliability, as follows:

$$\log[Chl - a\,(\mu g/L)] = 1.322 \times \log[TP\,(\mu g/L)] - 0.950 \tag{3}$$

Therefore, it can be seen that the control of nitrogen and phosphorus in urban water can reduce the value of SPI, and the reduction of SPI will also promote the increase of PVH to a certain extent, which is the improvement of recreational services provided by water bodies. Moreover, the progress in the public's sense of acquisition, happiness, and satisfaction will be enormous.

4.2 A Discussion on PVH

In this research, there are difficulties in acquiring some needed data directly. First, the water quality of the landscape and the personal attributes of visitors, including their tour behavior, must be provided simultaneously. Second, the water quality in the water landscape does not change much within a day. To obtain a wide range of water quality changes, it is necessary to acquire the water quality of several water bodies on several dates. In addition, it is essential to contain a wide enough range of water quality changes. That is, there are samples of poor and good water quality.

We have selected Tongzhou Grand Canal Forest Park as a case and conducted twice on-the-spot investigations in 2017 and 2018 [30]. We obtained the detailed personal attributes provided by more than 500 visitors and the tour tracks supplied by more than 300 visitors. However, the amount of data is far from enough. Furthermore, the data obtained by GPS positioning is actively collected, so the behavior of visitors may be influenced and changed subjectively, which is not conducive to getting accurate results. Furthermore, it is necessary to combine multiple parks with similar attributes to meet the spatial representativeness of water quality data. Hence, it is not feasible to further the study by survey and questionnaire. Many studies have regarded mobile phone self-report data as potential to fulfill these requirements because the data reflect human behavior richly and ubiquitously [31].

Moreover, the information obtained by smartphones belongs to a way of passive collection, which can objectively and genuinely reflect people's actual behavior. It is easy to find the universal law because of the large amount of data. However, mobile phone data is collected by base stations with a spatial accuracy of 10–20 m. We can determine whether visitors are in a park or not and when they enter when they leave. Nevertheless, we can not identify the accurate visitor trajectory. So we have not analyzed population distribution and dynamics and the change of PVH for a particular water landscape.

PVH seems rough, but it is an objective and concrete quantitative expression of human behavior. It is more realistic than questionnaires, interviews, and messages visitors post on the website after visiting. After all, there will inevitably be some deviation between people's cognitive feelings and actual behaviors. Moreover, PVH is simple enough and highly operable in practice. It is a well-understood and scientific conclusion based on the simplification of complex spatio-temporal big data. From this point of view, it has a specific value.

The diversity in education, occupation, and living environment will make people have different lifestyles, and the differences in lifestyles will lead to differences in behavior patterns. It is an interesting topic that the water quality of the water landscape affects the PVH of various groups. This research mainly divides the groups by age. If trying other schemes, we can also get valuable conclusions.

To sum up, the PVH index proposed in this paper proves the correlation between water quality and visitor behavior, and this correlation is statistically significant. The influence on different groups of people is distinct. However, suppose we can discuss it for a more extended period, we will be able to better and more effectively assist urban environmental governance, which is also the direction that we will strive for in the future next step.

5 Conclusions

Sightseeing behavior in water is expressed by PVH and PVA, which are measurable. Based on the two spatio-temporal big data of remote sensing observation and mobile phone signaling, the correlation analysis between visitors presence status and water quality in the urban water landscape parks can be realized.

From the research, we can see that SPI and PVH have a significant negative correlation, so the deterioration of water quality will significantly shorten the visiting time of visitors. Compared with different water quality conditions, the tour events with a longer duration will show an increasing trend with better water quality. There are significant differences in PVH between other groups of people when the water quality is excellent and poor.

References

1. Zhang, D., Shen, J., Sun, F.: Evaluation of water environment performance based on a DPSIR-SBM-Tobit model. KSCE J. Civ. Eng. 24(5), 1641–1654 (2020). https://doi.org/10.1007/s12205-020-2370-6

2. Lu, M., et al.: An assessment of temporal and spatial dynamics of regional water resources security in the DPSIR framework in Jiangxi Province, China. Int. J. Environ. Res. Public Health **19**(6), 3650 (2022)
3. Wu, H., et al.: Agricultural water and land resources allocation considering carbon sink/source and water scarcity/degradation footprint. Sci. Total Environ. **819**, 152058 (2022)
4. Fan, J.-L., et al.: Relationship between energy production and water resource utilization: a panel data analysis of 31 provinces in China. J. Clean. Prod. **167**, 88–96 (2017)
5. Peng, T., et al.: Assessment on water resources carrying capacity in karst areas by using an innovative DPESBRM concept model and cloud model. Sci. Total Environ. **767**, 144353 (2021)
6. Safavi, H.R., Mehrparvar, M., Szidarovszky, F.: Conjunctive management of surface and ground water resources using conflict resolution approach. J. Irrigat. Drainage Eng. **142**(4), 05016001 (2016)
7. Han, Y., et al.: Risk assessment of the water resources carrying capacity: a case study in North China. J. Am. Water Resour. Assoc. (2022)
8. Zhang, K., Wen, Z., Xhang, X.: China's water environment at the beginning of the 21st century: challenges and countermeasures. Water Sci. Technol. **46**(11–12), 245–251 (2002)
9. Pei, Y., et al.: Rehabilitation and improvement of Guilin urban water environment: function-oriented management. J. Environ. Sci. **25**(7), 1477–1482 (2013)
10. Wu, C., et al.: Regional water resource carrying capacity evaluation based on multi-dimensional precondition cloud and risk matrix coupling model. Sci. Total Environ. **710**, 136324 (2020)
11. Zhou, R., et al.: Forewarning model of regional water resources carrying capacity based on combination weights and entropy principles. Entropy **19**(11), 574 (2017)
12. Chen, Z., Wu, J., Wang, Y.: Analysis on water pollution control: a case study of industrial sewage leakage incident in china and its lessons learned. Res. J. Chem. Environ. **16**, 153–156 (2012)
13. Huo, S., et al.: The protection of high quality waters in China calls for antidegradation policy. Ecol. Ind. **46**, 119–120 (2014)
14. Zhou, Z., et al.: Does the "10-point water plan" reduce the intensity of industrial water pollution? Quasi-experimental evidence from China. J. Environ. Manag. **295**, 113048 (2021)
15. Boardman, J., Foster, I.D.L.: Run-off and sediment storage: the effectiveness of mitigation measures against soil erosion and freshwater pollution. Land Degrad. Dev. **32**(7), 2453–2455 (2021)
16. Pan, D., Hong, W., He, M.: Can campaign-style enforcement facilitate water pollution control? Learning from China's environmental protection interview. J. Environ. Manag. **301**, 113910 (2022)
17. Xu, X., et al.: Assessing the effect of the chinese river chief policy for water pollution control under uncertainty-using Chaohu Lake as a case. Int. J. Environ. Res. Public Health **17**(9), 3103 (2020)
18. Dong, J., Destech Publicat, I.: Research on the applications of cyclic water quality model and simulated annealing algorithm for water pollution control and planning. In: International Conference on Social Science, Management and Economics (SSME), Guangzhou, People's Republic China (2015)
19. Pan, D., Tang, J.: The effects of heterogeneous environmental regulations on water pollution control: quasi-natural experimental evidence from China. Sci. Total Environ. **751**, 141550 (2021)
20. Li, X., et al.: Rural households' willingness to accept compensation standards for controlling agricultural non-point source pollution: a case study of the Qinba water source area in Northwest China. Water **11**(6), 1251 (2019)

21. Whelton, A.J., et al.: Residential tap water contamination following the freedom industries chemical spill: perceptions, water quality, and health impacts. Environ. Sci. Technol. **49**(2), 813–823 (2015)
22. Shi, J., et al.: Estimation of chlorophyll-a concentrations in small water bodies: comparison of fused Gaofen-6 and Sentinel-2 sensors. Remote Sens. **14**(1), 229 (2022)
23. Beck, R., et al.: Comparison of satellite reflectance algorithms for estimating chlorophyll-a in a temperate reservoir using coincident hyperspectral aircraft imagery and dense coincident surface observations. Remote Sens. Environ. **178**, 15–30 (2016)
24. Xu, M., et al.: Regionally and locally adaptive models for retrieving Chlorophyll-a concentration in inland waters from remotely sensed multispectral and hyperspectral imagery. IEEE Trans. Geosci. Remote Sens. **57**(7), 4758–4774 (2019)
25. Wang, L., Hua, Z., Wang, Y.: Estimation of annual reference condition of Chlorophyll-a based on the segmental linear regression and power-law relationship in Taihu Lake. Water Supply **19**(1), 107–114 (2019)
26. Johansen, R., et al.: Evaluating the portability of satellite derived Chlorophyll-a algorithms for temperate inland lakes using airborne hyperspectral imagery and dense surface observations. Harmful Algae **76**, 35–46 (2018)
27. Xu, M., et al.: A spectral space partition guided ensemble method for retrieving chlorophyll-a concentration in inland waters from Sentinel-2A satellite imagery. J. Great Lakes Res. **45**(3), 454–465 (2019)
28. Prepas, E.E., Trew, D.O.: Evaluation of the phosphorus chlorophyll relationship for lakes off the precambrian shield in Western Canada. Can. J. Fisheries Aquatic Sci. **40**(1), 27–35 (1983)
29. Nicholls, K.H., Dillon, P.J.: Evaluation of phosphorus-chlorophyll-phytoplankton relationships for lakes. Int. Rev. Gesamten Hydrobiol. **63**(2), 141–154 (1978)
30. Meng, Y., et al.: To assess customers satisfaction at waterscape by sojourn time: case of the Beijing Grand Canal Forest Park. J. Beijing Norm. Univ. Nat. Sci. **57**(3), 424–432 (2021)
31. Wang, Y., et al.: Using mobile phone data for emergency management: a systematic literature review. Inf. Syst. Front. **22**(6), 1539–1559 (2020). https://doi.org/10.1007/s10796-020-100 57-w

MAHGE: Point-of-Interest Recommendation Using Meta-path Aggregated Heterogeneous Graph Embeddings

Jing Tian[1], Mengmeng Chang[1], Zhiming Ding[2(✉)], Xue Han[1], and Yajun Chen[1]

[1] Beijing University of Technology, Beijing 100124, China
{tianj,changmengmeng,hanxue,chenyajun}@emails.bjut.edu.cn
[2] Institute of Software, Chinese Academy of Sciences, Beijing 100190, China
zhiming@iscas.ac.cn

Abstract. The rapid growth of Location-Based Social Networks (LBSNs) has led to the generation of large amounts of users' check-in data, which has driven the development of many location-based recommendation services. Point-of-Interest (POI) recommendation is one such service that helps users find places they are interested in based on the current time and location. Unlike traditional recommendation tasks, users' check-in data contains rich heterogeneous data such as time, geographical information and social relationship information; thus it is challenging to capture the complex contextual relationships between these heterogeneous information for POI recommendation. To solve this problem, we propose a Metapath Aggregated Heterogeneous Graph Embeddings method(MAHGE). Specially, it firstly proposes a novel method to construct the heterogeneous LBSN graph which innovatively models time as the relationship on the edges of the graph in order to capture the complex dependency between user and time. Then, it proposes to profile the target node based on meta-paths because meta-path reflects the characteristics of target node from a multi-dimensional perspective. Moreover, it introduces a graph embedding method based on meta-path aggregation to learn the vector representation of the target node with attention mechanism. Finally, extensive experiments on two real-word datasets are conducted, and the results show the effectiveness of this method.

Keywords: POI Recommendation · Heterogeneous graph embeddings · Meta-paths aggregation · Attention mechanism

1 Introduction

Location-based social networks (LBSNs), such as Gowalla, Foursquare and Yelp, have become prevalent in our daily life. In LBSNs, users are allowed to share their real-time geospatial locations and experiences on POIs via check-in function [25]. It is evident that these large amounts of users' check-in data gives LBSN

© The Author(s), under exclusive license to Springer Nature Switzerland AG 2022
H. Wu et al. (Eds.): SpatialDI 2022, LNCS 13614, pp. 250–263, 2022.
https://doi.org/10.1007/978-3-031-24521-3_18

providers invaluable information to provide meaningful suggestions for users. However, it is challenging to incorporate all contextual factors for user and POI representation learning due to their heterogeneity and sparsity.

A large number of efforts have been devoted to dealing with this challenge, which primarily focuses on users' relations with geographical information over bipartite networks [2,3,22]. However, such approaches are typically effective for learning local graph structure, but the global nature of the graph, including the community structure of homogeneous nodes and the remote dependencies of heterogeneous nodes, is not well preserved. Considering the heterogeneity of users' check-in data, STA [12] takes location and time as a spatiotemporal pair <*time, location*> and uses the embedding of this pair as a relationship for connecting users and POIs. However, it ignores auxiliary information related to users' interactions. Moreover, research based on meta-paths [1,21] still failed to learn heterogeneous graph embeddings because they discard all intermediate nodes along the metapath by only considering two end nodes, which results in information loss.

In this paper, we propose a Metapath Aggregated Heterogeneous Graph Embeddings method (MAHGE) to incorporate all contextual factors for user and POI representation learning. Specifically, we firstly introduce a novel method to construct the heterogeneous LBSN graph which innovatively models time as the relationship on the edges of the graph in order to capture the complex dependency between user and time. To overcome the sparsity of users' check-in data, we introduce category and geographical region of POIs in heterogeneous LBSN graph construction. Then, we propose to profile the target node based on meta-paths because meta-paths reflect the characteristics of target node from a multi-dimensional perspective. Moreover, we introduce a graph embedding method based on meta-path aggregation to learn the vector representation of the target node with attention mechanism.

To summarize, our contributions are listed as follows:

- To emphasize the interdependence between user and time, a novel heterogeneous LBSN graph construction method is proposed based on users' historical check-in records, which innovatively models time as a relationship on the edges of the graph.
- We innovatively propose to profile the target node based on meta-paths and learn the embedding representation of the target node based on the meta-path aggregation, which includes intra-metapath aggregation and inter-metapath aggregation.
- We conduct extensive experiments on two real-world datasets, and the experimental results demonstrate the effectiveness as well as the accuracy of the model proposed in this paper.

2 Related Work

In this section, we discuss existing researches related to our work, including POI recommendation integrating various factors and heterogeneous graph embedding techniques.

POI Recommendation. Existing POI recommendation methods are based on the following factors: social, geographical, temporal, and semantic effects to analyze users' behavior and provide recommendations. Specifically, the social influence refers that users tend to be influenced by their friends and visit common locations [10,24] used social influence to improve the POI recommendation performance, and proposed to distinguish three types of friendships, that are i) linked, ii) co-located, and iii) proximate friends and combined matrix factorization models into a unified framework. The geographical influence refers to that users tend to visit places that are close to him/her or are close to the places already visited by that user. Liu et al. [13] proposed to encode the geographical influence and user mobility and adopted a Bayesian probabilistic non-negative latent factor model for encoding both the spatial influence and personalized preferences. The temporal influence refers to that users show distinct check-in preferences at different hours of the day and tend to have similar preferences in consecutive hours than non-consecutive hours [5]. Gao et al. [5] proposed a temporal regularization to minimize an objective function using temporal coefficients which introduces a temporal state to represent hours of the day and defines the time-dependent user check-in preferences using the temporal state. Baral et al. [8] proposed to explore the category of the attended locations during particular times of the day. Thus, the category of the visited POIs in the past history at specific times of the day is crucial along with all other factors. However, most of the existing approache lack a comprehensive way of personalizing their recommendations since they ignore one or more of them.

Heterogeneous Graph Embedding. The purpose of heterogeneous graph embedding is to project the nodes in a heterogeneous graph into a low-dimensional vector space. Dong et al. [4] proposed metapath2vec, which generates neighborhoods from random walks guided by a single meta-path, and then feeds these nodes into skip-gram model [15] to learn node embeddings. Models like DeepWalk [16], node2vec [6], and TADW [23] are also based on random walk over the graph to sample the nodes in the neighborhood. Tang [19] et al. proposed LINE, which learns node embeddings by exploiting the first-order and second-order proximity between nodes. Shang et al. [17] proposed ESim, which generates node embeddings by learning from sampled positive and negative meta-path instances. Shi et al. [18] proposed HERec, which converts heterogeneous graph to a homogeneous graph based on metapath-based neighbors and applies the DeepWalk model to learn the node embeddings of the target type. However, these approaches ignore modeling spatial and temporal factors and can not be used for POI recommendation.

Contrary to all the above studies, we present a novel unified framework for POI recommendations that takes into account all of the aforementioned factors described previously. We construct the heterogeneous LBSN graph based on the check-ins, temporal effects, social connections, and auxiliary geographical and semantic information. Inspired by the state-of-the-art performance of heterogeneous graph embedding, we propose a heterogeneous graph-based framework(MAHGE), which profiles the target node based on meta-paths and leverages meta-paths aggregation method to jointly learn the graph embedding.

3   Preliminaries

To formulate the problem, let $U = \{u_1, u_2, ..., u_{|U|}\}$ denote a set of users and $L = \{l_1, l_2, ..., l_{|L|}\}$ represent a set of POIs, where $|U|$ and $|L|$ are the total numbers of users and POIs, respectively. For the ease of illustration, we give the following definitions.

Definition 1 (POI): A POI is a spatial location(e.g., a park or a gym) with unique geographical coordinates (latitude and longitude). In this paper, it is denoted as a trituple $<l, lat, lon>$.

Definition 2 (Check-In): A user's check-in record is represented by a trituple $<u, l, t>$, which means that a user $u \in U$ visited a POI $l \in L$ at time t. Further, the set of POIs of user u can be represented as $P_u = \{l|\exists<u,l,t>\}$

Definition 3 (Social relationship): Social relationship means that users are friends with each other. For a pair of mutual friends u and m, the social relationship between them can be represented by a tuple $<u,m>$. Further, the set of friends of user u can be represented as $F_u = \{m|\exists<u,m>\}$.

Problem Statement. Given the check-in set P_u, friend set F_u of user u and the query time t, the goal is to recommend the top-K preferable POIs for user u at time t.

4   The Proposed Framework

In this section, we elaborate technical details for our proposed model MAHGE. It contains four layers: input layer, neighbors sampling layer, meta-path aggregation layer and prediction layer. The input layer presents the user record graph construction based on users' check-in records. The neighbors sampling layer is designed to sample a fixed number of neighbor nodes for each node at time slot t. The meta-path aggregation layer introduces a graph embedding method based on meta-path aggregation to learn the vector representation of the target node with attention mechanism. The prediction layer calculates preference scores for candidate POIs with inner product. The overall architecture of MAHGE is presented in Fig. 1.

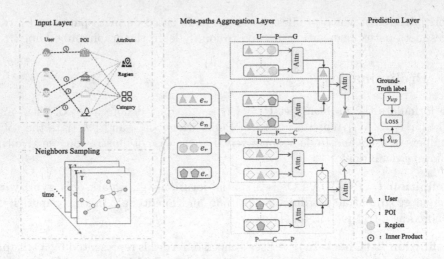

Fig. 1. The overview of the MAHGE model.

4.1 Heterogeneous LBSN Graph Construction

This section presents the user record graph construction based on users' check-in records. Specifically, in order to jointly learn the representations of the users and POIs, we construct $\mathcal{G}$ to represent the heterogeneous LBSN graph, $\mathcal{G} = <\mathcal{V}, \mathcal{E}>$, where $\mathcal{V}$ is the node set of the LBSN graph, which includes users, POIs, regions and categories. $\mathcal{E}$ denotes the edges of this LBSN graph, which includes users' check-in records with temporal information, social relationships among users, geographical information, and semantic information. Next, we explain each node and the type of edges.

The users node set, $\mathcal{U} = \{u_1, u_2, ..., u_M\}$, represents all the user entities in the check-in records, where M denotes the number of user entities.

The POIs node set, $\mathcal{L} = \{l_1, l_2, ..., l_N\}$, represents all the POI entities in the check-in records, where N denotes the number of POI entities.

The region node type $\mathcal{R}$ indicates the region to which the POIs belong. According to Tobler's first law of geography: users' check-in behavior tends to exhibit obvious geographic clustering, i.e., users prefer to visit POIs that are closer to their current geographic location [20]. In order to model the geographic clustering phenomenon, we propose to divide the geographic space where users check in into grids and map POIs into the grid so that POIs similar to each other locate in the same grid region.

User-User edge connects two users who have a social relationship.

User-POI edge connects users and POIs based on users' check-in data. $e_{i,j,t}$ represents user u_i visited p_j at t, if user u_i has visited p_j at different time, there will be multiple edges between two nodes, each edge represents a visited time.

POI-Region edge represents the subordination of the POI to the region, where $e_{i,j}$ denotes POI p_i is in region r_j.

Region-Region edge indicates the adjacency between regions, where $e_{i,j}$ denotes region r_i is geographically adjacent to region r_j.

POI-Category edge represents the subordination of the POI to the category, where $e_{i,j}$ denotes POI p_i belongs to c_j.

Time-Based Subgraph Sampling Algorithm. The heterogeneous LBSN graph contains edges at all times, however, we only need to focus on the part related to the target time slot t. Therefore, we introduce a time-based neighbor sampling algorithm to sample a fixed number of neighbor nodes for each node at time slot t. For neighboring nodes of the same type, the weight information of the edge is used to calculate the probability of being captured. For example, the weight w on the User-POI edge represents the association of the user node with the POI node, so the edge with a higher weight should have a higher probability of being captured when sampling. For different types of neighbor nodes, a normalization is introduced to ensure that each neighbor node type has equal probability of being captured. The regularization of an edge with relation r associated with node i is calculated as:

$$regular_{i,r} = \frac{1}{\sum_{k \in \mathcal{N}_i^r} w_{i,k}} \tag{1}$$

where $\mathcal{N}_i^r$ represents neighbor nodes which is related to node i, $w_{i,k}$ denotes the weight of edge $e_{i,k}$. Thus, the weight of each edge at time slot t is defined as:

$$w_{i,k} = w_t^{i,k} \times w_{i,k} \times regular_{i,r} \tag{2}$$

where $w_t^{i,k} = 1$ if the time slot of edge $e_{i,k}$ is t, otherwise $w_t^{i,k} = 0$.

4.2   Meta-path Aggregation Method

Inspired by the idea of generating node embeddings based on local neighbors of GCN, we propose a meta-path aggregation-based approach to learn the embedding of target nodes. Firstly, various different meta-paths are designed based on the target node. Then, given a meta-path, the embedding vector of the target node guided by this meta-path is obtained by aggregating the instances under this meta-path based on the attention mechanism. Finally, the semantic information of different meta-paths is aggregated to obtain the final embedding representation of the target node.

In this section, we describe the process of meta-path aggregation by learning the embedding vector E_{u_2} of user node u_2 as an example. Assuming that the meta-path based on user nodes is UPG and UPC, we introduce how to aggregate neighbor information based on the meta-path UPG and UPC. As is shown in Fig. 2, $<u_2, p_1, g_1>$, $<u_2, p_2, g_2>$ and $<u_2, p_2, g_3>$ are instances of metapath UPG. For each meta-path instance, it is aggregated into a single vector by taking the mean value of its internal nodes. Since different meta-path instances

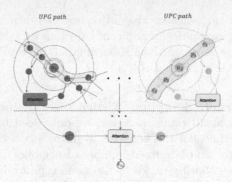

Fig. 2. An example of meta-paths aggregation method.

have different importance on user nodes, the graph attention mechanism is introduced to learn a normalized importance weight for each meta-path instance, and then weighted aggregation is used to obtain the embedding representation $E_{u_2}^{UPG}$ of user node u_2 under that meta-path. Similarly, we obtain the representation $E_{u_2}^{UPC}$ of user node u_2. Because different meta-paths have different impacts on the same target node, the attention mechanism is used to learn a normalized importance weight for each meta-path, and then weighted aggregation to obtain the final embedding representation of the target node.

4.3   User Modeling

In this section, we design meta-paths which start or end with user nodes, and profile user nodes with these meta-paths. The meta-paths selected are $\rho = \{UPG, UPC, UPGU, UPCU\}$, which represents geographical, semantic, and social influence, respectively. We extract the neighbors from meta-path instances which is obtained by random-walks on heterogeneous graphs, $I_{\rho_i} = p_1, p_2, ..., p_n$, and calculate the embedding representation of the target user node u under these meta-path instances by using Eq. (3):

$$E_u^{p_j^{\rho_i}} = \frac{1}{|p_j|} \sum_{v \in p_j^{\rho_i}} E_v. \tag{3}$$

Since different meta-path instances have different degrees of influence on user nodes, the graph attention mechanism is introduced to learn a normalized importance weight for each meta-path instance, and then the weighted aggregation yields the embedding representation of user node u under that meta-path:

$$e_u^{p_j^{\rho_i}} = LeakyReLU(W_{\rho_i}^T \cdot \left[E_u^{'} || E_u^{p_j^{\rho_i}} \right]), \tag{4}$$

$$\alpha_u^{p_j^{\rho_i}} = \frac{exp(e_u^{p_j^{\rho_i}})}{\sum_{p_k^{\rho_i} \in I_{\rho_i}} exp(e_u^{p_j^{\rho_i}})}, \tag{5}$$

$$E_u^{\rho_i} = \sigma\left(\sum_{p_j^{\rho_i} \in I_{\rho_i}} \alpha_u^{p_j^{\rho_i}} \cdot e_u^{p_j^{\rho_i}} \right). \tag{6}$$

where $E_u^{'} \in \mathbb{R}^d$ is the initial embedding vector of user u, $W_{\rho_i}^T$ is the attention mechanism parameters of metapath ρ_i, $\|$ is the concatenation operator. $e_u^{p_j^{\rho_i}}$ represents the importance of metapath instance ρ_i to target user node u. We then use softmax function to normalize all the meta-path instances weights, aggregate these metapath instances, and use activation function $\sigma(\cdot)$ to obtain the final embedding representation of the target node.

With Eq. (3)–Eq. (6), we obtain the embedding representation of user node u under meta-paths UPG, UPC, UPGU and UPCU respectively.

Next, we introduce an attention mechanism to aggregate the embeddings of target nodes under different meta-paths. Firstly, We obtain the vector of user type nodes under meta-path ρ_i by averaging the embedding vector of all user nodes:

$$E_U^{\rho_i} = \frac{1}{|U|} \sum_{u \in U} tanh(W_U \cdot E_u^{\rho_i} + b_U), \tag{7}$$

where $W_U \in \mathbb{R}^{d_n \times d}$ and $b_U \in d_n$ are learnable parameters. Then, we introduce attention mechanism to fuse different metapaths:

$$e_{\rho_i} = W_U^T \cdot E_U^{\rho_i} \tag{8}$$

$$\beta_{\rho_i} = \frac{exp(e_{\rho_i})}{\sum_{\rho_j \in \rho^u} exp(e_{\rho_j})} \tag{9}$$

$$E_u^{\rho_U} = \sum_{\rho_i \in \rho^U} \beta_{\rho_i} \cdot E_u^{\rho_i} \tag{10}$$

where $W_U^T \in \mathbb{R}^{d_n}$ is the attention parameters of user node type, β_{ρ_i} is the importance of meta-path ρ_i to user node type.

Finally, we use a non-linear function to project the embedding of the target user node u to a vector space of desired output dimensions:

$$E_u = \sigma(W_o \cdot E_u^{\rho^U}) \tag{11}$$

where $\sigma(\cdot)$ is activation function, $W_o \in \mathbb{R}^{d_n}$ is a linear mapping matrix.

4.4   POI Modeling

Similar to user node information aggregation, we use meta-paths PUP, PCP and PGP to aggregate POI nodes. The representations of POI node p_i is E_{p_i}.

4.5 Prediction and Training

After aggregating the meta-paths on user and POI nodes, we obtain the final representation of target nodes at the current time t. Given the representation E_u of user u and the representation E_p of POI p, we calculate the overall prediction score through Eq. (12), and then recommend the top-N POIs with the highest scores to the user.

$$y(u, p, t) = \sigma(E_u^T \cdot E_{(p_i)}) \tag{12}$$

where $\sigma(\cdot)$ is softmax function.

Given a set of training samples, we can optimize the model weights by minimizing the following loss function through negative sampling:

$$\mathcal{L} = - \sum_{(u,p)\in\mathcal{D}} log\sigma(y(u, p, t)) - \sum_{(u',p')\in\mathcal{D}^-} log\sigma(-y(u', p', t)),$$

where $\sigma(\cdot)$ is softmax function, D is the set of positive node pairs, D^- is the set of negative node pairs.

5 Experiments

In this section, we conduct various experiments on two real-world LBSN datasets to compare our proposed model MAHGE with baselines.

5.1 Experimental Setup

Datasets. We evaluate our proposed MAHGE model on two real-world datasets:(Gowalla and Weeplaces [14]). Both datasets contain records of users' check-ins to POIs, category information of POIs, and user-user social relationships. The basic information after pre-processing the data is shown in Table 1, where the sparsity is expressed as the ratio of blank items to all items in the user-POI check-in count matrix.

Table 1. Statistics of the four datasets

	Gowalla	Weeplaces
#users	319063	15799
#locations	2844076	971309
#check-ins	36001959	7658368
Sparsity	99.66%	99.65%

Comparison Methods. We compare our MAHGE with the following baselines:

(1) **GeoMF** [11]: It is based on weighted Matrix factorization which predicts users' preferences for POIs by considering their activity area preferences and the influence of POIs in the area.

(2) **LINE** [19]: It proposes a graph embedding learning method that considers the first-order and second-order proximity of nodes in a graph.

(3) **JLGE** [2]: It is a spatio-temporal graph model which applies the LINE [19] method to multiple bipartite graphs and jointly learns the embedding representation of each node.

(4) **RELINE** [3]: It is an extension of the JLGE [2] that takes user's POI path and stay point factors into account to better capture the user's dynamic preferences based on the JLGE.

(5) **STGCN** [7]: It takes the time factor into account when constructing the graph and incorporates GCNs to implement the embedding of the nodes in the graph.

Evaluation Metrics. We use the evaluation metric Accuracy@N (Acc@N) to measure the accuracy of the recommended tasks. In this case, $k = \{1, 5, 10\}$ is chosen for the experimental comparison.

Implementation Details. We implement the proposed method based on Pytorch. We employ the Adam [9] optimizer with the learning rate set to 0.005, the weight decay parameter set to 0.001. The dropout rate is set to 0.5. The meta-path intra-aggregate layer attention vector dimension is set to 128, and the meta-path inter-aggregate layer attention vector dimension is set to 64.

5.2   Recommendation Performance

Table 2 shows the performance of MAHGE method with other methods on two datasets, Gowalla and Weeplaces. MAHGE outperforms all the other models in all metrics. In particular, it improves 4.3%, 3.4%, 2.34% and 1.3%, 0.7%, 2.5% in terms of Acc@1, Acc@5, and Acc@10 on both datasets, respectively. In addition, the absolute performance of MAHGE is higher on Gowalla dataset than that on Weeplaces dataset, because the check-in and social information in the Gowalla dataset is richer than that in the Weeplaces dataset, which fully demonstrates the effectiveness of using meta-paths aggregation methods to fuse contextual information. Comparing with RELINE [3] and JLGE [2] which both consider time as an independent node when constructing the heterogeneous LBSN graph, we propose to consider the dependency of user and time factor as the relationship between user and POI and model time as the relationship between users and POIs, which improves the recommendation performance. The result that MAHGE outperforms the STGCN model indicates the effectiveness of the meta-path aggregation-based approach to embedding the target nodes.

Table 2. Recommendation performance. The best performing method in each row is boldfaced, and the second best method in each row is underlined. Improvements are shown in the last row respectively.

Model	Gowalla			Weeplaces		
	Acc@1	Acc@5	Acc@10	Acc@1	Acc@5	Acc@10
GeoMF	0.2980	0.3550	0.4060	0.2654	0.3201	0.3750
LINE	0.251	0.309	0.351	0.208	0.267	0.2250
JLGE	0.41	0.451	0.486	0.389	0.4182	0.4903
RELINE	0.408	0.435	0.477	0.386	0.421	0.488
STGCN	<u>0.43</u>	<u>0.4760</u>	<u>0.5340</u>	<u>0.4081</u>	<u>0.4729</u>	<u>0.5120</u>
MAHGE	**0.4730**	**0.5100**	**0.5574**	**0.4210**	**0.4800**	**0.5370**
%Improv.	4.3%	3.4%	2.34%	1.3%	0.7%	2.5%

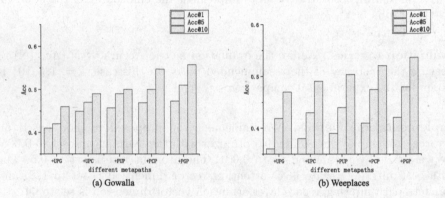

(a) Gowalla   (b) Weeplaces

Fig. 3. Performances of MAHGE with additive meta-paths.

5.3   Effect of Different Metapaths

The model MAHGE embeds target nodes by aggregating different meta-paths guided neighbors to improve recommendation performance. To further investigate the impact of different meta-paths on node embedding in the POI recommendation task, this subsection adds meta-paths UPG, UPC, PUP, PCP, and PGP sequentially in the model and observes the model performance.

Figure 3 shows the variation of model performance when adding meta-paths sequentially on the two datasets, where Fig. 3(a) shows the variation of model performance with sequential addition of meta-paths on the Gowalla dataset, and Fig. 3(b) shows the variation of model performance with sequential joining of meta-paths on the Weeplaces dataset. The results show that the performance of the model steadily improves as meta-paths are added to the model one by one, which indicates that adding new meta-paths plays an important role in learning the target node embedding. It should be noted that due to the limitation of the experimental setup, we only selected 5 representative meta-paths

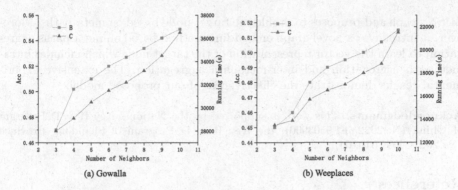

Fig. 4. Performances of MAHGE with different number of neighbors.

in our experiments. However, the MAHGE model provides a flexible framework to improve the recommendation performance by assembling more meta-paths as well as richer semantic information to characterize the target nodes.

5.4   Effect of the Number of Neighbors

In this subsection, a series of experiments are conducted on two datasets to evaluate the impact of the number of neighbor sampling on the POI recommendation performance. Specifically, for POI nodes, we set the number of neighbor nodes to a fixed value of 6, and for user nodes, we set the number of neighbor nodes to 3–10.

Figure 4 shows the variation of recommended performance and running time with the number of neighbors, where the red line indicates the recommended performance ACC and the green line indicates the running time. As shown in the Fig. 4, the performance of the model steadily improves as the number of neighbors increases. Note that the performance of the model continues to improve as the number of neighbors continues to increase, but tends to stabilize. Due to the constraints of the computational conditions, we set the maximum value of the neighbor variable to 10. This indicates that the neighbor information can effectively enhance the representation of user nodes. However, we can also note that as the number of neighbor samples increases, the running time of the model increases as well. Therefore, for the propose of keeping balance between accuracy and running time, we usually set the number of neighbors as 5.

6   Conclusions

In this paper, we study the POI recommendation problem in LBSNs. In order to incorporate these heterogeneous information in LBSNs, we model objects and interactions in POI recommendation system with a HIN and propose a meta-path aggregated heterogeneous graph embeddings method, called MAHGE. MAHGE introduces category and geographical region of POIs to construct heterogeneous

LBSN graph and proposes to profile the target node based on meta-paths. Moreover, it introduces a novel graph embedding method based on meta-paths aggregation to learn the vector representation of the target node which includes intra-metapath aggregation and inter-metapath aggregation. The extensive experimental results demonstrate the effectiveness of our proposed model.

Acknowledgments. This work is supported by the National Key R & D Program of China (No.2022YFF0503900), the Key R & D Program of Shandong Province (No.2021CXGC010104).

References

1. Canturk, D., Karagoz, P.: SgWalk: location recommendation by user subgraph-based graph embedding. IEEE Access **9**, 134858–134873 (2021)
2. Christoforidis, G., Kefalas, P., Papadopoulos, A., Manolopoulos, Y.: Recommendation of points-of-interest using graph embeddings. In: 2018 IEEE 5th International Conference on Data Science and Advanced Analytics (DSAA), pp. 31–40. IEEE (2018)
3. Christoforidis, G., Kefalas, P., Papadopoulos, A.N., Manolopoulos, Y.: Reline: point-of-interest recommendations using multiple network embeddings. Knowl. Inf. Syst. **63**(4), 791–817 (2021)
4. Dong, Y., Chawla, N.V., Swami, A.: metapath2vec: scalable representation learning for heterogeneous networks. In: Proceedings of the 23rd ACM SIGKDD International Conference on Knowledge Discovery and Data Mining, pp. 135–144 (2017)
5. Gao, H., Tang, J., Hu, X., Liu, H.: Exploring temporal effects for location recommendation on location-based social networks. In: Proceedings of the 7th ACM Conference on Recommender Systems, pp. 93–100 (2013)
6. Grover, A., Leskovec, J.: node2vec: scalable feature learning for networks. In: Proceedings of the 22nd ACM SIGKDD International Conference on Knowledge Discovery and Data Mining, pp. 855–864 (2016)
7. Han, H., et al.: STGCN: a spatial-temporal aware graph learning method for POI recommendation. In: 2020 IEEE International Conference on Data Mining (ICDM), pp. 1052–1057. IEEE (2020)
8. Kefalas, P., Manolopoulos, Y.: A time-aware spatio-textual recommender system. Expert Syst. Appl. **78**, 396–406 (2017)
9. Kingma, D.P., Ba, J.: Adam: a method for stochastic optimization. arXiv preprint arXiv:1412.6980 (2014)
10. Li, H., Ge, Y., Hong, R., Zhu, H.: Point-of-interest recommendations: learning potential check-ins from friends. In: Proceedings of the 22nd ACM SIGKDD International Conference on Knowledge Discovery and Data Mining, pp. 975–984 (2016)
11. Lian, D., Zhao, C., Xie, X., Sun, G., Chen, E., Rui, Y.: GeoMF: joint geographical modeling and matrix factorization for point-of-interest recommendation. In: Proceedings of the 20th ACM SIGKDD International Conference on Knowledge Discovery and Data Mining, pp. 831–840 (2014)
12. Liu, B., Qian, T., Liu, B., Hong, L., You, Z., Li, Y.: Learning spatiotemporal-aware representation for poi recommendation. arXiv preprint arXiv:1704.08853 (2017)
13. Liu, B., Fu, Y., Yao, Z., Xiong, H.: Learning geographical preferences for point-of-interest recommendation. In: Proceedings of the 19th ACM SIGKDD International Conference on Knowledge Discovery and Data Mining, pp. 1043–1051 (2013)

14. Liu, Y., Wei, W., Sun, A., Miao, C.: Exploiting geographical neighborhood characteristics for location recommendation. In: Proceedings of the 23rd ACM International Conference on Conference on Information and Knowledge Management, pp. 739–748 (2014)
15. Mikolov, T., Chen, K., Corrado, G., Dean, J.: Efficient estimation of word representations in vector space. arXiv preprint arXiv:1301.3781 (2013)
16. Perozzi, B., Al-Rfou, R., Skiena, S.: Deepwalk: online learning of social representations. In: Proceedings of the 20th ACM SIGKDD International Conference on Knowledge Discovery and Data Mining, pp. 701–710 (2014)
17. Shang, J., Qu, M., Liu, J., Kaplan, L.M., Han, J., Peng, J.: Meta-path guided embedding for similarity search in large-scale heterogeneous information networks. arXiv preprint arXiv:1610.09769 (2016)
18. Shi, C., Hu, B., Zhao, W.X., Philip, S.Y.: Heterogeneous information network embedding for recommendation. IEEE Trans. Knowl. Data Eng. **31**(2), 357–370 (2018)
19. Tang, J., Qu, M., Wang, M., Zhang, M., Yan, J., Mei, Q.: Line: large-scale information network embedding. In: Proceedings of the 24th International Conference on World Wide Web, pp. 1067–1077 (2015)
20. Wang, H., Shen, H., Ouyang, W., Cheng, X.: Exploiting poi-specific geographical influence for point-of-interest recommendation. In: IJCAI, pp. 3877–3883 (2018)
21. Wang, X., et al.: Heterogeneous graph attention network. In: The World Wide Web Conference, pp. 2022–2032 (2019)
22. Xie, M., Yin, H., Wang, H., Xu, F., Chen, W., Wang, S.: Learning graph-based poi embedding for location-based recommendation. In: Proceedings of the 25th ACM International on Conference on Information and Knowledge Management, pp. 15–24 (2016)
23. Yang, C., Liu, Z., Zhao, D., Sun, M., Chang, E.: Network representation learning with rich text information. In: Twenty-Fourth International Joint Conference on Artificial Intelligence (2015)
24. Zhang, J.D., Chow, C.Y.: Geosoca: exploiting geographical, social and categorical correlations for point-of-interest recommendations. In: Proceedings of the 38th International ACM SIGIR Conference on Research and Development in Information Retrieval, pp. 443–452 (2015)
25. Zheng, C., Tao, D., Wang, J., Cui, L., Ruan, W., Yu, S.: Memory augmented hierarchical attention network for next point-of-interest recommendation. IEEE Trans. Comput. Soc. Syst. **8**(2), 489–499 (2020)

A Novel Method for Groups Identification Based on Spatio-Temporal Trajectories

Zhi Cai[1], Meilin Ji[1], Hongbing Ren[2], Qing Mi[1(✉)], Limin Guo[1], and Zhiming Ding[1,3]

[1] The College of Computer Science, Beijing University of Technology, Beijing 100124, China
{caiz,miqing,guolimin,zmding}@bjut.edu.cn,
Jimeilin@emails.bjut.edu.cn
[2] Chengdu Micro-clouds Technology Co., Ltd., Chendu 610000, China
[3] Beijing Key Laboratory on Integration and Analysis of Large-Scale Stream Data, Chinese Academy of Sciences, Beijing 100144, China

Abstract. With the rapid development of sensing hard-devices, wireless communication technologies and smart mobile devices, a large number of data for moving objects have been collected, among which a group of high precision data (e.g., GPS) are widely used for traffic predictions and management. However, in modern city life, a large volume of positioning data of moving objects is collected with low-precision positions, which causes the difficulty for trajectory match, analysis or group identification. In view of this limitation, this paper proposes a novel method for the semantic trajectory based group identification. Specifically, the trajectory data are used to discover the spatial and semantic information of persons to calculate their similarities. Based on which, the groups of persons with strong correlations are identified. To evaluate our method, we conduct several experiments on Geolife dataset. The experimental results show that the proposed method has a significant effect on the group identification.

Keywords: Trajectory · Moving object data · Clustering analysis · Groups identification

1 Introduction

In recent years, the continuous development and wide application of the satellite communication, GPS equipments, RFID, wireless sensors, Internet of Things and video tracking have made the positioning and tracking of moving objects more accurate and effective. The trajectory data of the moving objects give us a new perspective for the data mining and analyzing. The study of persons' trajectories can help us to identify groups, understand group movements and analyze group behaviors. Moreover, we can do some targeted preparations and preventions for large-scale activities based on these information. However, there are still very few researches on the data mining and analyzing for the group identification of persons from the perspective of their historical trajectories and POIs. Meanwhile, there are some researches to analyze the behavior pattern of target persons. These studies provide us with some new perspectives to analyze the behaviors of groups.

© The Author(s), under exclusive license to Springer Nature Switzerland AG 2022
H. Wu et al. (Eds.): SpatialDI 2022, LNCS 13614, pp. 264–280, 2022.
https://doi.org/10.1007/978-3-031-24521-3_19

In this paper, we focus on the group identification by mining and analyzing the trajectory data of target persons. Specifically, the key groups identification is to divide target person into different groups and the persons in the same group have similar characteristics. Then, based on the characteristics of groups and application scenarios, we can focus on the selected key groups.

The contributions of this paper are summarized as follows.

1. The proposed method uses the geographic locations and temporal tags (i.e., spatio-temporal information) of persons' trajectories to detect their stay regions and their frequency in each stay region in a period of time;
2. Based on the semantic information extracted from stay regions, the proposed method further analyzes and accurately describes the characteristics of persons' behavior;
3. By using the characteristics of persons' behavior, the clustering mechanism is employed by the proposed method to divide target persons into different groups. Then, the key groups can be identified based on their characteristics and the application scenarios.

The rest of the paper is organized as follows. In Sect. 2, we review some works about the group identification and the data mining and analyzing methods for moving objects. In Sect. 3, we give some basic definitions that are used in the proposed method. Section 4 describes how we detect user's stay regions. In Sect. 5, we introduce how to extract the semantic information from the stay regions. In Sect. 6, we customize the similarity measures between persons, and then apply the clustering method for the key groups identification. Section 7 illustrates experiments and evaluations. Section 8 concludes this paper.

2 Related Work

In this section, we introduce some works related to the group identification and some data mining and analyzing methods for the moving objects. To the best of our knowledge, there is no existing work using the data of moving objects to identify the key groups from crowds.

2.1 The Group Identification

The key group identification technologies have played an important role in the decision making on security and emergency. In the context of social media [1–3], with the rapid development of information technologies, many social media platforms (e.g. apps on mobile terminals, websites, etc.) were built on Internet, where users can participate and establish their social networks. During this process, a lot of useful user data were generated, such as users' hot spots, behaviors, interaction information, etc. [4, 5]. Through the deep analyzing these data, we can identify the characteristics of individuals or groups and their social relationships, which can support and help us to make decisions in security and emergency scenarios.

Peng et al. used the clustering method and the non-negative matrix factorization to find the usage pattern of information from user tags [6]. Zhang et al. combined the author-top (AT) model with user relationship information to find the user community in online social networks [7]. Hu et al. considered each micro-blog user as an agent. Through mining and analyzing the data of these agents, the psychology and behavior patterns in the micro-blog information dissemination were found [8]. Yang et al. proposed the MABR algorithm, which found the behavioral rules of individuals, groups or countries through three steps, that were the finding of candidate behavioral rules, the pruning of behavioral rules and the generation of actionable behavioral behavioral rules [9]. Boratto et al. proposed the BaseGRA algorithm, which used the user shared information and clustering method to find relationships and groups of users and give recommendations to users [10].

2.2 The Mining and Analyzing for the Moving Object Data

Due to the development of positioning, tracking and telecommunication technologies, a large amount of data of moving objects are collected and employed by many applications. Recently, the data mining and analyzing for moving objects has attracted a lot of attentions from researchers. In the last ten years, many mining and analyzing approaches were proposed for the moving object data in a wide range of applications.

Pan et al. proposed a trace mining framework for smart cities to support the decision for the city's public security, transportation, health-care, commerce, etc. [11]. Zhou et al. used the clustering algorithm to discover meaningful places for individuals and propose the evaluation benchmarks and frameworks [12]. Shaw et al. proposed a modified Apriori algorithm to find the frequent coordinates from trajectories and reduce the searching time and space by pruning the coordinate sets [13]. Ye et al. proposed the LP-Mine framework to retrieve the persons' pattern from their raw GPS data [14]. Kalnis et al. proposed MC1, MC2 and MC3 three methods to identify the moving groups through calculating the moving similarity of objects in a long period [15]. The above approaches only analyze the trajectories of moving objects. However, they are lack of the analysis for the semantic information of trajectories and the temporal and spatial similarities of behaviors.

In recent years, some trajectory analysis approaches for the moving objects take the semantic information into account. In [17], Parent et al. summarized the construction, the semantic extension and behavior analysis approaches for the trajectory of moving objects. In 2014, Bogorny et al. proposed the CONSTAnT, an ontology-based model to describe the trajectory of moving objects and their semantic information [16]. Although the CONSTAnT can comprehensively describe the semantic and spatial information from the trajectory of moving objects, they do not specify how to obtain the semantic information from the trajectory of moving objects.

3 Definitions

In this section, we briefly describe some definitions of the proposed method.

By considering a person as a moving object, its location information in a period of time describes its trajectory. The location information can be obtained by GPS devices carried by the person, such as a mobile phone. Thus, the trajectory of a person in a range of time can be defined as a set.

$$T = (point_1, point_2, \ldots, point_n), \tag{1}$$

where $point_i$ contains the information of $\{lat, lon, timestamp\}$. lat and lon represent the coordinates of a location, where the person stays at and $timestamp$ represents the time when the person is at the location.

Based on the trajectory of the person, we only need to extract the Stay Regions from his/her trajectories, while given a set of trajectories, their corresponding SR are defined as follows:

$$SR = (lat, lon, (p_i)_{i=1}^n, r), \tag{2}$$

where $(p_i)_{i=1}^n$ represents the stay points in the stay region, r is the radius of the stay region, lat and lon represent the location (i.e., latitude and longitude) of the center of the stay region.

4 The Stay Region Extraction

The stay region extraction from person's trajectories is to find the geographic regions that the person pays special interests with. If a person stays in a region for a long period of time, it means that the person carries out some activities at the place and the information of the region of the place is meaningful to the person. We adopt a hierarchical method for the stay region extraction rather than the density-based clustering algorithm.

In the hierarchical method, the first step is to extract the stay points from a person's trajectory. A stay point is a geographic location where the person stays for a while. Since these stay points associated with the person's geographic locations, so they can reflect the person's activities to some extent. Zheng et al. proposed an algorithm to detect person's stay points. Given a trajectory of a person $T = (p_i, p_{i+1}, \ldots, p_{i+m})$ (see Definition 1), if $distance(p_i, p_x) \leq \theta_d$, $|t_i - t_x| \geq \theta_t$, $i \leq x \leq i + m$, then $p(lat, lon)$ is the stay point, where

$$p.lat = \frac{\sum_{k=i}^x p_k.lat}{x - i + 1}, p.lon = \frac{\sum_{k=i}^x p_k.lon}{x - i + 1} \tag{3}$$

In the hierarchical method, the second step is to extract the person's stay regions. In the previous step, we have got the stay points from a person's trajectory. Obviously, if a person goes somewhere frequently, his/her stay points at that place will be more. On the contrary, there will be less stay points at the place where the person seldom goes to. As shown in Fig. 1, the three colors represent the three trajectories of a person. The arrows represent the person's moving directions, the circles represent person's stay points and the black circles represent the average point of all stay points in the cluster. The person's stay points in the region which the person visits and stays frequently are close to each other. These stay points are clearly form a cluster, such as cluster 1, cluster 2, cluster 4, cluster 5 and cluster 7 in Fig. 1. There are also some regions where the person only visits for once, such as cluster 3 and cluster 6. Although there is only one stay point in these clusters, we cannot omit them so that we will not miss any region where the person has ever been to.

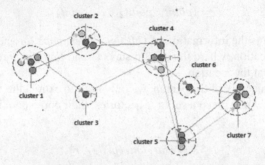

Fig. 1. The stay regions of a person

It seems that we can apply a density-based clustering algorithm DBSCAN 19 to these stay points. The DBSCAN algorithm requires two input parameters which are a radius *eps* and the minimum point number *minPts* of stay points within the radius, respectively. However, the DBSCAN algorithm is sensitive to input parameters and its time complexity is $O(n^2)$. So, we propose a novel Simple Clustering algorithm (denote as SC) that requires only one input parameter, that is the distance threshold τ. By traversing all stay points, we assign each stay point to a cluster whose distance to the stay point is less than the threshold τ, and if there is no cluster that satisfies the condition, then the stay point is regarded as a new cluster.

In Fig. 1, r is the radius of the cluster. As for those clusters that only contain one stay point, r is set to 50 m as the default value. The number of the cluster's stay points is recorded as the frequency that the person visits the stay region of them.

The usage of this hierarchical method to extract the stay regions not only improves the efficiency and accuracy of the algorithm, but also facilitates the follow-up experiments to discuss the impact of stay regions under different sizes on the similarity of person.

5   The Semantic Information Extraction

In this section, we introduce how to extract the basic semantic information from the stay regions.

In order to find the relationship between persons accurately, we cannot just study the geographic information. As shown is Fig. 2, the four colors represent the four person's stay regions, respectively. From the Fig. 2, it can be seen that Person 1 and Person 2 have more common stay regions, so they are similar. While for Person 3 and Person 4, there are no common stay region between them form the geographic information of stay regions. However, by considering the semantic information of stay regions of them, it can be found that both Person 3 and Person 4 usually goes to the school, gym and concert hall. Although geographic information of the two persons is different, their semantic information of them is almost same, so we consider they are similar too. From this point of view, simply comparing the geographic information of stay regions of persons is not enough to determine the similarity between them. In this section, we proposed a novel method to extract the semantic information of the stay regions of a person.

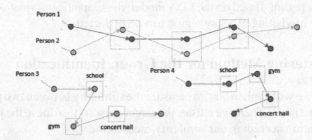

Fig. 2. The semantic information of persons' stay regions

We can use the categories of the point of interests (POIs) to represent the semantic information of the location. However, it is hard to extract POIs from the stay points of a person due to GPS positioning errors, calculation errors and crowded distribution of POIs in a city 20. The category of some stay regions is relatively simple, such as school, where the POIs belong to this category of the science and education service. In most cases, the categories of POIs in a stay region are diverse, especially when the size of the stay region is large. The proportions of POIs in a stay region indicate the likelihood that the person may perform different activities in the stay region, it is hard to use one category to describe all semantic information of a stay region. We have to record all POIs' categories and their ratios in a stay region, which are described as $sem = (\langle catg_1, freq_1 \rangle, \langle catg_2, freq_2 \rangle, \dots, \langle catg_n, freq_n \rangle)$, where $n \geq 1$.

Latent Dirichlet Allocation (LDA) is a generative probabilistic model for the collection of the discrete data, such as text corpora. The LDA model can calculate the multiple topics and their respective probabilities in a document in a corpus and can also fully extract the semantic information of a word or a sentence.

Obviously, we can consider the POI information in a stay region as a document, regard the semantic information of a stay region as the theme and take each POI as a word. We use the LDA model to extract the semantic information of POIs in a stay region. First, the POI information in all stay regions of a person is used as the input data to train the model, and then we use the trained model to extract the semantic information from each stay region.

After extracted the semantic information, a stay region (see Eq. 2) can be further described as follows.

$$SR = \left(lat, lon, (p_i)_{i=1}^{n}, (sem_i)_{i=1}^{m}, r\right), \tag{4}$$

where $(p_i)_{i=1}^{n}$ represents the stay points in the stay region and $(sem_i)_{i=1}^{m}$ represents the POI information in the stay region.

Now, we have extracted the characteristics of a person, which is the final information of the person's stay regions and the frequency of the person visits each stay region. The characteristics of a person is described as follows.

$$C = \left((SR_i)_{i=1}^n, (freq_i)_{i=1}^n\right), \tag{5}$$

where $(SR_i)_{i=1}^n$ represents the full information of a stay region which contains its geographic and semantic information and $(freq_i)_{i=1}^n$ represents the frequency of the person visiting the stay region. Based on the LDA model, the semantic information of POIs and their frequency of visiting in a stay region can be extracted.

6   The Clustering Method for the Group Identification

In this section, we will explain how to measure the similarity between two persons based on their characteristics. Then, we cluster the target persons to achieve the purpose of the group identification according our similarity measurement.

6.1   The Similarity Measurement

To compare persons' similarity, we first need to define the similarity measure between persons. In this paper, the similarity is used to measure the degree of interest of two persons to the certain stay regions, which includes two aspects, the geographic similarity and the semantic similarity.

First, we introduce the measure of the geographic similarity. If two persons have several the same geographic stay regions and their visiting frequencies are similar, we consider that the two persons are similar to some extent. The two persons may be neighbors or work together, they may have the same interests, but do not know each other, they may belong to the same group to do something, etc.

To accurately calculate the geographic similarity of two persons, we employ the extension of the cosine similarity (i.e., the tanimoto coefficient). Different with the cosine similarity, the tanimoto coefficient takes into account the visiting frequency and the length of vectors, which is described as follows.

$$tanimoto(A, B) = \frac{\sum_{i=1}^n la_i \cdot lb_i}{\sum_{i=1}^n la_i^2 + \sum_{i=1}^n lb_i^2 - \sum_{i=1}^n la_i \cdot lb_i}, \tag{6}$$

By using the tanimoto coefficient, the common stay regions of two persons are considered in the calculation of the geographic similarity of them. Here, a problem is how to judge whether two stay regions are common or the same. A simple method is to set a threshold and if the distance between two stay regions' centers is less than the threshold, we consider the two stay regions are common or the same. But this method is not adaptive, since if the radius of the stay region (i.e., r in Eq. 2) is changed in the stay region extraction step (i.e., see Sect. 4), the distance threshold should be changed according to r. In addition, due to the positioning error of the GPS devices, it is not accurate to judge whether two stay regions are common or the same through the above method in real applications. Therefore, the similarity of the two stay regions is used to judge whether the two stay regions are common or the same, which is calculated by the overlapping degree of stay points in two stay regions. The overlapping degree is calculated through the ratio between the number of stay points (of the stay region with less stay points) in the overlapping area and the number of all stay points (of the stay region with less stay points). Specifically, if there are two stay regions SR_1 and SR_2 (i.e., see Eq. 2) and $\left|(p_{i_1})_{i_1=1}^{n_1}\right| < \left|(p_{i_2})_{i_2=1}^{n_2}\right|$, the overlapping degree is calculated as follows.

$$w_i = \frac{\left|(p_{i_1})_{i_1=1}^{n_1} \in SR_1 \cap SR_2\right|}{\left|(p_{i_1})_{i_1=1}^{n_1}\right|}, \tag{7}$$

Weadd the stay region similarity as a weight to the tanimoto coefficient to form a new weighted geographic similarity measurement, which is expressed as follows.

$$sim_{loc}(A, B) = \frac{\sum_{i=1}^n la_i \cdot lb_i \cdot w_i}{\sum_{i=1}^n la_i^2 + \sum_{i=1}^n lb_i^2 - \sum_{i=1}^n la_i \cdot lb_i \cdot w_i}, \tag{8}$$

In the second aspect, we calculate the semantic similarity. Since the semantic information of a person in a stay region is not unique, we store all the semantic information and the frequency of a person's stay regions (see Sect. 5.1). Given the semantic information of a person's stay region $sem = (\langle c_1, f_1 \rangle, \langle c_2, f_2 \rangle, \ldots, \langle c_n, f_n \rangle), n \geq 1, f_i$ represents the probability for the person visiting c_i and $\sum_{i=1}^n f_i = 1$. If the semantic information of stay regions is unified, it is easy for us to determine their similarity through the tanimoto coefficient. However, since multiple semantic information of a stay region is stored, we should calculate the semantic similarity between two stay regions, rather than just determine whether their semantic is the same. *Sem* contains all semantic information and their probability distribution $(f_1, f_2, \ldots, f_n)$, we use the Kullback-Leibler divergence [26] or simply (i.e., the KL divergence) to calculate the probability distribution distance between two persons' stay regions.

In the probability theory, the KL divergence is used to measure the difference between two probability distributions in the same event space. Supposing the probability distributions of the semantic information in a stay region of Person A and Person B are $fa(x)$ and $fb(x)$, respectively. The KL divergence between their stay regions is expressed as:

$$D_{KL}(fa\|fb) = \sum_{x \in X} fa(x) log \frac{fa(x)}{fb(x)}, \tag{9}$$

However, the KL divergence is non-symmetric, that is, $D_{KL}(fa\|fb) \neq D_{KL}(fb\|fa)$, so it is not a good measurement. The Jensen-Shannon (JS) divergence is asymmetrical improvement of the KL divergence, which defines the distance between 0 to 1. If the semantic information of all stay regions of two persons (i.e., Person A and Person B) are *semA* and *semB*, respectively, the JS divergence of them is calculated as follows.

$$D_{JS}(fa\|fb) = \frac{1}{2}\left[D_{KL}\left(fa\|\frac{fa+fb}{2}\right) + D_{KL}\left(fb\|\frac{fa+fb}{2}\right)\right], \tag{10}$$

If $max_{fa \in semA, fb \in semB}\{D_{JS}(fa\|fb)\} \geq \delta$, where δ is the threshold of the semantic similarity, we can say that the semantic information of the two persons' stay regions are similar.

Since the semantic information is extracted from the stay regions, which also corresponds to the frequency that the person visits the stay regions. The same as the geographic similarity, the semantic similarity should also consider the overlap degree (i.e., see Eq. 8). The final equation to calculate the semantic information of Person A and Person B are described as follows.

$$sim_{sem}(A, B) = \frac{\sum_{i=1}^{n} sa_i \cdot sb_i \cdot w_i}{\sum_{i=1}^{n} sa_i^2 + \sum_{i=1}^{n} sb_i^2 - \sum_{i=1}^{n} sa_i \cdot sb_i \cdot w_i}, \tag{11}$$

where sa and sb are the semantic information frequency vectors of two persons and w is the vector which consists of D_{JS}. □

With the geographic and semantic similarity of two persons' stay regions, the person's similarity is defined as a combination of Eqs. 9 and 12, which is described as follows.

$$sim(A, B) = \alpha \cdot sim_{loc}(A, B) + (1 - \alpha) \cdot sim_{sem}(A, B), \tag{12}$$

where $\alpha \in [0, 1]$ determines the weights of the geographic and semantic similarities. The effect of α will be discussed in Sect. 7.

In the proposed method, the reason to separately calculate the geographic and semantic similarities is to evaluate the effect of α, and the influence of the two similarities on the final similarity.

6.2 The Clustering of Persons

In the proposed method, the group identification is achieved through clustering target persons, which divides target persons with similar characteristics into the same groups from the original dataset with lots of noise. The characteristics are derived from the geographic and semantic information of persons' stay regions rather than what they actually do. The objective of the person clustering is to find out the groups that the characteristic similarity among persons in the same group and the characteristic difference among persons between groups are as large as possible.

To achieve the above objective, we proposed a *SNN*-based clustering algorithm. The *SNN* similarity represents the number of common neighbors in the k nearest neighbors of two objects. Due to the features of the *SNN* similarity, it is good at dealing with noise and outliers and can handle clusters in different sizes, shapes and densities, especially for the clusters with strongly correlated objects.

The clustering-based group identification algorithm includes three steps. In the first step, according to the persons' characteristics and their similarity, the *SNN* proximity matrix is constructed. In the second step, the *SNN* similarity graph is constructed based on the *SNN* proximity matrix. In the third step, all connected components in the *SNN* similarity graph are found, each of which is a cluster. After removing the clusters with only one person, each remaining cluster with a high intra-cluster similarity is regarded as a group. By setting an appropriate value of k and the *SNN* similarity threshold γ, we can effectively identify groups, in which persons are closely related.

So far, we have found all clusters (i.e., groups) from the target persons. The clustering results under different values of k and γ will be discussed in the next section.

7 The Experiments and Analysis

In this section, we conduct a series of experiments to evaluate the effectiveness and efficiency of our method.

7.1 The Experimental Datasets

One of our experimental datasets is from Microsoft's open-source project Geolife 21. The dataset collects the GPS trajectories of 182 persons from April 2007 to August 2012, which contains17,621 trajectories with a total distance of 1,292,951 km and a total duration of 50176 h. Most of them are collected from persons in Haidian District of Beijing. Now, the dataset has been widely used in many research areas [18, 22–25]. In our experiments, we preprocess the trajectories in dataset by storing a person's daily trajectories in one file.

The POI data are collected from the Amap. Due to the network limitation, we only collected the POI data from Haidian District in Bejing.The POI dataset contains 156500 POIs, each of which includes name, address, categories and 3D coordinates.

7.2 The Experimental Results and Analysis

The Comparison of DBSCAN and the SC Algorithm. To compare the efficiency of the DBSCAN algorithm and the SC algorithm on the stay point extraction, we still use 180 persons' trajectories in Geolife and compare the running time of the two algorithms with different numbers of persons. We set the *eps* radius of two algorithms to 100 m. Figure 3 shows the comparison results.

From Fig. 3, it can be seen that although the running time of the two algorithms increase with the number of persons, the running time of SC is obviously less than the time consumed by DBSCAN with the same number of persons. This confirms our analysis in Sect. 4.

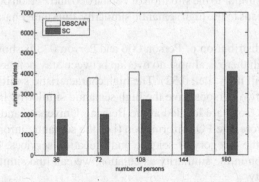

Fig. 3. Efficiency comparison between DBSCAN and SC

The Evaluation of the Semantic Information and the Coefficient α. In Sect. 6.1, we present our characteristic similarity calculation for persons, which integrates geographic and semantic similarities. In order to measure the impacts of two similarities on the characteristic similarity calculation, we select the trajectories of 8 persons to compare their characteristic similarity, where $\alpha = 0.3$. Later, we will explain why α is set to 0.3. The characteristic similarity matrix of the 8 persons is shown in Fig. 4.

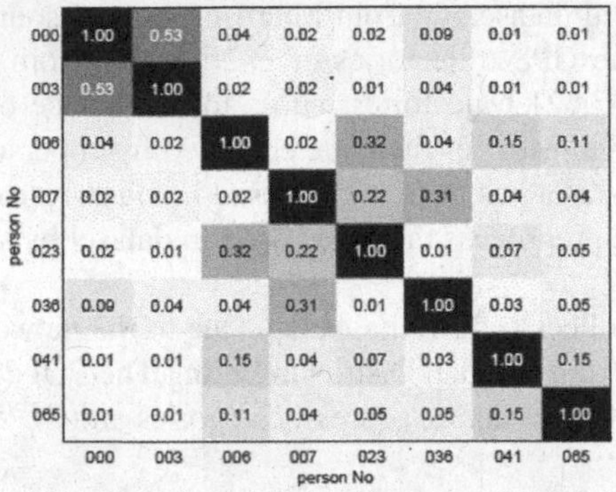

Fig. 4. The characteristic similarity matrix of persons

From Fig. 4, it can be seen that there are three pairs of similar persons, which are Person 000 and Person 003, Person 007 and Person 036, Person 006 and Person 023. The stay point distribution of Person 000 and Person 003 is shown in Fig. 5. Obviously, the stay points of the two persons have a lot of overlaps so that their geographic similarity is high. In addition, due to the semantic information that is extracted from the geographic stay regions, their semantic similarity is also high. Thus, the characteristic similarity of the two persons is 0.53, which is the same as our expectation.

The stay point distribution of Person 007 and Person 036 is shown in Fig. 6. The situation of them is similar to the situation of Person 000 and Person 003, where high geographic similarity leads to the high semantic similarity, thus their characteristic similarity is also high.

The stay point distribution of Person 006 and Person 023 is shown in Fig. 7. It can be seen that although there is almost no overlap between stay points of the two persons, their similarity is still high (i.e., 0.32). The high characteristic similarity is because the stay regions of the two persons have the high semantic similarity. In fact, most of stay points of the two persons are located at the Beihang University and Minzu University, respectively. Therefore, the POI information (i.e., the semantic information) of the two regions belongs to the category of science and education services. By considering the semantic information in the similarity calculation, we can find similar persons without geographic similarity.

Figure 8 shows the changes of characteristic similarity with the value changes of the coefficient α (i.e., see Eq. 12). From Fig. 8, it can be seen that the characteristic similarity between Person 000 and Person003 increases with the increase of α, so as the characteristic similarity of Person 007 and Person 036. This is because that the geographic similarities between these persons are larger than their semantic similarities. While the characteristic similarity between Person 006 and Person 023 decreases with the increase of α. This is because that the geographic similarity between them is almost 0 (i.e., see Fig. 7). But, the semantic similarity of the two persons is high, since all stay regions of them belong to the category of science and education services. In particular, the characteristic similarity is 0 when $\alpha = 1$, where the characteristic similarity is only calculated from the geographic similarity. In general, the value choice of α depends on the importance of the semantic information in the calculation of the characteristic similarity. Choosing an appropriate α can help us find the relationship among persons more accurately. In this study, we set α as 0.3.

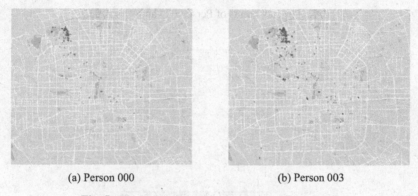

(a) Person 000   (b) Person 003

Fig. 5. The stay points of Person 000 and Person 003

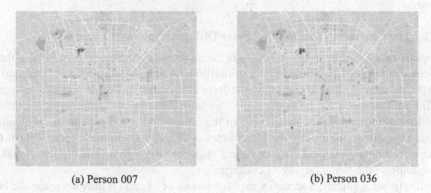

(a) Person 007   (b) Person 036

Fig. 6. The stay points of Person 007 and Person 036

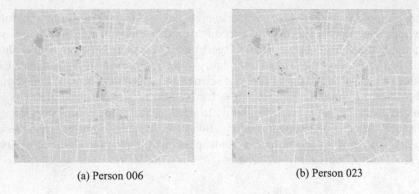

(a) Person 006   (b) Person 023

Fig. 7. The stay points of Person 006 and Person 023

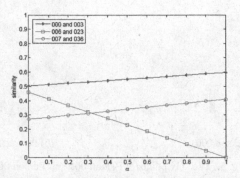

Fig. 8. The changes of characteristic similarity with different α

7.2.1 The Clustering Evaluation Under Different Values of k and γ

There are many validity indices to measure the quality of clustering results. Most of these indices can be roughly divided into external indices and internal indices. Considering that the persons in Geolife dataset do not have cluster labels (i.e., the external indices), the internal indices are used as the quality measurement for our clustering algorithm.

Most of internal indices are based on the compactness and separation of clusters. In our experiment, we choose the Dunn index (DI) and the Silhouette index (SI) as the criteria to evaluate the performance of our clustering algorithm. The higher DI and SI value indicate the better quality of clustering.

But, in our application scenario, the high values of SI and DI may not mean the best clustering results. Since the objective of the proposed method is to find a few groups of persons with potential bad behaviors from crowds, so there are a large number of noise persons in the crowds. Figure 9 shows the changes of DI and SI with the change of k (i.e., the number of nearest neighbors, see Sect. 6.2). In the figures, we choose the most representative values of k between 12 and 26 and the threshold of the SNN similarity γ is set to 10.

From Fig. 9, it can be seen that both of the two criteria are maximized when k is 12 or 13, where both of them have the same clustering results. There are two clusters which contain Persons 032, 044 and Persons 151, 162 respectively. The characteristic similarity matrix is shown in Fig. 10.

The experimental results indicate that the proposed clustering algorithm finds two groups of similar persons from 182 persons, two persons in each group and the rest 178 persons are considered as noise. From DI and SI criteria and the perspective of the clustering algorithm, this is the best clustering result. However, from the perspective of our application scenario, finding too few groups of persons is not good for our further group identification. The distributions of stay points of the two groups of persons are shown in Fig. 11 and Fig. 12.

From Fig. 11 and Fig. 12, it can be seen that Person 032 and Person 044 have several obviously overlapping stay regions with high visiting frequency. The geographic similarity of person 032 and person 044 is 0.781, the semantic similarity of them is 0.824, and the characteristic similarity of them is 0.881, which indicates that the two persons are highly similar. The geographic similarity of Person 151 and Person 162 is 0 since they do not have common stay regions. But the semantic similarity of them is 0.823. The semantic information of stay regions where Person 151 frequently visits are the restaurant, the public car park and the convenient store. The semantic information of stay regions where Person 162 frequently visits are the restaurant and the public car park. This indicates that the experimental results calculated by the proposed method are reasonable.

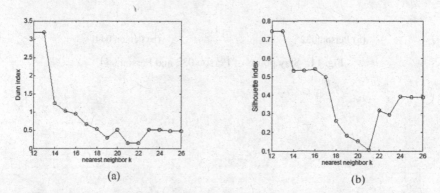

Fig. 9. (a) The relationship between DI and k; (b) The relationship between SI and k

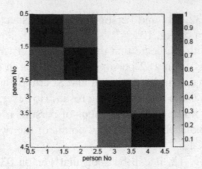

Fig. 10. The characteristic similarity of the two clusters

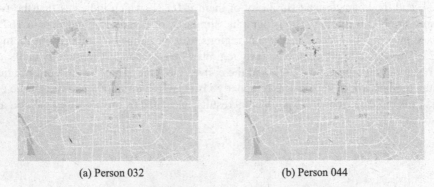

(a) Person 032   (b) Person 044

Fig. 11. Stay points of Person 032 and Person 044

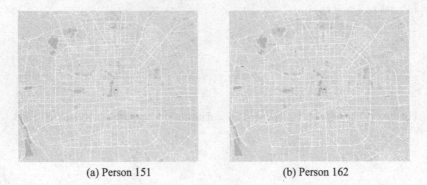

(a) Person 151   (b) Person 162

Fig. 12. Stay points of Person 151 and Person 162

From the experiments, it can be seen that the proposed method can effectively and efficiently identify the groups of persons with high characteristic similarity. The behaviors of persons in the identified groups are more similar to those in our experiments, indicating that our method is applicable in real application scenarios.

8 Conclusion

In this paper, we propose a method to identify key groups by using the trajectory data of persons or moving objects. In the proposed method, we first extract the stay regions and calculate their visiting frequencies from persons' trajectories. Compared with the traditional methods, such as DBSCAN, our method is simpler, faster and more effective. Then, to accurately describe persons' behavior, the semantic information of persons stay regions are extracted from POIs in the regions. After that, the geographic and semantic information of persons' stay regions are used to calculate the characteristic similarity of persons. Finally, the groups of persons are divided and identified based on their characteristic similarities. The experimental results show the effectiveness and efficiency of our method on the stay region extraction, semantic information extraction and the group identification.

In future work, we will try to add other information (e.g., social data) to the characteristic similarity calculation to accurately discover the relationships between persons.

Acknowledgment. This work is supported by National Science of Foundation of China (No. 62072016), the Beijing Natural Science Foundation (No. 4212016).

References

1. Li, Z., Ding, B., Han, J., Kays, R., Nye, P.: Mining periodic behaviors for moving objects. In: Proceedings of the 16th ACM SIGKDD International Conference on Knowledge Discovery and Data Mining, pp. 1099–1108 (2010)
2. Lv, M., Chen, L., Xu, Z., Li, Y., Chen, G.: The discovery of personally semantic places based on trajectory data mining. Neurocomputing **173**, 1142–1153 (2016)
3. Tang, L.-A., et al.: A framework of traveling companion discovery on trajectorydata streams. ACM Trans. Intell. Syst. Technol. **5**(1), 1–34 (2014)
4. Yan, Z., Chakraborty, D., Parent, C., Spaccapietra, S., Aberer, K.: Semantic trajectories: mobility data computation and annotation. ACM Trans. Intell. Syst. Technol. **4**(3), 1–39 (2013)
5. Zheng, Y.: Trajectory data mining: an overview. ACM Trans. Intell. Syst. Technol. **6**(3), 1–41 (2015)
6. Peng, J., Zeng, D.D.: Exploring information hidden in tags: a subject-based item recommendation approach. In: 19th Workshop on Information Technologies and Systems, pp. 73–78 (2009)
7. Zhang, Z., Li, Q., Zeng, D., Gao, H.: User community discovery from multi-relational networks. Decis. Support Syst. **54**(2), 870–879 (2013)
8. Hu, H.: Psychology and behavior mechanism of micro-blog information spreading. Afr. J. Bus. Manage. **6**(35), 9797–9807 (2012)
9. Yang, X., Wu, Y., Li, L.: Multiple active rescheduling algorithm in obs network. Comput. Eng. Appl. **47**(8), 90–92 (2011)
10. Boratto, L., Carta, S., Satta, M.: Groups identification and individual recommendations in group recommendation algorithms. In: Proceedings of the Workshop on the Practical Use of Recommender Systems, Algorithms and Technologies, vol. 676, pp. 27–34 (2010)

11. Pan, G., Qi, G., Zhang, W., Li, S.: Trace analysis and mining for smart cities: issues, methods, and applications. IEEE Commun. Mag. **51**(6), 120–126 (2013)
12. Zhou, C., Dan, F., Ludford, P., Shekhar, S., Terveen, L.: Discovering personally meaningful places. ACM Trans. Inf. Syst. 2029–2032 (2005)
13. Shaw, A.A., Gopalan, N.P.: Frequent pattern mining of trajectory coordinates using Apriori algorithm. Int. J. Comput. Appl. **22**(9), 1–7 (2011)
14. Ye, Y., Zheng, Y., Chen, Y., Feng, J., Xie, X.: Mining individual life pattern based on location history. In: Proceedings of the 10th International Conference on Mobile Data Management, pp. 1–10 (2009)
15. Kalnis, P., Mamoulis, N., Bakiras, S.: On discovering moving clusters in spatio-temporal data. In: Bauzer Medeiros, C., Egenhofer, M.J., Bertino, E. (eds.) SSTD 2005. LNCS, vol. 3633, pp. 364–381. Springer, Heidelberg (2005). https://doi.org/10.1007/11535331_21
16. Bogorny, V., Renso, C., Aquino, A.R.D., Siqueira, F.D.L., Alvares, L.O.: Constant - a conceptual data model for semantic trajectories of moving objects. Trans. GIS **18**(1), 66–88 (2014)
17. Parent, C., et al.: Semantic trajectories modeling and analysis. ACM Comput. Surv. **45**(4), 1–32 (2013)
18. Li, Q., Zheng, Y., Xie, X., Chen, Y., Liu, W., Ma, W.Y.: Mining user similarity based on location history. In: Proceedings of the 16th ACM SIGSPATIAL Conference on Advance in Geographical Information Systems, pp. 1–10 (2008)
19. Ester, M., Kriegel, H.-P., Sander, J., Xu, X.: A density-based algorithm for discovering clusters in large spatial databases with noise. In: Proceedings of the Second International Conference on Knowledge Discovery and Data Mining, pp. 226–231 (1996)
20. Xiao, X., Zheng, Y., Luo, Q., Xie, X.: Finding similar users using category-based location history. In: Proceedings of the 18th SIGSPATIAL International Conference on Advances in Geographic Information Systems, pp. 442–445 (2010)
21. Zheng, Y., Xie, X., Ma, W.: Geolife: a collaborative social networking service among user, location and trajectory. IEEE Data Eng. Bull. **33**(2), 32–39 (2010)
22. Chen, Z., Sanjabi, B., Papliatseyeu, A., Mayora, O.: A location-based user movement prediction approach for geolife project. Int. J. Comput. Eng. Res. **2**(7), 16–19 (2012)
23. Chen, X., Pang, J., Xue, R.: Constructing and comparing user mobility profiles. ACM Trans. Web **8**(4), 1–25 (2014)
24. Zheng, Y., Xie, X.: Learning travel recommendations from user-generated GPS traces. ACM Trans. Intell. Syst. Technol. **2**(1), 1–29 (2011)
25. Zheng, Y., Li, Q., Chen, Y., Xie, X., Ma, W.Y.: Understanding mobility based on GPS data. In: Proceedings of the 10th ACM Conference on Ubiquitous Computing, pp. 312–321 (2008)
26. Kullback, S., Leibler, R.A.: On information and sufficiency. Ann. Math. Stat. **22**(1), 79–86 (1951)

Correction to: Spatial Data and Intelligence

Huayi Wu, Yu Liu, Jianzhong Li, Xiaofeng Meng, Qingfeng Guan,
Xuan Song, Guoqiong Liao, and Guoliang Li

Correction to:
H. Wu et al. (Eds.): *Spatial Data and Intelligence*, **LNCS 13614,**
https://doi.org/10.1007/978-3-031-24521-3

In the originally published book wrong affiliation has been used for the Editor Huayi
Wu. The affiliation has been changed to "Wuhan University".

The updated original version of the book can be found at
https://doi.org/10.1007/978-3-031-24521-3

Author Index

Printed in the United States
by Baker & Taylor Publisher Services